ONWARD AND UPWARD

ONWARD AND UPWARD

*A Biography
of Katharine S. White*

Linda H. Davis

1817

HARPER & ROW, PUBLISHERS, New York
Cambridge, Philadelphia, San Francisco, Washington
London, Mexico City, São Paulo, Singapore, Sydney

ONWARD AND UPWARD. Copyright © 1987 by Linda H. Davis. All rights reserved. Printed in the United States of America. No part of this book may be used or reproduced in any manner whatsoever without written permission except in the case of brief quotations embodied in critical articles and reviews. For information address Harper & Row, Publishers, Inc., 10 East 53rd Street, New York, N.Y. 10022. Published simultaneously in Canada by Fitzhenry & Whiteside Limited, Toronto.

FIRST EDITION

Designer: Erich Hobbing
Copy editor: Margaret Cheney
Indexer: Sylvia Farrington

Library of Congress Cataloging-in-Publication Data

Davis, Linda H.
  Onward and upward.

  Bibliography: p.
  Includes index.
  1. White, Katharine Sergeant Angell. 2. Journalists—United States—Biography. I. Title.
PN4874.W516D38   1987   070.4'1'0924 [B]   86–46055
ISBN 0–06–015750–X

87 88 89 90 91 HC 10 9 8 7 6 5 4 3 2 1

For my grandmother
Honor Lister
With love and thanks

Contents

Illustrations

ILLUSTRATIONS

Preface

IN THE FALL OF 1977, when I was a graduate student at Simmons College in Boston and was casting about for an original idea for a master's thesis, Katharine White occurred to me. She had been on my mind since the previous winter, when, after reading the *Letters of E. B. White,* I wrote a complimentary letter to the author and received a thank you from his wife just six days later. The letter was typed on *New Yorker* stationery. In her shaky scrawl, Katharine White had interlined a few corrections, added a sentence, and signed her name. I was charmed and saddened by the letter, by the woman who apologized for the "secondhand reply" and was "a costly invalid now, with nurses day and night"—the woman of the sad-eyed, hauntingly beautiful portrait I had lingered over in the *Letters* book, taken when Katharine White (then Katharine Angell) was in her late thirties. And I felt that I had found a kindred spirit.

"Dear Ms. Davis," the letter began, "Forgive the 'Ms.' instead of 'Miss' or 'Mrs.' It is an abbreviation I despise although I have worked all my life and am a liberated woman. Possibly your envelope would have told whether you are married or not, but only the letter came to me." We were strangers, but she had written to me as to a friend. I sensed that she was lonely and feeling useless: "My husband's desk is deep in unanswered letters so he has agreed to let me help him." I wanted to comfort this elderly person; and at the same time, I was exhilarated by my first contact with a distinguished literary woman. I wrote again to thank her, and that ended our correspondence. When she died, five months later, I was traveling in England. It was not until I returned home that I learned of her death and thought of writing my thesis about her.

"Why Katharine White?" The question I have most often been asked over the years is unanswerable. I was only vaguely familiar with her work as a *New Yorker* editor and her life as the wife of E. B. White. And yet when she suggested herself to me (clearly, *she* had been the initiator), strolled serenely and imposingly into my head, I felt the thrill of recognition: this was what I was meant to do. I decided to write a biography instead of a thesis.

During the next six years I worked haltingly and intermittently on the biography until getting a contract for it in 1983. I amassed a small library of information about my subject, much of it attesting to her unique work as a literary editor. My research easily proved that I had been justified in undertaking such a risky project (assuming, of course, that I could pull it off). Undoubtedly, Katharine White had exerted a profound influence on American fiction, poetry, and humor—on the quality of English prose itself. Hers was an important enough life to justify a full-scale biography. And she was virtually unknown to the public. But it wasn't her impressive career that kept me going and held me fascinated over the course of almost nine years, years during which I matured and changed considerably, years when my private life underwent many revolutions, not least among them the transition from unmarried graduate student to married mother of two.

She was captivating, frustrating, endearing, inspiring, elusive, complex: I couldn't get to the bottom of her. There remained something mysterious about her, something essentially private and unknowable. And she was to me what William Faulkner was referring to in his 1950 Nobel Prize acceptance speech when he said that the only thing worth writing about is "the human heart in conflict with itself . . . love and honor and pity and pride and compassion and sacrifice." Katharine White was not closer to perfection than other human beings; she was fully human. As a mother she had serious failings. She had an unfortunate tendency to dwell on her own ill health and on that of her husband, giving her what one friend called "a gloomy side." A perfectionist, she could be overly demanding of people. She was slow to forgive. Many people thought her beautiful, but aristocratic and severe, and nearly everyone found her formidable. But, despite the impression Katharine White gave of enormous strength, she was a vulnerable, painfully sensitive woman who worried about nearly everyone, suffered inordinately for her private mistakes, and was crucially wounded by people's perception of her as "cold." What gives her life particular interest and value is the way in which she struggled with her faults and fears and ultimately triumphed over them to give herself generously to others, and to literature. She was truly Walt Whitman's "bold swimmer": an experiencing, curious, fully alert nature, unafraid of challenge, courageous in the face of illness and adversity. She never gave up on life; she never stopped trying to be the best she could be.

I am not sure why E. B. White decided to talk to me about his beloved Katharine. He did not know me, he had no real proof of my writing ability, and both he and his wife had felt betrayed by writers before, some of whom they had known personally. But White was a kind and trusting man, and I was young and well-meaning. More significantly, Katharine White had died only a few months before the day I arrived at their large white farmhouse in Maine. She was still very much on her lonely husband's mind, and he wanted to talk about her and keep her alive. He wanted people to know about the important work she had done (as a writer, *he* had always been the center of attention), and to rescue her from the shadows that editors work in. Before I fully grasped what I had gotten myself into, I had given up my plans to return to England and settled down with Katharine White. She has been a stimulating and durable companion.

ONWARD AND UPWARD

Prologue

KATHARINE WHITE WAS sixty-two years old in 1955—an imposing, aristocratic-looking woman with heavy-lidded gray eyes, an aquiline nose, and a heavy coil of gray hair, which had never been cut. Sitting at her desk in a large corner office above Forty-fourth Street, Fifth Avenue in the distance, she was forbidding to those meeting her for the first time. It was partly that she looked austere, with a patrician profile (but "pretty, like a cameo," said William Maxwell). And there was her voice: "low and strong," the broad *a*'s, precise diction, and a way of stressing a word's last syllable, as though, with a brown pencil, she were underlining it. She looked directly at you when you spoke, the gray eyes intent, the ash about to drop from her cigarette.

After thirty years as a *New Yorker* magazine editor, Katharine had decided to give up her job for one that would be less demanding on her energy and time. Beginning January 1, 1956, she would leave *The New Yorker*'s Fiction Department to work "on general magazine policy, new ideas, etc. for all departments of the New Yorker." It was a wrenching decision, one that oppressed her for months before it took effect. Throughout the summer and fall she had been "really obsessed with the details of this big change in [her] life, and buried in gloom."

Her life had been full and immensely rewarding. She had been happily married for twenty-six years to a man she adored. She had three children, all of whom now had families and successful careers of their own; and seven grandchildren. Perhaps to her disappointment, only one of her children had shown a professional interest in literature: Roger Angell, Katharine's thirty-five-year-old son from her first marriage, was a writer and an editor of *Holiday* magazine. Katharine's career, which she had pursued at some cost but without depriving herself of a personal life, was distinguished. Though largely unknown to the general public, she was highly respected and admired in literary circles. And her husband's place in literature—as an eminent prose stylist, essayist, and writer of children's books—was firmly established.

Though inclined to worry about money, Katharine was financially secure.

The Whites owned a gracious large farmhouse and thirty-six acres in Maine; they had always had a cook and other household help; and for the last ten years they had rented what Katharine described as "the loveliest apartment in New York" as well, in Turtle Bay Gardens at 229 East 48th Street. Turtle Bay was home to several of New York's literati and theatrical people—in the Whites' day, to the journalist Dorothy Thompson; Maxwell Perkins, the famous Scribner editor; and Katharine Hepburn (whom Katharine White had never met but greatly admired, "both as an actress and a person"), who lived across the garden from Katharine and Andy. In exalted and slightly exaggerated terms, the poet Louise Bogan described the Whites' beige-colored apartment as a "dream-duplex," with its bookcases, its "circle of lemon-colored couches; one fine painting over the fireplace; a broad black cocktail table; and, best of all, four windows (one of them behind a concert grand) onto the communal garden." In the summertime, if the mosquitoes weren't biting, Andy might mix their guests vermouth cassis cocktails on the terrace overlooking the garden. With its ancient elm, flowering shrubs, the "big sweet gum tree" that overhung the Whites' dwelling, and its "narrow and secret-looking gardens hidden from the city," Turtle Bay looked, to the South African short-story writer and novelist Nadine Gordimer, "like a New Yorker cover itself."

By 1955 Katharine White had reached that time of life, precarious to diligent, work-loving people, when she was expected to retire, or at least slow down. Retirement was unthinkable, but for her husband's sake she was determined to do less-demanding work.

Having worked for the magazine nearly as long as his wife (since 1926), Andy White felt that a permanent move to the old Maine farmhouse they had purchased in 1933 would provide a better writing environment for him than did year-round living in New York, which was beginning to wear on him. Katharine shared his love of the country, but she had always been a working woman, and she had built her life around *The New Yorker,* had thrived on her challenging, stimulating work. And leaving it—leaving the daily contact with other editors and writers—held another fear. "They are about the only friends I have left because of my thirty years of obsession with the New Yorker," she wrote the poet May Sarton, whose *New Yorker* work she edited, "so I hope you will remember that I still count on seeing you." It was not true that Katharine's friends were confined to *The New Yorker,* but it was with this group of people that she had most in common, and a woman of her interests and intellect was understandably fearful about leaving New York for the isolated, if lovely, life in Maine.

In a letter to Gordimer, another of her writers, Katharine explained her decision to leave editorial work. "The new work will give me—and Andy

—much more freedom of mind and spirit, and more freedom to move about as he may wish to for his writing, and I felt that I owed it to him as well as to myself after more than 30 years of my working such long hours and always under the unpredictable calls upon one's time that [manuscript] work is apt to impose." Until the end of December of that year, she wrote letters informing contributors and their agents of the imminent change in her job and their change in editor, and urged them to send her anything for the magazine they might have been holding back, so that she might "have the pleasure of reading and working on a story of yours one more time." The letters went quickly; she seemed to be racing against the new year.

Katharine found a sympathetic spirit in the literary agent Henry Volkening, who commiserated with her about the strain of such concentrated, responsible work, which "[becomes] too much for everyone of our generation, except those lucky few who were sort of *born* with a perpetual couple of martinis inside of them." Though equally sympathetic, *The New Yorker*'s writers and editors reacted differently. To these talented and often troubled people, Katharine White was more than a fine editor: she was a mother figure (in her husband's words, "a broody hen"). Whether fretting about Niccolò Tucci's "eating only a carrot for lunch" or worrying about Wolcott Gibbs's drinking; whether writing a letter to John Updike inquiring anxiously about the birth of his first baby, or defending her writers against the magazine's fact-checking department, she was always there, and many people had come to depend on her and to feel, somehow, that she would always be there. S. N. Behrman, whose nickname for Katharine was "Madam C,"* felt that she alone was responsible for his recent memoir, *The Worcester Account* (published in 1954), which he had written at her suggestion. And in 1955 Katharine and Frances Gray Patton had happily anticipated a new movie of *Good Morning, Miss Dove*, starring Jennifer Jones; Katharine had edited the story in its original *New Yorker* form.

Nineteen fifty-five had been an eventful year. That summer, she and Andy had taken their long-delayed trip to England. While there, they traveled to Oxford to finally meet the promising young writer whose stories and light verse Katharine had been editing for the past year: twenty-three-year-old John Updike, in England on a year's fellowship at Oxford's Ruskin School of Drawing and Fine Art following his 1954 graduation from Harvard. Katharine had offered Updike a job on the *New Yorker* staff, and because his year at Oxford was ending, he had accepted.

*The nickname, which Behrman appears to have given her in 1954, arose from Katharine's mispronunciation of the Yiddish colloquialism *chutzpah*, which the usually correct editor called "chootsbah." "It tickled Sam pink and he later told me I was known all over Broadway as Mme. C."

One of the most exciting literary events of the year had been the publication of Vladimir Nabokov's *Lolita*. It would later pain Katharine to remember that *The New Yorker* might have published part of this novel.

Lolita, Nabokov's seventh book and third novel in English (by 1955 he had published eighteen books in Russian), is the confession of the fictive Humbert Humbert, a middle-aged former English teacher obsessed with "nymphic," pubescent girls—specifically one, Lolita—whom he calls nymphets. Written in the first person as the hero is about to be tried for his crimes, the novel is at once a sexually explicit study in psychopathology and a complex blend of allusion, linguistics, parody, and word play. Its earnings, and the sale of the movie rights, allowed Nabokov to quit teaching and leave the United States in 1959 for Montreux, Switzerland, where for the rest of his life he lived with his family at the Montreux-Palace Hotel.

The book had been written in the early fifties, when Nabokov was teaching at Cornell. When the novel was rejected by four American publishers, Nabokov became afraid of losing his teaching job if the book was published in the United States. He consequently arranged publication through the Olympia Press in Paris, to which the manuscript was to be sent after Katharine White, his *New Yorker* editor, looked it over. Katharine later wrote:

> On Friday p.m. [early in 1954] I received a telegram from V. N. saying a manuscript would be at our Turtle Bay apartment delivered by Western Union. It commanded me to read the manuscript and said it would be picked up by Western Union on Monday morning. . . . All with no warning. It happened that I had a visiting grandchild for two days and was giving a family dinner on Saturday night. The telegram also said that I was never, never to show the manuscript to [*The New Yorker*'s editor, William Shawn] or even to speak of it because he was afraid it would offend him. I therefore never had time nor the desire to read under Vladimir's strict rules, so it left Monday morning for France.

Katharine did not read *Lolita* until March of 1957; Nabokov sent her the two-volume Olympia Press edition with the butterfly inscription he reserved for special friends.

Though deeply disturbed by the novel, Katharine regretted that Nabokov, a writer she greatly admired, had been "so fearful" about Shawn's reaction to it, and she thought that, had she been given the time to read the manuscript, *The New Yorker* could have published some of the funny chapters dealing with Humbert's travels with Lolita. In a characteristically frank letter written in March of 1957, Katharine told Nabokov her reaction.

Prologue

I have read "Lolita" in the past week; I couldn't put it down once I started it, which is a real tribute for no one can put a novel down easier than I can, and this is an extra tribute in this case because the book colored my days so darkly that I could well have avoided it in my escapist vacation mood. I don't suppose anyone like me, with five potential nymphets in the family—my granddaughters, one of whom, a golden-skinned, thin-armed nine-year-old, was visiting me at the time, would not find the book uncomfortable. You will gather that I don't like the book. It wouldn't be honest of me to say that I do, in spite of my constant recognition of its great virtuosity. It isn't because it shocked me and I don't think the book should be banned. That is all wrong. It is just that I have never been able to feel real sympathy and identification with psychopaths. To me they seem in the realm of medicine rather than in that of humanity and I've never liked fiction that is all out pathological. But I did enjoy and greatly admire your observation of, and comments, indirect, on the United States, and your allegory on our times. The second volume even aroused to a small degree my sympathy for Humbert. So you see you really completely achieved what you set out to: you raised my hair, gave me the horrors, stimulated my mind, aroused my antagonism and, grudgingly, my admiration. Reading the book is something I'll never forget though it made me thoroughly miserable and failed to elevate me, as it seems to have elevated many of your readers.

She ended the letter by saying that she was perhaps "a fool to go out on a limb like this for you are sure to be angry with me. But I like you too much and admire you too much to just pass it over politely with little or no comment. Please try to forgive my perversity on your perversity." It was signed with "many apologies" from Nabokov's "humble admirer, Katharine."

Some of Katharine's acquaintances may have wondered at Nabokov's confidence, what appears to be his complete lack of hesitation, in sending his manuscript (obscene, by that day's standards) to Katharine White, whom one friend likened, "in her refined quality," to Edith Wharton. Katharine *was* refined: well-bred; reserved; precise and cultivated in her speech; understated and elegant in her dress; instinctively polite. She was not the kind of woman one could imagine swearing or telling a dirty joke (some people mistakenly thought her humorless). But she was not prudish. As she told Nabokov, she abhorred censorship; and despite her repugnance toward *Lolita*'s psychopathic hero, she was objective and open-minded enough to feel that *The New Yorker* should have published some of the novel. Nabokov seems never to have had the notion that she, like William Shawn, might be offended by the book.

Katharine was not fastidious. E. B. White, who objected to people's perception of his wife as overly refined, loved to recall a story about her that became the favorite Katharine White story of her son-in-law, Louis Stableford. One year (the date is forgotten), as the Whites were making what became their annual migration to Sarasota, Florida, Katharine needed to urinate and she asked Andy to pull the car off the road. It was hunting season, and as Katharine disappeared over a wooded embankment, she began to sing, loudly, in her unmelodious singing voice, "Jesus Loves Me." Suddenly Andy heard his wife shouting for help and imploring him to come quickly. When he reached her she said that she had put her hand in a fox turd. Andy loved the image of his proper wife relieving herself in the woods; Louis Stableford · was proud of having the only mother-in-law in the world who could distinguish a fox turd from any other.

When Katharine's change of job became effective on January 1, 1956, Gustave Lobrano was to assume some of her duties. A close friend of the Whites (Andy was godfather of Lobrano's daughter, Dorothy), Gus Lobrano had been hired by Katharine to take over her job as Fiction Department head in 1938, when she and Andy had gone to live in Maine for several years. During the Second World War the Whites returned to New York, and Katharine went to work under Gus. Now, just when he was to assume her duties for good, Gus Lobrano fell ill. He died several months later.

And so, after months of preparing to leave the work that had obsessed her for over thirty years, on April 1 Katharine returned to the long hours, the unpredictable calls upon her time, and the additional task of comforting the writers who had worked with Gus Lobrano: S. J. Perelman, Ogden Nash, J. D. Salinger, and others. And she returned to the work with the unsettling knowledge that it was only temporary and she would again have to leave it.

In August of 1956 *The New Yorker* published a short story that recalled a curious incident from Katharine White's early life. Jean Stafford, a contributor to the magazine since 1948, had recently suffered a severe writer's block, and Katharine, her friend and editor, tried to help her by telling a story from her own life. She told about a lake where as a girl she had summered with her family—and where, one summer, something terrible had happened.

The lake was Chocorua, and it lay in eastern New Hampshire. Named for an Algonquin Indian chief, Chocorua means "sharp knife," but the lake was spoon-shaped and very blue; a thick fringe of trees veiled the summer homes surrounding it. The big lake yielded to a smaller one, and along the

Sandwich Range to the northwest rose Mount Chocorua, 3,475 feet in the air. Here Katharine Sergeant spent "the best summers" of her girlhood, summers of boating and hiking.

It was late July, 1913. Katharine was a junior at Bryn Mawr, engaged to a Harvard man named Ernest Angell. Like her, he had spent many summers at the lake; they were of a group of young people who came to the lake each year with their families. It had been a typical mountain day. Katharine and Ernest had returned from a hike, and upon entering the Sergeants' summer home were met by Katharine's Aunt Caroline, who was "walking about in distress." The family's two young Irish maids, who were friends and had come up with the family for the summer, had left the house at about four o'clock and had failed to return for supper. Would Katharine and Ernest look for them? They set off again, through the darkening woods and the vigorous mountain air, and began to circle the lake.

Katharine never recorded the events of that day in detail. What she saw on the lake was so shocking, so monstrous, she continued to dream of it until finally she broke down and confided in a friend at school. Jean Stafford may have imagined the untouched picnic that first alarmed Katharine and Ernest:

> its corners neatly held down with rocks, the tablecloth with a pattern of tulips
> . . . neatly set for two with blue willowware plates and kitchen silver and jelly
> glasses; in the middle of the tablecloth there was a Dundee marmalade jar filled
> with Mariposa lilies. But the embossed-paper napkins had not been unfolded,
> the glasses had not been filled from the thermos, and the hamper had not been
> opened.

Katharine and Ernest found the girls' clothing in the boathouse. Then they found the bodies, floating in about fifteen feet of water.

While Ernest dived in for the bodies, Katharine watched. The maids, she realized, had drowned; they had been just learning to swim. Katharine could not have been prepared for what she saw next. For the bodies that Ernest retrieved from the lake were not only dead, but ravaged, the young flesh ripped from their faces and limbs by the carnivorous turtles that lived in the shallow water.

The maids—twenty-three-year-old Margaret Hynes of Somerville, Massachusetts, and twenty-six-year-old Delia Sullivan of Cambridge—were Irish Catholic. Their families would not even be able to give them a proper wake: the pitiful condition of the bodies required that they be returned to Boston in closed caskets. It was a shock and a nightmare—"the most dreadful happening of my life," Katharine said later. This was the story she told Jean Stafford. It became "The Mountain Day" and was included in Stafford's

Collected Stories, which was dedicated to Katharine S. White and later won the Pulitzer Prize.

Katharine herself had always wanted to turn it into a short story, but she realized that she never could—perhaps because she had long since decided that she was an editor, not a writer, perhaps because she lacked the necessary distance to write about it. It had been a difficult story for her to edit; she was uncertain about the way Jean had described the maids' disfigurement, and considered herself "too close to the actual facts" to advise her. She was likewise unsure whether Jean should have included certain details, such as the sealed coffins, which the maids' families had taken hard. She was simply "too close to reality to judge what is best for this story."

Despite its inclusion in the collection that won Jean Stafford a Pulitzer (the book was also nominated for a National Book Award), "The Mountain Day," Katharine felt, was not "nearly as good as the stories based on Jean's own Colorado youth [the story's setting is changed from New Hampshire to Stafford's native Colorado], but at least it got her back to writing." Stafford's Judy Grayson (the Katharine Sergeant White figure in the story), a "giddy," pampered eighteen-year-old whose selfishness gives way to mature love when she watches her fiancé's terrible suffering after he retrieves the maids' mangled bodies from the lake, was entirely fictional. Many years after "The Mountain Day" was published Katharine wrote that "Jean took this dreadful story and made it completely her own. The girl of the story couldn't have been me at all."

Though an unusual example of what an editor could do for a writer, this was certainly not the only time Katharine helped a writer in some extraordinary way. Asking the right question could trigger as dramatic an effect: "My mother [Phyllis McGinley] has told me repeatedly how you changed the direction of her whole career," wrote Julie Hayden, "—by sending her a check with a note: 'We're buying this, but why do you sing the same sad songs all women sing?'"

When she was an old woman (a "long-winded *old* lady," she called herself), Katharine White's mind naturally returned to some of the writers she had edited during her thirty-six-year career at *The New Yorker.* John Updike, Vladimir Nabokov, Jean Stafford . . . They were among the writers she had most admired. She had had warm relationships with them all, particularly with Jean Stafford, who was a close friend. It was the writers and artists, the magazine's founding editor, Harold Ross, and his remarkable staff who had raised *The New Yorker* to something more than just a weekly magazine.

She had always felt that writers' work was far more important than hers.

But she was proud of her life's work, of the contribution she had made. Once, after she had retired and was admitted to the hospital with the rare skin disease that would plague her for the last thirteen years of her life, the admitting person who was filling out the customary forms said, "Occupation —housewife?" Katharine indignantly raised her abrading body from her chair and replied, "Semi-retired fiction editor."

Part One

1

Hawthorn Road

KATHARINE WHITE'S APPEARANCE was of the kind people make assumptions about. The unfashionable but handsome bun at the back of her head, the strong, classically beautiful features, the head itself like that on a Roman coin; the expensive, timeless clothes of tweed, wool, and silk, and in summer, the Liberty of London skirts and flowered-print dresses with complementary cashmere sweaters; the Sally Victor hats. "To me," said the writer Nancy Hale, "[she] simply looked the way distinguished women in Boston looked." She did not look like a New Yorker.

People assumed that she was a Boston Brahmin, a member of a fine old Boston family. "First the pilgrims, with a dead fish in every hill of corn," wrote E. B. White to James Thurber, "then the long winter at Valley Forge, then Emerson and the exaltation of those transcendental days when the Peabodys and the Hawthornes and the Hales were founding a pure blood-strain that finally produced Katharine." Always scrupulous and precise, Katharine would have set about correcting the facts.

She began life as Katharine Sergeant (pronounced Sur-jent), a name often confused with the more familiar "Sargent." The earliest-known Sergeants were pious Congregationalists who arrived in Branford, Connecticut, sometime before 1644 "in a company of Puritans." The first recorded generations were nearly all Johnathans and Johns, and included the first treasurer of the College of New Jersey (later, Princeton University). This Johnathan also chose Princeton's location, and founded the town's First Presbyterian Church. The Sergeants continued to play an important role in the growth of Princeton. Several attended the college; one married its first president. Another Sergeant helped write the constitution of the State of New Jersey. The Sergeant women, remembered for their "personal attraction and moral and Christian excellence," married well. One Hannah Sergeant married John Ewing, D.D., a noted Philadelphia educator and divine. And Hannah's nephew, Johnathan Dickenson Sergeant, married Sarah Bache, a granddaughter of Benjamin Franklin.

The most distinguished ancestor on Katharine's paternal side was the

Reverend John Sergeant, a Yale scholar who devoted his life to the education and conversion to Christianity of the Indians of Stockbridge, Massachusetts, a town he helped found.

John Sergeant's marriage, to Abigail Williams, produced three sons; it is from their son Erastus that Katharine was descended. A pioneer in the early days of American medicine, Dr. Erastus Sergeant practiced in Stockbridge and fought in the battle of Ticonderoga and in Shay's Rebellion. The doctor was progressive in his notions concerning women's education, a trait that was to reappear in his descendants. When his only daughter turned sixteen, she was dispatched to a female academy in Newark, New Jersey, where he wrote her a letter advising her to

> apply your mind to those branches of knowledge which you need most, writing, reading, spelling, and geography—and perhaps arithmetic and grammar for the next term—in the female department, you may take your own fancy and learn what you think will be most useful to you. You must be careful how you lay out your money and keep a regular account of it. If the gentlemen who instruct the dancing school are men of character, I shall have no objection to your attending a quarter. Don't forget to read your bible and attend the worship of God on Sundays.

The Sergeant women continued to pursue advanced educations—two of Katharine's paternal aunts were among the first graduates of Smith College —but the Sunday worship of God came to a halt in the eighth generation, that of Katharine Sergeant. Elsie Sergeant, Katharine's eldest sister, said that as a boy their father had been subjected to "such a severe dose of Congregational Puritanism . . . such a stern father, such heavy punishments for [every] minor error like not saying 'thank you,' which deprived him of a Thanksgiving dinner," that after his marriage and the birth of his first child, he seldom allowed his wife's mother, "in her black veil," to take Elsie to church. Katharine and her sisters grew up in a family in which Sundays were holidays and churchgoing was confined to Christmas and Easter.

Katharine's father, Charles Spencer Sergeant, was the third of seven children of a Northampton, Massachusetts, grain merchant, George Sergeant, and Lydia Ann Clark, daughter of the editor of the Hartford *Courant*. By the time Charles was seventeen, both of his parents had died, and as the eldest son he was left to support his five sisters and younger brother. There is no family account of how he did so, and how two sisters managed to attend, and graduate from, Smith College. The records show that after graduating from Northampton High School in 1868, Charles Sergeant spent four years working at a bank. This was followed by four years of railroad work in Michigan. Apparently he managed to teach himself engineering without benefit of a college education. By 1876 he had become chief clerk and auditor for Boston's Eastern Railroad. He later went on to become auditor, then second vice president, of the West End Street Railway Company.

In this age of spinsters, four of Charles's five sisters remained single (his brother never married, either). Two became teachers following their graduation from Smith. Catharine de Forest Sergeant (Aunt Kitty), for whom Katharine may have been named, was the eldest. She had become mother to her brothers and sisters at the age of fifteen, an early responsibility that seems to have overwhelmed her, for she became a semi-invalid who never moved away from the Northampton family home at 82 Bridge Street; in later years she was cared for by one of her sisters, Helen Cornelia Sergeant. For many years, a few Sergeants were always in residence on Bridge Street. As a child Katharine was deeply impressed by her visits to the house presided over by her two frail aunts, who "cultivated their own gardens, and . . . had strong opinions on Rights for Women." In their garden grew the sweetest of sweet peas. After receiving a copy of Elizabeth Gaskell's nineteenth-century novel *Cranford* for her twelfth birthday, Katharine imagined that Northampton, with the house inhabited by her unmarried aunts, was Mrs. Gaskell's fictional town "in possession of the Amazons." Like the Cranford ladies, the Northampton aunts practiced "elegant economies," paid calls, and presided over ladies' tea parties. There were committee meetings of the DAR, and "meetings of the Tuesday morning club, where previously prepared papers were read aloud, followed by discussion, and food."

Katharine's mother did not come from the world of ladies' clubs and tea parties, even that world restrained by "elegant economies." Elizabeth Blake Shepley, whom the family called Bessie, was the second child of a lawyer turned sheep rancher.

The Shepleys are traced to John Sheple of Wenham, Massachusetts, in 1636. Sheple or Shiply descendants continued to live in Massachusetts, in nearby towns, a few falling victim to Indian raids. The fourth John Sheple was carried into captivity by the Indians, and he remained with them for about four years. From him Katharine's Shepley ancestors were descended. Nineteenth-century Shepleys included lawyers, governors, and generals.

Katharine's maternal grandfather was James Cunningham Shepley. Born in Saco, Maine, James Shepley followed the family tradition and became a lawyer. He fought in the Civil War and further distinguished himself by helping to write the constitution of the State of Minnesota. He married Mary Barrows, a physician's daughter from Fryeburg, Maine. James and Mary had three children: Annie Barrows ("Aunt Poo" to Katharine and her sisters), Elizabeth Blake (Bessie), who became Katharine's mother, and George Barstow.

Following the Civil War, James Shepley, suffering from malaria, abandoned his law practice to become estate manager to a Barrows farmer cousin, "Uncle" Sam Perley. The family spent eight idyllic years living on the Perleys' large farm in Naples, Maine, before Shepley fully regained his health and decided to try his hand at sheep ranching. When Bessie was fifteen, her father bought a partnership in a sheep ranch in Fresno, California, and headed west with a friend, leaving his family behind to pack and follow as soon as he was settled. A year went by.

The sheep ranch lay in a secluded territory seven miles from the nearest railroad, in a place called Little Dry Creek. While sleeping at the camp one night, James was strangled to death. When his body was found several days later his money was discovered untouched, and his gold watch was still dangling from a hook on the wall. Two Portuguese sheepherders from a nearby camp were arrested and tried for the murder, then released without a conviction.

With the financial help of relatives, Aunt Poo and George were sent to school, she to art school in Lowell, Massachusetts; Bessie went to live temporarily with a childless aunt and uncle until her mother was resettled and could send for her. Mary Shepley went to Boston, where the educational opportunities for her children were better, and where she planned to support them by letting rooms.

Nearly eight years passed between James Shepley's murder and Bessie's marriage to Charles Sergeant in the spring of 1880. The Shepleys lived in "extreme poverty"; the boarding house was a disaster. "For one thing," wrote Aunt Poo, "[Mother] thought it was unprincipled to buy any but the best cuts of meat. She had very bad cooks and servants, not having had experience in choosing from employment offices." And "the way of life was foreign to all the family." George Shepley took a job as an errand boy at a bank, working six days a week for a salary of $2. Aunt Poo finished art school and got a $500-a-year job teaching drawing at the public school in Palatine Bridge, New York. Bessie remained at home.

In the memoir that Aunt Poo later wrote for her nieces, there is a photograph of Bessie taken in maturity, probably when she was in her early thirties. Except for her averted head and eyes she is turned toward the camera, and the portrait ends just below the waist, at the tips of her touching fingers. Aunt Poo said that as a girl Bessie looked ethereal—small and slender, with big blue eyes, a delicate pink and white complexion, "masses of pale hair," and "beautifully formed hands and feet." But, other than the reverent attitude of her hands, this woman with the swelling breasts and tightly laced bodice, the broad ruffled shoulders and large grave eyes, does not suggest the Victorian ideal of her sister's description.

It is hard to know what Katharine's mother was really like. Her sister's account of her—which, along with an autobiographical fragment penned by Katharine's sister, Elsie Sergeant, is all that apparently exists—is sentimental, and, noted Katharine, "maddeningly vague." As a child, said Aunt Poo, Bessie "had a clear understanding of the world's standards and wished to live up to them." And "not being so thrilled with life as I was, and more critical, she was more observant and therefore less naive than I, although in those days she did not know this, and I was the leader when I should have been the follower." Bessie liked canoeing, dancing, tennis, and Dickens; she was musical, a talented painter. But, unlike her artist sister, she had never wanted to be anything but "a common family woman, like my mother," and her family seems to have considered that her beauty would be her passport through life. In a letter he wrote to his wife shortly before his death, James Shepley had remarked: "Bessie, with her beauty, will be able to make her way in the world."

Bessie was twenty-three years old when she married Charles Sergeant, whom she had met when he became a boarder in her mother's house. Aunt Poo tells us that Charles was "a quiet young man with beautiful dark eyes," given to sketching in his leisure time. In the artistic Shepley sisters he found kindred souls. He was a self-made man whose future with the Eastern Railroad was promising. He persuaded his prospective mother-in-law to give up her foundering business and move in with him and Bess after their marriage. The engagement seems to have aroused a little snobbery in Charles's sisters, who may have considered the match socially less than all they desired. Aunt Poo writes that, though the lack of money in both families was regrettable, each considered the young couple's happiness to be most important. For their part, wrote Aunt Poo, the Shepleys took Charles to their hearts, "those narrow hearts which only beat for each other."

Aunt Poo told a story about her newly married sister, who was so lonely for her family on her honeymoon that she and her twenty-eight-year-old husband came home early, surprising her mother and sister, who had not finished fitting up the couple's new bedroom.

The Sergeants' first home was in Winchester, Massachusetts, and it was there that Katharine was born. Katharine was her parents' last child; Elizabeth Shepley (Elsie) had been born three years after their marriage, in 1883; Rosamond in 1890. When, in 1892, Katharine's birth drew near, her sisters were spirited away to Fryeburg, Maine, for the summer, a small town near the White Mountains where their maternal grandmother was born. Katharine's arrival was announced to her sisters by a telegram from their father, which Grandmother Shepley, whom the children called Gartie, read to them one Sunday after church. It said simply, "But yet a woman." Being the title of a popular novel, the message was quickly understood.

By 1898, the Boston Elevated Company had bought the lease of the West End Street Railway. Charles Sergeant was by then general manager of the West End in charge of stations, arrangement of tracks, etc. He and his family had left Winchester and were living in a house on Walnut Street in Brookline when they purchased a lovely new house in the same city.

It was proof of her father's success that seventeen years after his marriage he was able to buy a $23,500 home in "the rich men's town," as Brookline, Massachusetts, was then called: an 8,800-square-foot Georgian house on over a third of an acre. Katharine grew up in this house, and most of her memories began here, where she moved when she was eight. In later years, she loved to talk about her Boston girlhood, and she preferred to write about the past. Her memories of the house and garden, of the New England of her early life, shaped themselves, in the last quarter of her life, into a series of singular garden essays.

The house stood at the corner of a leafy residential street, Hawthorn Road —aptly named, Katharine recalled, for "the three huge English hawthorn trees that grew in our own yard—a red, a pink, and a white. Towering above the lilacs in the curving bed of shrubs, they were a sight to see in May." It was an austerely beautiful house, dusty pink brick surrounded by tall hedges, which parted briefly in front to admit a small curved drive. The façade was all windows, oculus and square. A carriage house stood to the right of the house; in back, the sloping lawn was "impeccably shorn and green." On the lawn Katharine and her next-eldest sister, Rosamond, played croquet, diabolo, baseball, ring toss, and shuttlecock, as badminton was then called, and their favorite game, statues. The tableau might have been by John Singer Sargent: the Sergeant girls in their crisp white pinafores and dark stockings balanced precariously on the lawn, that "soft carpet of grass [which] was a true necessity, for the little girl who was 'It' would seize each of the other girls in turn by the wrist and whirl her around and around until she was dizzy, and then, just as she flung her victim off, to stagger, and often to fall, on the grass, she would scream out an abstract noun—Grief, Anger, Grace, Hatred, Love, or Defiance—to indicate the pose and expression the living statue must freeze into." Katharine later thought that the Copley prints of classic Greek and Roman sculptures she was required to assemble for her ancient history class might have inspired this popular game. "Do Copley prints still figure in Boston education?" she wondered. "Do little girls still posture on the lawns of Hawthorn Road?"

In 1899, when Katharine was six years old, her mother died. Bessie had not been feeling well for some time, and she had taken a trip to New York, where Uncle George and Aunt Poo were then living, hoping that the change of air would help. By the time she arrived, her appendix had burst and she was rushed to the hospital; but her illness was misdiagnosed and she was given improper medical treatment before the real cause of illness was determined. Her last words were to her sister: "Nobody can say I didn't have courage." She died on the operating table ten minutes after Charles arrived from Boston. She was forty-one.

Katharine would scarcely remember her mother, and she had no conscious sense of loss. She later attributed this to age and circumstances: she was so young when her mother died. More significantly, one of Papa's sisters came to live with the family shortly afterward. Caroline Belle Sergeant (Aunt Crully), who was ten years to the day her brother's junior, became the only mother Katharine knew, and she was a godsend. "When my Aunt Caroline died at 93, I felt that there was no one left in the world in whose eyes I could do no wrong, no matter how badly I behaved."

Caroline—small, sweet-natured, refined, a black velvet choker around her neck—was one of the two Sergeant sisters who had graduated from Smith. A member of the college's fourth graduating class (1884), she had taught in a school for the deaf and served with another woman as headmistress of a girls' school before coming to live with her brother's family. E. B. White remembered her as "a marvelous person—extremely articulate. I remember her once saying, after I'd apologized for not taking her out to see the fall foliage, 'Remembrance is sufficient of the beauty we have seen.' That was the way she talked!" Her influence on Katharine must have been profound. At the impressionable age of six, Katharine had lost her mother and acquired a new mother who gave her unconditional love, a happy home, and a model —of literacy and achievement—to which she could aspire. When Bessie died, Katharine was young enough to attach herself easily to her aunt, and this softened the loss. But she was also young enough to pattern her personality on her aunt's, and this may not have been as favorable to her early development.

Bessie had been emotional, and had sometimes lost control. Elsie remembered her as a young wife and mother, a pretty woman in a blue cambric skirt crying over the household accounts, and sitting tearfully by her children's sickbeds after allowing them to overindulge in sweets, wishing aloud that she could be sick for them.* For all their kindness, the Sergeants, by contrast with the Shepleys, were a stiff, repressive lot. Aunt Crully, recalled

---

*One cannot be sure what is fact, what is fiction, what is exaggerated, in Elsie's written accounts of her mother, which were never finished. It is unclear whether she intended these scraps of autobiography for a novel or a memoir.

E. B. White, was "too upright, too under control to cry outright." And Charles, perhaps fearing his own loss of control, forbade seventeen-year-old Elsie to cry at her mother's funeral. With Bessie gone, there were now two inhibited people at the head of the family. Elsie rebelled against the Sergeant restraint, "had rages," and suffered from psychological problems all her adult life; Rosamond became "a flawed personality": a henpecking wife, an unaffectionate mother. Katharine, said E. B. White, "did not easily slip an arm around one of her children," and her tears were mostly "silent and lonely. She would sometimes awake in the morning, crying in bed about something she'd been thinking about, or dreaming." And when he asked her what was troubling her, she would not always tell him. At an early age she had learned self-control; and a part of her remained secret and private, even from her adored second husband. When Katharine was an old woman, she wrote: "I have always tended to forget purposely painful events." She repressed any memory of the death of her mother.

Aunt Poo offered only one observation of Bessie as a mother: that in the beginning she was timid, and, lacking confidence, "she never had as much pleasure in her babies as many mothers have. She was always too anxious, but she had gained experience and confidence by the time Katharine came, and she really took comfort in her."

Had Bessie lived, she might have exerted a softening influence on her daughters, and it is in this that Katharine was deprived, whether she was aware of it or not. Elsie and Rosamond might have been happier. Katharine might not have seemed forbidding.

Katharine's life, by her own account, was charmed. Flower-filled, comfortable, and gracious, these years of her girlhood emerge from the "Onward and Upward In The Garden" pieces and the letters she wrote for *The New Yorker*'s "Department of Amplification" as a series of Victorian postcards. A small girl carefully snips a backyard rosebud for the breakfast table; with her sister, trims their Boston schoolgirls' hats with flowers from the shrubbery; paddles in a canoe, in the glorious early-morning light, to pick water lilies on the lake at the foot of Mount Chocorua. There are scenes of girls riding bicycles through Holm Lea, the great 180-acre estate of Professor Charles Sprague Sargent of Harvard, whose mail is delivered to the home of Charles Spencer Sergeant—a confusion the two men are unable to straighten out; of carriage rides through the Arnold Arboretum in neighboring Jamaica Plain.

The Sergeant kitchen was presided over by a "talented, tyrannical" cook named Mary Hillen, whose strawberry shortcake "was a huge, round crusty *shortbread,* hot out of the oven, split and buttered and filled to bursting with juicy berries, which oozed onto the platter, the whole luscious structure topped with two inches of unpasteurized whipped cream." A neighborhood handyman, William Hickey, tended the lawn, shoveled the driveway in winter, stoked the coal stove and replenished the firewood, blacked the family's boots, and washed their fox terrier, Teddy. Each spring, to Katharine's delight, a team of horses pulled a heavy roller over the newly fertilized lawn, their hooves dressed in small leather boots to protect the turf.

A steady force and evidently delightful presence during these years was Papa—(accent on the second syllable)—Papa with his handlebar mustache and his fussiness about the lawn and flowers. By all accounts he was a fond and attentive father, a father in the old-fashioned sense, who read to his children and joined them in games and activities. In Elsie's few recorded recollections, he seems to have been impatient at times with his wife and her family, but protective and only sometimes stern with her. In Katharine's writings, her father is seen "inflamed" only once—at the sight of a dandelion on his beloved lawn. He was a small man—"impressive," said E. B. White, "in a small way." Katharine's daughter, Nancy Stableford, said that he gave the impression of being rich; White would have said "substantial. He was a man of substance." He was of the hard-working generation of men who toiled six days a week, leaving his house at eight o'clock in the morning and returning just before seven at night. "He was a typical Boston capitalist home man," said White. Except on the rarest occasions, he always wore a necktie or bow tie, and a vest. He belonged to the St. Botolph Club, the Country Club, the restrictive Exchange and Algonquin clubs, whose memberships included Coolidges, Saltonstalls, Searses, and at least one Cabot and a Lodge. He was listed in the Boston Blue Book.

Nancy Stableford and E. B. White, who of course knew Charles Sergeant only in later years, liked this man who liked his martini and awoke coughing in the morning with catarrh from cigarette smoking. Ashes would fall on his vest. He was terrified of bees—anything that buzzed. There is a memory of the small elderly man running from a bee swarm. But, for all his humanness, he could be frightening to his young granddaughter, scaring "the hell out of you because he was so formal." To Nancy, he was "loveable, though stiff," funny, pompous, and officious, "with strong opinions on all kinds of things." She recalled a Fourth of July when she was thirteen years old and her grandfather, then in his early seventies, ceremoniously instructed her in the proper use of a Roman candle—and promptly shot it off into her stomach.

From Katharine's early childhood on her father was a widower, a man whose sexual life had ended at forty-seven, and who thereafter lived, in a semblance of marriage, with his unmarried sister, sharing the rearing of his children. Whether or not he lived happily we do not know. But he and Aunt Crully managed to create a loving home for Katharine, giving her a sense of security and a strong sense of her own self-worth.

"I was the youngest in a family that read aloud," wrote Katharine in 1946. "I was continually listening to books that were 'too old' for me—or, at any rate, ones that would be called too old by today's educators. I heard 'Ivanhoe' at seven or eight and was alarmed by 'Oliver Twist' soon after. I made my first inquiry into the mystery of birth because of the puzzling phrase on the first pages of 'David Copperfield': 'I was born with a caul.' This sent me to the dictionary and Webster's own brand of puzzles." She learned the *New England Primer's* alphabet from her father, who delighted in reciting,

> Zaccheus *he*
> *Did climb the Tree*
> *Our Lord to see.*

"To which, according to my father, the children irreverently added:

> *The Tree did break*
> *And he did fall*
> *And never saw*
> *His Lord at all."*

Storytelling began in early childhood. Bessie talked to her children of her Minneapolis girlhood and the cats she had had; and returning home from the evening commuter train, Papa would sit with a daughter on his lap in the parlor, his mustache tickling her ear, his "very low" voice "affirmative" and "spellcasting" as he talked of an imaginary figure named Mr. Greenheart, "who lived in a little house in the crotch of a tree." During her visits, Aunt Poo joined in with her own stories, which contained "more of magic and romance." "She had, she assured me," said Elsie, "located a band of [fairies] who danced at night in a lovely green hollow called a 'dell' very near our house."

Katharine became an avid reader. She read the usual fairy tales of the day —most often Andrew Lang's colored fairy books, of which she owned seven. She had two of Walter Crane's illustrated English songbooks, and two of "Boutet de Monvel's lovely books of *Chansons pour les petits enfants."* She was scarcely interested in the popular *Heidi* and *Hans Brinker or the Silver Skates,* and was so repelled by one year's Christmas gift, a slim nonfiction volume called *Ten Boys on the Road from Long Ago to Now,* that as an adult she worried about giving children nonfiction books for Christmas. Among the favorite books of her childhood were *Black Beauty, The Rose and the Ring,* and Lily F. Wesselhoeft's talking-animal books, which gave Katharine her "first taste of realism. I have never forgotten the one about a man who was frozen in a blizzard and whose arm stuck up through the snow, a gruesome episode that seems to have left no emotional scar." And she memorized verses:

> *Come and see me, Mary Ann,*
> *This afternoon at three;*
> *Come as early as you can*
> *And stay till after tea.*
> *We'll jump the rope, we'll dress the doll,*
> *We'll feed my sister's birds,*
> *And read my little story books,*
> *All full of easy words.*

The illustrated books Katharine read helped her understand how art could fuse with literature to bring stories more vividly to life. Some pictures were "gloomy," even terrifying—like Arthur Rackham's illustrations, with their "darksome forests and tortured tree trunks." The beauty of others stayed with her all her life. She remembered once seeing the Gustave Doré–illustrated *Adventures of Baron Munchausen* at the home of a friend, where the book was ceremoniously brought out "and read aloud with many admonitions about not touching the precious engravings," which made the book the more enchanting.

As an older child and young woman, Katharine "dearly loved *The Wind in the Willows*" and the novels of Jane Austen, who remained her favorite novelist.* She particularly liked the somber *Mansfield Park,* and she considered *Emma* "the best picture of a managing woman (whose interest was other women), I have ever read." Charles Sergeant forbade his daughters to read Dumas, whose books he considered "racy," but otherwise appears to have given them free literary rein.

Children of Katharine's generation found a creative outlet in the *St. Nicholas Magazine,* a popular juvenile publication that encouraged young talent with competitions for badges in story writing, poetry, and drawing.

---

*In a 1944 letter to Edmund Wilson, Katharine wrote: "All my life I've been a Janeite (horrible word and I've never used it of myself before) and I read the novels over constantly, for solace, comfort, and pleasure. Andy has complained many times over having Miss Austen in bed with us, but just recently he has begun reading and adoring her himself. . . . In my silly moments I think of Jane Austen as the perfect New Yorker writer."

During the magazine's lifetime, from 1873 to 1940, the competitors and winners of the coveted badges included Edna St. Vincent Millay, Ring Lardner, Stephen Benét, Robert Benchley, Conrad Aiken, William Faulkner, Vita Sackville-West, E. B. White, and at least two of Katharine White's writers: Janet Flanner and Edmund Wilson. Katharine once received a silver badge for a given topic, "A Surprise." Her winning entry was on "the long nest of the Trap Door Spider, that some relative gave me when I was a little girl. The door part fascinated me with its perfect hinge and just enough space for the spider to stick her foot into and close the door behind her." Rosamond Sergeant competed too, and, said Katharine, won "a gold badge for a photograph of wild ducks, but I always thought it was a cheat because they were actually very tame ducks and were swimming in a park in Worcester, Mass., where our artist aunt lived for a few years. I think I was discouraged by Rosamond's gold badge—I never submitted anything else." Katharine certainly had a prim side, and it earned her a private nickname from some of her classmates, who called her Goody Sergeant.

"Katharine never did anything she shouldn't do—she was not very gay," recalled an alumna of Miss Winsor's School in Boston (now The Winsor School). "We called her Goody Sergeant behind her back, shortening it to Little Goody or simply Goody, because she was the goodest and the brightest in the class." Rosamond Sergeant "was gayer and more like the others" than her younger sister, the small girl with the long pigtails who went directly home from school rather than join in the after-school frolics in the Boston Public Garden, where other Winsor girls battled "with the boys from Noble & Greenough's who had no use for girls—nor we for them. We whacked them with our string bags, nubbly with books."

Katharine's was the class of 1909; she entered the school on Beacon Street in 1903, as a seventh grader (having apparently been educated at home before then), the third Sergeant child to attend Winsor's. A genteel private establishment typical of the better day schools attended by the daughters of middle-class and wealthy families, Winsor had a good reputation—"Winsor girls got into the college of their choice." Following Aunt Crully's and Elsie's example (Elsie had graduated from Bryn Mawr by the time Katharine entered Winsor's), Katharine enrolled in the college-preparatory program, which included French, Latin, and German. Weekdays she boarded the streetcar a couple of blocks from home, and "when I came home from Miss Winsor's School all full of excitement about a new science course (physiology and biology) . . . my father raised his hand wearily and stopped me, saying 'Do I have to go through that course a third time?' "

Katharine moved serenely through her school days, winning good grades and taking away the impression that "Miss Winsor's stimulating Summer Reading Lists must have been a powerful influence in my education." Another powerful—and less benign—influence was her eldest sister.

Among Katharine's letters and family papers, in her published writing, there are no descriptions of Elsie when young. It was Rosamond who figured in Katharine's childhood memories, Katharine and Rosamond who climbed the hawthorn trees and played lawn games, picked water lilies on Lake Chocorua and fruit "and unharvested tomatos and carrots" in the orchards and gardens of Woodstock, Connecticut, where Aunt Poo lived for a while. Elsie's absence from these scenes was inevitable: she was eleven years older than Katharine. And yet her early influence on her youngest sister—an influence that was to be lifelong—was profound. A story Katharine began to write many years later and left unfinished is testimony to this.

> So many things had happened that year, good things and bad things, that Kathy could never quite sort them out in her mind or know which had happened first. She couldn't even be sure they had all happened *that* year, when she was six, but she did know that the best of them all was the teacup. It was the most unexpected and the nicest of all her Christmas presents.

Thus begins "The Teacup," one of the few documents Katharine White left undated and unexplained at her death. It is unclear whether she originally intended the piece for publication, or whether she wrote it merely as an exercise, an attempt to express her deepest feelings about her overpowering eldest sister. E. B. White thought that his wife had intended the story for publication, and the third-person narrative supports the theory, as does the change in names: Aunt Caroline is represented by "Aunt Annie," Elsie by "Penelope." Penelope, however, is Kathy's next-eldest rather than eldest sister; the eldest sister of the story, who seems not to represent Rosamond but to be another extension of Elsie, is seventeen (Elsie's age when Katharine was six), and is called "Marguerite." If Katharine did not intend to publish the story, she may simply have found it easier to write about the incident from the distance that these fictional devices permitted.

A heavily revised and partly illegible draft of about four hundred words, "The Teacup" is based on a Christmas gift of china teacups Katharine and Elsie received when Katharine was a child. "Wrapped in white tissue paper and tied with narrow white satin ribbon," the package promises something wonderful. On the outside in gold letters is written "Marshall Field & Co., Chicago, Illinois." And then the contents are revealed, the cups of very fine and delicate English china—"bone." As the youngest child, Kathy is invited by her father to choose between the cups, which have come with a card from a distant aunt "For the two younger girls." But, before Kathy can make her selection, Penelope "snatche[s] up the cup with lavender and yellow pansies dotted on a white field," leaving Kathy with the cup she privately prefers, "the rosy cup with its blue ribbon pattern, its graceful curving lines, its elegant little foot. She had never seen anything so beautiful in her life." This is where the fragment ends.

Katharine left no account of the actual story, but according to E. B. White, when Elsie later went to college she took Katharine's teacup with her as well as her own. Whether Elsie deliberately took the cup because it was part of a set and she somehow felt entitled to it, or removed it accidentally, is unknown. But it was a bitter experience for Katharine, and she never forgot it.

Possessions were important to Katharine, as were things of quality; this was true of her even as a child. Reading "The Teacup," one is struck by the author's attention to the beauty of the cups and the fine quality of the china. (She twice mentions that they are bone china.) The cups are exquisite, but the adults react "scornfully." "It's perfectly obvious Emily hasn't the least idea what age the girls are," says Papa. "Teacups!" Marguerite, who at seventeen appears to Kathy as one of the grown-ups and has herself received a silver spoon from the aunt, says, "What a Christmas present for children!" But the teacup is not merely a beautiful object to be treasured for its own sake: it also makes Kathy feel grown-up. Viewed as autobiography, the fragment suggests that the subsequent loss of the cup may have underscored for Katharine the loss of her mother. Kathy is six and the year has been eventful; it has been a year of "good things and bad things." Kathy cannot remember which of the "things" happened first, but she associates the events with each other. Katharine was six when her mother died and Aunt Crully came to live with the family. If, like Kathy, Katharine received the cup at age six, it arrived on the first Christmas after her mother's death, and was therefore of special value.

One senses that throughout their lives Katharine and Elsie each felt that the other had "snatched" something away from her, or had something that the other wanted. In later years, it was Elsie who felt deprived. Family members perceived her as a lonely, troubled woman who envied Katharine her literary success, something that had eluded Elsie, though she wrote dozens of articles for *The New Republic* and other magazines and published half a dozen books; a woman who was jealous of Katharine's home and children, which she had likewise never had. But early in their lives it was Katharine who felt jealous and resentful.

Katharine's feelings were rooted partly in her own upbringing, and in an idea that she had not been wanted. "I was the third girl in our family and a disappointment," she would write, "& I realized this even when very young, but later on the family made up [for] this." She did not explain how she had known herself to be a disappointment, or how her family made it up to her. But she had heard about the telegram Charles Sergeant sent her sisters announcing her birth—"But yet a woman"—and she may have interpreted it to mean that he was disappointed in having yet another daughter. Then, too, there was Elsie's position in the Sergeant family, the ascendancy she had established over her younger sisters. In the house where Katharine and Rosamond shared a room, Elsie had her own bedroom and private study. Though Katharine was clearly not neglected and was undoubtedly loved, Elsie, said E. B. White, was "queen of the May." "Everything Elsie did was important, according to Elsie and the family." Once, Elsie was even allowed to take Noland, the family horse, and the buggy, and drive alone to Dublin, New Hampshire; Papa gave her a pistol with which to protect herself. Katharine, who "didn't think Elsie had any gift with horses," viewed the episode with contempt.

One remembers similar reactions—to the gold badge Rosamond won from the St. Nicholas League for her photograph of bogus wild ducks; to the repellent book Katharine received one year for Christmas. The picture is of a girl who was in some ways a curiously old child of impossibly high standards, easily disappointed in people, and judgmental.

Though Elsie was clearly Aunt Poo's favorite ("the most beloved after my brother," Aunt Poo writes in her memoir), it is impossible to determine whether she was also Charles and Caroline's favorite, or Charles and Bess's. But she was the first born—in fact, for nearly seven years, the only child in the whole family of Northampton aunts and uncle and the Boston Shepleys. And it is certain that by the time Elsie graduated from Bryn Mawr, when Katharine was ten years old, the family was aware that something was wrong with her.

Aunt Poo writes that at the time of Elsie's college graduation she was "in very bad shape physically. Her doctor recommended travel abroad, and Elsie thought I was the travelling companion she most wanted . . . we sailed away for Italy." During that warm Italian spring of 1903, aunt and niece met with "highly entertaining society," the beautiful niece winning admiring glances from the Italian men. They went first to Sicily, and finally north to Assisi, where in the Upper Church they saw the Giotto frescos that were a tribute to the life of St. Francis, who was "rather a hero" of Katharine's. But though they moved at a leisurely pace, stopping regularly for Elsie to rest, Elsie's "condition" became the worse for travel, and Aunt Poo took her to a sanitarium in Paris. The memoir does not name the sanitarium, it says nothing of Elsie's diagnosis, and no information is to be found among surviving family members, letters, or papers. Aunt Poo says only that she "could scarcely see [Elsie] and that after waiting for a time, having a studio and living at the American Club, I sailed for home." At some point Elsie appears to have been moved to a sanitarium in Zürich. Charles Sergeant, in London to supervise the building of that city's underground railway, now traveled to Zürich to watch over his eldest child.

Aunt Crully, Rosamond, and Katharine spent the summer of 1904 at the Chocorua Hotel. With two of the family missing, and perhaps because of the additional expenses incurred by Elsie's prolonged hospital stay, they decided against renting a cottage that year. At the hotel Katharine met and became friends with a girl named Hildegarde Angell, who was staying there with her widowed mother and older brother, Ernest, a good-looking boy of fifteen, "who was in pursuit of a much older girl than he—my distant cousin and later Elsie's Jungian friend, Hildegarde Nagel," recalled Katharine. Not yet twelve, Katharine was "too young to be interesting" to her friend's brother.

Elsie seems to have remained at the sanitarium throughout the winter of 1904–1905. She was in Europe for two years following her graduation from Bryn Mawr. It may have been while in Switzerland that she was analyzed by Dr. Carl Jung. Family papers reveal that this occurred sometime before the First World War.

The exact nature of Elsie's psychological problems remains unclear. Referring, apparently, to Jung, Elsie later wrote that "a great psychologist once described her as 'an egg without a shell.' " (Elsie was writing about herself in the third person.) Aunt Poo, in the vernacular of her time, wrote of Elsie's "long nervous illness," an illness that prevented her from beginning to write professionally until five or six years after her college graduation.

On the first day of October, 1907, "an extraordinary thing" happened at 4 Hawthorn Road. Fifty-one-year-old Aunt Poo, her "adored nieces" surrounding her, became the bride of a thirty-year-old Japanese, Hyozo Omori.

Aunt Poo met Mr. Omori when she hired him as a cook at her house in Woodstock, Connecticut, which she called Apple End. E. B. White later told the story of their courtship:

> It became apparent almost immediately that Mr. Omori and a kitchen were strangers of long standing. Aristocracy stuck out all over him. Although his efforts at cooking were preposterous, his conversation was charming. Aunt Poo saw in him a man who had been waited on all his life and who was clearly unsuited for any sudden reversal. So she set to and prepared Mr. Omori's meals

for him, and as soon as possible engaged a large colored woman to carry some of the rapidly mounting household burden.

Mr. Omori, it must be said, offered to leave, but she urged him to stay on and assume duties of a more wispy sort—poking about the flower garden and exchanging views on poetry. He consented. For a while the domestic situation at Apple End was confused; the Japanese student was unwilling to sit at table with the colored woman, and the mistress of the house was disinclined to sit at table with the Japanese student. Everybody was eating off trays, in aseptic splendor.

> In this way [writes Aunt Poo in her memorial volume] began my acquaintance with Hyozo Omori, a gentleman of ancient lineage and culture who, like most of the Japanese students of that day, regarded all Americans as quite inferior in culture but were quite ready, given a respect for all honest work, to earn money from us in a perfectly impersonal way, making a contact with unpleasant things for a moment for convenience, without feeling oneself degraded.

I take it what slight momentary degradation Mr. Omori had been subjected to during his first few days at Woodstock was forgotten in the ensuing weeks. Aunt Poo and he liked the same books. Together they walked in the garden and talked of Japanese art—which Mr. Omori knew a great deal about—and he told her of his two ambitions in life: to found a settlement house in Tokyo, and to increase the stature of the Japanese race. In the fall he returned to Springfield, she to Boston. They corresponded. He visited her several times, and finally asked her to marry him. She decided after a while to accept.

The wedding took place in the parlor, where the fireplace mantel, adorned with Mrs. Humphry Ward roses, served as an altar. Papa, who in Aunt Poo's words had "refused at first to have anything to do with [the match]," but had since come to regard it sympathetically, provided the wedding breakfast.

Given the time and the recent strain in United States relations with Japan, Charles Sergeant's first reaction to his sister-in-law's intended marriage is understandable. Only a year earlier, in 1906, the San Francisco school board had proposed an order segregating Asiatics, though few Japanese children were enrolled in the schools. The Japanese government protested the discrimination against its people. In 1907, with an eye on "this formidable new power" in the Orient, President Theodore Roosevelt carefully forged the Gentlemen's Agreement with Japan. Japan agreed to prevent her laborers from emigrating to the United States; in turn, the United States promised not to discriminate openly against the Japanese. But American animosity toward the country's Japanese citizens remained.

It is said that the Boston *American* "broke the story [of the engagement] with a mild flourish.* Family councils were held behind closed doors. The girls, bursting with direct questions, were put off with evasive answers. It was a time of incredible consternation and embarrassment." Since all of Aunt Poo's immediate family were now deceased, Mr. Omori desired Charles Sergeant's consent to the marriage. Charles Sergeant was a reasonable man, and he was finally won over by Omori's considerable charm, and his deep and obvious love for Aunt Poo. "[I]n the end," wrote Aunt Poo, "his greatest regret seemed to be for [Hyozo]. It seemed a pity to waste his lovely youth on me, and I agreed heartily but could not refuse him." As for Katharine and her sisters, they were delighted by the prospect of a wedding in the house, and enchanted with their refined and "celestial"-looking uncle-to-be, whose "slight beard . . . delicate features and sensitiveness, gave him a Christlike appearance," and who taught them to make green tea "in cups without handles."

Immediately after the wedding, the Omoris left for Tokyo. There they wasted no time fulfilling Uncle Hyo's dreams for the Japanese race, first founding a Japanese settlement house, which became the distinguished Yu-rin-En, Tokyo's Hull House. Theorizing that athletic prowess and competition would further advance his ambitions for his people, Uncle Hyo then organized the first Japanese Olympic team, which he and Aunt Poo proudly accompanied to the 1912 games in Stockholm. Afterward, the couple paid their last visit to the Brookline family; Uncle Hyo died of tuberculosis en route home to Tokyo. Aunt Poo returned to her adopted country and dedicated the rest of her life to the Japanese people, continuing her husband's work at Yurin-En, writing an English translation of *Lady Murasaki,* and, with another woman, *Diaries of Court Ladies of Old Japan,* and performing heroic service in the 1922 earthquake, for which she was given the Order of the Rising Sun by the government. With a faithful correspondence, she remained close to her American family, though her blind loyalty to Japan strained her relationship with her nieces during the events leading up to World War II. Aunt Poo acquired at least one Japanese relative, a nephew, Takecheyo Matsuda, who became Japan's cabinet minister for communications after the war. Many years later, Takecheyo, or Homer, as his aunt called him, visited some of his American relations.

One senses that for Katharine these events were something more than a merely colorful and amusing chapter in her family history: she seemed proud of her Japanese relatives, both for their own achievements and for the rich

*There is some doubt that this newspaper broke the story. A careful perusal of the Boston *American*'s 1907 issues has turned up no such story.

cultural heritage and aesthetic sensitivity that were theirs. In one of her gardening essays, she wrote at some length about *ikebana,* the Japanese art of flower arrangement, which she had studied a little. And she recalled the aunt who, so long ago, "had taken the then astounding step of marrying a Japanese."

It was taken for granted—by Katharine, and apparently by her family— that Katharine would go to college. As she wrote years later, "I can hardly remember a time in my childhood, absurd a child as I must sound to admit it, when my plans for myself 'grown-up' did not include both marriage and a definite career. At twelve years old, after a dose of Greek history, I was to be an archaeologist, a few years later a doctor"—her ambitions had always been serious. Having prepared at Miss Winsor's, having been encouraged by Elsie, whom she had visited when Elsie was herself a student there, Katharine settled on Bryn Mawr.

2

The Inner Shrine

B RYN MAWR COLLEGE, in the years 1910–14, consisted of nine buildings of gray stone. Surrounded by rolling land dotted with tidy country houses, the college sat on a small hill, though the words "Bryn Mawr," in Welsh, mean "high hill." The application here was intellectual rather than physical, the words denoting a high order of learning and the lofty aspirations of its students.

Under the ambitious tutelage of President M. Carey Thomas, Bryn Mawr strove to be an American counterpart to the great English universities of Oxford and Cambridge. The college was a mixture of venerable architectural styles—Gothic, American High-Victorian Gothic, Jacobean—but with something all its own, and built of a local gray mica schist called "Germantown stone." The buildings, roughly forming a U, were wrapped with a heavy blanket of wisteria and ivy, and framed with maples, dogwoods, and Japanese cherry trees. One entered the college through the leaf-covered Pembroke Arch, which joined the two residence halls, Pembrokes East and West, in the latter of which Katharine Sergeant lived. The campus included Taylor Hall, with its clock tower and spire, and the library (which Katharine and a friend haunted chiefly to read the celebrated and "wicked" English magazine *The Yellow Book*), fronted with battlements and turrets and containing a cloister, whose colonnade was adorned with gargoyles. The overall effect of these buildings was intended, in President Thomas's words, to "give a sense of quiet and peace peculiarly adapted to the life of college students."

In the Oxbridge tradition, Bryn Mawr students hurried to class in caps and gowns, theirs a long black serge, which reached the ankles. The British influence was observed in the library's reading room as well, where the desks, modeled on those in the British Museum reading room, were separated with two-foot-high wooden partitions to ensure the reader's privacy. Following the 1904 appointment of a British sportswoman as college athletic director, field hockey became an important campus activity. And it may have been Oxford's legendary Bull Dog, the man who chased tardy students back to their colleges before they were locked for the night, who inspired Bryn

Mawr's gentle counterpart, the Lantern Man, whose job it was to escort students back from the train station to campus at night.

M. Carey Thomas hoped that the Bryn Mawr graduate would "become as well known and universally admired a type as the Oxford and Cambridge man or the graduate of the great English public schools." It was in the high caliber of its students and the distinguished quality of its education that Bryn Mawr importantly resembled the famous British institutions. Two-thirds of the college's applicants failed to make it past the rigorous entrance examinations. Bryn Mawr gave its own exams, though students were later permitted to take those given by the College Entrance Examination Board instead. Unlike Vassar and Mount Holyoke, Bryn Mawr did not accept an approved school certificate in place of tests. The Bryn Mawr exams were fully as exacting as those given by the top-ranked men's universities, which set the school apart from the other women's colleges. The college's formidable prerequisites not only resulted in superior students entering Bryn Mawr; they raised the standards of American education, both at the college and secondary levels, with students demanding that they be prepared for the toughest examinations given: at the time, those of Bryn Mawr and Harvard.

Admission requirements included a knowledge of three of four languages —Latin, Greek, French, and German. Students missing a fourth language were required to take it at college. Particularly striking was the secondary-school requirement: 17.5 units (a unit representing about one-quarter of a year's work), though four years of high school typically amounted to 16. This was in contrast to other top schools—among them Dartmouth, Yale, Wellesley, Radcliffe, and Harvard—which required from 14.5 to 16 units.

At a time when fewer than 65,000 women attended college in the United States, both at the graduate and undergraduate levels (compared with more than 119,000 men), more than 42,000 of these women at coeducational institutions, Bryn Mawr students were an especially privileged lot. The privilege was paid for in fees ranging from $500 to $775 a year, according to the rooms one occupied. (Tuition was $200 a year, with board varying according to one's accommodations.) With another student Katharine occupied a two-bedroom suite and study in Pembroke West, which cost from $225 to $350 a year (compared with $75 to $175 for a single room). When one realizes that per capita income in America was about $300, or from $1100 to $1300 for a family of four, it is no wonder that Bryn Mawr was reputed to be a rich girl's school.

Bryn Mawr's curriculum was loosely modeled on that of Johns Hopkins, though M. Carey Thomas had made it her own. It was known as the Group System, which meant that students specialized in subjects which were taken in pairs or groups of three: Greek with Latin, German with modern history, economics with politics and philosophy—there were twenty-five different groupings taken in Katharine's graduating class of 1914. Required courses made up half of the students' work, all students taking English, philosophy, Greek, Latin, a science course, and French and German, if needed. M. Carey Thomas believed that French would be necessary for those pursuing careers in the humanities, with German serving those in the sciences. At the end of her senior year, each student was required to pass oral exams in both French and German. They were given four chances. If everyone in the class passed, they rolled hoops to celebrate.

Martha Carey Thomas was herself a formidable scholar. Following her graduation from Cornell, she had studied at Germany's University of Leipzig before going on to Zürich to earn a doctorate of philosophy *summa cum laude,* a highest honor rarely given. She appears to have been only the second woman anywhere to have received a doctorate of philosophy, and the first woman college president with a Ph.D. Handsome, severely plain in dress and style, her white hair pulled back for efficiency rather than effect, she walked with a limp from a childhood accident during which she had been burned nearly to death. This purposeful, formidable woman—the regal subject of the portrait John Singer Sargent considered his best—could scarcely be imagined young. Many years after Katharine's graduation from Bryn Mawr, she would write that she "was delighted to learn that M. Carey Thomas was able to flirt with anyone during her German student days. My memories of her as President are too austere to envisage her having ever given a sidewise glance to a young man!"

At fifty-seven, Dr. Thomas had been president of Bryn Mawr for twenty years (dean for eleven years before that) when Katharine Sergeant arrived at the college in the last months of 1910. Bryn Mawr's impressive standing in American education, its stringent admission requirements and staunchly classical curriculum, and even the tenor of its day-to-day college life bore the imprint of this extraordinary and determined personality. An ardent feminist, suspicious and resentful of the male-dominated world that held women back—a world that had forced her to go all the way to Zürich to find a university willing to award a doctorate of philosophy to a woman —she fought to prove women's superiority to men.

Thomas believed that women could best make their mark on the world in the areas of academics and research. To this aim, for three decades she had endeavored to create a female type in her own image: highly disciplined, unmarried, committed to a life of scholarship and "intellectual renunciation." She reasoned that her scholars would best be formed in the female world of a women's college, where they could study free from romantic distractions: "It is undesirable to have the problems of love and marriage presented for decision to a young girl during the four years when she ought to devote her energies to profiting by the only systematic intellectual training she is likely to receive during her life." Ideally, even after graduation the Bryn Mawr woman would resist the temptation to marry. But Thomas was aware that not all her graduates would distinguish themselves professionally, and that some, inevitably, would marry. By the time Katharine began her freshman year, Thomas's rhetoric had begun to soften, the passionate separatist now allowing that it might be possible to marry and still make a professional contribution to the world. But Thomas insisted that educated women who married should be "both economically and psychologically independent" from their husbands. They should be self-supporting, if only to be able to hire someone to do housework for them. Still, marriage was not the preferred route. One of Katharine's classmates remembered being taught to believe that the Bryn Mawr woman's place was not necessarily in the home, but rather in the world—as a person making a significant contribution to science or the humanities.

Sixty-five years after her 1914 graduation from Bryn Mawr, Leah Cadbury Furtmuller recalled a moment when she and Katharine Sergeant stood on the steps of Pembroke and Katharine announced, "I'm engaged to be married!" "Oh, Katharine, how perfectly awful!" was the grave reply.

Katharine began her freshman year an engaged woman. Ernest Angell, her friend of many summers at Chocorua, had proposed to her on her eighteenth birthday. Now twenty-one and a senior at Harvard, Ernest was extremely handsome, exactly six feet tall, and slender. His long, angular face and high cheekbones bespoke his Indian ancestry (he was one-eighth Seneca). It is the large dark eyes one is drawn to in his photographs—"Fine, frank, judicious brown eyes," Elsie would describe them. Not surprisingly, he had engaged in flirtations with other girls before Katharine, but the romance with her appears to have been first love for them both.

It was both natural and logical that Ernest Angell and Katharine Sergeant were attracted to each other. Since childhood, they had been thrown together during summers at Lake Chocorua; Katharine and Ernest's sister, Hildegarde, were friends; they had interests in common—the theater, books; and there must have been an intellectual attraction. Like Katharine, Ernest was highly intelligent, a good student who had won highest honors and a commencement prize in Greek and Latin at the progressive University School east of Cleveland, where he was born and had grown up. He had lived in Germany and attended school there for a year; he spoke German and beautiful French; he read Greek. At Harvard he won several scholarships, played baseball on his class team, and was on the Harvard *Advocate* with classmate Conrad Aiken and T. S. Eliot (class of 1910).

There is a striking similarity between Ernest Angell's University School record and Katharine's activities at Bryn Mawr. Like Katharine, Ernest showed an early aptitude for writing; he qualified as one of eight finalists in an essay competition, though he did not finish in the top three. To rave reviews in the school paper, he acted a comic part in a class play. Katharine acted in and directed plays. Both Katharine and Ernest were editors of their school literary magazines, to which they also contributed fiction and nonfiction. Ernest's writings included mysteries suggestive of Sherlock Holmes and Ellery Queen (one, like a story Katharine wrote at Bryn Mawr, ends with a hoax); and a piece about Lake Chocorua. Katharine also wrote a story about Chocorua.

When Ernest began to regard his sister's friend in a romantic light, and when the two fell in love, is unknown. We can only imagine their attraction to each other. He was tall and athletic, strikingly handsome; she was petite (just five feet tall), and feminine, holding a paper parasol against the sun, yet ready to participate in all the outdoor activities. Ernest and the other young men cleared two natural pools in the woods—one for the boys, the other for the girls—where they swam without clothes. (One of the young men, Stuart Chase, later a distinguished economist and author, insisted that "the privacy of the two pools was never violated.")

Katharine was in love. Enough in love to enter into an engagement she knew must be for years—until she graduated from Bryn Mawr, Ernest from college and law school, and until he obtained a job. All that is known of the engagement is learned from a few fragmented memories Katharine passed on to her children, and some letters she wrote to family and friends. There were dances at Harvard's Brattle Hall; there were letters Katharine described as infrequent on her part: "I guess there's no danger of my writing Ernest too much," she wrote Papa her junior year. "I'm ashamed, I am so horrid to him." There was the opera. To "Dearest Papa" Katharine wrote asking permission to attend the opera with Ernest. "Loads of girls do go with men, and we could go 2nd balcony & no one would see us. I'll write him to telephone Aunt C. and ask whether it's all right to get tickets."

Katharine's offhand remarks about neglecting Ernest notwithstanding, by her junior year she was compelled to reassure her father and aunt that she had not eloped.

The summer preceding Katharine's freshman year had been spent apart from Ernest, who had gone to work and herd reindeer at the distinguished Grenfell Mission in St. Anthony, near the northern tip of Newfoundland.

He returned with a pair of hairy sealskin mukluks, which Katharine "proudly" carried off to the mild winter climate of Pennsylvania. The shoes

> proved to be a bone of contention [Katharine recalled], for the hairy hides were improperly cured and exuded a rich and almost intolerable smell. Even though they were shut up in the closet of my bedroom they made our study and the whole end of the corridor smell to high heaven, not to speak of my clothes. Finally my dear roommate, Eleanor Washburn, rebelled and it became apparent that I would have to throw away the boots without ever wearing them. I can see them still! Ernest forgave me. . . . For months our college study and the two small bedrooms smelled like an Eskimo igloo.

At Bryn Mawr, as at Miss Winsor's, Katharine Sergeant was known as one of the brightest girls—"one of the leading intellectual Bryn Mawrtyrs of the class," said a classmate. Another alumna remembered Katharine as popular and well-liked, with about ten very close friends—not a mixer, but a contributor. Katharine belonged to the esoteric group of six "called 'The Inner Shrine'—yes, actually!" she wrote Mary McCarthy years later. She compared her clique to that in McCarthy's best-selling novel *The Group:*

> We even called ourselves, tongue in cheek, by this detestable name in defiance of a girl outside the group who scornfully gave us the name. We weren't so different from your girls after all, nor were our fates, but because of our romantic and do-good inheritance, there was a time lag before we began to overthrow the morals and mores of our parents. Ten years after our graduation and early marriages was when we began to come apart at the seams. If your girls had Freud and the Depression to contend with, we had Havelock Ellis and World War I.

During her senior year Katharine was a member of the elite nine-member English Club. Membership required that a girl have one A or two B's in English, and that she be either a junior or a senior. Apart from singing songs in the dining room and listening to an invited speaker discourse on women in journalism, the club's purpose is unclear. The Bryn Mawrtyrs who had twice flunked English established the antiphonal Hinglish Club and sang, "Here's to the English Club—God bless them, they need it!"

Though one of the brainier girls, Katharine—"Serge" to her friends—was not quite the Goody Sergeant of her Winsor years. She was not above playing tick-tack-toe in the English class of one particularly dull lecturer. Her letters to her father reveal a hard but not frantic studier: "Merit in Greek, —the saints be praised,—no one knows how it happened. . . . With Miss Donnelly in Poets I got credit,—and there goes my last chance for an H.C. [High Credit] but who cares." For a Shakespeare exam she was required to memorize three hundred lines of *Hamlet* to prepare for one question; she did not bother.

She was in many ways a typical college girl, busy with friends and campus activities. Despite "daily preparations in Greek plus Kant three times a week" (junior year), life was "jolly," "amusing," and "gay." There were tennis and cross-country walks. There was an odd stint teaching mandolin "to a group of Negro maids for *The Christian Association*." (How she acquired her knowledge of the mandolin she did not say.) She spoke at one Sunday-night chapel—the talk, perhaps, that ended future efforts. She was not a naturally good speaker, and after she spoke "passionately for or against some proposition," her best friend, who was sitting next to her, whispered, "I hope you realize that you were very ungrammatical."

The Quaker influence at Bryn Mawr forbade dancing with men; at the Promenade (junior prom) the girls walked around the room with their male partners. This taboo extended as well to the plays and dances the classes gave for each other, when the speech teacher, Mr. King, was the only male present; for some of the parts, the women wore trousers, which were not considered proper for men to see. Four hours of weekly exercise were required for graduation—field hockey in fall, basketball in winter, water polo in spring. Leah Furtmuller remembered feeling "wonderfully secure" the year Katharine played basketball each afternoon of her junior year. "Endless people are trying for the one position, side center [sic]," she wrote Papa. "They say I play a horrid rough game which is a disgrace, but I don't mean to."

An English and philosophy major, Katharine usually confined her extracurricular contributions to the literary-intellectual functions of the college: she was the class secretary and the philosophical club secretary during her sophomore and junior years and also a director of plays in which she sometimes had small parts—a Shakespeare play sophomore year, *Cyrano de Bergerac* in her junior year.

During Katharine's last two years at Bryn Mawr her efforts took a significant turn. With a friend, she revived and became coeditor of a biweekly school magazine called *Tipyn O'Bob* (from the Welsh, "a bit of everything"), and she became an editor of *The Lantern,* the college's literary annual. In her senior year she was editor-in-chief of both magazines. As editor of *The Lantern* Katharine managed "to wheedle a contribution out of [Marianne Moore]" (class of '09), and she fought her first battles against censorship. "She took exception to the college's practice of reading and censoring material that was to be printed in the magazine," said Nancy Stableford. "Mother went right to the top with her complaint—she appealed to M. Carey Thomas. . . . Miss Thomas's reply, as told to me by Mother, was 'You are entirely right, my dear. Hereafter, I will read the material myself.' " Katharine herself recalled a day when President Thomas "summoned me about one word in an article on Christopher Marlowe . . . 'he died in a brawl in the stews of London.' She asked if I knew what the word 'stews' meant and I gulped and said I did and said it had to be in there because it was a fact. I won out."

Katharine was more interested in writing than in editing. To the *Typ* she contributed editorials, fiction, and verse. Her editorials were collegiate meditations on the usual topics—the future, the past—well-written overall, but scarred with the heavy-handed sentimentality of school-paper journalists and poets: "We are growing old, some of us, and philosophic-minded as the year draws to a close." From the same editorial: "We cannot now feel with poetic temperament the sadness of mutability nor the majesty of permanence."

Except for a rather good poem titled "The Hermit Saint," Katharine's verse was negligible. Her fiction was better.

"The Bullet-Head" (1913) is a tongue-in-cheek suspense tale about young people's overactive imaginations. It is weak in characterization but entertaining, and effective in its attempt to be suspenseful. The description of Tokyo, where the final action occurs, is sprinkled with Japanese words, and sounds authentic. (Katharine undoubtedly was both inspired and informed by Aunt Poo.) And the story is funny. Catlin, a student who never studies and is always on academic probation, is a prodigious reader and has "acquired the greatest amount of stray information on obscure subjects." Among his talents is "a speaking knowledge of the language of the Labrador Esquimaux."

"In the Lumber Camp" (1914) is about sacrifice and egoistic youth. While not such pleasant reading as "The Bullet-Head," the story is well-written, and the Chocorua region in which the lumber camp is set is evocatively described.

The best of these stories is "The Theorist" (1914), a satiric tale about an idle and pretentious young man named Hasrick, who fancies himself an aesthete. Hasrick is engaged to the decorative Claire, who is "always effective, her clothes . . . always aesthetic, strikingly so, her poses always [making] the best of her white arms and hands, and slim, languorous body." For Hasrick, there is no love where there is no beauty. Claire, "the latest beautiful object to be added to his collection," will be the crowning touch to the summer villa with its new Matisse and other precious *objets d'art.*

Hasrick's ambition is to have Claire's portrait painted by the premier American portrait painter, Gerome Kane, who lives in the neighboring town. Following a slight acquaintance with the celebrated artist, Hasrick is invited to the Kane house for tea. Upon his arrival Hasrick finds that the master's dwelling is only "a plain frame house, not even a picturesque vine-grown cottage." More surprising, a few minutes' conversation about art and beauty destroys Hasrick's expectations of finding in Gerome Kane a kindred soul. The venerable painter not only disclaims Hasrick's foolish theories, he insists that he has never painted anyone who was not in some way beautiful. Beauty, Kane asserts, grows out of love. Hasrick's most shocking discovery comes with his introduction to the artist's wife, whom he had never seen except in Kane's exquisite "Madonna" painting.

> Hasrick shook hands in a daze, his fascinated glance became fastened on the shabby little hat with its dowdy trimming of gay, nodding flowers, above the worn, plain face, wrinkled, sun-burned. It was the face of the "Madonna" secularized, grown homely and commonplace, quite congruous with the ill-fitting coat, and cotton gloves, and outrageous green bow at the throat and the crude dowdy hat—the clothes and whole appearance of a farmer's wife.

Overcome by this last revelation, Hasrick excuses himself and hurries away from the Kane residence, with a parting invitation to his villa for tea. The invitation is fulfilled; the Kanes pass a pleasant time on Hasrick's loggia, where Claire, a vision in "a pale green gown with a diaphanous scarf over her shoulders," pours tea from an old silver service. The story ends with Gerome Kane and his wife wondering how he is ever to paint the vapid Claire, whose face the artist has searched in vain for real beauty.

Reading this early fiction of Katharine White, one is impressed by the stories' diversity. Their young author seems determined to show that she is not only prolific but imaginative. Except for the Tokyo scenes in "The Bullet-Head," the New Hampshire setting of "In the Lumber Camp," and the occupation of the latter story's narrator (he is an engineer, like Charles Sergeant), the tales are far removed from the limited experiences of a Boston-reared and Bryn Mawr–educated girl. Each protagonist is a man. Though sometimes predictable and marked by some clumsy sentences, the stories are more than competent. There are some fine descriptions, the dialogue is handled smoothly, and, for the most part, the reader's attention is sustained. Like all writers, Katharine was at her best when she wrote about what she knew. "The Theorist," the tale that would have most naturally evolved from her thinking and experience, is the most skillfully written of the three. Though it is impossible to tell how far her talent would have taken her had she made the writing of fiction her career, these youthful efforts are promising.

Katharine's senior year did not begin altogether happily. She returned to school troubled by dreams about Margaret and Delia, who had drowned that summer at Chocorua. Added to the devastating, hideous, unforgettable sight of their mutilated bodies was her own overwhelming shame: after Aunt

Crully sent her and Ernest to look for the maids, she had rushed off to check all the neighboring houses to see if they were there, in the hope of pleasing Ernest. It was this girlish vainglory about her own helpfulness that she had been preoccupied with, not the poor dead girls.

What Katharine did not mention in her later written accounts of the incident is that the newspapers ran a story of the drowning identifying the maids' employer as "Charles S. Sargent of Brookline"—one article even pointing out that he was "Professor Sargent of Harvard and the Arnold Arboretum." This latest confusion of Charles S. Sergeant with Charles S. Sargent must have added embarrassment to the anguish and shock the family already felt. At least six newspapers carried the story. It made the first page of two Boston newspapers (the Boston *Daily Globe* gave it a three-quarter-inch headline) and one New Hampshire paper.

Katharine ended her college career in the spring of 1914 as number four in a graduating class of seventy-nine and as undergraduate director of the college's fourth May Day festival, an event that attracted thousands of spectators.

Every four years Bryn Mawr welcomed the spring with an Elizabethan pageant known as Big May Day. Originally conceived as a way to raise money for a students' building, the event was now less a fundraiser than an amusement. For months, students devoted their free time to elaborate preparations for the festive day of revelers, musicians, Elizabethan and pre-Elizabethan plays, and Maypole dancers. A big Maypole surrounded by four smaller poles was erected on a large lawn; around the Maypoles danced gaily attired chimney sweeps and white-gowned milkmaids, while the crowd milled about, singing or joining in the dancing. Katharine's job as director "was so big that I paid much more attention to it than I did to my classes that senior year," she later said. She assisted the alumnae director in finding a part in the celebration for every student in the college, and she helped cast and train the companies of many of the plays, including *A Midsummer Night's Dream*. Leah Furtmuller, who played Thisbe, remembered Katharine ordering her to return to her place on stage. "When Katharine said to do something, you did it."

For her class yearbook Katharine wrote a light-hearted, funny piece about May Day—the exhilaration and frustration of casting and rehearsals, the feminine outbursts and quarrels, the offended participants ("When we poor females were assured that the homeliest girl in college was 'a type that appeals to men,' what *could* we say? Even Feminism had no answer."). And there was "the expanse of fat thighs," the "sandals that pinched," and Mr. King, "who berated fiancés, engaged committee members and lovesick mortals in general, [and] was himself surprised into quite a new state of mind."

Bryn Mawr, May Day, and Katharine White later tickled the imaginations of *New Yorker* artists and humorists. In cartoons by Peter Arno, James Thurber, and Carl Rose, and in an essay by E. B. White, the Bryn Mawr woman emerges as a comically audacious, properly heeled enchantress. Arno's 1955 drawing shows a young woman—tight sweater, high heels, fake eyelashes, cigarette holder—sitting on the lap of a Frenchman in a Paris café, her arm draped about his shoulder. They are both drinking. Another girl (pony tail and glasses) gasps: "But Mary Lou! You mean you're not going back to Bryn Mawr *ever*?" In the same vein, Thurber's drawing depicts a woman immodestly cavorting with a group of men while several women look on. Says one woman to another: "She's all I know about Bryn Mawr and she's all I need to know." A 1936 drawing by Carl Rose consists of a girl walking across campus. The caption reads: "The Renascence of Rugged Individualism—The Bryn Mawr Sophomore Who Wore a Town Ensemble and Correct Accessories on the Campus." E. B. White's adoring evocation in prose, "Call Me Ishmael, Or How I Feel About Being Married to a Bryn Mawr Graduate," was altogether different.

3

Divertissement

KATHARINE AND ERNEST were married on Saturday, May 22, 1915, in the home of the bride. A thirty-seven-word announcement in the Brookline *Chronicle,* which misspelled Katharine's name and neglected to mention that she was a graduate of Bryn Mawr (the groom was accorded a "Harvard, 1911"), said that the ceremony was performed by the Reverend Frederick M. Eliot. (Frederick May Eliot, who later became the president of the Unitarian Church, was a classmate, clubmate, and close friend of Ernest Angell. Ernest liked to call him the "Unitarian Pope.") There was no mention of bridesmaids, no details of the bride's dress and flowers. They were married ten days before Ernest's twenty-sixth birthday; Katharine was twenty-two.

The honeymoon, Ernest Angell style, was spent canoeing and camping at isolated Timagami Lake in northern Ontario, to which the couple traveled by train. Afterward, they settled in Cleveland.

Katharine had spent the year between her college graduation and marriage at home and in travel. She would tell her daughter that during that time she attended Miss Fannie Farmer's School of Cookery, "which is really pretty funny," said Nancy Stableford, who did not think that her mother "ever could or did boil an egg!" And there was a trip abroad, apparently with a relative or friend, from which Katharine was summoned home by her father when world war became imminent. During the winter of 1914–15, Katharine became a volunteer at Massachusetts General Hospital's large outpatient department, where she interviewed patients suspected of suffering from occupational diseases. She held the job for six months, until her marriage.

Ernest had completed his Harvard Law studies in two years (three years was standard), graduating in 1913, then returning to Cleveland to work "in general practice as an underling" in the large law firm that had been his father's. "There," he would write twenty-five years after his college graduation, "I learned more about the law, something about men in action, not nearly enough about myself in relation to them, and developed a growing

43

bewilderment, occasionally indignant, over the supposed civilization of our day."

By temperament, by a kind of birthright, Ernest Angell was a natural for the law. Those who knew him professionally later stressed his persistence, his dedication, his fair-mindedness, his enthusiasm. He was judicious, prudent, a man of "outstanding legal ability" and "infinite patience, willing to listen to the expression of every point of view." Ernest was particularly and passionately concerned about the advancement of human rights, and this interest, together with his "willingness to take risks for liberty," eventually found a compelling and satisfying outlet in the American Civil Liberties Union.

His father had been Elgin Adelbert Angell, a native of Chautauqua County, New York, a Harvard man, an 1875 graduate of the law school; like his son later on, Angell took his law degree in two years, but two years was then the standard period of legal education. There are other father-son parallels. As a student, the senior Angell had won academic honors and prizes for writing (for a dissertation; for an essay on Goldsmith's *Poems*). He later wrote an article on taxation published in the *Yale Review;* Ernest would write many magazine articles. Elgin Angell was endowed with a penchant for hard work, a tender love for his family. Ernest shared these qualities as well.

When Ernest was nine years old and away at school, his father was lost at sea in the collision of *La Bourgogne,* on which he was traveling, with the *Cromartyshire* in the Gulf of St. Lawrence. After that, Ernest became "the man of the family," a position he seems to have borne with remarkable patience. His mother, Lily Curtis Angell—a formidable woman, "tall and thin and humorless"—apparently dominated her son's early life. "Mrs. Angell, long widowed, followed her children wherever they went," recalled Katharine. "All of Ernest's Harvard years, when Hildegarde was living at Dana Hall [in Andover, Massachusetts], she lived in Cambridge, hovering over them." After his graduation from law school, Ernest lived in Cleveland with his mother. After his marriage, he and Katharine lived in a house around the corner.

Ernest put in long days at the firm, and devoted much of his leisure time to studying and writing. Katharine spent the first four months of her marriage caring for the house, the next eight months working part time (doing what is unknown) "to earn a maid."

During the first year of their marriage, Katharine and Ernest found a focus for their interest in the theater. It began one day in 1915, when Katharine encountered a woman named Grace Treat at the headquarters of the Woman's-suffrage Party. (Katharine's presence there is unexplained.) Grace was excited about a theatrical presentation she had witnessed the previous night at the home of Raymond O'Neil, drama and music critic for the Cleveland *Leader.* With Henry Keller, a painter who taught at the Cleveland School of Art, O'Neil had built a cardboard cyclorama to surround a tiny stage. Cutout figures or other objects were placed on stage while lights controlled with a rheostat projected their silhouettes against the cyclorama, producing shadowgraphs. Thus a craggy rock became a mountain peak at the break of dawn, the morning sky gradually darkening to dusk, and finally midnight. In these modern techniques, O'Neil had been influenced by the Moscow Art Theatre, and the revolutionary ideas of stage design espoused by Max Reinhardt and Gordon Craig.

As Grace Treat, a student of Henry Keller, described what she had seen, Katharine Angell and Minerva Brooks, chairman of the Woman's-suffrage Party, became intrigued. A performance was arranged for them and their husbands.

The Cleveland Play House was born one autumn night in 1915, when ten people, including Katharine and Ernest Angell, gathered at the home of Charles and Minerva Brooks. At Mrs. Brooks's suggestion, the group agreed to form a theater company, with Raymond O'Neil serving as director. Ernest Angell was elected treasurer and helped create a constitution.

There were no aspiring thespians in the original group; as a later member recalled, these energetic young men and women were simply interested in the theater, but theater in all its forms—"its relation to art, the dance, music, drama, community relations." The Play House members agreed to produce plays in three different groups. The first, "carrying out Gordon Craig's theory of the impersonal actor," would employ marionettes; the second would use shadowgraphs; the third would perform plays, with an emphasis on contemporary works.

It was to the marionette group that Katharine attached herself. The Play House's first production, in May of 1916, was Maurice Maeterlinck's play for puppets, *The Death of Tintagiles.* Katharine was one of six reader-manipulators who "labored tirelessly" for months "to achieve the perfection of production demanded by O'Neil." Katharine later thought it was she who had been the voice of Tintagiles, whose final scream gave her vocal cords "their first roughening." A witness to the performance described the result as "completely breathtaking."

Katharine was about two months pregnant when the Cleveland Play House made its debut with the Maeterlinck play. The Angells' daughter,

Nancy, was born on December 7, 1916. Eleven months later, in November of 1917, Ernest enlisted in the army as a first lieutenant.

Willard Straight, a former journalist and diplomat, now a major in charge of the War Risk Bureau in Washington, had been sent to France to organize the overseas branch. He asked Ernest to be part of a team of young lawyers who would organize "the first insurance system ever devised for American troops at war." Ernest accepted the offer and soon found himself in France. Katharine received half her husband's salary, but found it inadequate to support herself and Nancy. She looked for a job.

Katharine later wrote to a granddaughter, Caroline "Callie" Angell, about the jobs she held during the next two years. She got a job working for the woman she had worked directly under at Mass. General, who now hired her to make a survey of all the crippled and handicapped people living in Cleveland. Armed with a list of addresses and a card of identification, Katharine traveled door to door and questioned the mistress of each specified house to determine the handicapped person's living conditions, the kind of care he or she was given, the family's income, etc., after which she would judge whether the person in question might be trained to work. In the poor areas of the city, the job was often made difficult by a language barrier because of the many transplanted Hungarians who lived there. This job, which Katharine later thought had "taught [her] a great deal," required that she enter Cleveland's worst slums as well as its wealthy district. Katharine preferred the slums. "Usually in a tenement house I was well received. In a mansion of the rich it was hard to get my foot in the door but I always managed to."

Katharine did not recollect how long she had this job, but before she left Cleveland she held another paid job working for Mrs. Florence Kelley, the national head of the Consumer's League. The League's office was headed in Washington by Dr. Alice Hamilton, who was working as a special investigator of poisonous trades for the United States Department of Labor. Katharine, with an Ohio State inspection badge, gained entrée to various factories, which she inspected for unsafe working conditions. Here she was able to draw on her volunteer job determining occupational diseases—"For instance, [in recognizing] workers using lead paints who had no chance to wash their hands before eating their lunch pail lunches or workers spraying banana oil on airplanes, the fumes of which are very dangerous for the lungs." She represented the league at hearings for new legislation on child labor, sweatshops, and the like, and traveled to Columbus to lobby for worker-protection laws. "I had a small triumph here: the Great American Can Co. had a calldown from Washington and a threat that their war contract would be removed unless they improved conditions, and also a similar warning and reprimand was sent to an airplane factory because of my reports." Katharine's efforts were additionally rewarded by a letter from Dr. Hamilton, who praised her reports as among the best she received.

Katharine would look back on this period of her life as tiring but happy, lived "in a fever of energy that was almost exaltation." By late 1917, she and Ernest had moved into a pleasant frame house in Cleveland Heights, purchased with Lily Angell's help. With its tree-lined streets and neat, modest homes framed by the stately houses of Shaker Heights, the suburb was a step up for the family. Katharine commuted an hour to work by trolley, leaving Nancy in the care of "a young girl" named Sophie Novèlli, who had "six weeks training as a baby nurse." After a five-hour working day Katharine made the long journey home, returning in the late afternoon to the baby and garden, to cutting the small lawn; evenings were for letters to Ernest in France.

In *Late Innings,* Roger Angell tells a story from this period of Katharine's life. She was, he notes, "a true Red Sox fan, even though young women didn't go to many games then. My father grew up in Cleveland, so he was an Indians rooter, of course." In 1916 the Red Sox player Tris Speaker was traded to the Indians.

> My mother once told me that in the summer afternoons of 1917 she would often push a baby carriage past League Park, the Indians' home field, out on Linwood Avenue, which was a block or two away from my parents' house. Sometimes there was a game going on, and if she heard a roar of pleasure from the fans inside she would tell herself that probably Tris Speaker had just done something special. She was lonely in Cleveland, she told me, and it made her feel good to know that Tris Speaker was there in the same town with her. "Tris Speaker and I were traded to Cleveland in the same year," she said.

During this time, Katharine continued to do volunteer work for the Cleveland Play House. And with Ida Treat O'Neil, Raymond O'Neil's wife, she edited a book of poetry by local talent (published about 1918), her first editing job since Bryn Mawr. Two of Katharine's own poems were included in the book. With some skill but to little effect, they express a mother's delight in her curious child, for whom a garden is "A color harvest for your shining eyes," and an appreciation "for the golden presence of my friend." The friend to whom Katharine was referring is unknown.

During the winter of 1918–19, Katharine was forced to leave Cleveland for her girlhood home in Brookline, when the city's war factories created a shortage of natural gas and the temperature in her house plummeted to 32 degrees. Settled in Brookline with Nancy, Sophie, Aunt Crully, and Papa, Katharine busied herself auditing writing courses at Boston University, volunteering at a Brookline school playground, and reading to children at Boston's Children's Hospital.

There had been a change in affairs at Hawthorn Road—specifically, in those of Katharine's father.

In 1916, a Massachusetts commission had been formed to investigate the finances and operations of the Boston Elevated Railway Company. In recent years, facilities and equipment had become unusable or obsolete, maintenance had deteriorated, and the company's deficits had mounted. Though the Elevated was taking in enough money to meet daily operating expenses, it was not setting aside sufficient funds for repairs and replacement of equip-ment—all of which was a matter of considerable concern both to the company's shareholders and to the citizens of Boston who were dependent upon public transportation.

Hearings were held in the fall of 1916, with Lieutenant Governor Calvin Coolidge serving as chairman of the commission. Among the many matters discussed were the salaries of the Elevated's management, which were consid-ered so high as to be "indefensible." Charles Sergeant, vice president of the company since 1900, and the person in charge of operations, was then earning the immense annual sum of $20,000 (equivalent to about $200,000 today). Though Sergeant himself was not named in the commission's report, some of its criticisms—specifically, the salary issue, and the company's methods of management and operation—seemed to have been aimed at him. In 1918, the Boston Elevated came under public control. Charles Sergeant's salary was reduced to $6,000, cut by a staggering 70 percent. He retired the same year.*

By Katharine's account, and in those of the newspapers following his death, Charles Sergeant had been an inventive and brilliant force in the development of street railways—a pioneer. He was a banking and rapid-transit expert with a "genius for organizing," who was often called to Europe for consultation. He was even offered the presidency of the London Rapid Transit System, which he refused. "It was because of his vision," said the Boston *Sunday Globe*, "that the [Boston Elevated] system maintains the high standard for which it is known throughout the world."

And yet both the investigating committee and a consulting engineer from New York appointed to undertake a thorough study of the Elevated painted a much different picture, partly by what they did not say. The engineer's report, for instance, praised certain members of the company's management by name; Charles Sergeant was not mentioned. Furthermore, newspaper

*The library of the Massachusetts Bay Transportation Authority lists two different dates for Charles Sergeant's retirement, November 25, 1918, and February 1, 1920. In 1918 he may have left to work part time or as a consultant until his retirement in 1920. In any case, in 1918 he was sixty-six years old and of retirement age. By 1919 Sergeant was no longer listed as a top officer of the company.

accounts of various tunnel openings, etc., do not mention Sergeant as having made important contributions to any projects.

It is unlikely that Katharine would have deliberately exaggerated her father's achievements and misrepresented him. But one may at least argue that, as the man in charge of operations and a former auditor as well, Sergeant should have insisted upon adequate depreciation allowances and other financial arrangements, which would have prevented the problems that caused the company's downfall as a private corporation. Yet, in the end, Charles Sergeant may have fallen victim to the political process, to the ambitions of younger men who were contemptuous of the Elevated's old guard. He may thus have been made a scapegoat for problems not entirely of his own making.

In 1921, Charles Sergeant sold his house and moved with Aunt Crully back to their childhood home at 82 Bridge Street, in Northampton, where Aunt Helen and Aunt Mollie were still in residence. Katharine either helped to support him, or sent him money on occasion—although when she began to do this, and in what amounts, is unknown. Nancy Angell Stableford understood that her grandfather retired after he had been told he was going to die ("I don't know what he was going to die of"), and that he retired long before he was sixty-five, having made enough money to live comfortably, if not elaborately.

Nancy Stableford has surmised that the reason for her mother's silence about what appear to be the true events leading up to Charles Sergeant's retirement came from Katharine's belief that "There were things you didn't need to know," and from an idea that her children might not have thought well of Grandpa if they had known, which wouldn't have been fair to him. But Nancy Stableford was sure that had she confronted her mother with the truth Katharine would have answered her honestly. Katharine usually answered direct questions directly.

For Katharine, working—at the very least, keeping busy—was a fundamental need. "I have and always have had, a personal need for the opportunity to follow my own bent," she would write. "One hesitates to use that much overworked and now somewhat ludicrous term 'self-expression'—but if honest, I must admit to a distinct personal ambition that is thwarted and an underlying cause for unhappiness when I cannot do the work of mind, not hands, for which I am best fitted." Katharine was the product of a diligent family, an inner restlessness. And the need to work had been reinforced at Bryn Mawr: she was, after all, supposed to be doing something useful; she was expected to make a contribution to the world. Staying home, keeping house and caring for a baby, did not qualify. Katharine admitted that she was "easily tired and frazzled by the steady care or teaching of children (although intellectually there is nothing that interests me more than the psychology of bringing up and educating young children—a paradox, perhaps, but not an unusual one.)"

Katharine's assertions that she had to work to help support her family (and therefore required a baby nurse) are questionable. To be sure, Ernest, even when he was promoted to captain in 1919, was earning only about $2400 annually (taking war inflation into consideration, worth about $16,000 today). It was a small income, meager for a woman of Katharine's background. But even in Brookline, when Katharine was apparently unable to get a paid job, Sophie was employed to take care of two-year-old Nancy so that Katharine could do volunteer work.

Katharine's maternal feelings did not require that she be with her child full time; she felt a greater need to do something outside the home. Thus she was able to justify paying (probably very little) for the services of a baby nurse when she herself was not earning money, had only one child, and received an income she considered inadequate. It apparently never occurred to her that Nancy might have been better off in the care of her mother. Katharine, as her Angell children said, was in some ways insensitive to the needs of a child—"except if you'd skinned a knee," said Nancy Stableford. This failing is perhaps partly attributable to circumstances: Katharine had been married only nineteen months when, at age twenty-four, she became pregnant with her first child. She had not had much time alone with her husband; she had not yet had time to establish herself in a career. But she was also bored at home, and she put her own needs first.

Ernest was not the only member of Katharine's family caught in the war raging overseas. Elsie, now a journalist, had gone to France in September of 1917 to write a series of articles for *The New Republic.* In October, 1918, she was one of a group of correspondents sent by the French Maison de la Presse to visit Rheims and the American battlefields of the Marne. While touring the recaptured battlefield of Mont-Bligny, Elsie was seriously injured. A French woman journalist had picked up a German "potato-masher" grenade, which the lieutenant who was guiding the party ordered her to put down. It exploded, hurling Elsie to the ground, and fracturing both her ankles. Elsie was the lucky one. The lieutenant lost an arm, the Frenchwoman was killed. Elsie was taken to a military hospital for surgery, then transferred to the American hospital at Neuilly, where she spent the next seven months recuperating. Ernest came up from Dijon to visit her, "the affection in his eyes sustain[ing] me," she later wrote.

"Your grandfather was overseas longer than almost anybody I knew,"

Katharine would write to Callie Angell. Ernest was discharged from the army on September 15, 1919, nearly ten months after the armistice and two days before Katharine's twenty-seventh birthday. Ernest had not long been overseas when he left the insurance team to do counter-espionage for the army in Dijon, a job in which he was well served by his pluck and his excellent speaking French. He caught two German spies, and was decorated for it. "After twenty long months he returned," wrote Katharine. He was a changed man.

The change was immediately reflected in his determination to leave Cleveland for New York. For Ernest, the Midwest had been "a pleasant place to practice law, but a terrible place for the young man with a 'civic conscience' such as blessed or afflicted me in those medieval days before the war." And he had felt oppressed by four years "of an unending and overlapping series of committee meetings and committee reports." Before the war, he had not paused to dispute these circuitous procedures. But the war changed everything, setting "all of [his] previous life against the background of questioning." Returning to the Midwest now was "unthinkable." New York, if not providing the answers, "at least [had] the merit of affording a wider field of choice for the exercise of those war-questionings."

The decision to leave Cleveland was motivated by other factors, too, in which Katharine shared—including, one suspects, the need to put a greater distance between herself and her nearby mother-in-law. After four years of marriage, Katharine needed to be free to lead the life of her choice, away from the watchful eyes of Lily Curtis Angell, away from community life and "the parochialism and inhibitory traditions of the Main Street on which [Ernest] had been reared." New York offered freedom, greater intellectual resources for them both, and "the opportunity for a richer and more gracious existence." One month after Ernest's discharge, they moved to New York and, as Katharine later wrote, found themselves "engaged in the most stirring adventure thus far of our marriage."

Upon their arrival in New York, Katharine, Ernest, Nancy, and a nurse-maid got into a taxi at Grand Central Terminal and "drove grandly" up to the door of a furnished apartment that Elsie had found for them on East 81st Street. They had taken it sight unseen, the Cleveland house still unsold, both Ernest and Katharine out of work. Within two weeks' time Ernest obtained a new job in a law firm in the city. "We were very short of money and New York was expensive so I needed a job again," Katharine recalled. During the winter of 1919–20, Katharine was offered a paid job working for the newly formed Bryn Mawr Alumna Endowment Fund, which she gladly accepted. Her willingness to take the job, which required that she frequently travel across the country, suggests that Ernest's return had no material effect upon her determination to pursue her own interests. But a second pregnancy interrupted the work, and she was forced to quit the job before it was finished. On September 19, 1920, two days after Katharine's twenty-eighth birthday, her son Roger was born.

The war, and France, had caused Ernest to question more than the midwestern style of practicing law. Observing him in France, Elsie sketched the following portrait of him, circa 1918.

> Ernest: he will have been drinking to victory in some tapestry-hung salon of the *noblesse* of Dijon. And when he gets back to his humble billet he will pause, as he begins to remove his huge military boots—wrinkling his nose characteristically—to wonder what he is to do and what Katharine and Nancy are to do with the series of aesthetic and leisurely reactions on life, the taste for old wines and rare etchings, the love of the French humanities, the French tongue, and the French race that he has suddenly substituted for the hard drive of a law office in a rather barren Middle-Western city.

During his nearly two years in France, Ernest had acquired a taste for *l'amour,* as well. "World War II soldiers who went to France, as your grandfather Angell did, came back with the French idea that a wife and a mistress was the way to live," Katharine wrote to her granddaughter, Callie. When, exactly, Katharine was apprised of her husband's unfaithfulness is uncertain; she seems to have known by 1922.

During the next five years the Angells divided their time between New York and a rented summer house north of the city in an area Katharine described as "an amusing place called Sneden's Landing," where Papa and Aunt Crully would also rent a summer home. It was a snug, secret-looking place, overrun with vines, trees, and shrubbery, situated on a steep hillside along the Palisades across the Hudson from Dobbs Ferry; the Angells' seventeenth-century Dutch fieldstone house sat right on the bank of the river. Here "we garden, swim, play tennis, and make wine," wrote Katharine. Here, one Fourth of July, a balloonist crashed into the Hudson River, was fished out and brought into the Angells' house unconscious. When he revived, Katharine was standing over him. "Where am I?" "Why, you're with the Angells," came the soft reply.

With the birth of Roger, the furnished apartment had given way to a six-room modern apartment, and the Angells sent for their furniture stored in Cleveland. But without Katharine working the rent was too high, and after six months they left to live year round at Sneden's, where they remained for the next two years. Finally came a sixteen-foot-wide, three-story house of their own, at 61 East 93rd Street ("almost on the East River," wrote Katharine inaccurately), half the purchase price given by Lily. By 1921 Lily

Angell had herself moved to New York—to an apartment at 1192 Park Avenue, on the same block as her son and daughter-in-law's, the back of whose house her building literally overlooked.

Katharine, meanwhile, was breaking into print in a more ambitious way than she had done before, with two articles in *The New Republic* (a magazine to which Elsie may have helped her gain entrée) and book reviews in the *Atlantic Monthly* and the *Saturday Review of Literature.*

The *New Republic* articles, published in May and July of 1922, grew out of a trip to Haiti and Santo Domingo. Ernest had been appointed to represent the Haitians and the Dominicans in the U.S. Senate investigation of the United States occupation of Haiti and the Dominican Republic. Senator Joseph Medill McCormick, who was heading the Senate committee, asked Ernest if he would like to bring his wife along. Ernest's way was to be paid, but Katharine's was not. Her "bad mathematics" having persuaded her that she had an extra $1,000 in the bank, she accompanied Ernest, leaving the children with Aunt Crully. Katharine later recovered the cost of the trip when she sold the articles to *The New Republic.*

"The Great Ditch in Haiti" and "On Trial in Santo Domingo" are passionate indictments of the occupation and the racial prejudice and segregation in Haiti, which had caused the great dividing ditch, or "grand fossé," between the American military and the native Haitians. Both pieces are bold, resonant with descriptions of the local settings and the flavor of occupied life. Katharine condemns President Harding's appointment of Brigadier General Russell as Haitian High Commissioner, which "if not so tragic would be comic,—for he is the officer above all hated and distrusted by the Haitians ... the man under whose leadership 'the great ditch' was finally completed." Though highly complimentary of Senator McCormick's "masterly" chairmanship of the Santo Domingo hearing, she is self-assured enough to describe him eyeing a pretty occupation wife who entered the room.

Katharine wanted to be a writer, and she was a good one. The following passage ends the Santo Domingo article.

> The Dominicans have a habit of walking or driving in their open carriages at the end of the afternoon out past the signal tower onto the malecon, the terraced esplanade above the rocks that edge the open ocean. There they see the waves dash and the sharks play and watch the hot sun set behind the two black etched towers of a great battleship wrecked on those red rocks. That ship is the United States battleship Memphis, a former pride of the Navy. To the Dominicans there must be a poetic justice in seeing it stranded there, high and dry on their own rocky coast, swept up by a tidal wave in 1916 just when it was bringing more American troops to occupy the republic. It is not happy

for Americans to see it rusting and rotting away nor to remember the many American sailors who lost their lives, for the experienced Dominican swimmers could save only a few. Yet if the Dominicans find in the sight a poetic justice, it is but natural, and it remains for Americans to change the meaning of that symbol and to assure Santo Domingo a justice more substantial than that of the waves.

Katharine wrote the *New Republic* pieces as if she were a journalist who was in Haiti and Santo Domingo solely to cover the occupation and trial. She refrained from connecting herself with her husband, but offered this view of him in the Santo Domingo article. Describing Ernest only as "the counsel for the former Dominican government," she recalled a moment during the trial when he was asked whether he was aware of the tradition that when a stronger country takes control of a weaker, the latter picks up the tab for the occupation. Counsel replies: "I am aware that such has been the case in darkest Africa, in faraway China, in backward Egypt and India. But I am willing to state that the American people will not allow such a perversion of justice to be carried out now in this present day. We shall set a new precedent if necessary, of justice and honor towards small nations."

Katharine was to have two more jobs before she met her destiny. One was a two-week stint working for a woman she later described only as "a psychoanalyst whose name was well known at the time. She had written a book in very Germanic English and I was supposed to turn it into good English. I gave it up after two weeks because I found out that she was more messed up than her patients were—having an affair with another woman, oppressing her son, etc." Katharine's last pre–*New Yorker* job was part time, working as an errand girl and shopkeeper for an interior decorator named Amy Colton, a Sneden's neighbor and friend.

> Amy's idea of decoration was to make everything brown and green and very drab, and another young girl who worked for her and I thought this very funny. "Just an autumn leaf" was what the other girl called her. . . . I remember once being sent way downtown by subway and having to bring back in my arms an awful objet d'art or antique that still had its price label on it. I thought surely I would be arrested for shoplifting but I made it back to the 57th Street shop without being questioned.

Her life, as she described it in a light-hearted letter to her Bryn Mawr classmates (late 1924), was filled with "domesticity, gayety, work." She was having fun with the interior-decorating job, but she missed her "old pursuit of book reviewing and desultory writing of one sort or other." Her children, now eight and four, were thriving, she loved her summers at Sneden's Landing, she was often at Bryn Mawr on Alumnae Board business, and she had just returned from a council meeting in Washington. She said nothing of Ernest. She sounded cheerful and a trifle bored.

It was the summer of 1925. A Sneden's neighbor named Fillmore Hyde, who was working for the newborn *New Yorker* magazine, told Katharine he thought she would make a good first reader, and he suggested she go to see the editor, Harold Ross. "Before applying at *The New Yorker,* I asked the advice of Henry Seidel Canby, then editor of the *Saturday Review of Literature.* He said that *The New Yorker* was nothing and that I would make a great mistake to join it because he thought it would never amount to anything. I listened to him and then went back and immediately applied for the job."

PART TWO

4

Rewriting

THE MAGAZINE Henry Seidel Canby pronounced "nothing" had made a promising debut on February 15, 1925. In six months—from its premier fifteen-cent issue to the issues of August, when Katharine Angell joined the staff—*The New Yorker* had grown from a funny, unformed weekly of good quality to something more mature. Its tone was now less collegiate and sarcastic, more metropolitan and restrained. The humor that had sometimes expressed itself as lampoons or gags was more sophisticated and wry: less likely to poke fun at someone and more inclined to entertain by revealing man's follies, which were addressed with a barbed, but seldom sophomoric, comment. *The New Yorker* was attracting talented contributors—Dorothy Parker, Frank Sullivan, and Corey Ford, among others; the artists Helen Hokinson, Peter Arno, and Rea Irvin, who drew the Regency dandy that appeared on the cover of *The New Yorker*'s first issue (which is reprinted on each anniversary) and was later named Eustace Tilley. The text, consisting of humor, satire, light verse, profiles of well-known New Yorkers, reviews (the theater, music, art, books, moving pictures), and sports commentary, was well written and short, each item typically covering one-half to two pages. The magazine itself ran to only about twenty-four pages. The cover art and drawings (as *New Yorker* cartoons were called) were attractive and funny. The nonfiction was mostly limited to humorous trivia or anecdotes about local celebrities; the fiction consisted of brief satire rather than short stories; and the poetry, which from the beginning had been usually humorous light verse, had practically disappeared. It was a young magazine searching for its voice. The layout was evolving; many features had been dropped or changed. But *The New Yorker* was not nothing. In disregarding Henry Seidel Canby's advice, Katharine was plucky, but more reasonable than defiant.

Financially, Katharine's decision to join *The New Yorker* indeed seemed reckless: the new magazine was deep in the red, starved for advertising and struggling to stay alive. When Katharine arrived on staff *The New Yorker*'s chief financier, Raoul Fleischmann, and Harold Ross, its thirty-two-year-old founder and editor, were trying to save *The New Yorker* with a campaign to attract advertisers. Years later, Fleischmann attributed *The New Yorker*'s wonderfully successful advertising to Katharine:

> Being a sensitive, cultured New Englander, imbued with the fine conscience characteristic of that famed rock-ribbed area, you had strong feelings involving honesty, decency and believability in the advertising we should accept, and you got Harold seriously interested. In spite of a few fumbles at the outset, [the rest of us], when we got a bit educated, were all for your ideas, and it evolved that our current acceptance of advertising is based solidly on certain musts and must-nots.

Harold Ross hired Katharine Angell as a part-time reader of manuscripts, at a weekly salary of $25. Two weeks later she was working full time at double the salary. By fall she was an editor "doing everything—as we all did at the start," she wrote Callie. "Everything" included sitting in on the weekly art meetings, during which drawings and covers were voted on and edited for effectiveness and clarity. "Ross felt that artists would resent rejections and suggestions for corrections coming from a fellow artist," recalled Katharine, "so the job of talking to the artists each week, giving them new ideas, encouraging them, handing them rejections, and sending them checks fell to me"—and eventually to the man who would become her right-hand assistant, Wolcott Gibbs.

There is no record of the day Katharine Angell walked into the offices of *The New Yorker* magazine and applied for a job, no account of her introduction to Harold Ross and her first impression of him. She was apparently hired on the spot—a supposition that concurs with other accounts of Ross's hiring people on impulse, trusting his instincts more than an applicant's credentials, which is not to discount Katharine's credentials. It is not surprising that he gave her the job: Katharine Angell would have been hard to turn down. That he quickly recognized in her a person of taste, intelligence, and refinement, someone who could be of immense value to his fledgling magazine, was natural more because "quality" was written all over the thirty-two-year-old Mrs. Angell than because of Ross's intuitive gifts.

Much has been written—and exaggerated—about Harold Ross's intellectual and personal deficiences, his lack of formal education (he did not finish high school), his intractable hair and teeth, his profanity, his uncouth manner and appearance. Ross's façade belied his intelligence and his considerable talent as an editor, as Katharine's aristocratic and cultivated appearance confirmed hers. The published accounts of Ross—many of them smirking and snobbish—rarely penetrate the surface, with the result that Ross survives as a caricature rather than as the human being he was. Though Katharine would later say that she "never felt any attraction to Ross as a male [;] in fact I couldn't see how anybody could bear to be married to him"—even at that first meeting she would not have stopped at the surface. She was not a snob; like the true aristocrat, she did not need to be. Although she could be amused by people, and she was often amused by Ross, she was perceptive and inherently fair-minded, willing to trouble herself to get to know someone rather than brand him a roughneck or a country bumpkin. (And Katharine could hardly be supposed willing to take a job working for someone she considered ridiculous or offensive.) She was unimpressed by polish or dress or show. What mattered was the person inside the shell.

She got past the shell, past "the barrier reef of noisy shallows that ringed him into the lagoon that was Ross himself—a rewarding, and even enchanting, and relatively quiet place, utterly trustworthy as an anchorage." Here was a man of energy and "endless curiosity," a persevering, restless spirit not so unlike herself. Here was a man passionately dedicated to the achievement of clear, precise, grammatical English prose, someone intrigued by facts and determined that they should be accurate (part of his system of continual self-education, Katharine recognized). The woman with the Bryn Mawr education was not put off by her employer's unfamiliarity with the classics. When, during the twenties, Ross was about to depart for Europe, Katharine asked him what she could give him to read on the ship. "Send me a Dickens novel. I have never read Dickens and I want to." Touched by his honesty and his humility, she sent him two of Dickens's best-known novels.

In the lagoon she found a friend. He was fun—"best of all," possessing "the rarest of all the great qualities of mind," a subtle sense of humor. He was kind, loyal. In time to come he would make a great many concessions to her personal and domestic life, to the illnesses and family responsibilities that took her away from *The New Yorker*. She felt the freedom one knows with a true friend, the freedom to be oneself, to be direct, to disagree without hard feelings. "All right, all right, but you needn't be so goddam rude about it," she exclaimed during one verbal battle. (She had become profane because of him, she later said.)

"I have two entirely different vocabularies, one for men, the other for mixed company and women, children, and ministers," Ross wrote to Katharine, apparently unaware that he did not always employ the second vocabulary when addressing her. One suspects that, in Katharine, Ross had found a friend too, so that he could sometimes forget himself. He seems never to have precisely articulated his feelings about her (one close observer, William Shawn, has called those feelings "ambiguous"). More comfortable with men than with women, Ross was prone to exclaim in frustration, "I am surrounded by women and children!" Katharine was sure she was the "women." Ross may have partly explained his "women problem" himself—at least as it pertained to Katharine—in an introductory letter he once gave her to take on a trip abroad. "This is to introduce Mrs. Angell, who is not unattractive."

She was not sure, but she thought Ross was fond of her, as she was of him. The introductory letter was "the highest personal compliment I ever got from him." What is certain is that Harold Ross respected Katharine's literary judgment, perhaps as much as he ever respected anyone's. He relied on her for almost everything connected with *The New Yorker*. He repeatedly sought her advice about his daughter, Patty, and we know that he took at least some of that advice to heart. Certainly his letters to Katharine—chatty, confiding, advising—are written in friendship, though the friend is almost invariably "Mrs. Angell," a professional habit, probably, which carried into his personal correspondence as well. (Her Christian name, when used, is misspelled, even as "Kathryn.") Katharine might not have been a Ross friend in the sense of a favored companion; Ross might not have been attached to her through affection; but he was certainly, indisputably, bound to her through esteem.

Both the state of Katharine's marriage and her feelings about her new editorial job may be gauged by two articles she wrote during her first year at *The New Yorker*.

The first, published anonymously in *Harper's Magazine* in December of 1925, is titled "Living on the Ragged Edge," and subtitled "Family Income Vs. Family Expenses." That Katharine wrote this intriguing story anonymously is not surprising: the information was highly personal, and Katharine possessed the Old New England disdain of talking about money. (One did not discuss sex, either.) And yet money—precisely, the lack of it—would become a recurring theme in the letters Katharine wrote later in life.

The title refers to the ragged edge of debt on which Katharine and Ernest had been teetering for the past two years in New York. The article itself, which proposes, "from the highest of motives," to share a story with other empathic couples in their mid-thirties who are likewise living beyond their incomes, is actually a passionate plea for understanding of the anonymous Angells' financial dilemma. On a deeper level, it is an effort to justify a style of life expensive beyond one's means, and in this it resembles an article of the following year, published in 1926, in which Katharine defended her life as a working wife and mother.

One wonders why Katharine wrote the narrative at this time, what factors had just then worked to provoke such a detailed review—some four thousand words—of her ten-year marriage. She was engaged in challenging new work—literary work. Things would seem to have been going right for her. Perhaps it was that very rightness that enabled her to release the tightly coiled emotions that inevitably had accumulated from years of worrying about money, and other, nameless things.

She seems to have been releasing, if not actually acknowledging, her feelings about the nameless things as well—about Ernest's unfaithfulness and her father's downfall at the Elevated. She describes "Tom's" (as Ernest is called) time in France as "the excitement of living up to his rather arduous resolve to be a cosmopolitan sort of person and yet remain faithful to his wife." And she observes elsewhere that "It is hard for two people to gauge to the same instant the indiscretions that repression is bound to foster. At times flirtation or the other man's flask will appear to be the least expensive anodyne for financial worry." It is likely that by now Katharine was aware that her husband had been fully cosmopolitan in France, and that she was but too conscious of his "flirtations" close to home—an anodyne to Ernest, perhaps, but not to her. As for her father, among the few details Katharine changes from her life to disguise her identity is his survival: she makes herself an orphan, *both* parents having died before her marriage (Tom, like Ernest, has a widowed mother). And she adds, "circumstances so fell that my financial inheritance was so small as to be almost negligible." It is a revealing change in fact.

Katharine's inheritance, or trust, had actually amounted to a considerable sum (a supplementary income of roughly $3,500 a year for the first three years of her marriage), and this she had in addition to her husband's, admittedly small, salary, and the financial assistance from her mother-in-law toward the purchase of the Cleveland and New York houses. Given the alteration in her biography and the comment about her "negligible" inheritance, one senses that she may have felt resentful not only about the circumstances that drastically reduced Charles Sergeant's salary but also about the resulting loss of money to herself. (Presumably, she would have inherited far more had her father retired later, at his earlier high salary.) Her resentment may have been aggravated by disappointment or anxiety about Ernest's low earnings. Her later comments, and the impressions of Nancy and Roger Angell, suggest that she was thus disappointed, and Katharine writes that she married "on an income that is now considered a bare living wage." She fails to mention her own supplementary income.

More than anything, "Ragged Edge" reflects Katharine's concern about what other people think of her. Katharine several times pauses to defend herself outright.

> "Which one of you is the extravagant one?" a friend once asked me, and I could reply in all honesty that both my husband and myself are really economical, that we spend a minimum on ourselves, our clothes, our pleasures.

"Then the answer must be that you have too high a standard of living for your income." Perhaps, but the problem is not quite so simple.

The problem *was* that simple. To begin at the lesser end of the balance sheet, the Angells bought expensive clothes and shoes.

> Instinctively [writes Katharine], we feel that the quality of our food and clothes and house furnishing must be, while not luxurious, never cheap. According to the foolish tradition we both inherited, quality, even in so small a matter as shoes, becomes a matter of character. Though we have gradually learned that everything that is not the best is not therefore *ipso facto* shoddy, we are constantly running into our own deep-rooted standards of expense.

Furniture, Katharine notes, is not an expense, since she has inherited more than she needs. And the cost of apparel is tempered by the generosity of their relatives, who give them most of their clothes. ("I could discourse eloquently on the doubtful joy of receiving clothing which is not one's taste or choice, either for oneself or for one's children.") Katharine and Ernest saved money on books; rather than buy them, they rented or borrowed them. They did not spend on music lessons for the children, but taught them the piano "very feebly ourselves." They rarely gave gifts to each other or to friends; they seldom took vacations or spent on weekends away together ("the spiritual renewals so necessary to marriage"). Although their charitable contributions were "absurdly irregular," some years they gave "far too much—all depending on how flush we happen to be when approached." They had given the largest sums to their colleges, to which they "pledged for a period of years more than we could possibly afford to give."

But they led an active social life. During the winter months they went out two or three times a week, sometimes in evening dress, Katharine wearing long white gloves, and they gave dinner parties about twice a month. When they entertained, their habits were "lavish" when uncurbed. But they saved money on theater tickets, which they purchased only a few times yearly ("and it is not much happier to be always *taken* to the theater than to be given one's party clothes"). Their cab fares for evenings out, however, were high.

Their insurance was high; it was their only way of saving. Doctors' and dentists' bills were high. They sent their children to "the best modern schools that New York City offers" (but these were not necessarily the most expensive). They lived in New York City rather than in the suburbs. ("Tom and I are not made temperamentally for suburban life, for neighborliness, or for a life of country clubs, bridge, and automobiles.")

For reasons that Katharine does not explain, but that seem attributable to her dislike of this chore, she did all her food shopping by telephone, which was the most expensive way to do it. Though the Sneden's house was rented for "an incredibly small sum" and the fruits and vegetables Ernest grew there (Katharine devoted herself to the flowers) markedly reduced their summer food bills, they rented the place year round. And last, in town they had a cook, a maid, and a nurse. In the country they employed two maids.*

The Angells' problem, as Katharine viewed it, was that by virtue of their upbringings (this factor is stressed), educations, and personalities, they required a certain style of life in order to be happy, but their income could not quite support it. Thus the last two years had been "thoroughly unhappy." "Two years of misery, of bills that mount beyond income, of carrying over from one month to the next the less urgent bills, of paying a small amount on a large bill, of last-moment frantic borrowings from capital or on life insurance, of months of fooling ourselves with the vain hope, 'Next month we shall get caught up.'" Their attempts to reduce expenses had failed— "we are either too obstinate or too weak to alter our most fundamental ideals of what life should afford us and our children." What Katharine does not acknowledge, what she apparently does not see, is that, for all their little economies, such as teaching the children the piano themselves, she and Ernest are extravagant. Katharine writes of the need for servants, for instance, as if it were a given. (Servants were of course very common then, even in lower-income families.) She is not self-conscious about having them, as she is about having the Sneden's house; she is unembarrassed by her cook, maid, and nurse in town, her two maids in the country. And in analyzing where she and Ernest may have erred, she never mentions the servants; they are "a necessary concomitant to the *economy* of buying the house."

Katharine's servants were not attributable to her upbringing or Ernest's. Nancy Stableford has recalled that Charles Sergeant and Aunt Crully had one helper, probably part-time; Aunt Crully did the cooking. (During Katharine's girlhood there had been the tyrannical cook, Mary Hillen, and the part-time handyman, William Hickey.) The Northampton house had at most one part-time servant; Aunt Helen was a great cook and cooked by choice. Lily Curtis Angell had only a part-time maid. Katharine simply disliked housework and cooking (she was nearly incapable in the kitchen), her aversion fueled by a sense of her greater destiny. But Katharine implies that the servants are there partly because of her own uncertain health: "To be sure I am not very robust, I cannot do domestic work steadily." The

*Roger Angell is certain that this was not most of the time. Usually, the Angells employed only an occasional cook, perhaps a housekeeper, and a summer nursemaid for Roger.

excuse of health would become a familiar refrain as Katharine aged. But it was no more than an excuse. Since her marriage, she had held down a number of jobs, some of them demanding; she played tennis occasionally (and not very well—"She always licked her right thumb before serving!" said Roger Angell); she took very good care of herself.

In their daughter's view, the Angells' problem was compounded by their financial incompetency: Ernest was "lousy at handling money." He was "on the fringe of being dishonest to himself about being such a bad manager." Katharine was "naive about money"—or absent-minded, "above money," in her second husband's view. (According to E. B. White, though good at making money, Katharine, in her natural elevation of mind, was impervious to the mundane business of managing it.)

Katharine continued:

> When I re-read the surface story of our financial history as I have written it down, it seems to have almost no relation to our essential married life, to mirror not at all the real Tom and the real me, the family of four we now are, nor the rises and falls of happiness and discontent, and the sweeps of emotion and activity or barren stretches of inhibition or of drifting that go to make up ten years of life. Behind the bare financial facts there have been profound stirrings of spirit at both achievements and failures, but our present situation produces only a dull, nagging, insistent hurt. We are at an impasse.

Katharine's efforts at sounding a reassuring note about her marriage are not helped by the "barren stretches of inhibition"; it is the falls, not the rises of happiness, one steadily feels in the article. "The psychological effect of the economic strain is incalculably deep," she continues. "It is hardest for Tom." He, according to his anonymous wife, had done "remarkably well in the law," and was respected by his peers. But he had not done remarkably well financially, not well enough to support the two homes, the servants, the rest.

> . . . he now talks of "the bitterness of failure"; he who has always had such a happy and sane self-confidence is building up an inferiority complex which it is agony for me to watch. He rails against what he has fabricated into "the shame" of accepting money from his mother or of "allowing" his wife to work; he has ceased to believe in the future. The actual worry of whether bills can be met is in his mind and mine constantly. It will invade our most foolish and light-hearted moments. Tom would here insist that light-hearted moments

no longer exist for him, and he has always been the gay and optimistic member of the family.

The article ends hopefully, with Katharine's assertion that she and her husband "are very well balanced people. . . . The abnormalities of the situation are not often to the fore, and the very real depth of our relationship and our own essential happiness keep us going."

The New Yorker kept her going. By the following year, Katharine felt herself to be moving in an ascent.

There is a startling difference between "Living on the Ragged Edge" and the next article, "Home and Office," written in *The Survey* just six months later, under her own name, during the summer of 1926. Though both efforts are defensive about Katharine's way of life, the former is a grinding tale of distress ending on a falsely cheerful note, the latter an exhilarated discourse on the life of a working wife and mother—A Day in the Life of a Liberated Woman.

"Home and Office" begins serenely, wonderingly, its mood as upbeat, its voice as secure as "Ragged Edge" is pessimistic and fragile (the fragility is better disguised here). Katharine writes with the satisfied, sure strokes of one who has finally arrived at her destination: "And now after eleven years of marriage I find myself, strangely enough, actually living to some degree the life I had visualized for myself fifteen or more years ago." Her new, full-time editorial job has given her "a way of life infinitely more satisfying than any I have yet known."

The bulk of the piece is devoted to an elucidation of Katharine's need to work, and to a sketch of her domestic game plan: Katharine is seen juggling her office duties with her role as wife and mother, the emphasis being on home.

Written sixty years ago, "Home and Office" sounds curiously contemporary; it is only by a few social signposts (Katharine and her children are seen taking tea together and reading aloud), and the writer's perception that in both desiring a full-time career and having one she is doing something out of the ordinary (as she was in 1926), that it is dated.

Her job did not require that she be at her desk early in the morning, which is perhaps another way of saying that Harold Ross accommodated the Woman on his staff.* In winter, when she lived in New York, there was

---

*"Home and Office" closes with a smile at Ross: "I may perhaps add that the chief interference [with work] I have encountered has been the psychological fear of my employers, who have sometimes trembled at their own temerity in hiring a married woman."

time to see the children off to school and give directions to the household staff before leaving for work; her West Forty-fifth Street office (*The New Yorker*'s first address) was near enough for her to lunch at home with five-year-old Roger, which she did occasionally despite the long cab ride. She arrived home at five. Having a cook, she was relieved of the rush to get dinner on the table, and she and Nancy and Roger would "tell each other the adventures of the day, have tea together and read aloud or play games." The children sometimes dined separately from their parents. Evenings at home were often spent working, Katharine on manuscripts, Ernest on his own office work. Weekends were largely devoted to the children, at Sneden's in good weather. At Sneden's during the summer months Katharine was required to leave home earlier to allow for the longer commute, by way of an ancient motorboat taken across the Hudson to Dobbs Ferry, and then by the New York Central to Grand Central, and she returned later—

> but theoretically I am supposed to be able to work two or three days at home into which I can sandwich some good hours with the children. I say theoretically, because I have just finished two summer months of comparative failure in my system, months when through unusual circumstances, I have had to be more regularly at my desk than I like, with too few days for work at home. But this has been an emergency and as such, one that can be met and prepared against another time.

Like "Ragged Edge," "Home and Office" is inherently defensive. In addition to pointing out that she is often able to bring her work home, that she spends two hours of concentrated companionship with Nancy and Roger each working day in winter and most of her time with them on weekends, Katharine explains that she can take time off from work to visit her children's schools or accompany them on important expeditions, and that she is careful about whom she entrusts them to. "I feel strongly that they must not be left to unintelligent servants, and I should be sorry ever to turn my children over whole-heartedly to a governess or mother's helper." And she reasons that the time she spends with her children is of a higher quality than the time many nonprofessional mothers spend with theirs—a thought as little likely to please the majority of that era'a female readers as was, perhaps, the article itself.

But the piece is not entirely an effort at self-assurance. "To be a working mother is not easy," Katharine confesses, "even for a professional woman."

> Aside from the fatigue there are countless pulls against it, the overwhelming one being the eternal questioning: Am I seeing enough of my children? Am I giving them enough of my time? Am I always there when they need me? However much one is convinced in principle, there is the constant tug the

other way, too, of tradition, inheritance, and custom which manifests itself in one's approach to life and in what other people think of you (a factor even for a woman of the most ardent convictions).

Though Katharine reports that her children were not troubled by having a working mother, that her daughter, whom she had questioned about it, actually preferred that her mother work, Nancy Stableford would remember it differently. To Nancy, Mother was someone she never really knew. "For most of the time, there was a governess to cope with every day matters until I went away to boarding school. I never felt particularly well understood as a child or as an adult." When sick, she had felt like a "terrible nuisance, disrupting the household" and her mother's work. Katharine would come home early and read to her. A hired nurse stayed with Nancy during the day. Roger Angell, who was four years younger than his sister, reacted differently to his working mother. He never felt that he wanted his mother not to work; working was such a part of her that it was hard to imagine her not working. She would have been a completely different person. He never felt that she thought her work was more important than he was. He felt that she cared about him. If he suffered, it was from a lack of physical affection from both parents. Neither Katharine nor Ernest was a hugger or kisser, though Ernest was a bit more open in his affections, and quite a bit more when he got older.

Contradicting what she would say later in life, and contrary to the frantic financial picture of "Living on the Ragged Edge," Katharine writes that she does not need to work for money; she simply needs to work. Her "honest attempts at the domestic life" have failed; she needs to work—full time.

> I imagine that I find all-day work more satisfying than part-time work just because it requires that I make a complete psychological adjustment to the combination of home and job, whereas in the past I have found that I usually tried to add my part-time work as an "extra" to the average mother-housewife existence. Moreover, part-time work is unsatisfactory because, except in the most rare cases, no serious professional career can be achieved by it. There is, too, the tendency to give to the fractional job more hours than are required for a salary only too apt to be small. And in my experience, just because it demands a scattering of attention and effort, part-time work is more fatiguing and less rewarding than the longer working day.

In "Home and Office" Katharine portrays her husband as both enlightened and accommodating, a willing partner in their very modern marriage. Having overcome society's expectations of what a wife provides for her husband, having survived the inevitable comparisons with other married men, whose nonprofessional wives are free to "grease every wheel" and relieve them of all domestic care, Ernest accepts that Katharine "has not time to perform small personal services for him." He understands that "she must entrust to a mere servant this matter of holes in the socks." Husband and wife even agree that other men "[do] not necessarily have the largest or most rewarding [lives]." And of their working evenings at home, Katharine writes, "neither one of us finds that working side by side is any less companionable than reading our separate novels, or even than playing bridge together." Ernest shares equally in the domestic duties that are not performed by servants; in addition to dividing these chores with Katharine, he too visits the children's schools and attends them on weekend expeditions, "and he has even been known to invade on the sacred duties of the mother to the point of taking a child to the dentist or doctor, although he is still to come to the point of purchasing their clothes!" But "Tom" of "Ragged Edge," who talks of the shame of allowing his wife to work, is perhaps the truer portrait. Nancy Stableford viewed her father as a liberal *in part*. Like the civil libertarian who defends the constitutional rights of one whose views he personally disapproves, Ernest supported women's right to work, perhaps—intellectually— even approved of women working. But at heart, so his daughter suspected, he wasn't convinced that they shouldn't be sitting at home. (Roger Angell did not agree with this view of his father at all.)

When Nancy got married years later, Ernest advised her that it was all right if she worked outside the home, but that she should not bring her work home with her; the difference between men and women, he maintained, is that women bring their work home with them. (So much for the companionableness of working side by side.) Katharine self-consciously observes, "In the psychology of all marriages the subtle balance of values and emphasis is of the utmost importance and women, who plunge emotionally so deeply into all their activities, open themselves to the danger of being too much wedded to their work. A certain masculine detachment is a virtue much to be sought." It was a virtue neither Katharine Angell nor Katharine White ever achieved.

Katharine had, in a sense, detached herself financially, with a separate checking account. When she went to work for *The New Yorker* she soon began to earn more money than Ernest; this, of which the separate accounts were a reproachful reminder, greatly bothered Ernest and hurt his pride. There was perhaps some underlying resentment in one of his nicknames for her, Katrinka, after the Fontaine Fox cartoon character, the Powerful Katrinka.* But Ernest much more often called her Katrina, a term of affection to Roger Angell's young ears.

But he had hurt her pride, too. He was energetically, audaciously unfaithful, at one point even living with someone Katharine later described as "a much older woman all his working week" and returning to Katharine and the children in Sneden's on weekends. For the sake of the children she tolerated it, and when she could endure it no longer Ernest gave up his mistress. But the philandering continued, discretion abandoned. Nancy knew of an incident when her father was robbed while out with another woman (one of Katharine's friends). The gold watch that had belonged to his father, which Ernest wore on a chain attached to his suit, was taken. When one day Katharine noticed that he wasn't wearing it, and inquired about it, Ernest told her the story honestly. At one time, perhaps the same time, he even suggested that she have an affair. She was horrified, she later told Roger.

Writing about these events many years later, Katharine noted that she and Ernest were happy together up until the seventh year of their marriage; the last seven years were unhappy. Until 1922, that is, three and four years before the two articles were published. "So I began to work & hold down several jobs before The New Yorker was founded, then we got to quarreling (and this was bad for Nancy and Roger)." The implication that she went to work to escape her unhappy marriage was one of Katharine's self-deceptions—she would have worked anyway—though working must have served that need, too. Her suggestion that the quarreling started because of Ernest's infidelities is questionable.

Nancy Stableford and Roger Angell retained a childhood impression of their parents quarreling "all the time," but not about anything in particular. There were sharp words on both sides. Ernest was by nature "very argumentative," and he was possessed of "a scary, violent temper"; Roger thought that Ernest had slapped Katharine a couple of times. When angry, Katharine "didn't scream so that you could hear her down the street, but she raised her voice, and their fighting was the kind of thing that makes me want to cringe," said Nancy. Roger recalled once waking up in the middle of the night to the sound of his parents fighting—his father shouting, mother crying. To stop the fight Roger called out that he was just getting a glass of water.

Roger thought that one of the problems between his parents was that their

*From the newspaper comic strip "Toonerville Folks." In an installment of 1921, the brawny Katrinka, her hair worn in a bun in back of her head, is seen charging over a lawn while balancing a balloon-toting baby in a helmet in a contraption atop a long stick. The caption says, "Mother would probably have thrown a duck fit if she could have seen Katrinka and the baby going over to the ice plant fire."

views, though not completely opposite, "didn't intersect." Nancy Stableford saw it differently. Communication between husband and wife "was not very good on a marital level. They didn't give and take; they each acted as individuals." Given their backgrounds, the problem was perhaps inevitable. Neither Katharine nor Ernest had grown up in a household where they could observe and model themselves on a married couple living together; he had no father, she had no mother. Roger Angell thought that this common history had helped bring his parents together in the first place, and that it also helped to destroy, or at least damage, their marriage.

By 1926, Katharine was writing for *The New Yorker*—trifles, above her initials or the pseudonym Angelina.

[January 2, 1926]

THE MEN I HATE TO GO OUT WITH

The one who shows off his bad French to the waiter (I having a husband who speaks perfect French he never wastes on the waiter).

The one who tells me I sit on the wrong side of the taxi (I having a husband who never reads etiquette books).

The tall one whose dancing gives me a crick in the neck (I having a six-foot two husband with whom dancing is restful).

THE MEN I LIKE TO GO OUT WITH

The one who likes concerts (I having a husband who is tone deaf).

The one who tells me the latest "off-color" (I having a husband without Rabelaisian tastes).

The one with whom dancing is not restful (I having a husband with whom dancing is as per above). —ANGELINA

Katharine's earliest *New Yorker* writings, which included verse, one brief obituary of a *New Yorker* artist, and two "casuals" (Ross's word for essays, memoirs, and humor), were more effective as space fillers than as literature. She was obviously enjoying herself—the writing is light-hearted—and writing to have fun and to help the struggling magazine rather than make her mark on the world of literature. "We all had a very merry time," she would say, "and we were a light-hearted bunch."

Though Katharine continued to write, she had settled on editing, had apparently made her choice. She had perhaps already realized that she was, by nature, more of an editor than a writer. She was indeed a natural editor, in her feeling for literature, and in a complex, inborn need: to be challenged, intellectually and creatively; to work with people (work to which she had earlier been drawn, in different forms); to nurture others. In her contact with writers, whom she endlessly reassured, counseled, encouraged, and comforted, and to whom she was always available, Katharine was essentially maternal; paradoxically, she was unable to mother her own children. She was compelled to express her maternity by leaving her family, as, years earlier, she had left Nancy in the care of a nurse so that she could do volunteer work with children. Perhaps only a psychologist who had treated Katharine could say why this was so, but one guesses that it had something to do with her intrinsic reserve, her inability to express her deepest feelings intimately: editing gave her the distance she required while simultaneously allowing her to free her abundant warmth and gregariousness. Editing was also easier than writing, and more fun.

A *New Yorker* Opinion Sheet to her fellow editor Wolcott Gibbs:

> From FPA*
> Come three a day

To Katharine from Gibbs:

> Ruth McKenney
> Writes too many.

And in Katharine's handwriting:

> Phyllis McGinley
> Writes too thinly

> FPA

Katharine herself did not attempt to analyze her choice, but she considered herself a more skillful editor than writer. Still, she never lost the need to write (a large part of her gift as an editor, and a hallmark of her editorial work, was the remarkable long letters she wrote to writers), and she continued to write professionally for *The New Yorker*. "Ideally," she would say years later, "all editors should also be writers."

Of the details of Katharine's editing during the 1920s, little is known. During her first several years on staff, before she knew what she or the magazine was going to turn out to be, Katharine did not keep copies for herself of her correspondence with writers, as she did later, but apparently left them at *The New Yorker*, where they have remained in closed files. Neither did she record her memories of these years, except in a general way.

*Franklin P. Adams

Only two letters, both to Katharine Angell from William Rose Benét, directly reveal Katharine's editorial work during this period.

The Benét letters are of interest to us because they affirm that part of what distinguished Katharine White's work as an editor was, in the 1920s, already present: her persuasiveness and her writers' warm responsiveness to her. Benét's letters are typical of the familiar, unbusinesslike letters Katharine's writers wrote her (and she them). As Harriet Walden, a secretary of Katharine's, later observed, "She knew the whole person, not just the manuscript in front of her."

Benét began by responding to a compliment and a query Katharine had sent him on his story "Queer Birds," and by thanking her for a check. He went on to write about his wife, Elinor Wylie.

June 12, 1928

> About Elinor, even though you spoil her, spare the rod, as the child gets some awfully bright ideas every once in a while and is really worth the retaining fee, as you know. I shall be going over to England to see her the end of July and maybe before then I may be able to extract . . . some bright quips. Sometimes when she and I are having a holiday we get some fairly funny ideas together, being too lazy to write them up. But I shall really endeavor to turn her thoughts toward you, as she has a little more time just now.

The second letter from Benét, written in December of that year, is about Elinor Wylie's death. He thanks Katharine and the rest of *The New Yorker* staff for their expressions of sympathy, and he writes of his feelings about his wife's death.

In May of 1928 the stories of John O'Hara began to appear in *The New Yorker*; they were edited by Katharine Angell. Though O'Hara has since acquired a reputation as difficult, Katharine found him easy to get along with and work with—"Like every good writer, he welcomed questions if they made sense to him and he was glad to have his very semi-occasional errors of syntax, style, or lack of clarity pointed out." He required little editing, and "except for minor corrections in O'Hara's manuscripts I always asked that he make any rewordings himself." He was able to revise his work quickly, and even during periods when he was drinking heavily, he was always sober when he came to *The New Yorker* for an editing session with Katharine, which took place at a big table in her office.

Years later Katharine would remember only two occasions when O'Hara was upset with her. Once, during a slump, after several of his stories were rejected, he informed her that *The New Yorker* would have to pay him for rejected stories as well as accepted work, or he could not afford to continue writing for the magazine. Katharine laughingly referred him to Harold Ross, the two men fought it out, and though Ross refused to accede to O'Hara's ridiculous demand, he gave him a peace offering of a jeweled watch on a heavy chain, which O'Hara afterward wore in his vest pocket. On another occasion, O'Hara "stormed into [Katharine's] office and said, 'Katharine, O'Hara doesn't run in the second position.' I said, 'Well, O'Hara *has* run in the second position,' and explained to him that position [the placing of a story in the magazine] had nothing to do with merit. . . . It's usually a matter of length and how things fit in." There were times O'Hara left the office in a sulk about editorial queries, and his first wife, Belle, would talk him out of his mood and telephone Katharine to say that John was willing to cooperate. But Katharine mostly recalled their meetings as pleasurable. She was not put off by his "prickly qualities"; she considered him very lovable, his faults innocent.

O'Hara seems to have responded to Katharine Angell with equal affection. He was "unfailingly polite"; he could not bear to let her take him to lunch —it was humiliating to let a woman sign a check—though he knew she had an expense account, and he always took her to New York's most exclusive restaurant, the 21 Club, which was filled with celebrities, and where he delighted in getting a good table.

Incoming O'Hara stories were read first by Katharine's assistant, Wolcott Gibbs, who wrote an opinion on them and passed them along to Katharine. After adding her own opinion Katharine sent them to Ross. Gibbs and O'Hara were close friends, and because Katharine thought that O'Hara was the kind of writer one should work with in person, Gibbs edited O'Hara's stories when Katharine was on vacation or working at home.

During Katharine's absences, Gibbs also served as Alexander Woollcott's editor. A more difficult and less endearing writer to Katharine than John O'Hara, Woollcott began writing a regular column for *The New Yorker* in 1929—an anecdotal, gossiping feature titled "Shouts and Murmurs," which Ross, who shared a sometimes hostile friendship with Woollcott, had approved only on the condition that Katharine serve as Woollcott's editor and assume full responsibility for the column.

Though Woollcott disliked being edited, and delighted in trying to shock Katharine by sneaking double entendres into his column or once answering the door to his apartment in the nude ("Go back and put your clothes on, Mr. Woollcott"), Katharine edited his copy without much difficulty and maintained a friendly relationship with him. Unlike O'Hara and other writers who lived in New York, Woollcott did not come to Katharine's office to discuss editorial changes, but handled them over the telephone or at his apartment if she had to persuade him on some point. Katharine's week began with a Monday-morning telephone call from Bill Levick, head of *The New Yorker*'s makeup department, who inquired, "Old Foolish this week?" Levick's call was shortly followed by one from Woollcott to tell Katharine whether he would submit a column that week. After editing Woollcott's copy, Katharine sent it on to the magazine's copy editors, who picked up any errors in usage, grammar, or syntax that she had missed. After getting it back—Ross having added his notes—Katharine would discuss further changes with Woollcott, whose copy was on the whole "clean," though the content was trifling: whatever Katharine's view of it at the time, she came to regard "Shouts and Murmurs" as unmemorable and "silly." And, as well as they got along, she could not quite forgive Woollcott, in later years, for gossiping meanly to her and others about Ross's second wife, Frances.

By 1928, Wolcott Gibbs was one of three young men at *The New Yorker* who were becoming important in Katharine's life. Twenty-six-year-old Gibbs had come to the magazine in 1927 and become Katharine's assistant in running the Fiction Department (which then included poetry and verse, memoirs, casual essays, and humor), a position he retained until the late thirties, when he left to do his own writing. He was bright, witty, talented, high-strung, and thoroughly professional; of the early staff members he seemed one of the most promising. From the beginning Katharine seems to have befriended him and regarded him as a valuable asset, both to the magazine and to herself.

James Thurber, who was thirty-four, had also joined the staff in 1927. Ross had mistakenly hired Thurber as an editor, a job to which he was ill suited and which made him unhappy, but a few months later Thurber got his way and became a full-time writer (he had done some writing for *The New Yorker* while serving as an editor). Katharine was his editor, and would edit all of Thurber's famous *My Life and Hard Times* as it first appeared in *The New Yorker*, in 1933. Thurber and his first wife, Althea, were friendly with Katharine and Ernest Angell. But it was Thurber's friendship with the young writer who shared his office, E. B. White, that most affected Katharine.

The first stirrings of Katharine's romance with E. B. White are as difficult to pinpoint on the calendar as is the period she and Ernest began to love each other. Asked about it some fifty years after his marriage to Katharine, White could not recall when he had fallen in love with her. He was "half in love with her for a long time." He went away once and then looked at her face when he returned, and he knew. He knew he loved her and that she was the right one.

Rewriting

They met in 1926, just before or shortly after Katharine wrote "Home and Office." White had been sending short prose pieces to *The New Yorker* since the previous year, the writing beautifully clear and relaxed, in the style that appealed to Harold Ross. After the magazine had published about a dozen of these contributions, Katharine suggested that Ross offer White a job as a staff writer. Ross invited White to drop by the office. When he did, he was met in the reception area by Mrs. Angell. "Are you Elwyn Brooks White?" His impression of her after this first meeting was simply "that she had a lot of back hair and the knack of making a young contributor feel at ease."

Scott Elledge, E. B. White's biographer, dates White's attraction to Katharine as late 1927; his feelings for her seem to have been recorded first in a series of verses published in *The New Yorker* early in 1928.* Titled "Notes from a Desk Calendar," the stanzas move within the framework of the workdays Monday through Saturday to chart the poet's quickening awareness of the person he thinks he is falling in love with. He wonders whether she feels the same; he ponders her glance, and self-consciously considers being observed together: "—have they guessed / There stands so much between us / Which has not been confessed?" Though the would-be lovers have not acknowledged their love, the poet suspects that his love is returned. Taken as autobiography, the poem, with its sense of the watching eyes, and the guilty-sounding word "blame" ("And if I love you truly / Is anyone to blame?") seems to fit the response of a sensitive man in love with a married woman.

E. B. White—Andy to his friends—was keenly sensitive: not only to the feelings and attitudes of others, but to the natural world, to beauty in the commonplace. This quality, united with his intelligence, his integrity, the clarity and grace of his writing, and above all his delicious sense of humor, was by 1928 infusing the pages of *The New Yorker* with a new, distinctive voice. In casuals and unsigned paragraphs in the magazine's lead "Notes and Comment" section, with humor White expressed compassion for a miserable waitress who had spilled a glass of buttermilk on his suit; worried about pollutants to the environment and diseased trees; and in an echo of Ernest Angell's work with the ACLU, warned against oppressors of civil liberties. He could handle, often brilliantly, almost any form of writing the magazine needed: he parodied advertisements, wrote cartoon captions, wrote tag lines for newsbreaks† and invented headings for them ("Uh Huh Department" and "Neatest Trick of the Week"). By 1927, when *The New Yorker*'s

*The verses appear above the pseudonym "Beppo," the name of White's boyhood dog.

†Ludicrous bits of writing and typographical errors garnered from newspapers, magazines, office memos, and other sources, used as space fillers at the ends of columns.

circulation exceeded fifty thousand and the magazine was starting to make a profit, White was becoming an indispensable part of it.

Andy White, a good-looking, boyish twenty-eight in early 1928, was seven years Katharine's junior. He was shy, modest about his talent, and funny. With three Cornell fraternity brothers, he shared a furnished walk-up apartment in Greenwich Village. He was unsettled. In the six years since his college graduation, he had drifted from one writing job to another, working briefly for United Press; writing press releases; working as a reporter, as a layout man in a production department, as an advertising copy writer. He had wandered from Ithaca, in upstate New York, to Seattle, Alaska, then back to his hometown, Mount Vernon, New York, before coming to New York City. Perhaps fearing another detour on the road to writing what he wanted to write, he had been reluctant to commit himself to a job at *The New Yorker*. There were lunches with Ross and Mrs. Angell. When he finally accepted the job, it was for part-time work; he retained his other part-time job at an advertising agency for several months.

Seven days before the poem presumably addressed to Katharine appeared in *The New Yorker* (January, 1928), the magazine published a White poem titled "Belated Christmas Card," which tells of a romance that is not working out. The poem, which apparently refers to someone other than Katharine, reveals a great deal about its author. Being both drawn to the experience of loving someone and fearful of it, being afflicted with "Too small a heart, too large a pen," the poet has loved "aimlessly." For him, love has been but "a small divertissement."

Andy's attraction to Katharine Angell likewise appeared to be a small divertissement, for he was soon in love with a pretty nineteen-year-old *New Yorker* secretary, whom he considered marrying. But by the late spring of 1928 he had resumed writing poems to Katharine.

Apparently in an attempt to save their foundering marriage, or so Ernest seems to have considered it, the Angells planned to sail to Europe with Katharine's sister Rosamond and her husband, John Newberry, in the summer. Andy was going too, on a separate ship, with one of his roommates, Gus Lobrano. He and Katharine arranged to meet in Paris.

The Angells, including Nancy and Roger and their French governess, who was going home for the summer, departed in grand style, with a queue of taxis in front of the house to take the luggage to Pier 54 and the S.S. *France*. At the pier there was a feeling of elegance and excitement, friends arriving to see them off, people drinking, celebrating. Caught up in the party's festive mood, Ernest, who rarely drank to excess, got drunk before the ship left, and sick at his stomach. Katharine lost her temper to the point that she became "absolutely livid."

Rewriting

Once they were in France, the children were left with a French family in St. Tropez, where they would learn to speak French. At some point Katharine and Ernest parted company (it is unclear whether Ernest left to meet another woman, returned home early, or both), and Katharine met Andy.

However certain she was of her love for Andy, and regardless of her husband's erotic adventures, it must have been difficult for Katharine to have a love affair. For the rest of her life she would suffer the psychological fallout of her own adultery, and seek to mask her guilt by denying that the affair had occurred. Adultery, though not a religious scruple for her, violated her nineteenth-century Boston upbringing and the principles with which she had been raised (her father, after all, had been faithful to her mother even after Bess's death). Most of all, perhaps, infidelity and its lies betrayed Katharine's character and her integrity. But she was in love with Andy, and, as White later observed, she "had to become a bad girl in order to survive in her marriage."

What is known of Katharine's rendezvous with Andy in France comes from Scott Elledge and E. B. White.

Katharine and Andy went canoeing on the Seine. They started from St. Tropez, then went on to Corsica, where they stayed at the small Hôtel des Étrangers. There they found a fragrant garden filled with sunshine and lizards, orange trees, winging swallows, and climbing vines. There they drank white wine (Andy, drinking too much and trying to ride a bicycle, landed in a "cactus coppice"), and were visited by "the sound of someone practicing the piano in the dead afternoon." It was their secret place to stand and love in for a day. When the day was over, they went back to New York, and separate lives.

Either because Katharine was not yet ready to give up on her marriage or because Andy was fearful of commitment and had proven fickle in love before, they agreed not to continue the affair. They would remain friends at the office. It was a hard, unhappy resolution for them both, and it could not last.

Andy, apparently still "guard[ing] the most difficult part of [him]," the part "that [had] left [him] free," continued to write poems to Katharine, published at a distance in F.P.A.'s column "The Conning Tower" in the New York *World*. The "nearness," "the animal alertness to the other's heart" have been muffled by "the broad impertinences" they now speak. "I take your hand / Merely to help you cross the street / (We are such friends), / Choosing the long and formal phrase / Deliberately." These poems expressing White's loneliness for the days when he had "walk[ed] with love" continued to appear as late as January, 1929. Katharine, keeping abreast of

79

what was published where, must have seen them. She cannot have failed to be affected, and at least partly swayed, by them.

Katharine and Ernest continued to argue violently. By now Ernest must have been lashing out at her for her affair with Andy. (Nancy Stableford remembered once making the mistake of asking her father why E. B. White was always at their house when he was out of town.) Nancy overheard her mother saying that she didn't want the children.

Andy did not ask her to leave Ernest; he did not offer her marriage. But in late February (1929), after a quarrel during which Ernest slapped her across the face and knocked her to the floor, Katharine walked out. She decided, irrevocably, on divorce.

"I am very much grieved that you should have been subjected to the additional strain of K's affairs just at this time," Charles Sergeant wrote Elsie two months later.

> I do hope you are wrong as to the finality of K's decision and that I may by sympathetic argument persuade her to delay because, as I have written her she is not in a state of mind or health to make so vital a decision. I wrote that I should ask for delay for this reason. I wrote nothing else except a desire to hear from her all the story and to assure her of love and sympathy. To me it seems incredible that without consulting me, of all people, she should so decide. I shall try to disguise my own hurt on this account but it does hurt very terribly. Of course I can form no opinion in the matter until I learn more details. It has come to me as a terrible shock and I cannot get used to the thought. The woman always suffers in divorce whether right or wrong yet I may agree that it should be when I learn the facts. It will be a sad homecoming [to Sneden's] indeed.
>
> I hate to see these dear children become victims to these modern ideas of individuality. I believe that family is of vastly more importance than the happiness of anyone of its members yet I am terribly sorry for Katharine and worried lest in some way I am at fault about it.

When Katharine hastily left her home, she went to the Thurbers' apartment in the Village and stayed with them briefly, until Jim and Andy could help her move some of her things to the Sneden's house. Katharine stayed at Sneden's for the next few months, Nancy and Roger remaining with Ernest. Years later, Ernest Angell told Roger that he had talked to Thurber when things between husband and wife had reached a crisis, and that Thurber said something to him "that wounded me more than anything I've ever heard in my life." He did not say what it was. E. B. White could not remember what it was, though he remembered the incident. He thought that Ernest had summoned Thurber. "Ernest," said White, "was always summoning people" to his office, including White, who felt that Ernest's eyes were "like headlights" looking at him.

Jim, now separated from Althea, and Andy often came out to Sneden's to visit Katharine. On one such occasion in February, shortly after Katharine left Ernest, the threesome sat for photographs—in pairs, since someone had to hold the camera. The photograph of Andy and Thurber shows Andy sitting frontally, looking rather sensually and penetratingly into the camera —through the camera and into Katharine, it seems—looking confident and happy. In the other picture, Katharine sits with her head turned away from Andy's camera, toward Thurber. There are no pictures of Katharine and Andy together.

He loaned her his camera. Now, in May, in Nevada, there was still no picture of them together; they, or Andy, had still not decided what their future was to be, or if in fact they had a future together. They had talked about marriage, which made things worse—in Andy's words, they got "all mixed up just from saying good night."

Having arrived in Nevada for the three months required to establish residency and get a divorce, Katharine carefully avoided mixing things up further. The letters she began writing every few days (it seems not to have occurred to her that the frequency of her letters might mix things up) tended to be newsy rather than personal. Though it seemed like months since she had left New York, three weeks after her May 11th departure on the opulent *20th Century Limited,* where she had said good-bye to Andy and Ross at the station, she was able to report that she was "healthy and normal," a very different creature from "the abnormal half mad woman I was those last months in New York."

She wanted Andy to see her as she was now, four pounds heavier.

> By the time you get here I'll be disgustingly fat. Also I must warn you that I'm wearing my hair in [a] braid around my head in order to give it a rest and prevent the weight of it pulling all the hair on my forehead out. So you won't like the looks of me even tho' I'm not so remarkably funny in breeches as you surmise. Just for that I won't send you a picture.

(Her expectation of a visit was not unreasonable: clearly he loved her. The night after saying good-bye to Katharine, Andy had fallen into a troubled sleep. The telephone rang; not fully awake when he answered, he mistakenly thought it was Katharine and that she needed him. He chartered a plane in Long Island and flew to Cleveland, where Katharine was stopping to visit friends. The dream, now reality, turned nightmare. A snowstorm engulfed the plane. The pilot, unable to see, handed the chart to Andy and told him to find the airport. Having safely landed and been assured of Katharine's safety, Andy returned to New York by train.)

After briefly touching base in Reno, where she conferred with the judge, Katharine settled in at the Circle S Ranch outside of town, near Pyramid Lake. Two other women waiting out divorces were also staying there. In 1929, it was tough to get a divorce in New York. The New York laws were very restrictive, and Katharine would have had to prove adultery. Nevada's liberal divorce laws, which included a comparatively short waiting period, would certainly have been more appealing to Katharine, who, having made up her mind about something, tended to act quickly. We do not know the grounds on which she was divorced, though they would have been either adultery or extreme cruelty.

In going to Reno for her divorce, Katharine was making the choice that most people seeking divorces were then making; Nevada was the fastest and easiest route. Katharine may have decided on Nevada also to keep this part of the divorce private and to minimize embarrassment to herself and her family. Considering her family's opposition and Katharine's own dignity, and given the infrequency of divorce at that time (in the United States, in 1930, 7.7 per 1,000 marriages ended in divorce), it was a bold action. Bolder still—even shocking—was her custody arrangement.

The overwhelming majority of women of that era sought and were awarded custody of their children. Most cases of custody awarded to the husband seem to have been in divorce complaints filed by the husbands on moral grounds. Many years later, Katharine claimed that her lawyer, Morris Ernst, had persuaded her "that joint custody was the civilized kind of divorce."

Roger Angell was always told that his father said he would *never* part with the children and that he would drag Katharine, E. B. White, and even Roger and Nancy into court if it ever came to that. It was because of this that Morris Ernst persuaded Katharine to sign the joint custody compromise. Katharine was bitter about it.

Nancy Stableford had of course overheard her mother tell her father that she didn't want the children. But this may have been the utterance of an angry moment, perhaps a response to a threat from Ernest about dragging her and Andy and the children into court—for Katharine suffered terrible guilt feelings about the custody arrangement the rest of her life. Roger Angell was certain that his mother would not have agreed to give up her children if she had not hoped to marry Andy. But she was never able to admit this, even though it made no sense for her to part with the children unless Ernest had insisted on it because of Andy.

Rewriting

Katharine's letters to Andy, the only available letters she wrote during this time, evoke her life from without: long horseback rides, her first in fourteen years, through Left Side Jigger Joe's Canyon, where wild onion grew and "the sage was bright with flowers"; playing Red Dog, sometimes "at huge stakes"; corn whiskey, which she tasted and liked; people named Elky and Hy and Mae West (not the actress). Mae's Kentucky hunter, The Lord, had followed some wild horses into the hills. "All morning was spent in motoring to Round Hole Ranch to inquire for The Lord—(no sign of him). Round Hole is the first habitation north of us,—one small oasis set down in a vast sand desert fifty miles long. The strange dramatic quality of the countryside, I never seem to get accustomed to."

In her letters to Andy she often stressed the humorous side of life at the Circle S, as Andy would have done. "A regular Ring Lardner horse-dealer turned up here yesterday, a superb person in checks. Yesterday the pigs escaped into the hills and The Lord is still lost." She advised Andy to get inoculated for horse asthma before he came to visit her, and she gave him instructions about Daisy, her Scottish terrier puppy who had come from Thurber's bitch, Jeannie. Daisy should stay with Nancy when Andy came to visit. Katharine's health was "superb"; she was drinking milk and going to bed "religiously" at nine. She was enjoying her horseback rides—up to twenty-five miles one day—and wanted to purchase a pair of spurs "to become thoroughly professional." She was reading Sinclair Lewis's new novel, *Dodsworth*, and *The Innocent Voyage*, by Richard Arthur Warren Hughes, which she recommended to Andy, and she was waiting for a Beerbohm book Andy had sent her. She commented on *The New Yorker* only briefly, almost as an afterthought, at the end of her letters. "Ross writes me at length and with astonishing regularity. He sounds happy to be working hard & to have me out of the way." She was "a flourishing vegetable who only occasionally gets a little lonely or restless or something."

Her letters provide glimpses, and sometimes more, into her life within:

Ⓢ Ranch
May 25 [1929]

The mail has come & both yesterday's & today's has made me wonder why the post, that here one waits for for the breath of life, can sometimes be so horrible a poison. If only they'd leave me *alone*—letters & letters that almost drive one frantic,—even my sister's mother-in-law whom I haven't seen in years & who is blind, dictates a letter begging me "to forgive Ernest & reconsider this terrible step I am taking." It is too much. These letters make no impression on one's mind or feelings but they, cumulatively, do have a horribly depressing effect. And I haven't had any counteractive cheer in a letter from you (or from anyone else at the office) since I got here to Pyramid . . . you can see how much better off I am emotionally that I can get letters calculated to stir one up, & still remain comparatively calm and cheerful. You & everyone else at the N. Yorker (except Jim the meanie) have been so grand about writing me that it's been the greatest help.

The words of Rosamond's blind mother-in-law—in effect, that Katharine had reason "to forgive" Ernest—suggest how widespread was the knowledge of Ernest's philandering (and apparently how little known was Katharine's affair with Andy). Even the daughter of one of Katharine's Bryn Mawr friends, upon asking her mother about the divorce, was told: "Mr. Angell was unfaithful." Katharine later confirmed this reason for her divorce, adding that the pressures of a long separation during the war, and their having married too young, before she and Ernest knew what they were going to be, had also helped destroy the marriage. All of this was undoubtedly true. And yet to Andy Katharine confided something altogether different: that she was not divorcing Ernest for his infidelities; she could have put up with that. Asked about it years later, Andy could not remember what Katharine had confided to him. She was, he said, divorcing Ernest for some small thing. What it amounted to was that Katharine knew that Ernest just wasn't right for her. Perhaps it had to do with Ernest's reaction to *The Great Gatsby,* a book he disliked because "there was not one admirable person in it." How could she be compatible with a man who thus responded to a work so alive? Andy thought Katharine considered herself brighter than Ernest.

Katharine always vigorously denied that Andy had had anything to do with the break-up of her marriage, or that she and Andy had even fallen in love until her marriage had ended. Given what is known about her marriage to Ernest Angell and her feelings about her fulfilling work at *The New Yorker,* she would very likely have divorced Ernest even without Andy, though perhaps at a later time. As it was, she had held on to the marriage for a long time before finally letting go. Katharine was truthful in saying that Andy did not cause the divorce; but he probably hastened it.

"I went to Reno with no idea that Andy and I would be married," Katharine wrote to Callie in 1976. "I had been hurt too much & saw no future in a marriage with a man nearly 7 years younger than I. He felt the same reservations."

Andy had decided not to come to Reno. He was thinking of going to Europe instead, with Gus Lobrano.

Katharine tried to control her disappointment, but it insistently broke through in her letter. She began by saying that she had had "two bad days," which she attributed to some problems her horse, Snowball, was having, and to her own health. She was depressed "due to indigestion, heart, hernia or bladder trouble, I can't decide which . . . [and] because the months seem so long, the people at Circle S bore me so, and your letter came saying you couldn't come to Nevada. I'd been looking forward to it so, but you're certainly right *not* to come if you don't want to."

Except for two impersonal notes, the letters White wrote to Katharine in Nevada either have not survived or are unavailable. Katharine's letter suggests that he had cited his hay fever as a reason for not coming. Katharine assured him that his hay fever would not bother him in this weed-free, hay-free country, its climate so like Corsica's.

Frid[ay]
May 31 [1929]
Reno

I think I can imagine some of the reasons why you don't want to come. It is, of course, entirely different, your coming to the Wests, than if I were living at a hotel in town. A man came out to visit Margaret Morgan & no one thought anything of it. No one would know that you'd been here but the Wests, & your coming would be as a guest in their house. Mae asked me to ask anyone I wanted—she loves visitors—I asked her about appearances (she has a lot of sense) [and] she assured me that noone would think anything of it here & that noone in the East would know. I wouldn't want you to come if I didn't really believe it was a perfectly natural & comfortable thing—with no sentiment, emotion or such like, assumed or taken for granted by other people. As for ourselves, you may assume that it would complicate us still further, get us involved in endless pros & cons of behavior, make me take for granted more for the future. Well, it wouldn't. I'm living right now in a state of suspended animation, with no past and no future and all I want is a little companionship to help the present to pass,—the present that is often dreary because of loneliness but often so nice I want to share it with you. Also, of course I do want to see *you*. . . . Oh, Andy, we could have such fun—and three months is such a long time. I thought it would be great too, if you could bring Ross with you. I know he'd love the Wests & Nevada. I wrote him suggesting he should come out with you or someone else to keep up my morale by paying me a visit. If he couldn't leave, is there any chance of getting anyone else to come with you,—Cushman or Thurber or who? We could give 'em a good time. I'll find lots of girls for Jim but I suppose he & you couldn't be away together. Well, I promise not to say anything more about it so don't worry that you'll be getting nagging letters but I did just once want to say that if I knew your reasons for *not* wanting to come, maybe I could remove them all. I wouldn't want you if I felt your visit would be surreptitious, in bad taste. A ranch wipes out intellectual & emotional complications—everything is simple & spread out like the land. Here's a man I could have a swell time with, & he with me, why shouldn't he visit me? I *know* here we would not get "all mixed up just from saying good night"—as you once put it. I don't want to and won't.

. . . And if you come out, you may be sure of one thing—there's one subject that I would refuse to converse upon—i.e., whether or not you & I should ever get married.

She tried to change the subject. She thanked him for some clothes he had selected for her and sent at her request. She drew him a large, unflattering profile of her peeling, sunburnt nose, and scolded him for not sending her the notices of his first book, a collection of verse titled *The Lady Is Cold*. And she tried again to persuade him to come. "How'm I ever going to learn to drive a car or see Nevada if you don't come?" "Horrid letter—excuse it. Don't for Heaven's sake come out if you don't honestly want to. I'm all right." Feeling sick, she went to bed with a headache.

The next morning she regretted her letter and wrote another.

Circle S—Sat June 1 [1929]

I got sick from a number of reasons, maybe ptomaine, maybe catching cold, maybe various indigestion from anxiety over the children. My own family seem bound to torture me in every way they can conjure up. They write of Roger and Willie's going adrift in a boat down the Hudson which is somewhat worrying but worse, my sister writes she thinks Nancy ought to be taken to see a psycho-analyst—just because Nancy won't talk about this all to any of the family. It drives one frantic. If only they'd leave the child alone or arrange to have her come out here. I don't believe in analysts for most people. Elsie lives by them & not having me there to urge into seeing one (tho' she does it by letter) she has to pick on Nancy. A child of twelve, of all things. I hope I can make them keep their hands off her. Nancy writes me long, quite happy & normal letters—she's been doing better work than ever in school, —I'm *sure* she's all right. But this exile at such a distance is awful.

She had had a change of heart about sending him a photograph of herself, and enclosed a flattering picture of her slender self on horseback—it "is so good of Snowball & the breeches don't show much."

"The hot desert summer is winging along with a certain slow brilliant monotony that makes one long for a cloud or a shower," she wrote in June. But her letters—vivid, stirring, amusing, constantly interesting evocations of her new life on the ranch, a life utterly unlike the one she had left in New York, utterly different from all her previous life—are far from monotonous. The narrative skill and eye for telling detail that strengthen her published writing are alive in these letters to Andy.

Horses—in round-up, in service, in flight—gallop through the letters of June. Round-ups are "as good as Greek games. I never saw anything more beautiful than Russell, Ray and Ligi, who are tall god-like creatures anyway, in action roping and cutting in." Katharine, brimming with enthusiasm and needing to be involved with something, had become part of the equine action at Circle S. She had been kicked by a horse—"a distinction of which I'm a trifle vain." She had gained enough experience or confidence to herd horses by moonlight, participate in a search for missing horses, and assist in some of the round-ups. (She was so thrilled by one round-up that she sent Andy a telegram.) She won second prize in a potato race on horseback. A horse had been named for her, Pyramid Angel. But she was also appalled by the "wholesale handling of horses," by the dead colts left along the road following a stampede, and the rejected animals sent to the chicken feed factory in Reno; by the ranch dogs gorging themselves on the carcasses of dead colts. One of the ranch's best bitches had thus died from satiation. "Sustenance, birth, death are brutal & ever present—yet there is a sort of beauty to it all,—with the sun so strong and persistent."

She was learning horse breeding and terminology; she had watched her first branding, of cattle and a bull. She had lunched with a sheep rancher, "as engaging a person as I've seen in many a day." Less engaging was one of the new women waiting out a divorce at Circle S. "Bobby I hate with a growing passion and everyone feels about the same way. We're hoping Reno may somehow hold out greater inducements to her." But she loved Betty, the other new woman, who was "constantly amusing and nice to be with," and whom she went swimming with every morning. Katharine had taken to sunbathing nude on Pyramid beach. Bobby and Betty spent

> most of their time sewing on lacy underwear and I'm actually inspired and calm enough (a great sign of a vegetable state of mind) to sew also and have started on a birthday present for my sister. I haven't sewed to really make anything in years, certainly not since I was on The New Yorker. Do you suppose it will ruin me forever for any so-called mental work? I wonder if I'll ever be able to earn my living with my head again.

Katharine's mood continued to fluctuate. She was full of health and energy; then her spirits ebbed. She had received final word that Nancy would not be coming out to visit her in July, "for which I'd been hoping for and pulling hard." And she had "abandoned, antagonized, and lost as friends the major portion of my family and acquaintance all at one fell swoop. And I'm likely to finish the rest before I get through." Despite the vigorous days on the ranch she felt that "most of my life has been going on inside of myself."

She missed Andy "still, in spite of this vast Nevada." He clipped Baby's* tail feathers to his letters to her; she sent him a sage blossom. She missed New York. She was "homesick for a hot New York park bench, and cool summer alleys." She was "too disgusted for words at Ross' going to a sanitarium for his vacation. I should like to send him a little piece of tatting or a kindergarten mat to weave. If that isn't intellectual poverty for you." She suffered from indigestion and insomnia. In Reno she visited the doctor again

> for my own satisfaction and [I] find my pulse is normal, my pulse strength which was one half of what it should be when I left Reno is now normal, and my blood pressure is better. Now I can forget doctors forever.

She missed Thurber. He was about to do a radio show, and Katharine hoped to pick it up.

> Jim on sex would give me a great kick. I got into a state of hysterics from amusement and emotion yesterday describing to someone here the man with one eye who could draw Early Woman, act like a Scottie, go into a fit over a no-hit-no-run dice baseball game etc. There should be more Thurbers around.

Thurber had written her a letter enclosing two letters he'd received from girlfriends. Katharine parodied one of them—"perhaps that's the kind of letter men like to get . . . I should take a lesson," she wrote Andy.

Saturday, June 22 [1929]

> Andy, when you're around the world looks all silver and mauve and opalescent. I'm looking very beautiful today, Andy, and I love you—that other girl there in New York, you tell her from a lady of taste and one who knows how to dress, even if she is in Nevada, you tell her that sun tan powder and a coral pink dress make her look sick.

*White's canary.

88

Rewriting

She did not write love letters. She was cautious. Even if she had not been married, getting divorced in 1929, and in love with a young man wary of commitment, she would not have been comfortable expressing her most intimate feelings on paper. These letters to Andy might have been written to a brother or friend. Though she still longed to have him (and "Mr. Ross") visit her—"It would be kind of a triumph to" get Ross to visit—after the begging letter of May 31 she seldom mentioned it.

Ceasing to count on Andy's teaching her to drive, and showing him her independence, Katharine purchased a rumble-seat Model A Ford for the summer and enlisted two high school boys for drives along the rough country roads of Pyramid and the more intimidating city roads of Reno. She named the Ford Bonnie Gray.

Katharine had asked Andy to look for an apartment for her in New York. He found an attractive place on East Eighth Street, and after satisfying her questions as to rent, lease, light, air, sun, etc., secured it for her. Her letters concerning the apartment sound matter-of-fact and warily optimistic. They scarcely betray her anxiety about the new life alone the apartment represented. She conceded only that she thought she'd feel "far less homeless if I had a definite place to look forward to in N.Y."

She did not know whether she had Andy to look forward to. She did not know how much she would see him, or whether he would even be there to greet her upon her return. He was talking of going to Camp Otter, a boys' camp in Ontario where he had worked when in his early twenties, and in which he was thinking of buying an interest.

[August, 1929]

I don't suppose you know how long you'll be gone [wrote Katharine]. Will you be apt to be back when I arrive on the 23rd of August? Probably not. Maybe Daisy will go to Ontario with you. You must leave me elaborate instructions as to her health,—pills, skin lotions & all if you won't be there and she will. I'll feel rather guilty taking her over from you anyway for I can never do so good a job by her and she will miss you and you her. I get back on a Friday morning by the Twentieth Century and will find a deserted Sneden's,—my family & Nancy away till after Labor Day and Roger not arriving till five days after I do. If you were to be around I thought maybe I'd get you to take me out that empty Sunday (that is, if you wanted to) for [a trip] in your canoe on the Sound, of whose existence (the canoe's, not the Sound's) I have some doubts. Or maybe Jim & Althea would let me go to Silvermine and see the poodles—for I must plan to be very busy I can see when I first get back and not just sit at home and mope. . . . I certainly don't plan any moping . . . I've heard from Ross from Stockbridge, quite a cheery letter & two telegrams saying "Just Relax"—He's used that phrase so often that it begins to assume the proportions of "Events Leading Up to a Tragedy." I'll stand it just once more. And such words to come from him too. To tell the truth I'm so relaxed he'll find it hard to get me [keyed] up to his degree of energy ever again.

Andy had been getting restless. From camp he wrote Ross that he would be away from his job longer than expected, and that when he returned to New York he would reduce his writing load. "On account of the fact that The New Yorker has a tendency to make me morose and surly, the farther I stay away the better." Though he considered his feeling for the magazine "as tender" as Ross's or anybody's, for him *The New Yorker*

> [wasn't] a complete life . . . and that's one reason why returning to this place where I worked during the summers of 1920–21 has been such a satisfying experience. In ten years Dorset hasn't changed—it's almost the only place I've ever come back to that hasn't given me an empty feeling from discovering that nothing can be the same again.

Andy may have also been discovering that, with Katharine soon to be divorced, their love and his life could not be the same. His refusal to visit her in Reno, his flight instead to a boys' camp (a literal return to carefree boyhood), was timely.

Katharine entered into Andy's *New Yorker* malaise.

> You may dislike the idea of The New Yorker. To me it's poison. Never did I less want to work there. Now, when I begin to feel I may be able to live again I realize The New Yorker was an escape from the life I didn't like; but now, of course, I seem to have to keep on from economic necessity.

One suspects that Katharine was trying to reassure Andy that the absorption in her work that had beset her first marriage, an absorption that Andy had daily observed at the office, would not be part of their marriage should a union between them take place. "I can't and won't ever go back to such a grind and so much routine and I feel sure I've learned to limit myself on what I take on. It may even be fun—who can tell." She would learn that desirable virtue of masculine detachment.

Andy wrote Katharine of his other concerns about marriage. Only part of her reply has survived.

Rewriting

[July 12?] 1929

I am more shocked & overwhelmed at the part in your letter about my letter
to you, than I can say. If you can think those are my ideas, if I write so badly
that you can so misunderstand me, I give up. I thought perhaps you were the
one person in the world who understood that ease, safety, income & locality
were so little a part of my own desires for life that I'd never recommend them
to anyone else.

Andy, do you honestly think I meant or said that?

He knew her, he understood her contradictions, the desire for simplicity
that expressed itself in a maid, a cook, a governess for the children. She could
not afford to gamble, but she could pay a couple of hundred dollars for a
rumble-seat Ford. In Reno she stayed at the town's new luxury hotel, the
Riverside, and, for the remainder of her Nevada stay, she put up at a ranch,
the costlier way to wait out a divorce. And hadn't she traveled west on the
20th Century Limited, the higher-priced luxury train whence came the expression "the red-carpet treatment"? A life with Katharine would be complicated, and expensive.

A life with Andy would demand a different kind of understanding, an
appreciation of his insecurities (these she knew already), and of his need to
be free, unfettered by a full-time job. That summer he had turned thirty and
reached a crisis of indecision about his future. "You say you're a failure at
the writing racket and that you could be contented in your present job if
you didn't mind being just a hack," wrote Katharine.

I know what you mean by this even if I don't agree and I admire you for
not being content to do what seems to you, just a small thing in writing, well.
You feel that in thirty years you haven't produced a really important book,
poem or piece of prose—Most people haven't by then. It seems to me, though,
that you are preeminently a writer—everything you do has a certain perfection that is rare. You have made the Comment page of the New Yorker the
most distinguished part of that magazine—this is not just my opinion; many
people who did not know who wrote that page and whose opinions I value
have said so to me. . . . Your comments grow better and better—this last year's
have been more important than the year's before—Aside from that you've
written most of your best poems in the last year and a half so far as I can see.
Now I quite understand why you don't want to go on writing what you call
"palpitating paragraphs" all your life and appreciate your feeling that writing
is fun when you don't have to do it, when you do it as an amateur and not

because you must sit before a typewriter and turn out so many words a week. Whether you should keep the New Yorker job I can't say,—certainly you shouldn't if it prevents you from writing things you care about more but it seems to me that that job, properly held down so you control it and not it you,—so you don't give all your life to it and allow it to harass and burden you, seems to me to have a lot to be said for it for the next few years anyway. After all it's a pretty pleasant job as things go,—allows you to live a comparatively gracious and free life. Your hours are your own with certain exceptions, you have some fun out of it you must admit; you have, I should guess, a life that would please you more than another sort of office job would give you. You might go into farming, ferry-boating what not and write when you felt like it. That has a lot to be said for it, too, but I do know this: there's no real freedom or happiness in life for the person who just vagabonds, throws over the idea of being a responsible member of society and says "This year I can live on 50¢ a day and work my way to the coast." Everyone of your temperament should do that once in a while but a lifetime of it would leave you pretty blank after a year or two. . . . If you do keep on the New Yorker job, why not limit yourself definitely to, say three days in the office,—and give yourself a real break in writing something you want to, the rest of the time—or not writing at all if you don't want to. For you to give up writing now would be like a violinist so good that he could always be the Concert Master of one of the four or five leading orchestras of the world, giving up fiddling because he couldn't be Heifetz. Perhaps you'll never be a Heifetz, perhaps you will, I can't say. . . . But it doesn't seem sensible for a concert master to throw over music, the thing he most loved in the world, because he can't be Heifetz. The least you'll ever be, in my estimation, is a concert master. You know there's a kind of vanity in underestimating yourself. . . . Oh, stop preaching, Katharine. I ought to be the last person in the world to hold forth on how to arrange one's life, I having made a pretty disgusting mess of my own and other people's—Do please forgive me—I'll bet on you whatever you do.

And then the words he had misunderstood:

I'm with you more heartily than I can say in being against success that is economic only, and against loading one's life with possessions, routines and riches of one sort or another, that only tie one down and keep one from really living. How I long for a *simple,* decent life of my own,—with a few things for the soul to feed on. You can have it anyway, my dear,—and *please* don't be unhappy or worried now. At least don't create unhappinesses for yourself where they don't exist—there are enough necessary ones around for everyone.

Rewriting

She was leaving Reno. The August 18th issue of the *New York Times* announced her impending divorce, the child-custody arrangement, and the alimony agreement.* To her last, vulnerable letter to Andy expressing her dreams of a reunion with him upon her return to a Sneden's bereft of family and children, Katharine added an inviting postscript. "Maybe it's as well I'm leaving. I was discovered naked on Pyramid beach by an Indian today. It's *their* lake, too."

Before leaving, Katharine visited a fortuneteller with filthy hands who told the events of Katharine's life without making a single mistake. The fortuneteller told Katharine about her son and daughter, and the big office she worked in. And she said that her future "will be everything I want— smooth, calm, quiet & happy! Oh yes, I'm to live till 81, which is the only gloomy thing she predicted!"

*The AP item ran under the heading "Wife Sues Ernest Angell. Files for Divorce from New York Lawyer at Reno."

5

Real and Incontrovertible

Back in new york, Katharine settled into her new apartment in Greenwich Village, at 16 East 8th Street. She engaged a housekeeper and returned to the poisonous *New Yorker.* In September, she passed her thirty-seventh birthday.

When Nancy and Roger Angell were first informed of their parents' impending divorce, Katharine and Ernest told them how much time they would be spending with their mother and how often they would be seeing her. Remembering these events many years later, Roger Angell could not picture his mother in a particular place between the time she left their New York house and when she moved into the East Eighth Street apartment, though she had lived at Sneden's for several months before going to Reno. He had been happy when his mother moved into the new apartment and he could attach her to a place.

Though Katharine was awarded $5,000-a-year alimony, joint custody of the children actually meant that Nancy and Roger lived with their father during the week and went to their mother's apartment weekends, holidays, and during the summer months. Father's house at East Ninety-third Street was their "official home."

Ernest tried hard to maintain a sense of normality and to compensate for their suffering. Nine-year-old Roger, a handsome, beautifully behaved boy with a great shock of brown hair, was permitted to keep a rather alarming menagerie in the house: two dogs, including the Boston terrier Roger had been given on his fifth birthday (named Tunney, after the prizefighter); a monkey, a gift from the writer Emily Hahn; cats and kittens; an assortment of snakes—one a king snake, which guests often observed slithering around the bookcases in the living room. Nancy Stableford later remembered that all the attention made her little brother "act like an adult. He thought he was the cat's pajamas. . . . But it was good for him, too. He needed it."

Andy had not received Katharine's last letter telling him that she would be without the children and alone at Sneden's on the weekend following her return from Reno. He did not know about her fantasies of a canoe trip with him on the Sound. His breezy letter written in August sounded as though he were concerned with more important things: "I haven't heard from you in a dog's age, but my mail seems to be scattered around a bit anyway. I have succeeded in losing track of about everything—people, dates, friends, mail, jobs, home. And it feels good."

On September 11, Andy wrote again, extolling the pleasures and beauties of camp life, and "the handsome new canoe" he had had built for himself. He wanted to return home in the canoe, paddling "down the Erie canal and Hudson to surprise central New York people and to give myself a good time."

After investing $8,000 (a sizable part of his savings) in Camp Otter, which he seems to have viewed as an eventual escape from *The New Yorker* and the grind of weekly deadlines, Andy returned to the magazine, and to the light writing schedule he had earlier outlined to Harold Ross. In November, White's second book, a collaborative effort with James Thurber, was published by Harper & Brothers. *Is Sex Necessary? Or Why You Feel the Way You Do* parodied the current proliferation of sex books by various authorities.

Katharine and Andy soon resumed their discussion of marriage. E. B. White recalled the conversation that proved the turning point. It was a Wednesday, November 13.

> I don't remember how ivy got into the discussion but potted plants have never been far removed from Katharine's thoughts. Anyway, when I heard the word "ivy," I said petulantly, "Oh, let the ivy rest!" K's whole manner changed. Instead of slamming the ball back over the net at me, she replied in a mild and thoughtful voice: "That sounds like the name of an English country house."
>
> At this point, I decided that she was the girl for me and the hell with the obstacles. So, after some badgering, she agreed to it, and we spent the rest of the day getting married—no mean feat.

They were married the same day.* It was a hasty day crowded with last-minute errands—to the bank, for Katharine's divorce papers; to City Hall, for the marriage license; to a cheap jewelry store to look at rings (passed over, temporarily, in favor of Katharine's college ring). Katharine canceled a dinner engagement and the cooking services of her housekeeper. She and Andy lunched at a speakeasy. Then, taking Daisy along, they drove fifty

*A day whose details we again owe to Scott Elledge.

miles north to Bedford Village, where, having first tried to find a justice of the peace, they were finally married by a minister in the Presbyterian Church on the village green, next to the minister's house. The church was decorated with autumn leaves left over from a funeral. E. B. White recalled that "It was a very nice wedding—nobody threw anything, and there was a dog fight." The wedding dinner for two took place in a back room of an Italian restaurant in Manhattan. The Whites went to work the next day.

Katharine's writers were informed by a typewritten announcement that "Mrs. Angell is now Mrs. White." Two days after the wedding Walter Winchell reported the event in his column in the New York *Daily Mirror.*

> News that couldn't wait until Monday: E. B. White, of The New Yorker's comical department and one of the better wits in the town, and Katharine Angell, the managing editor of The New Yorker, eloped Tuesday and were sealed up-state.
>
> The groom recently co-authored a book titled (heh-heh): "Is Sex Necessary?"*

Katharine was not amused.

Katharine's Angell relatives were not amused by the announcement of her marriage, either. Hildegarde Angell read about it in the society section, and informed Nancy.

Fearing that their marriage plans, if revealed beforehand, would open them up to "an endless round of debates"—fearing, perhaps, that the marriage would not come off at all—Katharine and Andy had driven to Bedford Village without telling anyone of their plans. Katharine's foolish decision not to enlighten or even prepare her children, who were freshly wounded by their parents' separation and divorce, is probably explained by her intense desire to marry Andy, which made her self-centered, and by a blind spot in her own perceptiveness. It was evident in the letter Katharine had written to Andy during the summer, when she insisted that Nancy, "a child of twelve," did not need psychological help, and was in fact adjusting well to the divorce. Katharine, understandably, wanted to believe that was true, needed to believe that twelve-year-old Nancy was and would be all right. If it wasn't true, if in fact Elsie was right about Nancy's being so troubled that she required psychoanalysis, how was Katharine to bear her own guilt? And so Katharine had responded to the surface of Nancy; she grasped at the

---

*Out of Katharine's earshot, members of the Inner Shrine said, "First she married an earnest angel, then she married the author of *Is Sex Necessary?*"

external signs, at her daughter's good performance in school, and the normal-sounding letters Nancy wrote her in Reno. Speaking of her parents years later, Nancy Stableford said, "Part of their philosophy of life, in raising children, I think, was that you didn't expose them to unpleasant things, especially when you got divorced! You didn't let them go to funerals, didn't stress them with real life—which didn't help to prepare you for the world."

That Katharine allowed her children to hear of her marriage from someone other than herself is also likely attributable to Katharine's having married Andy on a Wednesday, when the children were with Ernest. She may not have wanted to call on them there; she perhaps reasoned that Saturday, when they would arrive as usual on the weekend, was soon enough. On the weekend, Nancy and Roger, accompanied by Aunt Hildegarde, visited their mother and new stepfather.

E. B. White's marriage to Katharine fueled Ernest's bitterness toward the younger man. Here was proof that Katharine had left him for someone else. The rejection triggered dark thoughts. Ernest informed Andy that he would not allow Nancy to be in the house with him unless Katharine was present. He put it in writing, into long letters to Katharine and Andy, detailing the things Andy was not to do with Nancy and Roger. The children observed their father writing the long letters to their mother. Nancy was dimly aware of the contents. "Father could never be even quietly civil about E. B. White," she said later. "He went out of his way to say uncivil things," reacting with nastiness to anything associated with *The New Yorker* or E. B. White. "She left me for another man" was, of course, "a way he could kid himself." Returning home from their visits to the Whites, Nancy and Roger quickly learned not to volunteer anything about Mother and Andy. "Pretty soon," said Nancy, "after we got used to Father's reaction, we didn't say anything at all."

Borrowing a piece of an old Rea Irvin drawing and paraphrasing its caption (quoting Albert Einstein, "People slowly accustomed themselves to the idea that the physical states of space itself were the final physical reality"), Andy left a memo on Katharine's desk: "E. B. White slowly accustomed himself to the idea that he had made the most beautiful decision of his life."

Ernest's attitude bothered Andy, but the instructions about the children, the dirty insinuations regarding Nancy, were "all blows around the head." They didn't really get to him or crush him because he knew how Katharine felt about him. In the "yellow lamplight / On the fields of our room," he would write, "all is certain."

[Late November, 1929]
Saturday night

Dear Katharine (very dear):

I've had moments of despair during the last week which have added years to my life and put many new thoughts in my head. Always, however, I have ended on a cheerful note of hope, based on the realization that you are the person to whom I return and that you are the recurrent phrase in my life. I realized that so strongly one day a couple of weeks ago when, after being away among people I wasn't sure of and in circumstances I had doubts about, I came back and walked into your office and saw how real and incontrovertible you seemed. I don't know whether you know just what I mean or whether you experience, ever, the same feeling; but what I mean is, that being with you is like walking on a very clear morning—definitely the sensation of belonging there.

This marriage is a terrible challenge: everyone wishing us well, and all with their tongues in their cheeks. What other people think, or wish, or prophesy, is not particularly important, except as it tends to work on our minds. I think you have the same intuitive hesitancy that I have—about pushing anything too hard, and the immediate problem surely is that we recognize & respect each other's identity. That I could assimilate Nancy overnight is obviously out of the question—or that she could me. In things like that we gain ground slowly. By and large, our respective families had probably best be kept in their respective places during the pumpkin weather—and gradually, like the Einstein drawing of Rea Irvin's, people will become accustomed to the idea that etc. etc.

I'm just writing this haphazard for no reason other than that I felt like writing you a letter before going to bed.

I love you. And that's a break.

Andy

Andy had gone to bed alone that night, the second Saturday after their marriage. Thinking that it would be easier on Nancy and Roger if they were alone with their mother, he had returned to his bachelor apartment for the weekend.

He wrote love letters and poetry. No one had ever done that for Katharine. No longer guarding the most difficult part of himself, he loved her openly, irresistibly, with a directness she herself could not commit to paper, though she was dearly, irrevocably committed to him. Deeply moved by her marriage to Andy but intuitively hesitant about expressing her feelings,

Katharine responded with cautious abandon—"If it lasts only a year, it will be worth it," she told Ann Honeycutt, a writer and Thurber girlfriend.

From the King Edward Hotel in Toronto, where he had gone on Camp Otter business, Andy wrote Katharine a poem that came to symbolize their marriage—its closeness and its separations.

November 30, 1929

NATURAL HISTORY

The spider, dropping down from twig,
Unwinds a thread of his devising:
A thin, premeditated rig
To use in rising.

And all the journey down through space,
In cool descent, and loyal-hearted,
He builds a ladder to the place
From which he started.

Thus I, gone forth, as spiders do,
In spider's web a truth discerning,
Attach one silken strand to you
For my returning.

In the fall of 1930 Nancy went away to Concord Academy. Ernest did not want his daughter to live away from home, but he thought she needed a woman's guidance, which she was not getting from her mother, and to be with girls her own age. There was talk, intermittently, of sending Roger to boarding school also, even to military school, to which Katharine was opposed. Following an exchange of letters between Katharine and Ernest, the idea was dropped. Ernest had not wanted Roger to go away anyway, and he may have recognized that Roger was just missing his mother.

Ernest realized that his ten-year-old son needed someone other than his father around, especially with Nancy gone. An observer during this time remembers that Ernest "would get kind of rigid with Roger." He sometimes had very little patience with his son, and would get upset at small things. Ernest himself knew that there should be someone to provide a buffer, a lightening of the atmosphere. He thought that Roger needed the companionship of a young man—a sort of older brother.

Arthur Goldschmidt, whom everyone called Tex because he came from San Antonio, Texas, had been tutoring on the side at Columbia University, where he was a junior, majoring in economics, when someone in the college office informed him, "There's a man who wants someone to come and have dinner with him and his son every night, and stay until the son goes to bed." The man had specifically requested a Christian student (a fact that later struck Tex as odd, since Ernest was not religious and had a lot of Jewish friends). Tutoring jobs had become scarce, and Tex went down to Wall Street to see Ernest Angell. They immediately got along. They talked for about twenty minutes—Did Arthur like to read? Did he like sports? Finally, giving Tex the house key, Ernest told him to go to the house at about four o'clock. Ernest would dine at the Harvard Club and come home later, after Arthur and Roger had had a chance to get acquainted. Tex was flat broke—it was the Depression. And he was delighted with the dinner invitation, because he didn't have enough money that week to buy himself a decent meal. Ernest was concerned that his son and this student hit it off: it was important to find the right person for Roger.

Thereafter, Tex came to the Angells' house as often as five nights a week, for several hours each night. He had been getting three or four dollars an hour tutoring; Ernest paid him about $15 a week. After a few months, when Tex quit living in his fraternity house, Ernest suggested that he move into Nancy's room. Roger Angell later said that "Tex really saved my life. For one thing (a very big thing), he showed me that it was all right to take life lightly at times—to laugh and enjoy a joke or a game. It lifted my heart. He was a sweet and bright man, full of affection and good will."

In his son's eyes, Ernest was very fair-minded, open to all kinds of ideas, his ideas sometimes "brilliant": Tex was one of them. Roger Angell thought it would not have occurred to his mother to get a student to look after him. Ernest was in many ways far more sensitive to human needs and complexities than Katharine was. Nancy Stableford agreed. "Some of it may have come about through circumstances. He was lonely a long time. And he was sensitive."

Katharine never came to the house. For Roger's weekend visits Tex took him down to the Village. The Whites were "terribly nice." Tex was later surprised to learn that others regarded Mrs. White as formidable, for he found her motherly. Tex had a kind of idealized view because of her work at *The New Yorker,* a magazine he read and admired. Once, Tex happened to be on the same train as Morris Ernst, who had represented Mrs. White in her divorce, and Ernst talked to him about the Angells' divorce. "She was a great earth mother," said Ernst, by way of explaining E. B. White's attraction to Katharine Angell. "She had those great bosoms," continued the lawyer, pushing his hands out from his chest and curling them under. Tex, who respected and even idolized Mrs. White, was offended by the older man's crude way of talking about her.

It seemed to Tex "so terrible that such nice people were divorced." He never had an unpleasant moment with Ernest, even though he didn't share Ernest's rigid personal style. Though not a New Englander, Ernest Angell was Tex's idea of the proper Bostonian: outwardly stiff, with a little bit of snobbery and propriety about things. He had a live-in French couple, Joseph and Edmonde Petrognani, to attend to the housework and cooking. His house itself was a brownstone; inside were books all around, and a marvelous library. Dinner, cooked by Joseph, was served by candlelight, coffee brought up to the library.

Now in his early forties, Ernest Angell was a formidable man of great vitality who kept late hours socializing or working at home, writing articles for law journals, his yellow legal pads scattered about on the floor. He was busy all the time. He enjoyed good conversation, but he was not a man for small talk, and this could make him seem arrogant. Vigorous himself, he was unsympathetic with the illnesses of others. He had an abrupt "lawyer manner": he would ask questions and could be cold and withering. But he had a good sense of humor (in the opinion of his daughter-in-law Evelyn Angell, it was better than Andy's), and he could tell stories on himself. His uncomfortable manner belied his essential kindness and warmth.

To Tex Goldschmidt, who was very involved in radical campus politics, Ernest Angell was a model of intellectual freedom. Despite Ernest's own middle-of-the-road liberalism, he constantly encouraged Tex's radical political involvements. Goldschmidt later thought that by example Ernest had saved him from joining the Communist party.

Tex knew that Ernest liked him, though Ernest wasn't affectionate. He was, rather, quietly considerate, dividing up the *Tribune* and the *Times* with Tex, sharing his bathroom with him because Tex liked to take showers and didn't have a shower on the third floor, where his bedroom was. Mornings, after they had gotten Roger off to school, one would shave while the other showered, the two men talking and arguing about politics all the while. When Tex and a group of students went down to participate in the Holland County mine workers' strike, Ernest cheered him on, gave a small dinner party for him when he returned, and presented him with a watch for bravery. There was never a question in Ernest's mind or Tex's that if there was a dinner party at the house Tex would be included. (So was Roger, quite often; the boy was encouraged to speak his mind, even to adults.)

Ernest never spoke to Tex about the divorce; theirs was an intellectual relationship. "We were good friends," recalled Goldschmidt, "but there was no emotional content on either side." Tex never heard Ernest say anything bad about Katharine to the children or in front of them, but he sensed a kind of bitterness in Ernest about the divorce, especially in the way he held it all at arm's length. And he realized that Ernest resented E. B. White more than he did Mrs. White. When Nancy and Roger brought up Katharine's name, it was usually because they were going to see her, and she was not dwelt on.

In the spring the Whites took a delayed honeymoon to Bermuda; in May Katharine learned she was pregnant. As in his first verses to Katharine, signed "Beppo," Andy used a guise of a dog (their dog Daisy) to express his feelings about impending fatherhood. In a letter to "Mrs. White" from Daisy, Andy worried that he had not told Katharine how glad he was about the baby; he "[held] himself back, not wanting to appear ludicrous to a veteran mother." Rather than feeling overwhelmed by having a child so soon after his marriage, Andy said that "it seemed so good that everything was starting at once."

Katharine was presumably happy about having a child with Andy and beginning a family of their own. At thirty-eight, she would again become a mother, but things would be different now, with her nourishing work at *The New Yorker,* and her happy new life with this man she loved above all others. It was right this time.

Nancy and Roger were excited about their mother's pregnancy. Nancy, who had hoped that her parents would be reconciled, was gradually recovering from their divorce, a delicate process made easier by Andy, who was wonderful with children, and by her father's tireless hostility toward E. B. White: there was a point at which Nancy became defensive of Andy, who could not be, and clearly was not, the evil figure of Father's rhetoric. Nancy would slowly realize that in some respects Mother's marriage to Andy had a lot to offer that the old way of life hadn't. She and Roger could both see that their mother was happier, and "it was always more fun at the Whites'." Their home was filled with laughter; they had a bigger Christmas tree. Andy soon taught Nancy to drive; he was patient and she learned well. And Andy had of course long been well-known to both children, having often been at their house before their parents were separated. Back then, before Reno, when Andy was teaching Mother to drive a car, they had taken Roger along in the Angells' Franklin, and Mother had stripped the gears on the Bronx River Parkway. Another time Roger had gone coasting with Andy at Sneden's on a snowy day. Andy was nice, and fun to be with.

In the summer of 1930 Katharine decided to spend some extra time alone with her children. Taking along her housekeeper-cook, Josephine Buffa, and a governess borrowed from Rosamond, she and the children removed to a rented house in Bedford Village. Andy returned to Camp Otter.

During their month-long separation, Andy wrote Katharine the same evocative, excited, boyish letters about camp life that he had written to her in Reno the previous summer, only somewhat more personal and openly loving. He missed his wife and future baby, who, if female, was to be called Serena; for a boy they were favoring Joel. He was glad things were going well for her in Bedford Village, "but it is foolish of you to be anywhere but here, with your tumultuous little Joe whom I love so and who must hear the great frogs of July at their love-making and see the lights in the north. Even at long distance it is good to know you."

On December 21, Katharine gave birth to a son, Joel McCoun White, by an emergency Caesarean section. The baby was healthy, but Katharine required an immediate blood transfusion, got from a cab driver hailed on the street. The doctors and nurses at New York's Harbor Hospital expected Katharine to die, but as Andy would recount, she "bounced back after a nurse had whispered in her ear, 'Do you want to say a little prayer, dearie?' 'Certainly not,' she replied, in her clear Boston voice."

Katharine recovered quickly and returned home with Joel. She then became ill with pyelitis, inflammation of a kidney pelvis, and was forced to enter another hospital. Though not in danger or pain, she was depressed from six weeks of bed rest.

Following her hospitalization, Katharine seems to have remained at home or worked part time until the fall, when she left Joel in the care of Andy and a nursemaid and returned to *The New Yorker* full time.

Katharine continued to write for *The New Yorker,* but just one more bit of verse appeared above her initials (printed backward).

NOTE AT FIFTH AVENUE
AND TWENTY-SIXTH STREET

Once more the autumn windows drape
Themselves in orange paper crêpe
For Halloween—the yearly benison
Of the well-known tag man, Mr. Dennison.

The two last casuals Katharine wrote for the magazine, in 1934 and 1935, are equally forgettable.

In December of 1933 she began writing something to which her talents were better suited: reviews of children's books. Before Katharine White, children's books were given only superficial treatment in the magazine, in an annual "Children's Toys and Books" section. The focus was on toys, the discussions of children's books few and brief—there was no real criticism—with the concentration being on where to buy them. The feature was unsigned.

For Katharine, the reviews were an addition to her full-time editorial work, which she did "with my left hand," until 1948. Katharine left no explanation of why she assumed this extra task, which greatly increased her heavy workload, except that she was interested in what children were reading and in what was being written for them. But she also had a need to write, to keep her hand in formal composition. And reviewing children's books provided her with an intimate activity with Joel, to whom she read many of the books before he could read them himself. She observed his reactions and duly recorded them in her reviews, usually keeping him anonymous ("my three year old critic"). She gave Roger many of the books for older children, and listened to and quoted his responses to them. Roger loved this; it made him feel close to his mother, and important to her.

She read everything, reviewed every worthy juvenile (a term she disliked, but used) that came her way, from fables to books about fighting planes. She read with a keen discrimination and an unabashed prejudice, openly preferring, and occasionally reminiscing about, the traditional books of her childhood, and decrying the newer, inferior illustrations given those beloved classics. To Katharine, a book's illustrations were very important, and she scrutinized them with nearly the same attention she gave the text. Hers was the attention of someone reared on beautifully illustrated books, like those of Gustave Doré, that of a literary editor whose early professional training had encompassed the editing of art work (*New Yorker* covers and drawings). One children's book contained "ingratiatingly simple pictures in clear, pale colors"; in another, "the pictures are gaily colored and straightforward." But in one unfortunate book "the pictures are so spectacular as to be unconvincing and sometimes confusing. I wish they could have been done by Hendrik Van Loon, preferably using a match dipped in colored ink." Katharine complained that "the artists have it all over the writers in the quality of their work for the young. First rate artists draw for them constantly, first-rate writers write for them seldom."

The critic who signed herself K. S. W. (later, K. S. White) was equally attentive to typography and paper. "This book is worthy of better type and paper, more margin, more space to turn around in." She disliked books printed in "manuscript writing," colored print as opposed to black, print that switched to "enormous capital letters to emphasize a point." Such devices were unnecessary. One must not underestimate children.

Neither should one write down to them. "It is a pity that Miss Singer has chosen to chop her prose into sentences so short that many of them are not sentences at all. Children can take subordinate clauses in their stride." Katharine worried about the so-called poetry written for children; and she fretted about the critical blindness of her fellow reviewers.

> With a few exceptions, the critics of children's books are remarkably lenient souls. They seem to regard books for children with the same tolerant tenderness with which nearly any adult regards a child. Most of us assume there is something good in every child; the critics go on from this to assume there is something good in every book written for a child. It is not a sound theory.

During the fifteen years Katharine reviewed children's books, she consistently alerted her readers to the inferior quality of much of the literature, and hammered away with particular zest at the books' sentimentality and similar subject matter.

> The rank-and-file books . . . for children of every age, are constantly invaded by the three major vices of the writer of juveniles: sentimentality, coyness, and moralizing. Too often there is among them a dreary similarity of subject matter. The monotony of little pioneer after little pioneer, of stories so continuously placed in the quainter periods of American history, is appalling.

> There are too many coy books full of talking animals, whimsical children, and condescending adults. (Some of the most famous animals in the world have talked, but they talked real talk and they weren't called silly names like Doody and Mooloo. They were called names like The Cheshire Cat and they asked sensible questions like "Did you say pig, or fig?") There is also too much effort to be informative and to widen the horizons of the pre-school child.

And yet, she thought, one must not shy away from widening the horizons of the very young; it is a mistake to protect children from books that are too old for them. Katharine worried that the profusion of attractive juveniles on the market diverted children from adult books; she thought writers were being too careful not to overstimulate children, too leery of scaring the child, of leaving him in doubt. "The child has become sacrosanct, and, by extension, so has the children's book." "It has always seemed to us that boys and girls worth their salt begin at twelve or thirteen to read, with a brilliant indiscrimination, every book they can lay their hands on." She envisioned twelve-year-old girls taking up Austen, and boys, Dickens. "You wonder how writers of juveniles have the brass to compete in this field, blithely announcing their works as 'suitable for the child of twelve to fourteen.' Their implication is that everything else is distinctly *un*suitable."

"The hardy, and we sometimes think presumptuous, writers of children's books are back this year sinning in a multitude of covers." Katharine routinely condemned books that had been critically applauded and awarded—Antoine de Saint-Exupéry's *The Little Prince* (1943), for instance, which she considered neither a good book nor a book for children; and Gertrude Stein's *The World Is Round* (1939), "listed for parents who don't want to miss the latest trick." For her evaluation of *The Little Prince* Katharine called on Joel.

> The only youthful appraisal I can offer is that of a twelve-year-old boy, who likes almost all kinds of books and usually reads at top speed. After dragging through this one, he said, "He seems to be writing about grownup things in a childish way." Possibly this judgment has some merit because, when you come to think of it, the best children's books are those which treat child-like things in an adult way. "The Little Prince" unquestionably has its moments of charm and point and its naive drawings have occasional humor and grace, but as a fairy tale, whether for adults or children, it seems to me to lack the simplicity and clarity all fairy tales must have in order to create their magic, and too often its charm turns into coyness and its point is lost in cloudy and boring elaboration. The jury will now retire to a locked hotel room for the night while the arguments continue.

The self-admittedly prejudiced reviewer thought that no adult knew what was suitable for the child mind. She herself tried to select books that were attractive and amusing (to Joel as well as herself), and timeless, likely to appeal to any age—such as *The White Deer,* Thurber's 1945 fairy tale for adults. She regularly reviewed children's books by *New Yorker* writers, and though she tried harder to like these she did not shy away from criticizing them, even if the author belonged to K. S. White's stable. Though she praised a children's book by her own Kay Boyle, "I don't feel that children in general will take it to their hearts. It . . . grows overpreachy, even for a fable."

During her tenure as reviewer of children's books for *The New Yorker,* Katharine covered from twenty-plus to more than eighty books a review, including reprints. She averaged about fifty books a review. (Many titles were simply listed.) In time, the reviews gathered speed and ambition, gradually becoming longer and more comprehensive. What began as a pre-Christmas annual became a twice-yearly feature, covering spring and summer books too. A typically brief introductory passage was followed by a list of books with concise summaries. At her best, K. S. W. was opinionated and crisp.

> *The Travels of Babar,* by Jean de Brunhoff. This year Babar is officially blessed by A. A. Milne in a prefatory paragraph, an unnecessary and misleading condescension, since de Brunhoff is witty without being Poohish, and Babar is an elephant who can stand on his own feet.
>
> *The Pied Piper of Hamelin,* by Robert Browning, illustrated in color and black-and-white by Arthur Rackham. It doesn't seem possible that Rackham has waited until now to illustrate the "Piper."

It had taken until now for Katharine to find her own genre. Her introductory paragraphs became graceful essays salted with reviews. The writing was at once formal and casual, informed and conjecturing, spirited and gently reminiscent, personal ("a sinister little set of volumes") and conversational —"Dear me!" The voice was Katharine White's, and it was yet to have its aria.

In January of 1933, the same year Katharine began her children's book reviews, *The New Yorker* published a short humorous piece about a long-married elderly couple, titled "Father and the French Court." It was the first of what was to be a long series of Father stories, the reminiscent works by Clarence Day that became *Life with Father.* * Katharine White was Day's editor and friend.

She and Day wrote to each other often, he frequently writing her personal letters during her summer vacations. Crippled and bedridden with arthritis since his twenties—his writing was achieved by flexing his shoulder muscle, which caused the pencil held stiffly in his hand to move—Clarence Day loved to hold court with a select group of friends in his bedroom facing the East River. Katharine was of this favored group. She handled the editing and scheduling of Day's stories and poems in letters, or discussed *New Yorker* matters with him during her visits to him at his home.

Only a few of Katharine's editorial letters to Clarence Day, and one of his letters to her—all of them from a later period, 1935—are available. They do not tell us to what extent Katharine edited Day's work or how much revision his work underwent before publication. But, taken altogether, this fragment of correspondence reveals much about Katharine White as an editor.

---

*Most, but not all, of Day's "Father" stories first appeared in *The New Yorker,* some of them under different titles from those in the *Life with Father* book. The others were published in *Harper's Magazine* and *The New Republic.*

April 11, 1935

Dear Clarence:

We think that the revised story of Father's old age is delightful and I enclose our check for it now. This piece is paid for complete. There will be no further checks due you on it as I believe there still are on at least one and possibly two manuscripts which are being held up because I have just not had time to edit and get them set in type.

Now on "Father Objects to Exploring," Mr. Ross asks whether you would be willing with this one to hold it awhile and resubmit for our final decision somewhat later. If we used it, we would want to have it follow the other story about boating. I hope we can use that one this summer, though I can't promise, but if we do schedule it we can give you warning so that you can send this in again. The reason for asking you to hold it is that it seems more of a personal reminiscence and less of a Father story than some others. It is charming and pleasant, but it is milder than some of the others. There is a very good chance that we might have space and might be crying for it when the time comes around, but Ross doesn't feel that we ought to promise to take it now. Somehow in tone it is more of a quiet childhood story than a character piece or an amusing anecdotal narrative.

However, if sending it back and asking you to hold embarrasses you financially, let us know and we can always give you an advance. I *am* sorry about the whole thing . . .

I had thought that perhaps I could pay you a visit this evening, if you want to see me, but now Andy's sister from Washington has turned up and we have to help her get a manic-depressive husband into Bloomingdale's.* He has seven children and no funds. Oh, Lord, what next?

Careful to point out when she had not proofread one of her letters and when the signature at bottom was a secretary's and not her own, Katharine closed the letter with "Dictated but not read & signed Katharine by?"—she had forgotten which secretary.

This personal editorial letter, with its mixture of business and news about Katharine's private life, was both natural and studied: it naturally evolved from Katharine's gregariousness, her intense need for friendship and approval, and yet was a deliberately and carefully honed technique for maintaining close contact with writers, and for encouraging them to continue contributing to *The New Yorker*. Katharine invented this brand of editorial letter for herself, and was proud of it. It "was a habit [she] tried to instill in everyone" of the editors she worked with.

*The New York Hospital on Bloomingdale Road in White Plains.

Real and Incontrovertible

As an editor Katharine was required to write her official letters in the editorial "we"; the device told the writer that the opinions or queries Katharine was sending him were not always hers alone, but the combined reaction of several editors, the magazine's copy readers, and the editor-in-chief. (Katharine was not allowed to tell a writer she liked a submitted piece until Ross had read it.) Her frequent references to Harold Ross also reminded the writer who at the magazine had final say (and helped deflect blame from herself). And yet the warmth of her tone ("Now what do you think we had better do about it, between us?" Katharine wrote in another letter to Clarence Day), her confidence about a manic-depressive relative, reassured the writer that though Katharine White had a job to do, she was on his side.

Her letters to Clarence Day are typical of Katharine's editorial letters: filled with suggestions and thoughtful ideas about how the writer might go about a particular piece, concerned with his feelings—"*Please* don't get excited about it, and if it would be better I will come up and talk about the whole thing." She enclosed fan letters, passed on compliments from other *New Yorker* staff members. Her rejection letters were straightforward, but sympathetic and apologetic, sometimes irresistible.

October 22, 1935

Dear Clarence:

You are one of the people that I want to see the most of all, both as a friend and as a contributor, and I promise to be there by hook or crook before very long to discuss the whole plan for the Father series. We had a good deal of talk about it yesterday and as soon as I can get your ideas very definitely down on paper, I think we can come to some arrangement that will be satisfactory.

In the meantime I have to tell you the bad news that the final decision on "Father Expects Every Tree to do its Duty" is a "no" just because the theme of this story is really too much like "Father and Old Mother Earth." The essential idea of both of them is Father disciplining nature. As you know, I had thought the two might be combined and we could pay you for the extra work so that you would not suffer, but you didn't want that and the scheme fell by the boards because of lack of cooperation here, the right hand not knowing what the left was doing. Mr. Ross was considering the suggestion and meanwhile Gibbs had scheduled and used in the magazine "Father and Old Mother Earth." I do feel that the first page of "Father Expects Every Tree . . ." could be part of another Father piece for us. . . . Do think it over in the midst of your wrath. If you are too cross with me I shall weep, so don't be. As an editor, one has to steel one's self in sending unpleasant news to contributors, especially after three months of country calm and a month of illness when no such tasks came up.

> Much love to you and
> I will see you soon.
> Katharine

Her rejection letters were not always so tender.

October 30, 1935

Dear Clarence:

Mr. Ross says about this poem and picture: "Too clinical for me. And, post scripturally, its not only the woman poet but all the psychiatrists who recognize this womb yearning and brand it the greatest cause of drunkenness." I would go even farther and say that the lady poet caught it from the psychiatrists, & that it's perhaps confusing to put it on the poet. It is too bad because it is a neatly turned poem and a good idea, but it does seem to give people the willies.

I am hoping really to be able to see you tomorrow, but I have a bad cold still and don't want to give it to you. It is clearing up, though.

> Affly,
> Katharine

Day seems to have taken the rejections in stride, or at least not held them against Katharine. In the deferential, reassuring manner in which so many of Katharine's writers and colleagues addressed her, Clarence Day wrote to Katharine in July of 1935 about *Life with Father,* now a Book of the Month Club selection with good reviews and Hollywood interest.

My God, if I were not a magazine contributor, my head would be turned. But a magazine contrib's head is kept cooled off by the buckets of cold water he gets, from editors who are always rewriting or rejecting his stuff, just to let him know he's a worm. (N.B., this *doesn't* mean *you.*)

I wish editors were always right about everything, or else always wrong.

I wish Ross and you and the copy room never caught me with my pants down.

Sometimes when Ross opens his box of little grammatical rules and disallows my best blasts of music and punctures my bag-pipes I wish to God I could exchange places with him a minute. (At other times, however, I'm obliged to him. Damn it. And I'm often grateful to *you.*)

Real and Incontrovertible

The affectionate inscription in the Whites' copy of *Life with Father* again expressed the author's gratitude "To K. S. W., both for warming me up, AND for toasting out my impurities." Day's accompanying illustration depicts Katharine as a graceful figure with a huge bun at the back of her head, literally toasting Day, held aloft on a long stick over a fire, as a reclining E. B. White watches.

The "impurities" in Clarence Day's prose seem to have been minor, though it is hard to tell from the few manuscripts of posthumously published Father stories that somehow found their way into Katharine White's possession. The pieces were in various stages of completion upon Day's death, those in the lesser stages naturally requiring more editing. But Katharine noted that the editing of all these manuscripts was much as it had been during Day's lifetime.

Typically, Katharine's editing of Day consisted of proofreaders' marks indicating many deletions of commas, and lines that should be indented or set farther to the left. Occasionally she changes a verb tense. Many pages bear her clarifications. Day's

> In the afternoon, the calls were much more formal and everyone was suitably dressed in stiff, rustling dresses

was altered at the end to

> . . . the ladies were suitably dressed . . .

Occasionally Katharine rewrote a sentence (something she probably asked Day to do himself when he was alive).

> Nearby, on St. Mark's Place, was a girl's school, kept by Madame Hix. One of the pupils was a little Spanish girl named Ermina de Verona. Father called her his sweetheart and watched for her from a front window.

Katharine's revision of the last sentence reads:

> Father called her his sweetheart, and, from a front window, watched for her to pass the house.

The editing reflects her careful reading, and her eye for detail. A stepladder standing on one side of a shop becomes a stepladder standing near the wall on one side of a shop. In the margin next to a passage describing Father unlocking a safe, she writes: "Check. Did safes ever have keys & doors to unlock? Usually it's just the combination that opens the door." Occasionally —as in her substitution of "the following morning" for "the next morning" —her changes are questionable, but overall the editing is sound and concerned mainly with clarifying the prose.

In December of 1935 Clarence Day died of pneumonia at the age of fifty-one, just before *Life with Father* became a commercial success. Though he had received a number of rejections from *The New Yorker,* the magazine had published more than eighty of his stories and poems (many of them illustrated by Day), all within a two-year period (1933–35). More of Day's stories were published posthumously.

Clarence Day's brief, gently humorous tales about his father were somewhat typical of *New Yorker* fiction in the 1930s, most of it sketches rather than short stories, one to two pages in length (few stories exceeded two or three pages), and light-hearted. By the mid-thirties the magazine was also publishing a good deal more serious, even grim, fiction. The poetry was now a neat mixture of both light and serious work, the former gradually giving way to the latter as the decade progressed. *The New Yorker* was a more mature, sophisticated, urbane publication—and longer, reaching sixty pages by mid-decade, eighty or more by decade's end.

Katharine White's influence on the changing *New Yorker* was subtle, obvious, far-reaching—it is in some ways difficult to pinpoint. During the first, formative years of *The New Yorker*'s life, Katharine, like others on staff, did a little of everything; when she became head of Fiction, her efforts became more focused. But she always worked closely with Harold Ross as an adviser on nearly all facets of *The New Yorker;* she quickly became his literary counterpart, completing his education, supplying what he lacked in taste, tact, and literary judgment.

She was largely responsible for the improvement in *New Yorker* poetry. In founding *The New Yorker,* Ross had thought that the magazine should publish no poetry except light verse; Katharine "finally persuaded him that serious poetry would be not only useful but important to the magazine."

> Ross [she later wrote] had very little feeling for poetry and left it to his other editors to work on. It was a concession on his part to run any serious verse, and I recall a long session with him when he said he couldn't publish an Aiken poem because he didn't understand it. I changed his mind by saying that it was the sound that mattered here, not the sense, and wondered if it made any difference if he understood it or not. To my astonishment he agreed to buy it and other Aiken poems.

Having convinced Ross, Katharine began writing "to all the good poets" —she later thought that this may have elicited Louise Bogan's first contributions.

Though Katharine White has been credited as being the main force behind *The New Yorker*'s increasing seriousness and ambition, this cannot yet be

*Elizabeth Blake
Shepley Sergeant,
Katharine's mother.*

*Charles Spencer
Sergeant, Katharine's
father.*

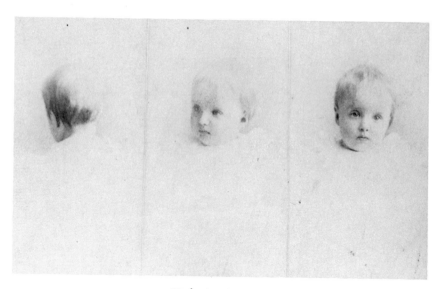

Katharine Sergeant.

Katharine Sergeant.

Number 4 Hawthorn Road.

Caroline Belle Sergeant
(Aunt Crully).

Charles Sergeant with Katharine.

Katharine Sergeant.

The Sergeant sisters: from left, Elizabeth (Elsie), Rosamond, and Katharine.

Katharine Sergeant.

(Harvard University Archives)

Katharine Angell with Nancy.

Ernest Angell with Nancy and Aunt Poo.

Nancy and Roger Angell.

Katharine Angell in Reno.

Katharine Angell.

E. B. White, around 1930.

proved; without documentation, such as correspondence between Katharine White and Harold Ross—only a fragment of which is available to scholars and writers, none of it expressing such an influence—there is no solid evidence that it was she alone who was responsible for this change in the magazine, even in its fiction, though as a strong-minded head of Fiction she certainly had an effect. We have no evidence of Katharine White arguing for a different kind of fiction in the magazine, though after the 1930s her editorial and personal letters sometimes convey her hopes that the magazine will accept a particular story or poem, and she has elsewhere noted her attempts to convince Ross to purchase particular works—such as the stories of Eudora Welty, some of which Ross vetoed. And she, along with a few of the other editors, gradually persuaded Ross to become more permissive about allowing possibly offensive language in the dialogue of stories in which the words were used to create character ("Nuts!" for instance, "which still retained its dirty connotation")—as in John O'Hara's stories. But she did not have to convince Ross to publish important fiction, and she defended him against the critics who said that he was intimidated by it. "I do not believe that Ross had a fear of publishing anything more literary than 'casuals,' " Katharine wrote, "—in fact, the moment fiction began to be turned in, he grabbed it eagerly. The only thing I persuaded him to do was to publish serious poetry."

In Katharine's view, Ross's reputed disdain of serious fiction came from others' too literal acceptance of his talk. "For instance, Ross would rail in public at grim or sordid stories but his public rantings seldom represented his literary feelings. Take Robert Coates—his best short stories were grim and violent indeed and Ross rejoiced in them, as he did in O'Hara's early grim stories and many others."

However Katharine attempted to persuade Ross to publish, or not publish, particular works of fiction or poetry, however persuasive she was, the final decision regarding a work's acceptance and publication was Ross's. And he read everything that *The New Yorker* published.

Six years after the Whites' marriage, Katharine's vow never to return "to such a grind and so much routine" seemed, with the dusty Reno summer of 1929, part of the hazy past. With the many boxes of children's books to read and review added to her full-time editorial duties, her domestic concerns and family life, Katharine was busier than ever, though she still made occasional noises of protest: "Gibbs and I rebelled on overwork and Ross only says 'Tell *Fleischmann*,' "* she wrote Andy. "—Wolcott and I have

*Raoul Fleischmann, publisher of *The New Yorker.*

decided they've got to hire another man to see artists so he can help me more on editing manuscripts. We looked at 839 idea pictures this PM & Gibbs read about 500 art ideas this morning." E. B. White painted a portrait of his wife as she was during these early exhausting, "fumbling and impoverished" years of *The New Yorker*'s existence, a picture, in words, of their life together.

> Katharine was soon sitting in on art sessions and planning sessions, editing fiction and poetry, cheering and steering authors and artists along the paths they were eager to follow, learning make-up, learning pencil editing, heading the Fiction Department, sharing the personal woes and dilemmas of innumerable contributors and staff people who were in trouble or despair, and, in short, accepting the whole unruly business of a tottering magazine with the warmth and dedication of a broody hen.
>
> I had a bird's-eye view of all this because, in the midst of it, I became her husband. During the day, I saw her in operation at the office. At the end of the day, I watched her bring the whole mess home with her in a cheap and bulging portfolio. The light burned late, our bed was lumpy with page proofs, and our home was alive with laughter and the pervasive spirit of her dedication and her industry.

Though she had once assured Andy that "ease, safety, income & locality [are] so little a part of my own desires for life that I'd never recommend them to anyone else," her life was made considerably easier (Andy's life, more complicated) by household help and child care, an income splendid by Depression standards (together, the Whites are thought to have earned between $23,000 and $30,000 in 1935), and two residences. Having outgrown their beloved Village apartment, which had twice been enlarged (their ping-pong room was the site of some wild and funny ping-pong games among the adults, including Thurber and the *New Yorker* crowd), they were about to move (in 1935) to a rented house with servants' quarters, at Turtle Bay Gardens on 48th and 49th streets, between Third and Second avenues. And they now owned a farmhouse in Maine. Taking Nancy and Roger along, they had begun summering far up on the Maine coast in 1931, when Joel was six months old. After three summers of renting a cottage in East Blue Hill, they bought a twelve-room farmhouse, circa 1800, and thirty-six acres in nearby North Brooklin.*

Money bought expensive clothes for Katharine, a thirty-foot cruising boat

---

*"I had a good tho. brief visit with K and Andy and enjoyed seeing the children," wrote Charles Sergeant to Elsie. "Little Joe is quite beautiful and charming. . . . K's new house seems quite ideal of its kind and is a very complete establishment, including a private bathing beach and pier. Lovely views from the house looking over Blue Hill bay toward Mt. Desert. Rather high and windy perhaps the only criticism."

for Andy (*Astrid*), and freedom—the freedom to go to Florida to recover from the flu, and to an inn in South Carolina to write. Andy made these trips without Katharine, who was constrained by her job. If she resented her husband's enjoying himself while she worked hard in New York, she seems not to have expressed it. "It's almost worth having you go away to have your letters which are so wonderful, though I admit I'd rather have *you* than the letters." She understood Andy, she comprehended his need to be at liberty when he felt trapped by life; and she appreciated the sensitive, fragile nature of the writer, which needed protecting. As Andy had written shortly after their marriage, Katharine perceived the danger of pushing anything too hard. And she knew that he left always with one silken strand attached to her for his returning. Marriage, like the spider's web, was delicate.

Marriage had not stilled Andy's urge to leave New York for a less-pressured existence. Now that he had a wife and son to support, Camp Otter was no longer a realizable dream; the farm in Maine took its place. Happy in marriage and fatherhood, Andy was increasingly restless in his job as *The New Yorker*'s anonymous Notes and Comment writer. Writing Comment had become a "frightful grind"; and it seemed to him that he had written nothing really important, no *magnum opus*. His anxieties released themselves physically, in psychosomatic illnesses, including chronic gastritis. "You say nothing about nasal discharge or stomach upheavals," wrote Katharine, typically, when Andy was away. "How are you—*really?*" A Florida sun-burn became, in Andy's mind, a brain tumor. Writing a half-laughing account of the episode to Katharine, he told of how he had "prepared for the end—wrote a brief note to you, unlocked the door to save the hotel people the trouble of breaking in, and went to bed, full of flatulence, dizziness & fear." His dying thoughts had been of her. "I have long thought he suffers mainly from Repression of Writing Instincts, which can be a much worse repression than that of sex," wrote Thurber in a letter to Katharine several years later. "I think now that he is writing more he will find that street dizziness and the ear trouble vanishing." But Andy's troubles did not vanish.

Nineteen thirty-five, which had ended with the death of their friend Clarence Day, had seen more private losses for the Whites as well. Andy's father died that summer, and in September Katharine suffered a miscarriage. With the move to Turtle Bay imminent, Katharine and Andy had gone to Maine in the hope that, with rest, Katharine could prevent the threatened miscarriage. While the pregnancy's future was still uncertain, Andy returned alone to New York. "It is probably wrong to go away and leave you when you are sick this way, but I didn't seem to be making matters any better when I was there, and perhaps I can make myself useful in New York. What a feverish summer this has been, so full of death and distemper!" Writing to Andy about the miscarriage, Katharine—now forty-three—said that she was not discouraged and wanted "to start fresh on a little Serena."

Despite the nesting, despite the increasing rootedness, the children, the two homes, and other possessions—or perhaps, in part, because of it all—Andy's psychosomatic illnesses worsened, and in the spring of 1937 things reached a crisis.

He decided to take a year off from *The New Yorker,* and in a sense, from his family. This time, Katharine did not assent. Her attempts to discuss the plan with Andy were unsatisfying to them both, he feeling inarticulate, she finding it difficult to express her anger and unhappiness at the prospect of being abandoned. "Whenever the subject has come up," Andy wrote her in May, "I have noticed an ever so slight chill seize you, as though you felt a draught and wished someone would shut a door." Addressing Katharine as "My dear Mrs. White," Andy outlined his plan in a letter—committing to paper, as he was wont to do, what he was unable to say to his wife directly. It is a revealing letter, one of the most telling documents White ever wrote about himself or his marriage. It's tone is self-mocking and playfully formal, selfish and immature. Imagining Katharine's point of view, the letter is altogether so disagreeable that the reader temporarily forgets that White was experiencing an emotional crisis.

His plan was as follows. For a twelvemonth he would travel, visit zoos and railway stations, Mount Vernon and favorite haunts, move when and where he was inclined—"my plan is to have none." He would be bound neither to office nor to household routines; "I seek the important privilege of not coming home to supper unless I happen to." He had a literary project in mind, which he would not define.

Financially, he would manage by living and traveling cheaply, by drawing on his savings, and by selling their Pierce Arrow convertible roadster for $2,000, three-quarters of which would go to Katharine. He would still have money enough "to continue in the same fifty-fifty arrangement with you in all matters of maintenance, recreation, and love." (As she had done in her marriage to Ernest, Katharine kept her earnings in a separate account.) He assumed that neither one of them would indulge in unnecessary expenses, such as a wine cellar or a broadloom carpet.

> Well, this about covers My Year. I urge you not to take it too seriously, or me. I am the same old fellow. I hope I shall give and receive the same old attentions and trifles. I don't want you tiptoeing around the halls telling people not to annoy me—the chances are I won't be doing anything anyway, except changing a bird's water. But I do want you to have some general conception

of my internal processes during this odd term of grace. I want you to be able to face my departure for Bellport on a rainy Thursday afternoon with an equanimity of spirit bordering on coma.

> Yrs with love and grace,
> Mr. White

In a postscript he added that he realized

> that the whole plan sounds selfish and not much fun for you; but that's the way art goes. You let yourself in for this, marrying a man who is supposed to write something, even though he never does.

And then, briefly letting down his guard, he added a second postscript expressing a desire for a sign of her good will; a third postscript voiced his willingness

> to answer any questions, or argue the whole matter out if it fails to meet with your approval or pleasure. I do not, however, want to discuss the literary nature of the project: for altho you are my b.f. and s.c. [best friend and severest critic], I will just have to do my own writing; as always.

The literary project Andy was contemplating was never completed, but in "Zoo Revisited" one finds a clue to the crisis that precipitated his flight. It begins on a buffalo range, where a bull, "with his expended fire . . . in the twilight of desire"—the bull who is also "Myself," the narrator—"stands . . . alone, with his torrential need, / At home with living death, at rest with reservoirs of seed." Though there is considerably more to the poem, the potent, powerfully felt metaphor of the "finished bison by the last water hole" who, though finished, retains his sexual desire and his fertility, evokes the frustration and fears of a man approaching forty (White was thirty-eight) who feels that he has accomplished nothing of real importance, except, perhaps, the begetting of a son, who is also his only child. The poem's narrator addresses himself to his son, "my self, my soul, my son."

That Andy needed to live out his term of grace alone, away from Katharine, perhaps says more about Andy than it does about his marriage: one observes in his life a pattern of separating—from people, from jobs, from responsibilities. His planned year-long abdication is reminiscent of a cross-country venture he undertook following his college graduation (he was gone for eighteen months), and, more pertinently, the summer of 1929, spent at Camp Otter while Katharine was in Reno. What one might consider a more troubling departure had occurred less than two years earlier, when he left

Katharine alone in Maine while her pregnancy was threatened. She was alone when she lost the baby. Even the month-long separation during the summer of 1930, when the Whites were newly married and Katharine was pregnant with their first child, seems odd, though they considered it important that Katharine spend some much-needed time alone with Nancy and Roger. Illness, or restlessness, prompted other partings, Andy sleeping alone in his study because of his bowels, Andy vacationing alone in Florida. That the White marriage was close and deeply satisfying for both Katharine and Andy is indisputable, but they, or Andy, required spaces in their togetherness. For private, forever hidden emotional reasons, they tended to separate at times when one would expect a happily married couple to draw closer.

Whether or not Katharine actually faced Andy's July departure with equanimity, she tried to, and restlessly settled down to her work. She was now associate editor of *The New Yorker,* earning $15,000 annually, plus stock.* By 1937 Katharine owned 350 shares of *New Yorker* stock; under a new plan which was to take effect at the end of the year, in addition to her salary she would receive 100 shares of stock each year for the next five years.† In 1943 she would be given an additional 50 shares as extra compensation. Further, she was to receive as added salary an amount of money equal to any dividends paid on stock that had not been issued to her. She stood to earn $275 more the following year, if the company declared its regular fifty-cent dividend payable at the end of March. "This arrangement," wrote Raoul Fleischmann, "puts you at once into the position of participating importantly in the company's success, or, God forbid, the lack thereof." Should Katharine take a leave of absence from the magazine, the plan would be suspended and the extra dividend salary reduced in the proportion her absence bore to the entire year. "You in turn agree to keep out of drafts and not try to cross when the lights are against you, thus helping insure continuation of your very keen interest in and most valuable work for The New Yorker," concluded Fleischmann.

Though appreciated most within the corridors of *The New Yorker,* Katharine's valuable work for the magazine was earning the recognition of others, including the publisher of a proposed book to be titled *Women of Achievement.* His request to include Katharine in the book as a woman of outstanding achievement in the field of literature drew a response that would become typical of her in years to come, when she was increasingly flattered with invitations to speak, sit on committees, or be otherwise honored.

---

*Katharine White has often been listed as managing editor, but she never was.

†The market value was probably at least $100 a share in early 1937, and quite possibly in the $150 to $175 range. The stock was not yet trading in the public market so it is difficult to be certain.

I am sorry that I shall have to say that I don't want to be included in your book, *Women of Achievement.* I can't see any reason for such a book, other than to satisfy the vanity of the ladies described in it, and can't imagine that such a book would be of any value to students, or as a reference book. I am sure that my own daughter would not receive any inspiration by reading about the successful careers of other women. Because I hold these beliefs I am probably not one of "America's representative women." I doubt if I am from any other point of view either.

In 1937 Katharine was still fighting for serious poetry, Ross having continued to be troubled by it since he began purchasing Conrad Aiken poems, and in September matters came to a head.

Having told Katharine of some serious personal problems the lyric poet and critic Louise Bogan was suffering, which had been upsetting some members of *The New Yorker* staff, Ross then used the occasion to again raise the issue of whether the magazine should publish serious poetry at all. Bogan, *The New Yorker*'s poetry critic since 1931, had also been a contributor since late in 1929—mainly of poetry, but of fiction and fact pieces as well. Katharine was Bogan's editor on poetry and fiction, and her "friend at court on all matters for her first decade of contributing." She had earlier managed to get Bogan a salary, which, though meager, raised her income: she now took up Bogan's cause—and that of serious poetry—in a five-page confidential memo to Ross, Gibbs, St. Clair McKelway (managing editor), and the editor Ik Shuman.

> As a critic of poetry I think [Bogan] is distinguished and sound. If her departments have ever been too cryptic I think that's the fault of our editing. [Janet] Flanner is just as cryptic, but we edit her obscurities out. Ross is definitely mistaken, I think, when he says Bogan covers only one or two schools or cults of poetry. She covers everything but light verse and the only reason she doesn't cover that is our rule that we cannot review what we have printed. The New Yorker publishes practically all the good light verse being written in America, with only one exception I can think of—a so-so poet named Leonard Bacon.

Apparently addressing herself to Ross, Katharine lectured,

> Now you can't say poetry isn't read. Look at Edna Millay now on the best seller lists with her poorest volume.
>
> Poets always start in by being little read, even when they're good. Yet they must be reviewed then, and if they're really good they get to be widely read eventually. I'll bet you'll find that Robert Frost, Stephen Benet, Jeffers, MacLeish, are a profit to their publishers and therefore are read widely—ditto

in England, Auden, Spender, Housman (tho' dead) and the others. We have to remember we're a pretty special group of factual-minded editors or editors with a sense for humour, irony, and satire. We're not representative of the world in general. How many of us read detective stories for that matter— mighty few I bet. Yet the mystery detective books sell by the millions and we recognize it and cover them. College courses in the appreciation and even in the writing of poetry are crammed these days. Poetry is actually popular.

Ross thought that Clifton Fadiman (*The New Yorker*'s book reviewer) could review poetry for the magazine, apparently as a replacement for Louise Bogan. Katharine thought Fadiman unequal to the task: he was not expert in poetry nor did he like it.

> He's also woefully weak on humor when the rare book of humor comes along that he can review, because it's not by a New Yorker writer. (And just as an aside I think as a humorous writer himself he's a bust, and as a writer of light verse he's so technically weak I don't see how he could even tell good light verse from bad). Very likely we'll soon need a new poetry critic if Bogan gets worse in her state of mind, but I don't think it should be Fadiman.

Making a final plea against Ross's wish that *The New Yorker* cease buying poetry and buy only verse, Katharine concluded:

> I am against buying poetry that is obscure, against buying any that seems too hard going to too many editors, but I'm certainly not for saying that hereafter we'll only buy verse. First of all, how can we decide where poetry begins and verse ends? You'd be pretty much up against it to decide this in 75% of the contributions of Stephen Benet and Dorothy Parker, for example. Also, there are only a half dozen good light verse writers alive apparently. . . . A more serious reason for publishing some poetry, tho', seems to me that it is effective as a change in mood and tempo. We use serious fiction to counterbalance humor for this same reason. Granted that we're a humorous magazine, I think the very reason we've been able to survive so long, "keep up the standard" as the phrase goes, is that we never set out to be exclusively humorous, like the old Life, or Judge. We'd be bound to get lousy if we published only humor, both prose and verse, because humorists and light verse writers are scarce as hen's teeth and they don't turn out enough good stuff to fill ou[r] pages. Curiously enough, we have turned into a magazine which according to as distinguished a critic as Carl Van Doren, publishes the best in all fields, humor, fiction, verse and poetry and articles. He said we were comparable to the Atlantic in its great days when it was publishing Oliver Wendell Holmes, Emerson, Longfellow, Lowell, Hawthorne, Whittier, and the others of that day. . . . Well, I don't know about that but I do know The New Yorker is

a better magazine if it has fiction, articles and poetry in it as well as humor and verse. But there's no reason for our using obscure, heavy, or esoteric poetry. . . . Poetry and verse . . . go together and make a readable blend. I often think we use too much poetry, but that's because we have so few decent writers of light verse that produce anything . . . Gibbs says he's for abandoning buying "advanced and intellectual verse." If by that he means queer, heavy, or obscure poetry I'm with him. If he means he wouldn't buy a good Edna Millay sonnet if it came our way, or the Elinor Wylie we published in her lifetime, etc. etc., I don't agree.

The poetry problem at *The New Yorker* would continue to irritate Katharine, in one way or another. When, in the late 1940s, Ross and two other editors devised a new system whereby poetry would be paid for according to its width, Katharine responded with a four-page memorandum to the editors in which she assailed "the basic absurdity" of this plan, which would reward excess more than quality.

> Think of it from the poet's point of view. If he had in mind a lyric (say in the Housman vein), he might say to himself that, for the sake of his family, it would be up to him to turn it into 6 beat Alexandrine meter (like Pope) or a 7 beat Sapphic line. Some of the best poetry and verse ever written has been written in very narrow measure. . . . Narrow-measure verse is often harder to write than wide-measure verse. Why should we penalize a poet for writing narrow-measure verse?

She cited the works of W. H. Auden, Emily Dickinson, Edna St. Vincent Millay: under this new system, they would earn *The New Yorker*'s lowest rate of pay, while a poem the magazine had recently bought by "a rank amateur," which the editors had even rewritten, "would, under the new system, receive a bonus for width." The magazine paid a bonus for compression and brevity in prose, and now it intended to penalize its poets for the same virtues. "Andy, when he heard of it, said he was going to write a poem with the longest lines ever known and with a title called something like 'On Learning That The New Yorker Pays More for Wide-Measure Verse than for Narrow-Measure Verse.' He said we might just as well pay for manuscripts by weighing them as by measuring their width."

She considered this plan "a drastic mistake" (why hadn't she been consulted about it?) that would furthermore make *The New Yorker* a laughing-stock in the literary world. "It will certainly figure as a high point in humor in all the memoirs that will eventually be written by the New Yorker staff." She was "worried about this new system's coming to the ears of someone like Bennett Cerf—who'll be sure to write it up."

Katharine suggested that they continue to figure poetry with a $1.50-a-line minimum (in 1947), and that the Fiction Department editors make "the same old arbitrary line rate suggestions on each payment." She lost the battle. Ross informed her by letter that the new system was the only way in which he could operate, since everything else in the magazine was paid for or measured by space.

While Katharine was fighting for poetry, editing, coping with extra work brought on by Wolcott Gibbs's departure as an editor, and tending to the household and Joel, Andy was fishing for mackerel, digging for clams, making an ax handle, worming the dog, cleaning out the vegetable garden, and writing her the local news of North Brooklin. He advised her not to work too hard—"It would embarrass me to have you working too hard." In an effort to save money, he wished to discontinue Joe's piano lessons, and teach him the piano himself. Where Katharine's money alone was concerned, he was carefree—at least as it applied to Aunt Caroline, approving of Katharine's having given money to her (of which Katharine informed Andy by letter), and advising her to give her elderly aunt as much money as she wished.

> You can't take it with you, as Ol' Sage Kaufman pointed out (at considerable profit to himself, I understand). My interest in money is at an extremely low ebb at the moment—I am surrounded by hundreds of bottles of new crabapple ¡jelly, and pears in jars, and ripening cranberries, and turkeys on the hoof, and ducks in the cove, and deer in the alders, and my own mackerel shining in air-tight glory. I wouldn't know what to do with a dollar even if I could remember which pants it was in.

He had abandoned his nine-to-one writing schedule, which was making him irritable; he "had never written anything between nine and one anyway." He wished Kay could share the spectacular October days; he enclosed in his letter the last pansy of the year and a brilliant red leaf from the maple tree in the front yard.

Restless with Andy away, Katharine was unsettled by his visits. The holidays brought her internal struggle and her frustration to the surface. When, in November, an argument erupted between Katharine's beloved old housekeeper, Josephine Buffa, and the new cook, Katharine burst into tears, "saying she was no good as a housewife (she said she was no good as a mother either, just for heightened effect)," Andy wrote to a friend, "and that she would have to give up her job and make a decent home for me. I told her to get the hell over to the office and win some more bread and stop her blubbering." At Christmas Katharine and Andy fought about the meaning of Christmas, which left them "in a limp beaten state"; Katharine then came down with a cold, Andy with a sore throat, after which he took Joel off to Maine for a few days' vacation.

"I read today of the death of Don Marquis and Alden Freeman,* both of whom I guess are happier dead," Katharine wrote Andy on December 30. "I wish you were writing Notes and C. to say something about Don Marquis." During the holidays she and Andy had discussed Andy's Year, Katharine saying they needed to make some plans. With Andy gone again, she worried that she had pushed him too hard.

> It's what I care most about, that things should be right for you, even though I seem to show it in curious and disagreeable ways. I know I can do better from now on. I have the feeling now that 1938 can be a very exciting or at least a very good year for us, whether it brings a wholly new way of life or continues with the old one improved, and I'm not worrying about it at all. It begins to me to seem good to be alive in these queer times, which is a big gain.

Writing to Katharine the following day, Andy concluded:

> This is the last day of 1937, and this letter is full of my love for you and hopes for the new year. I have had plenty of time for reflection in the last day or two and have decided that you are right about the necessity for planning. A single person can act aimlessly, but where lives mingle and merge there has to be scheme in advance.

By January 1938 he decided that he had made "an unholy mess" out of his five-month Year, breaking Katharine's health and his own spirit. He and Katharine began to consider leaving New York altogether to live year round in Maine.

They decided on Maine.

Gus Lobrano, Andy's old friend from Cornell and former Village room-mate, now an assistant editor at *Town & Country,* was invited to work for *The New Yorker,* with the idea that he would take Katharine's place as head of Fiction. During a try-out period, Katharine gave him stories and proofs to edit, adding her suggestions on how to handle them, and passing along Ross's opinions of the work in question. Lobrano having quickly proved to be an excellent editor, Katharine worked out an arrangement with Ross whereby she would edit part time from Maine and return to New York occasionally throughout the year. *The New Yorker*'s company officers and

---

*Donald Robert Perry Marquis was a well-known literary journalist whose column, "The Sun Dial," appeared in the New York *Evening Sun* from 1912 to 1920. He later wrote a column for the New York *Tribune* ("The Lantern"). Alden Freeman was a political reformer.

directors voted to continue paying her the same extra compensation of one hundred shares of *New Yorker* stock in addition to her salary. (It is unknown whether Katharine's full-time salary was reduced.) Should she die, *The New Yorker* would pay the stock due her to her estate.

In the summer of 1938, the Whites moved to North Brooklin.

6

~

The Imperfect Script

SEVERAL MONTHS BEFORE Katharine and Andy moved to Maine, Charles Sergeant fell ill in Hibernia, Florida, where he now lived, and Katharine went to see him. He was nearly eighty-six, and Katharine had visited him with Nancy the year before, finding him little changed in appearance and spirit (he "leaped on our running board when we arrived," she wrote Andy), but his life otherwise curtailed. He slept most of the time now, taking only a little exercise and enjoying a game of cards after dinner. Papa and Aunt Crully had remained together all these years. Papa had taken up watercolors; Aunt Crully, ten years younger, was engaged in literary pursuits. She had recently written a paper on Poe and Whitman—"not their lives . . . but their contribution to America." Brother and sister lived most of the year at their parental home at 82 Bridge Street in Northampton, where Aunt Helen also remained in residence and was delivering speeches to the Historical Society. Katharine still loved her visits there, and the house with its happy childhood memories, the attic with its child's log cabin, which she had played in . . . This visit with Papa in Florida was her last. He died in February.

Leaving *The New Yorker* was another—perhaps harder—kind of death. It was not that she had been there nearly thirteen years, though time had helped cement the bond, but that her involvement with it was so complete. It was a large part of what completed her—the magazine, its staff, and its writers, above all its quest for perfection in the English language, its disdain of sham, its love of humor. It was part of what made her tick. "If someone had said to her that they were just getting out a weekly magazine there, she would have been shocked," said Roger Angell. "And of course they weren't." E. B. White captured it, and Katharine, in a poem written at about this time. Katharine is called Serena, his poem name for her, the name that was to have been given their daughter.

LADY BEFORE BREAKFAST

On the white page of this unwritten day
Serena, waking, sees the imperfect script:

The misspelled word of circumstance, the play
Of error, and places where the pen slipped.
And having thus turned loose her fears to follow
The hapless scrawl of the long day along,
Lets fall an early tear on the warm pillow,
Weeping that no song is the perfect song.

By eight o'clock she has rewritten noon
For faults in style, in taste, in fact, in spelling;
Suspicious of the sleazy phrase so soon,
She's edited the tale before its telling.
Luckily Life's her darling: she'll forgive it.
See how she throws the covers off and starts to live it!

Had Katharine needed a reason to stay, her writers were ready to supply one. Patricia Collinge wrote to say that she not only appreciated Katharine's many pleasant letters to her, her kindness and encouragement, but that "there have been times when you have taken the place of the Marines in my life." Echoing a letter from Thurber, in which he had described Katharine as "the fountain and shrine" of *The New Yorker,* Frank Sullivan sent her the following:

February 9, 1938

Dear Katharine,

The more I think about you leaving, the more depressed I become over it. I wish you weren't. I make that simple declarative statement with every fibre of my being. You have been a friend, and a guide, and counsellor, and prop and Rock of Gibraltar to me for so long that I don't know just how I am going to manage without you. It will be something to know that you are at least going to keep an eye on things from Maine, but it won't seem quite like the New Yorker office to go in there and not find you. I have got my voodoo book out, and have made two wax images, of you and Andy, and I mutter certain incantations over them every night, the object being to bring an attack of nostalgia on you and Andy that will bring you both flying back to the magazine. I have set the alarm for this attack to take place next fall some time, so that you can at least get a summer of rest.

I always sign my letters to you "Love" but I never meant it more than this time. If this be sentiment, make the most of it.

Love, Frank

Like Frank Sullivan, Janet Flanner was a particular friend among the contributors, whose reaction to Katharine tended to be worshipful. Katharine's secretary, Daise Terry, wrote her of running into Flanner in *The New Yorker* halls, "when she was on her way from the checkers to Shawn, her arms filled with books, looking very harassed and cross. She stopped me and said (and this at least the 3rd time she's said it) 'I just can't forgive Mrs. White for deserting the office. She is the best woman editor in the world, had the best editor's job in the world, and what does she do, leave it all and retire to a farm in Maine. It's just too awful!' " Part of Flanner's remark—that Katharine had the best editor's job in the world—was repeated and later garbled, appearing in print years later as "Mrs. White believed herself to be giving up the best job held by any woman in America when she followed her husband to Maine." This corrupted version of Flanner's comment, together with the same person's misrepresentation of Katharine White as having reluctantly consented to move with Andy to Maine, would cause her considerable distress.

Katharine later said that she was not unwilling to move to Maine. "I wanted to go for my own sake as well as for Andy's. He had got to the point where he no longer enjoyed writing Comment and needed to write in the first person. I naturally felt sad at leaving, but I was not reluctant to go." Katharine did not explain what she meant by going to Maine "for my own sake," but she may have been referring to giving up the demands of working in New York for a calm existence; she had, after all, been working very hard for years, and she might reasonably have felt that as much as she loved the life, thrived on it, she could benefit from a respite. We will never know what she was thinking in 1938 or almost forty years later, when she reflected on this period. What we do know is that Andy's aborted year off had strained her, that she made her decision to leave New York after months of a stressful separation from him, and at a time when she was pressing him to make some definite plans for the future. And crucially, simply, Katharine loved Andy and needed him more than she did *The New Yorker*. She could not have chosen otherwise.

"I wasn't at all unhappy," Katharine wrote of these years in Maine.

I still had my half-time job with *The New Yorker* and still had my close connection there. Every day I spent a half day reading or editing manuscripts sent me by Ross, Lobrano, Maxwell . . . et al. I had time to go on with my children's book reviews, and Andy and I compiled the *Subtreasury of American*

Humor. I turned to gardening here in Maine, and it helped me later on when I wrote the series "Onward and Upward in the Garden." I was also running our big vegetable garden and the freezing and canning program [at our home]. Those four or five years before Ross called us back because of the War were among the happiest of my life.

Andy was writing monthly essays for *Harper's Magazine,* under the title "One Man's Meat."

Their happiness, their country mood, wrote Andy, "rang[ed] from bewilderment to a well-disciplined New England rapture." They adapted to distances—to the nine-mile drive to the grocery store in Blue Hill, the twenty-three miles to the train, the fifty-six-mile round trip to the movie house, the forty-seven-mile journey to the Frances Fox Institute in Bar Harbor, where Katharine got her hair washed. They adjusted to the old farmhouse with its freezing water pipes and to the problems of winterizing it; they accommodated the pullets and dogs, the pig in the barn cellar, the spiders and black flies, the pregnant cat. They accepted the claims upon their time of the local PTA; they embraced the new cook, who talked to herself in the kitchen (and were themselves embraced at Christmastime by the washerwoman, who presented Katharine with two cactus blossoms and a venison pie). "Am convinced that the greatest hazard of life in North Brooklin is the disparity between our scale of living and that of the [X's], our nearest neighbor," Andy had written Katharine shortly before their move. "[Mr. X] went down the road yesterday with a sack of straw on his back, like a character out of 'Tobacco Road.' Sprawled in our driveway were materials worth more than his entire dwelling. In New York these extremes are present, but do not obtrude."

By the time the Whites moved to Maine, Katharine's Angell children ("my Angell children and my White child," she called them) were nearly grown-up. Roger was about to enter Harvard; Nancy, newly graduated from Bryn Mawr, was continuing in the college's master's program in biology.

Glad to hear Nancy's abandoning medicine [wrote Thurber]. Why not biochemistry or bacteriology? I should think that hunting for the cancer bug or some other undiscovered thing would be the greatest excitement in the world. She has behind her your keen intelligence and Ernest's glowering vitality, both of which a bacteriologist has to have. I don't mean to say she glowers, but when confronted with an evasive problem in the laboratory a little glowering in the background is fine. Ernest should probably have turned his powers to the lab.

Thurber's enthusiasm notwithstanding, neither Katharine nor Ernest was able to comprehend their daughter's gravitation toward science, but Ernest was more accepting of it. Therefore, though they could well afford it, Nancy's parents refused to pay her tuition, and she relied on scholarships during her first two years of graduate work. Finally, when the scholarships were exhausted, Nancy told her parents that they would have to pay her tuition, and they did.

Nancy's relationship with her mother had always been lived at a distance. Katharine had worked throughout Nancy's childhood and after the divorce had seen her only on weekends and holidays and during the summer—about three months yearly. The distance was lengthened by a lack of physical affection when mother and daughter were together, and by their conflicting needs and interests. When Nancy first went to Bryn Mawr to register for courses, Katharine attended her. As Nancy emerged from her interview with the dean, Katharine asked, "Well now, what courses are you taking?" "English, German, Calculus, and Physics." "Nancy, I never heard of anything more horrible in my life." Nancy thought her mother was surprised when she graduated *cum laude;* Katharine herself admitted that she considered Nancy "good enough at her lessons (though by no means brilliant)," and had wondered "whether the poor child . . . could [ever] pass her [Bryn Mawr] entrance exams." She would never tell Nancy what her IQ was, and when asked why, said, "Well, it isn't terribly good." In other words, thought Nancy, not good enough. Not brilliant.

Of her three children, Roger was indisputably Katharine's favorite, though she tried hard not to show it. (If Roger needed money for something, Katharine would write to Nancy at great length, explaining why he needed money and that she was therefore sending Nancy the same amount.) He was literary, the most like her in interests. (In his self-pitying mood, Andy would say that the most important things to Kay were (1) *The New Yorker,* (2) Roger, (3) Andy.) Katharine appears not to have directly expressed her feelings for Nancy, though her consciousness of her daughter's tall, slender figure, so much more attractive than her own thickset body, and her lack of interest in what Nancy wore, which was so unlike her attention to her own clothing from Saks and Bergdorf Goodman, bespoke a feminine rivalry. In her cautiousness, Katharine seemed to reveal much about her feelings for Nancy in a 1961 letter to a friend: "One of my three children—my daughter —is very unlike me in many respects but we do have much in common even so and enjoy being together. . . . I think it is interesting to have children who are not like oneself." A few years earlier, Elsie had written to one of her friends, "I think I told you that I have drawn Nancy Stableford into a closer (family) relation than Katharine's ambiguity makes possible with her —by asking her (Nancy) to take the role of executor of my will." Elsie's view of Katharine's maternity was necessarily distorted by her own troubled relationship with Katharine, but she may have struck the right word with "ambiguity."

Katharine's feminine reaction to Nancy was visible when Nancy became engaged in 1941. Unable to decide on a mother-of-the-bride ensemble, Katharine finally purchased two complete outfits, including hats made to order. There was to be a church wedding in Maine, with Ernest in attendance.

Now twenty-four and a Ph.D. in biology, Nancy Angell was to marry a fellow Yale graduate student, Louis Stableford, also a doctor in biology, who had gotten a teaching job at Lafayette College, in Easton, Pennsylvania. Nancy brought Louis to Maine to meet her mother, who asked him in all seriousness: "Are you sure you want to marry Nancy? Do you know what she's like first thing in the morning?" When mother and daughter were alone, Katharine asked Nancy if she was a virgin. "No." "Good—that will make things a lot easier." And she volunteered to make an appointment with her gynecologist in New York. Though uncomfortable discussing sex, Katharine conscientiously tried to do as she ought for her daughter. With Andy present, she asked Nancy if she had any questions about marriage. "Yes. How often do you have sex?" "Once or twice a week." Privately Katharine offered that you do not have sex during your menstrual period.

"To negate my somewhat chaotic childhood," Nancy wanted a traditional wedding. Both parents and stepparents, all of whom, except Andy, had been married before, were against it and urged the couple to elope. Nancy "understood their reactions but held fast, and they humored me." Katharine's letters to her daughter during this time were warm-hearted, Victorian compositions about a trousseau, silver, and linen. Linen hand towels were later purchased, and Katharine taught Nancy how to embroider them.

Of Nancy's four parents, only Ernest's second wife, Betty, whom he had married two years earlier, in 1939, bore the approaching wedding with equanimity. Because of "that man White," Ernest did not want to go to Maine to give his daughter away. Betty finally persuaded him to go, just ten days before the wedding. Andy, always jittery at large social occasions, and probably disturbed by the prospect of seeing Ernest, got drunk the night before the wedding, and suffered such a severe hangover the next day that he was forced to excuse himself as wedding photographer.

Nancy Angell and Louis Stableford were married at the Blue Hill Congregational Church. One of Nancy's bridesmaids, Evelyn Baker, was Roger Angell's girlfriend, whom he would marry the following year. The catered reception, which took place without incident, was held on the lawn at the Whites' house in North Brooklin, Katharine and Ernest dividing all the costs.

Writing nearly thirty years later of the Second World War, Katharine White remembered this period in her life as "not at all unpleasant." The gasoline shortage had forced her to do a lot of walking and biking, but she got into the spirit of things and did not much mind. Katharine did mind not being called by the town for volunteer work when everyone else who volunteered was called. "I give up," she wrote Andy, who was away from home. "The home nursing course has started too and I am scorned for not being at it. Well. I always thought I might be useful as a warden as I have a car and the work would be at night mostly but I guess I shall just sit back and resign myself to being a conscientious objector." (Andy must have smiled at the idea of his short wife, such a terrible driver, cruising about Maine's country roads in the capacity of a warden.) The would-be warden, rallying to the cause as she had in the days when she inspected factories for safety hazards and lobbied for worker-protection laws, felt "a little too remote" in Maine. "I'd rather be near a bombing objective," she wrote Gene Saxton at Harper & Brothers. And to Andy, in March of 1942: "I could hardly go to bed last night, the news was so exciting with the Channel battle and our raid on the Japanese naval stations. The whole thing ruined my digestion once more."

In 1942 Ralph Ingersoll, a former managing editor of *The New Yorker* now with the newspaper *PM,* appealed to Katharine White in the name of her "own special literary genius" to help him launch a series of *PM* profiles of "the 50 worst bastards in Congress." Her answer was no. The extent of Katharine's political activism during the Second World War seems to have been an indignant letter written to Eleanor Roosevelt following the publication of Mrs. Roosevelt's column in the *World Telegram* on March 20, 1945. The offending piece, titled "Perfectionism," began with an innocuous calendar account of the First Lady's recent social activities, then abruptly shifted gears.

> In one of the papers the other day the results of a poll of the Senate on the question of setting up some machinery for international co-operation were published. It is interesting to note that the real difficulty of getting a plan for some kind of organization through the Senate will not come from those who want no such organization. It will come from the perfectionists and reservationists, who want an organization very badly, but who want only their own

kind of organization or one that is in some respect different from what the other United Nations agree on.

When you realize that other nations must have the same anxieties about subordinating their sovereignty that we have, one almost despairs of this effort to set up co-operative machinery on which to build peace. It is going to be well nigh impossible unless the people of this country state in no uncertain terms to their representatives that no one will be forgiven who prevents the setting up of some international machinery because of any specific objection.

Compromise means that everybody gives way a little. Those who cannot compromise should be looked down upon by their neighbors and their constituents.

March 24, 1945

Dear Mrs. Roosevelt:

In your column of March 20, which in the World-Telegram was titled "Perfectionism," your last two paragraphs and especially your last sentence are deeply disturbing. Usually I admire and respect your point of view but here I feel you are being strangely unAmerican and undemocratic, and even dangerously misleading. Every thinking person knows that a perfect international organization cannot be set up now—it may take centuries for that—and that compromises must be made to suit the different problems and ideologies of the fourty[sic]-four United Nations. But surely always, and especially in these months before the San Francisco preliminary conference, every difference of opinion on the peace must be aired and listened to with respect—even the opinions of those you label "perfectionists" and those you condemn for not being willing to compromise. It seems to me amazing that you should tell your readers—many of them simple people who are likely to take the words of the wife of the President as official—to "look down upon" their neighbors and the editorial writers who refuse to compromise. As I see it, the uncompromising idealists, the uncompromising thinkers, the uncompromising good people, are in the end the ones who have been our great political, religious, and philosophical leaders. They are often momentarily unpopular but in going back over history, it is evident they have been the ones who have showed the rest of us the right paths. It has never been American to disdain uncompromising thought or virtue.

Your use of the word "perfectionism" seems to show that, to your way of thinking, anyone who disagrees with any detail of the world structure outlined at Dumbarton Oaks or at Yalta is a "perfectionist," or a person who will not compromise and whom you therefore urge other Americans to look down upon. Since the meeting at San Francisco is one to which delegates are going to [sic] for the purpose of expressing the thoughts and will of their own peoples, since it is really merely a preliminary peace talk, is not this the moment when the wife of the head of a democracy should be urging expression of popular opinion, in all its various shadings, rather than suggesting that such expression be suppressed?

Once a peace plan is decided upon by our duly selected delegates, then, it seems to me, is the moment for differences of opinion to be subordinated and for all of us American citizens to ask our elected senators to support the new international organization. But not until then. I believe you will find that your perfectionists, for the most part, will do this in no uncertain terms, when this time comes.

Sincerely yours,
Katharine S. White

Apart from her spirited prose, Katharine's emotion—and her anger—are conveyed in her letter's rather sloppy appearance, in its several typographical errors, crossed-out and interlined words, and one misspelling and syntactical error. There is no existing or available reply to Katharine's letter, though Eleanor Roosevelt seems to have written one. For Katharine's letter not only found its way into the Roosevelt Library at Hyde Park, but according to a hand-written notation in its upper left-hand corner, was acknowledged on March 31, three days after Mrs. Roosevelt received it. That Katharine's letter aroused some emotion in the First Lady is indicated by an almost illegible note written in Eleanor Roosevelt's own hand across the top of the letter, which reads, roughly, "I never said they should not be aired and talked over and argued [,] only [that] they should not in their way prevent any set-up of an organization of this kind."

Coming across his wife's letter many years later, E. B. White interpreted it as a defense of him. In the 1940s White's *New Yorker* comment often spoke out in favor of world government (the pieces were later collected in *The Wild Flag*), and he later thought that Katharine assumed that the First Lady was putting him down.

During the early 1940s, Katharine resigned herself, not unhappily, to working indirectly to save the world, by "trying to make *The New Yorker* a good magazine." From North Brooklin came envelopes of edited stories, children's book reviews, memos, letters, and advice. She was brimming with ideas for saving money at *The New Yorker,* which could be done by cutting down on unnecessary staff and making better use of the others' time, with business-office economies, and by making changes in *New Yorker* advertising and promotion. She had been thinking about changing the payment for manuscripts.

To Ross, she sent an essay on paragraphing in *The New Yorker* and other magazines ("One of the most satisfying, eloquent, and amusing documents of the year," he responded); a memo on the use of verse in the magazine ("wise and constructive"); a memorandum on the follow-up of contributors ("putting a writer like Schulberg on your list was bad, it seems to me, and is disquieting"); and suggestions for *New Yorker* covers (Eustace Tilley in a helmet was rejected) and profiles.

> Your remarks about our profiles alarm me somewhat, for you seem to want us to go out for national figures, competing with Life and all the other magazines. You suggest Kaiser, for instance. I have said no to Kaiser at least twelve times, on the grounds that he's non-New York and out. Ditto some of your others. . . . Moreover, our best profile writers are gone, or mostly gone, and what can you do? The magazine is running us; we aren't running it. I do think, though, that you're right in saying we've gone in for too many obscure, freak people.

Katharine could never be glad to accept third or even second best if first was to be got. And, without first expressing her opinion, she was incapable of going along with Ross's policies and practices she considered unwise. It was frustrating to have to fight for her beliefs at long distance, and she thought she would have been more effective in bringing about change if she had been at her desk in New York.

Whether Katharine was in Maine or New York, Ross welcomed her opinions, and sought them, but he sometimes despaired over the manner in which they were conveyed.

> I have a proof of a poem . . . upon which you have written "I still think this is terribly childish and shouldn't have been bought." This is an iteration of an earlier opinion and, since we've bought the thing, entirely academic and a waste of time. I bring it up because I think you'd cut down your work by omitting such repetitions except in cases where you think our mistakes so serious that you want to urge that something be killed.

Ross regretted Katharine's habit of stating "general after-the-fact" opinions: that a drawing already purchased by the magazine was weak, "that a story sounded better (or worse) than when you'd read it before. Interesting, perhaps, but time-consuming and needless." He wished she would refrain from opinions that did not include recommendations; he wished she would be brief.

One of Katharine's *New Yorker* chores was to read every word of the magazine's *X* issue (just out), and identify its typos, faults, repetitions, merits, and failings—including those in the ads. She continued to do this from Maine as part of her "part-time work." Ross came to feel that he was getting more than he desired.

Mrs. White:

> As to your sharp-shooting of the issues, and your recent memo about this, I say do it your way. I deplore your way, but since you can't do it another way, I'll settle on it.

But he would not answer personal questions inserted in her reports; this habit of hers was "preposterously unfair." She should follow his example and write personal questions on a separate piece of paper. She should likewise keep separate her other ideas and suggestions for new departments (such as the camera department mentioned in her latest report, which Ross considered a good idea but only for an occasional piece). Henceforth, if Katharine was in agreement, she should confine her sharp-shooting to one issue a month.

Katharine was amused, rather than annoyed, by Ross's "wonderfully censorious memo." She appreciated his frankness, and their ability to call each other "crazy," which they managed to do without getting really angry. Still, Ross could be trying.

He implemented many time-consuming schemes, not all of which Katharine agreed with. For instance, she thought it a waste of her time to edit a piece that any one of the editors in the Fiction Department considered borderline or thought that Ross would not like. Ross insisted that "the time would be wasted only if such pieces were killed by me in proof after editing, and that almost never happens." Ross had also devised an elaborate system for following up on contributors ("follo"), which resulted in a list of contributors' names divided into categories to determine how often the editors should telephone them or take them out to lunch to ask for submissions. The editors' follow-up efforts—the dates of their telephone calls, letters to and lunches with contributors—were recorded, along with a list of received and rejected manuscripts. Occasionally Ross would call a meeting of the top editors in the Fiction-and-Verse Department to discover if they were doing their duty. As Katharine later remembered them, "in these meetings we'd discuss categories and change authors about or cross out some hopeless ones we'd rather *not* get manuscripts from. We also had a list of potential writers and would decide who was to approach them. All these meetings took time few of us could spare in office hours so they were sometimes held in the evenings or on holidays. Holidays meant little to

H.W.R., who had an erratic family life and only one child." Katharine was particularly indignant when Ross once called a two-hour meeting on Thanksgiving morning. Though she needed to prepare to receive guests, decorate the dinner table, and hover over pots and pans with her cook, she had to attend.

She disliked doing his dirty work, much of which he handed over to her. Ross, for instance, shrank from rejections, whether a letter that needed to be written or an employee who needed to be fired; Katharine was often dispatched to handle them. And, with the exception of a few old friends, he did not work directly with writers and artists; Ross relied on Katharine in the extreme. When in the late 1930s Janet Flanner was offered a job with *Time* as Paris correspondent and wrote a letter to Ross and Katharine asking a lot of questions, Ross fled to the country, leaving Katharine to answer it.

He had other quirks. He did not want to hear anything about a story until he had read it, and he would not annotate a piece in manuscript, only in proof. Ross was well known for his copious notes and queries, which could run to several pages and which presented Katharine (and the other editors) with the problem of how to pass them on tactfully to contributors. The problem was sometimes solved by simply drawing a line through the notes she considered "silly or unimportant"; Katharine was one of several editors to whom Ross gave blanket permission to disregard his notes, which he humbly considered only suggestions anyway. "I could tell when he thought a query was important," Katharine said later, "and if I didn't agree with him I always went to him and talked it over and explained why I didn't."

"No two people in the world could be more different than she and Ross," said E. B. White, "but they met at one point (they both thought the same things were funny), and the collision at this point sent up sparks." The sparks were variously interpreted, those who saw Katharine White and Harold Ross together carrying away different impressions: she intimidated him; he respected her; she tolerated him; in the eyes of Joel White, who as a boy was often at *The New Yorker,* there was great love between them—partly, he thought, because Ross liked Katharine for standing up to him. It was, on the surface, a curious alliance, a harmonious marriage of opposites. "I didn't give a hoot about the Harper's article," Ross wrote her in 1943. "Somebody told me it said I roared around and upset everything and that you kept things going with your tact. I don't give a damn what they said. . . . I gather that it tends to perpetuate all the old anecdotes, most of which weren't true, or funny either."

In 1942, Ross asked Katharine to keep her eye on the entire magazine field and advise him of anything she thought he should know about. She could not, of course, be expected to do this on a full-time basis, in addition to her other duties. Ross's idea was to have her occasionally take a dollar from the office and buy the new magazines at the newsstands. When she protested that magazines didn't get to Maine, Ross insisted that some of them did. He was reluctant to have someone else select them and mail them to her. "It takes an old-timer around here to do it and a person of comparatively great judgement. My only idea of euchring you into doing this job is that you qualify in both respects."

Harold Ross's letters to Katharine White reflect the unconstrained familiarity of one who has for years been a colleague and friend. He writes of everything from his teeth problems ("Dear Mrs W: The tooth dope is this . . .") and travel plans, to Wolcott Gibbs's pregnant wife. Ross had run into Max Schorr, who "wanted to know what becomes of magazine editors in their old age. Well, what does?" Mostly he writes of the office ("Thurber did a piece, very good, except for paragraphing"), of *New Yorker* plans and problems—chief among the latter, during the early forties, was the need for Comment from Andy. "Comment is by far the most glaringly weak thing now, and if White should write some it would save the day." Andy saved the day—or did he? Katharine conveyed her husband's worries to Ross.

> Andy did not do a shamefully bad job [he replied]. At least three of those
> comments were superb, absolutely first class White and there's nothing better.
> The rest were all right certainly, and all told they were a God-send. . . . We
> are not well enough ahead to ease up all summer, though, so for God's sake
> don't do anything to discourage White from writing more.

Katharine was a go-between for Ross and Andy, someone through whom Ross could send distress signals and reassurance. Through Katharine, Andy could transmit his insecurity. Ross felt free enough with Katharine to tell her not to discourage Andy from writing. He knew her, he understood the Whites' marriage well enough to realize that Katharine's sympathy with her husband's anxieties could lead her to baby him, and encourage him not to write if he didn't want to. Ross was comfortable enough with Katharine and sure enough of their relationship to openly criticize even her attitude toward her husband: he considered certain of her opinions "warped by self-consciousness, both as to White and to the magazine."

Katharine objected to *The New Yorker*'s failure to accommodate late-breaking Comment. There was a particularly important comment of Andy's, which should have been rushed through. (She was apparently referring to White's piece about the appointment of the news commentator Elmer Davis to be director of the newly formed Office of War Information.) Ross replied that he didn't mind being a week late with the comment, and that attempts to get it out quickly would probably have flubbed it, caused them to run into prohibitive overtime, and certainly have entailed hundreds of dollars in extra costs to reopen the plant. Although the magazine had occasionally rushed pieces through, Ross did not consider the Davis appointment important enough, and he thought it generally "better to take it in a leisurely stride, than to tear things open." He may have also considered Katharine's reaction typical of her "warped" attitude toward Andy.

"How are you doing with me away and no help and me complaining you sent me too much?" Katharine had written Gus Lobrano earlier that year (1941). She was distressed to hear about Ross's ulcer and she worried "all the time" about Gus's overworking and getting sick, and not finding an assistant ("I well remember when Ross told me in the early days that I would not be worth my salt until I found an assistant and trained him"), and she continued, in her chatty, friendly way, to dispense advice, anecdotes, and offers of help. Lobrano wrote Katharine of his efforts to get into the Navy, about the tests he had been taking (he feared that poor eyesight would keep him out of the service) and the prospective set-up at the office should he be called away. "I know (because he has told me so) that Ross depends upon your readiness to come back here, at least temporarily, if a real emergency should develop, and that he won't ask you to make such a revolution in your life unless he is convinced that there is a real emergency in prospect."

In the meantime, while waiting—and perhaps hoping—to be called back to New York, Katharine filled up her time. In addition to editing the manuscripts sent her by mail, reading children's books and reviewing them, and working for Ross and *The New Yorker* in many other capacities, she was working for her local library, finishing up work on *A Subtreasury of American Humor,* and assisting Andy in his work.

On behalf of the Friend Memorial Public Library in Brooklin she asked local (Maine) authors to get their publishers to contribute books, and wrote to Gene Saxton at Harper & Brothers requesting copies of E. B. White books, though she feared they would "baffle" her neighbors. "I don't know whether I dare ask for 'Is Sex Necessary?' because it would probably scandalize them so we'd have to move out of town. Better omit it." For her part, she gave the library a subscription to *Harper's* (because "One Man's Meat" was "avidly" read), contributed magazines, and donated her review copies of children's books to the local schools.

For the *Subtreasury* she wrote to H. L. Mencken, with whom she appears to have been slightly acquainted.* She wished to have a copy of a

---

*Writing to Katharine in 1955, Mencken's secretary said, "He asks me to say that he has always had a great admiration for you."

story of his for possible inclusion in the book; in addition, she would welcome any Mencken tips on funny stories or even book reviews—"I never did hold with the theory that an author is not a good judge of his own work and think you can make the best recommendations on Mencken as a humorist. . . . I should tell you . . . how much I have enjoyed the Baltimore stories, both the childhood ones and the current series which I read in proof or manuscript as they come along in my New Yorker daily envelope of work, for, though living in Maine, I still edit at long distance." It was important to Katharine, necessary to her self-esteem, that people know that she had not retired and was still part of *The New Yorker*.

Published by Coward-McCann in November of 1941, *A Subtreasury of American Humor,* edited by E. B. and Katharine S. White, was a personal collection of humor—writing from three centuries that appealed to and amused the Whites. It was decidedly " 'literary'—that is, it has been written down on paper, in words, to be read," wrote Andy in the preface. They had "made no attempt to throw in anything to please anybody else. This is a subtreasury designed for the safekeeping of our own valuables." The cautious "subtreasury" of the title warned the reader that the 804 pages of text were neither comprehensive nor comprised of general or well-known favorites (though some of the entries were). Grouped into thirteen categories—Stories and People, Fables and Other Moral Tales, For (and Against) Children, Nonsense, Verse, The Reporters at Work, to name a few—the *Subtreasury* was heavily populated with work by *New Yorker* writers and contributors, more by Thurber than by anyone else. (According to Wolcott Gibbs, John O'Hara was upset about not being included, was drunk most of the time and saying, "more or less dispassionately," that "he [was] a God damn sight funnier than Clarence Day." But O'Hara's reaction seems not to have touched his good relationship with Katharine White.) After writing the preface, Andy turned it over to Katharine, telling her to "get right after it and give it the works. I trust you absolutely to doctor it any way you think it should be doctored. . . . The most important thing, of course, is that you bring a ruthlessly critical mind to my facts and my theories."

E. B. White's willingness to subject his prose to his wife's brown pencil may have been a first and last: years later he would say that he never allowed Katharine to read his work until it was ready to depart for the publisher. He "would not want to tangle with Mrs. Katharine White." She had a bad poker face and he always knew if she didn't think something was very good. When Katharine read Andy's unpublished work, she did not touch a word —"She knew better than to touch it."

White need not have been fearful. Katharine White was his most fervent fan, and his protector. During the 1940s she assumed "the terrible responsibility" of becoming his agent, handling his contracts and editorial difficulties; and his work always took precedence in their family life. If Andy needed to work out of town, she and Joe would travel to meet him. She would rather have Joe miss school than see Andy's work interrupted. She steadily defended Andy against those who criticized his writing; a written assault on E. B. White could bring an impassioned and lengthy reply from his wife. "The tone and the gist of your and Mr. Murray's replies to him are still almost unbelievable to me," she wrote a woman who had written a letter to the editor of the *New York Times* about the primitive lifestyle of Brooklin, Maine, to which Andy had replied. Andy's letter was also published in the *Times,* and the woman took exception to it.

> They have shocked me greatly and I feel as if the whole tiny episode had assumed nightmare proportions. There is so much hatred in the world that where I see any chance of preventing it, I'll at least make a stab at it. . . . As a wife I naturally resent your implications about my husband's motives. . . . Also, as both an editor and a wife, I can't help saying too that I resent Mr. Murray's slurs on Andy's writing. The words he uses are fighting words —words like "racket," "sop," "soft soap," and "hogwash." But I am not going to fight about them because A's letter to the Times needs no defense against such words, nor does anything he has ever written. They are not words that should be applied to anyone who is an honest man and an honest writer. Andy is both.

Two years later (1945), when Andy's first book for children, *Stuart Little,* was published and came under an insistent attack by the influential former children's book librarian of the New York Public Library, Anne Carroll Moore, Katharine felt called upon to defend her husband. Having read *Stuart* in proof, Miss Moore, who knew Katharine from the library's Candlelight Meetings, wrote a fourteen-page letter to Katharine explaining why *Stuart* should not be published. Among her lengthy objections, Miss Moore cited that the story does not follow conventional patterns for fantasy, and she thought it would be sexually confusing to children if they were told that a human couple could give birth to a mouse. She claimed that the book would be damaging to E. B. White if published. Though Katharine "detested" Anne Carroll Moore, because of both her campaign against *Stuart* (Miss Moore's letter to Katharine was supported by a letter to the children's book editor of *Stuart*'s publisher, Harper & Brothers) and "the false sentimentality she taught the children's librarians," her reply was a model of restrained and intelligent dissent.

Whatever Andy's sentiments about such wifely rescues (Katharine did not always share her letters), he remained a romantic husband. On November 13, 1943, their fourteenth wedding anniversary, he could say that

> *The scenic points of love have not grown stale*
> *For that my mind in yours has found diversion*
> *And in your heart my heart could never fail.*

Ross finally sent out a distress signal, and in the winter of 1943–44 the Whites returned to New York, to their *New Yorker* desks, and, having refused Ross's offer of his Stamford house, to a furnished apartment on East Thirty-fifth Street.* Joel was at Exeter.

The return had followed a decline in health for them both, in the spring of 1943, when Katharine had gone back to New York for a hysterectomy and Andy, suffering from depression, was (Scott Elledge tells us) taking strychnine under a physician's care. Though at fifty Katharine had certainly long since realized that there would be no little Serena, the hysterectomy depressed her. As a young woman she had not been eager for children; the longing came in her late thirties and early forties, when she was feeling settled in her life and was married to a younger man, when she had begun to realize the mistakes she had made with Nancy and Roger. After Joel, she had wanted to give Andy a daughter; he loved children and she wanted, perhaps, to give him as much as she had given Ernest. She was feeling unusually vulnerable, suffering "all the trials of Job," and less energetic "thanks to the depleting effects of the Mt. Sinai mattress," she wrote Andy. She cried a lot, complained about her digestion, her nerves ("still shot"), the other patients, and, in a rare lapse of self-control, wrote her husband that she lived for his letters. "All I need is a woman friend or two which seems to be my great NYC lack."

The lack may have been due to the war, to its having temporarily removed Katharine's friends from the area. But the writer Faith McNulty, who met Katharine White at about this time, suggested another reason:

> She gave an impression of strength and of a person who cared very deeply and felt very deeply. I had a slight hint that she would have liked to be better understood. I suspect that she did a lot of understanding of other people who leaned on her in various ways, but she looked so capable that it would not occur to one that she might need any sort of support. But once when I had lunch with her she asked me a lot of personal questions and spoke of herself

---

*Ross suggested to Fleischmann that *The New Yorker* pay the Whites' expenses while they were in New York. Whether or not this happened is unknown.

in a way that made me think she liked and needed warmth from others just
as much as any other human being.

Katharine was among colleagues and writers again. There were exciting
new writers to edit and bring into her fold—Vladimir Nabokov and, by
1948, Jean Stafford—and a somewhat different job as one among *The New
Yorker*'s editorial staff rather than head of Fiction, the post Gus Lobrano
continued to hold. Katharine later described this role reversal as "a difficult,
sticky situation calling for tact on both our parts. I had trained Lobrano to
be an editor, and now he was my boss." Katharine felt that "it was awkward
for him that I had to reappear at that point," when Lobrano was still settling
into his role as head of Fiction, and that this was complicated by Ross's
continuing reliance on her. "Ross would sometimes consult me for an
opinion on a manuscript after Lobrano had sent it to him. Sometimes I would
agree with Lobrano's opinion and sometimes not, and this must have been
very trying for him, but it was not my fault. For the most part, our opinions
coincided, and we had many, many happy times together during that period." Whatever the tensions, they maintained an intimate working relationship, Lobrano stopping into Katharine's office first thing in the morning most
mornings to discuss personal as well as professional problems.

What mattered to Katharine was not the change in her job but her ability
to work more effectively for *The New Yorker* now that she was in New York
again. During her years away, Katharine had felt frustrated by what she
considered to be her ineffectiveness as an editor working at long distance.
As she wrote Edmund Wilson (in reference to an Anaïs Nin story she
recommended the magazine buy),

> When I'm at long distance I am at a disadvantage in getting anything which
> is out of the ordinary run accepted. When I'm on the spot I can go in and
> argue with Ross, or line up votes from people who don't usually read
> manuscript, or talk to the men who are against a piece and sometimes bring
> them around. I so wanted to be there to argue for the Nabokov one, for
> instance. Things like this continually give me pause as to the value of any work
> I do from [Maine], for no one pays as much attention to a written opinion
> as to the spoken word, or to a fighting female on the spot.

In the minds of a few of the men who worked with her, this self-portrait
of Katharine White as a fighting female would have seemed unpleasantly
characteristic. Bernard Bergman, who briefly worked for *The New Yorker*
during the thirties as managing editor, considered Katharine difficult to work
for. She was, he said, very much in control, in charge, preeminently the boss.
He considered her duplicitous as well: he thought that it was she who had

been responsible for getting him fired from his job. Bergman maintained that he and Ross were the best of friends, but that Katharine talked Ross into firing him. Bergman thought Katharine White very hypocritical—nice to his face, while privately disliking him, giving a party for him and his new wife when he knew Katharine disapproved of him and had called his wife "crazy." He said that Thurber and Wolcott Gibbs were likewise not thrilled about working for Katharine. He thought that her strong personality overwhelmed the weaker, less assertive Gibbs.

There is no evidence to support Bergman's suspicions about Katharine's getting him fired, though Ross typically assigned firings to her, perhaps giving others (or just Bergman) the impression that she was responsible. As for Wolcott Gibbs's discomfort working for Katharine, this has not been corroborated (the writer Nancy Hale said that Gibbs considered Katharine "the most ravishing creature he ever knew"). And Gibbs's ill feelings, assuming he had them, did not reflect those of at least two other editors who worked closely with her—William Shawn and William Maxwell, the latter of whom, like Gibbs, Katharine had trained as an editor (Maxwell found her "an excellent teacher, very maternal"). Still, he would not be the first instance of a colleague whom Katharine considered a close friend and ally harboring ill feelings toward her, or at least feeling ambivalent about her. She regarded St. Clair McKelway as a good friend, and he, too, seems to have resented her and tried to avoid working with her. Thurber had troubles of his own.

Since the 1920s, James Thurber had continued to be close to both Whites, maintaining an affectionate and loquacious correspondence with them when at a distance, some of his letters addressed to Katharine alone. He was wildly funny, and darkly troubled; Katharine and Andy considered him a dear and wonderful friend, when sober. Thurber suffered from a barely repressed hostility toward women, for which his art provided one outlet. E. B. White later spoke of two occasions when an intoxicated Thurber vented his women problem on Katharine, which contributed to the erosion of the Whites' friendship with him. (Thurber seems to have harbored some ill feelings toward Andy as well: "Don't fire until you see the Whites of *The New Yorker!*" he had said in a speakeasy during the thirties.) Bernard Bergman recalled Thurber telling him that Katharine had chased Andy until she got him. Andy, said Thurber, had been far too shy to initiate the relationship. (Even Bergman was not persuaded by this claim, or quite certain of Thurber's honesty.)

Consider Katharine White from the perspective of a weaker, or insecure, man. To begin with, she had been a part of *The New Yorker* almost since its inception; Harold Ross relied on her judgment and habitually deferred to her; the magazine had matured largely because of the endowment she had given it—of her taste and her standard of excellence. And there was Katharine herself: supremely self-confident, a woman of seemingly unshakable poise. Her absorption in the work—which for her was a necessity, an intellectual and emotional lifeline—was easily misconstrued. Though it would have grieved her had she realized it, Katharine White, by virtue of her personality and her appearance, was intimidating. Given any insecurity, a man would inevitably feel her presence as hovering oppressively over his job, and be threatened by it.

Even those who admired her, and most people did, could find her overwhelming at times. To the writer Niccolò Tucci, Katharine White was "a strong woman—too strong." Said a friend, "It is very hard for me to know what to say about Katharine. How one felt about her is not easy to describe."

Katharine White was not actually supremely self-confident; she suffered many self-doubts. In the words of Louis Stableford, she was "a velvet hand in an iron glove." But the impression persisted: a 1934 *Fortune* article about *The New Yorker* had described her as "hard, suave, ambitious." Katharine herself knew that she looked "New England and austere," and she thought that her reserve could prevent someone from knowing her affection for him. It prevented many people from calling her Kay, or even Katharine; even her daughter-in-law, Evelyn Angell, could never bring herself to address Katharine as anything more familiar than Mrs. White, though Katharine kept encouraging her to (Andy, by contrast, was always Andy). "She had a lot of armor," said a *New Yorker* colleague. "You had to know her before you perceived that the hand was made of velvet."

Curiously, Katharine White's letters give no indication of her formidableness: one who knew her only through her letters would find there a freer and more openly affectionate person than the woman others knew in life. In her letters, which gave her a distance from people while simultaneously providing her with an intimate and tangible means of communication, she was able to put her arm around you, a gesture she found difficult in the flesh.

In early June of 1944 Katharine wrote to Edmund Wilson to tell him that an advance of $500 had been approved for Vladimir Nabokov. Nabokov, it seems, was desperately in need of money; Wilson had requested a *New Yorker* contract on his behalf, which the editors felt they could not give him, since Nabokov had published only a few poems in the magazine. But to encourage him to contribute more (fiction and humor, preferably, since *The New Yorker* needed those more than poetry) they advanced him the money. In return, Katharine wrote to Wilson, they wanted a first-reading agreement "on all [Nabokov's] output of fiction, humor, satire, and reminiscence, until the advance [was] repaid." Wilson made the arrangements through Katharine, who was both concerned about Nabokov's financial distress and eager that he contribute more to *The New Yorker*.

Katharine had first met Nabokov in the early forties at the New York apartment hotel of Edmund Wilson and his wife Mary McCarthy. An image from this introductory meeting remained in her mind: that of Wilson and Nabokov engaged in "electrifying" conversation.

Katharine White had been Edmund Wilson's editor on nonfactual material (poetry, fiction, and some of the chapters *The New Yorker* published from *To the Finland Station*) since he began contributing to the magazine in 1934. Their relationship was one of editor to author, Wilson sometimes assuming the role of editor. He made suggestions on at least one of her children's book reviews and advised her on other areas where he thought *The New Yorker* wanted improving ("It will be of the greatest advantage to the magazine to have editorial criticism of this sort from you," wrote Katharine, "and it is good of you to take the time for it"). Their association was also that of colleague to colleague, with perhaps more respect on Katharine's side, for her letters betray a hint of wariness, or intimidation, and his could be arrogant.

Wilson was inclined to be pompous, and, in the opinion of *New Yorker* writer Joseph Mitchell, Katharine egged him on, and was entertained by him. When Wilson's *Memoirs of Hecate County* was published, Mitchell overheard Katharine White and another woman talking about it. In the book Wilson had used the expression "the club" as a euphemism for the male organs, and as the two women walked down the *New Yorker* corridor, Katharine said "the *club*," and they laughed, without viciousness or sarcasm, and in a friendly way, laughing at the male and at humanity.

Mary McCarthy, whose *New Yorker* fiction Katharine edited, perceived that the relationship between her husband and Katharine White was not an easy one. Katharine "was not the kind of woman Wilson got along with" —she was perhaps too "aunt-like," literary but "in a ladies' club style." Nevertheless, Wilson referred Anaïs Nin and Vladimir Nabokov to her. In Mary McCarthy's view, Wilson "would have thought that Katharine was the only one [at *The New Yorker*] who would be receptive to Nabokov, which was true. The other editors were all sort of squares, and would have stamped on a butterfly like Nabokov." Wilson also seems to have regarded Katharine as the least interfering of *The New Yorker*'s editors—he once referred in a letter to her "anti-editing campaign," and indeed several of Katharine's writers have praised her for the very little editing she applied to their work. And, as Mary McCarthy observed, Katharine had "all the literary writers under her wing." Mary McCarthy had the impression that

Katharine "didn't care for [Wilson]," though "I really [didn't] know the strength of her feelings, which I'd probably inferred anyway from small remarks of hers and from my sense of both their characters."

Wilson was never shy about telling Katharine what he considered wrong with *The New Yorker*—the fiction is "pointless and inane"; "the editors are so afraid of anything that is unusual, that is not expected, that they put a premium on insipidity and banality"—and she (so the available letters show) resisted her defensive tendency toward the magazine and submitted to the assaults with silence or gratitude: "What are we going to do to get any life into New Yorker fiction? I'm afraid you're only too right about it. Now that I'm away from the office I have more detachment."

It was not, apparently, until 1950 that Katharine's "Dear Edmund Wilson" gave way to "Edmund" (with an "E. W." in between); she never did work up the nerve to call him by his nickname, Bunny, though she once threatened to.

Vladimir Nabokov had come to the United States in 1940. His first piece submitted to *The New Yorker,* a story called "Mademoiselle," was rejected without having reached Katharine's desk. (Most unsolicited material was read by two other people before it came to Katharine. She was first reader of manuscripts submitted by agents and *The New Yorker*'s regular contributors.) When the Nabokov story appeared in the *Atlantic Monthly* in January 1943 Katharine clipped it and sent it to Ross, saying that she thought Nabokov would be right for *The New Yorker.* Afterward, Edmund Wilson suggested that Nabokov send his work directly to Katharine; thus began a long and sometimes difficult association.

The difficulty lay in Nabokov's elaborate prose style (he described it as a "web"), made arduous by foreign, archaic, and esoteric words, obscure or highly scientific passages; and in his resistance to editing, to relinquishing the problem words for words that were clearer and simpler.

> At last [Katharine wrote] I enclose the annotated "Portrait of My Mother" and I'm afraid that the very sight of all these notes will fill you with despair, anger, or at the very least, irritation. I know they would me. As I said in my letter, we like the piece enormously in many ways—to me it evokes a person and a period extraordinarily well and, besides, has unusual tenderness and beauty. However, the long unfamiliar words and the many foreign words do bother us all, especially in the first half of the manuscript. How I have wished I might talk with you about this manuscript instead of having to write so ponderously and finickingly! Also if I talked, I feel sure I could explain better than in a letter our reason for asking your cooperation in simplifying the

vocabulary wherever possible and wherever it does not hurt your literary effect. We often like the unusual and the unfamiliar word of course (and have no quarrel with the greater number of yours) and we like a literary style, but here it does seem to all of us that you have rather overloaded the dice against your reader and have detracted rather than added to the literary effect of your memoir by making it a bit too hard going and by making it just on the edge of sounding like academic rather than literary writing. (I am being very frank and I hope you won't fly into a passion against me!) I think this happened only because it must be sometimes impossible for you to know which of your unfamiliar English words send an English speaking and reasonably well educated person to a dictionary and which don't. And if one must seek the dictionary it mars the pleasure of reading your story. You must remember that you are a scientist to whom, for example, words like *synesthete, palpabral, photism,* and *asemia* are as familiar as *cat* and *dog.* But neither your readers nor your editors are scientists. Mr. Ross says that he would feel self-conscious and embarrassed to use all of your big words, especially since the New Yorker has always strived for simplicity and for the simple way of saying the hard thing.

I would understand if you thought you did not want it changed at all, but all of us would be frightfully grieved if this were your decision. (I couldn't *bear* to lose this perhaps most moving of all your memory pieces!) So do see if you can, and are willing to, cooperate with us, and please remember that all our pencilled changes are *merely suggestions.* We would always rather have the changes in your own words. Please feel free, too, to argue if you think we are frightfully wrong in any instance. I have really tried to think of *you* as well as The New Yorker, and I honestly feel we are sound in thinking that in this one instance your learning and knowledge of languages has just a trifle worked to defeat the emotional and literary effect you want to achieve. We don't want to be lowbrow but we do want our readers to be able to read what we publish without recourse to dictionaries.

Since Nabokov had learned English primarily, it seems, from studying the unabridged Oxford English Dictionary (and perhaps studying Latin simultaneously, Katharine theorized), his use of obsolete words and words with Latin roots rather than their Anglo-Saxon equivalents was, Katharine thought, perhaps inevitable. In any case, editing Nabokov could be a headache. In a letter to Andy Katharine wrote that she was swamped with work from contributors, including "a very long and very badly written but funny and bitter one by Nabokov who does not want me to edit it except for a word or two whereas it has to be turned by me into English and cut and transferred from the past to the present." Though he admired Nabokov's work, Ross shared Katharine's frustration about editing him. "Mrs. White: Would appreciate being notified if he's going to become a professor of English. I may cut my throat. We seem to have played a part in getting him the job, or the offer."

Nabokov's web frequently entangled writer and editor. "I do not understand what you mean by 'overwhelming style,'" Nabokov wrote after a story was rejected.* "All my stories are webs of style, and none seems at first blush to contain much kinetic matter. Several pieces of 'Conclusive Evidence,' for instance, which you were kind to admire, were merely a series of impressions held together by means of 'style.' For me 'style' *is* matter." "I think it's fine to have your style a web, when your web is an ornament, or a beautiful housing, for the content of your text, as it was in 'Conclusive Evidence,'" Katharine answered, "but a web can also be a trap when it gets snarled or becomes too involved, and readers can die like flies in a writer's style if it is unsuitable for its matter. I shall have to stick to my guns on that and on the fact that we did not think these Vane girls worthy of their web."

They debated English usage. "You want to say 'the anonymous roller that imparted upon my life, etc.," wrote Katharine. "The difficulty with this is that the [preposition] that follows the verb *impart* is 'to'—not 'upon,' yet it's not idiomatic to say 'imparted to my life a watermark,' etc. If you don't like 'stamped' (which is only partially correct as of watermarks apparently), can we make it 'pressed upon my life'? This is wholly correct of the roller-watermark process, I conclude, after studying Webster. Anyway I've changed it to 'pressed' but let me know if you object to this. We just don't want to use the ungrammatical 'imparted upon' and I'm sure you don't either." "All right, I surrender 'impart,' let us have 'press' or 'impress,'" Nabokov replied, adding that he would not give in on another point.†

In an effort to reduce last-minute editing problems, Katharine got into the habit of sending Nabokov a Varitype or typescript copy of his manuscript, a step omitted with most *New Yorker* writers, who were usually sent only the final "author's proof." The Varitype not only showed Katharine's "suggested editing and queries," but asked for Nabokov's "help or approval on every word changed from [his] original—all this before we put the piece into type or buy it," Katharine explained. Having received Nabokov's

---

*"The Vane Sisters," 1951.

†In a similar instance, Nabokov refused to submit to Edmund Wilson's emendation. (Wilson, of course, was not paying Nabokov for his work.) A female character in Nabokov's novel *Bend Sinister* says: "I must say, your new steady has a regular sense of humor." Wilson pointed out that "regular" was incorrect, that the girl would have said "wonderful" or something else. Nabokov retained "regular." See *The Nabokov-Wilson Letters, 1940–1971,* edited by Simon Karlinsky, Harper & Row, New York, 1980, p. 184.

approval and cooperation, Katharine bought the piece, had it set in type, and sent Nabokov his author's proof. As Katharine delicately explained to Nabokov, "We . . . put in this extra step in your case because your writing is particularly complex and subtle, and your idiom and style is particularly personal"—and then, more frankly, "and too often includes foreign words, matters of English usage, etc." *New Yorker* editing, it should be observed, could be exhaustive and considerable, and Nabokov understandably felt that what remained was not his work as he had written it and conceived it.

Katharine handled this prized writer carefully, like an exotic hothouse flower. She wrote to him respectfully, deferentially, and with a seemingly inexhaustible fund of maternal solicitude and reassurance—and kept him writing for *The New Yorker*. * She understood that Mr. Nabokov would be "annoyed" if she had misinterpreted a story; she asked his "indulgence" on the delay in getting back to him. Notes and queries on his stories (which were "unimportant") were sent for his "consideration"; editing was done only with Mr. Nabokov's "approval" and "permission"—though it was clear that if Nabokov refused to submit to the editing *The New Yorker* considered essential the magazine would refuse to publish his work. There were many small and large extras Katharine provided: seeing to it that Nabokov got his *New Yorker*s faster; nominating him for fellowships and grants (the Saxton and Ford); advising him about press agents, publishers, and advances; talking with influential people on his behalf; serving as mediator between Nabokov and other *New Yorker* editors, smoothing Nabokov's ruffled feathers when Gus Lobrano angered him with queries on proofs while Katharine vacationed one summer ("[Nabokov] was merely used to me," Katharine explained) and when Ross stepped into the editing of a Nabokov story.†

When Nabokov was suffering personal problems and Katharine was at a long distance, she urged him to telephone her collect. Most of all, though, there were the words of encouragement and praise ("I think this is perhaps

---

*Nabokov's uncertain finances, and *The New Yorker*'s high payment and other benefits also kept him contributing to the magazine. Another factor, notes Andrew Field, was Nabokov's respect for "the over-all level of the magazine," and his sense of pleasure and privilege in being a *New Yorker* writer. See *Nabokov: His Life in Part* (paperback edition), p. 246.

†"Two or three weeks ago," Nabokov wrote to Wilson (1945), "I sold a story to *The New Yorker*—was paid very handsomely for it. Unfortunately, a man called Ross started to 'edit' it, and I wrote to Mrs. White telling her that I could not accept *any* of those ridiculous and exasperating alterations (odds and ends inserted in order to 'link up' ideas and make them clear to the 'average reader'). Nothing like it has ever happened to me in my life and I was on the point of calling the deal off when they suddenly yielded and, except for one little 'bridge' which Mrs. White asked as a personal favor, the story is more or less intact. I am always quite willing to have my grammar corrected—but have now made it quite clear to the *New Yorker* that there will be no 'revising' and 'editing' of my stories henceforth. [I was terribly angry.] Mrs. White wrote me several letters and telephoned twice, and finally came to see me here (on her way to Maine). We have made it up now." Karlinsky, p. 154. The bracketed words are, in Nabokov's original, in French and Russian.

the most subtle and beautiful of all your memoirs," Katharine wrote of "The Perfect Past" [1949]. "Anyway it is to me. It's a privilege to be able to publish it"); the personal concern ("I am getting more and more worried about both you and Vera and will sleep better when I hear that you have both conquered the virus"). She longed for more Nabokov stories ("It is a devastating thought that we haven't got a Nabokov manuscript in the bank"; "I am in New York and looking at every morning's batch of mail, hoping it will bring us the promised Pnin piece"). *The New Yorker* wasn't the same without him ("There has been a long, painful gap for us since your last manuscript. We miss you terribly. Dare we hope for a story or poem soon? I hope so. *Do* take a little time off to write us something").

> Dear Vladimir:
>
> Where are you? What are you doing? Are you and Vera well? And your son? I do long for a bit of news and just as much I long for another Pnin story. Dare we hope? It has been far too long since we had something of yours and I do hate to see you not continue with that wonderful character. I just thought I should tell you that we badly miss your manuscripts.

Money was not only an inducement for Nabokov to contribute to *The New Yorker,* it was the plum Katharine White dangled, not unkindly, before the writer. Sensing that Nabokov would not cooperate with editing, she would withhold full payment on a piece; when Nabokov's mood was more favorable, she sent the whole check. Nabokov's willingness to be edited could make the difference between earning nothing and receiving "his quantity bonus of 25% retroactively on all the last six purchases."* At one point Nabokov was ill and unable to work on revisions. Though she could not send him the regular payment until he had revised his new story, Katharine sent him a $350 check "against future work as I know you must be having extra heavy expenses right now." A kind gesture voluntarily given was also a wise investment for *The New Yorker.* Warm-hearted and ever eager to help a writer in distress, Katharine White was also shrewd.

The effect of Katharine White on Vladimir Nabokov is perhaps best expressed by Andrew Field: "It is characteristic of the relationship between Nabokov and *The New Yorker* that he accepted occasional emendations, something he has never done for any other publisher or journal." (Katharine

---

*In December of 1947 six stories purchased from a contributor within a twelve-month period added 25 percent to the original purchase price of each story, and on any additional stories. *The New Yorker* also provided the contributors with whom they had first-reading agreements a discretionary cost-of-living adjustment, which could add another 25 percent to a story's purchase price.

The Imperfect Script

White could have argued with "occasional emendations": "Nabokov's early pieces in *The New Yorker* required an enormous amount of editing for English usage and for his use of English words no one had ever heard of.") Nabokov delighted in, was grateful for her friendship, enjoyed the company of "the very, very nice Whites," and disliked hurting Katharine's feelings, though on at least one occasion, early in their work together, he had "told poor Mrs. White off rather rudely" after *The New Yorker* "had the gall to send me back my story, accompanied by a letter filled with a farrago of nonsense." But he appreciated her—"such a subtle and loving reader"; he felt free with her. Looking back over their years of working together, Nabokov would describe it as a "cloudless association." He sent her his work first, before he sent it anywhere else, and when Katharine finally retired from *The New Yorker* she had edited about thirty of the forty-five Nabokovs published by the magazine (nearly all of the post-K.S.W. contributions were translations from the Russian, many of them by others or in collaboration with Nabokov). Nabokov was a lepidopterist, and his letters to Katharine were signed with his special butterfly signature.

It came naturally to writers, to nearly everyone who entered Katharine White's orbit, to be devoted to her. Her former daughter-in-law, Evelyn Angell Nelson, said that she never knew anyone who worked for Katharine "who didn't worship the ground she walked on." Katharine's secretaries seem not to have resented mailing her Christmas cards for her or shopping for her, whether the shopping entailed selecting a birthday gift for one of Katharine's relatives or taking her corset to Saks to have new bones put in it. (Katharine gave them generous checks and cashmere sweaters.) Writers confided in her about their personal problems and their struggles to write; they chatted to her about each other, dedicated books to her, sought her approval ("I hope you like the Bullitt piece," Janet Flanner once wrote. "If you don't, then I can't").

It is hard to conceive how Katharine White could have been surpassed in sheer solicitude: she wrote countless letters to both *New Yorker* contributors and noncontributors, asking them to submit their work to *The New Yorker,* praising them in precisely the words a writer dreams of hearing (to James F. Powers: "You are one of our most gifted fiction writers"). A poet was moved to write verse; a fiction writer given "an energy I find difficult to supply from other sources." "Her praise," wrote Faith McNulty, "was the best of Christmas presents." That she sent these missives even when she was hospitalized, and to writers she didn't know who were themselves ill, made the attention more significant, and genuine.

Katharine's dedication to her work was part of it too, part of why she inspired devotion in her writers, and stimulated them to write. She could spend hours working on a story, would try to edit a piece she considered likely to be rejected, in the hope of saving it. She vigilantly protected her writers from the "attempted improvements" of Harold Ross and *The New Yorker*'s scrupulous (Fact) Checking Department—"She was always putting her spokes in those wheels," said Mary McCarthy. But, despite Katharine's strength and her image as "a defensive bulwark against such assaults," she had a touching vulnerability, evident in her worries about her health, surfacing in her expressed self-doubts: Mary McCarthy recalled Katharine once asking her opinion about a Salinger story, which the other editors had overanalyzed, and to which they attributed symbolism Katharine didn't see. She was "upset by the fear that she might be wrong." And Katharine was unsure about her contributors' affection for her. But her writers adored her. Nabokov sent butterflies; Jean Stafford, homemade potpourris.

Jean Stafford, whose famous short story "Children Are Bored on Sunday," appeared in *The New Yorker* in February of 1948, soon became "one of [Katharine's] best friends among the contributors." The two women came together at a critical time in their lives, during a time of pain—the pain of divorce for thirty-three-year-old Jean Stafford; the physical agonies of a spinal operation for Katharine, now fifty-five.

In April, 1948 Katharine underwent a spinal-fusion operation. A piece of her pelvic bone was removed and placed over two crumbling vertebrae, then attached and held in place by two metal screws. The trouble had begun five years earlier, after a fall on winter ice, the fall later found to be complicated by curvature of the spine. For the past four years Katharine had been in constant pain, finally unable to walk a city block, ride in a car, or sit at a typewriter "without agonizing sciatica." Nevertheless, she remained at her *New Yorker* desk until April 12, three days before the surgery. The operation was followed by a long discouraging period, first under heavy sedation, lying perfectly still; there were eight months in an aluminum brace, and a full year of gradually lessening pain. A year later, in a letter to her Bryn Mawr class, Katharine wrote a detailed account of her surgery and recovery, adding that she had returned to her *New Yorker* desk three months after surgery (she was working at home two months after). Typically, she had never really left her desk; shortly after the operation, letters to *New Yorker* contributors began to sail forth from Room 1044 of Presbyterian Hospital's Harkness Pavilion, the room number and hospital noted at the upper right-hand corner of *The New Yorker* stationery.

The Imperfect Script

(To Jean Stafford)

April 30, 1948

Dear Jean:

If I may call you that—I always think of you as Jean and perhaps the drugs I am under have made me weak-headed enough to break down the barrier.

I got your letter today and was so glad to have it, but sorry to hear of your not too happy flight and not too happy state of mind. I hope that St. Thomas will prove soothing and that the perfect hell will end. My hell goes on, quite violently. The spine operation has gone wonderfully and if I didn't have every complication known to man I would be in fine shape. But I have them all and most of them torturing. Letters therefore are particularly helpful. It is good news that you are going to work on a new short story for The New Yorker.

Faithfully,
Katharine

Jean Stafford's "perfect hell" did not end with her trip to St. Thomas, where she had traveled to get a divorce from the poet Robert Lowell. Katharine sympathized with her, as she always sympathized with women getting divorced, writing in August that "I find myself unable to say how sorry I am about what you must have been through this summer. I know how frightfully my divorce upset me and I did not at that time have much if any feeling left for my husband. If you do, it must be hell itself." It was, perhaps, the younger woman's suffering that had first drawn Katharine to her: Katharine was attracted to suffering, in sympathy with it. And a suffering soul required maternal comfort, which Katharine needed to be able to give. Jean Stafford was also a witty, funny, highly intelligent woman, an articulate conversationalist and an extremely talented writer—like Louise Bogan, she was the kind of woman who naturally appealed to Katharine. Reading Katharine White's letters to Jean Stafford, letters spanning thirty years, one notices a somewhat different Katharine, someone less self-centered about her own health than Katharine was inclined to be, more selflessly concerned with another person's suffering, and yet freer about her own feelings, which could lead her to be more openly complaining and critical.

I was delighted with your account of the evening at the Ross's, and so was Andy to whom I read it. Andy contends that Ariane's accent is not an accent at all but just a general lack of coordination between brain and tongue. But

I say it's an accent and sit bemused as you did, trying to figure it out. California is in there and so is a general effort at elegance, and on top of that, long stays with the Kennedys—ex-Ambassador-to-England Kennedy—perhaps in Boston and perhaps in England. So Irish-American plus British haute-monde enters in. It is an endless study. Also, of course, she has stage and screen aspirations, which call for "tone." Was Ross nasty to her? That's one of the embarrassments of seeing them together.

Between February 1948 and August 1949 Katharine edited four of Stafford's stunning tales of displaced persons—characters ranging from an orphaned Indian boy ("A Summer Day") to divorcées in the Carribean ("The Cavalier"). The publication of "A Summer Day" brought a letter of protest from the National Association for the Advancement of Colored People to the editor of *The New Yorker,* which Katharine tried to reassure Jean about.

> Every time we use the word "nigger" in the magazine we get such a letter. We have a rule of course against using the word except for a literary purpose as you used it. It would have been absurd to change it in your story and the National Association for the Advancement of Colored People is certainly wrong in this instance when they say that the word "serves no particular essential need and is offensive and derogatory." Don't let it get you down. The same sort of letters come in from the Jewish Association which is against racial discrimination and they write us attacking stories that are written in the cause of racial toleration. They don't seem to want the subject mentioned.

From the beginning, and during the nine years in which Katharine served as Jean Stafford's editor, Stafford was completely cooperative about editing, even when the "editing" required that she entirely rewrite or reconceive a story. Unlike Vladimir Nabokov, Stafford seems not to have been insulted by editorial suggestions and emendations, even when her editor was preposterously wrong. (Not realizing that "Children Are Bored on Sunday" was the title of a popular French song, and thinking the "are bored" not "entirely apt" for Stafford's story, Katharine had advised her to retitle the story, and herself suggested "Children Cry on Sunday.") Jean Stafford was, in Katharine's words, "a remarkable reviser. Stories would come in with very hopeful material that hadn't quite jelled; and . . . over and over again I [would] ask her to rewrite a story, and over and over again she [did] so successfully." Unlike Nabokov, and many other *New Yorker* contributors, Jean Stafford was edited very little—if at all—for grammar and syntax (the one available manuscript bearing Katharine White's editorial comments contains no grammatical or syntactical emendations, and Katharine's editorial letters to Jean Stafford only occasionally talk of making a sentence or paragraph clearer);

Stafford's manuscripts were highly polished. The editing of Stafford was subtler, having to do with character or plot development, clarification of certain details. A Ross query on one story notes: "It seems to swing back to the particular, at the end here. It is unlikely that the boy would halt and be looked at by a policeman several times, as a general matter, isn't it?" To which Katharine responded: "No—it isn't unlikely in Germany—Stet the passage as is."

Katharine defended Stafford, protected her, tried to make her life easier. Jean wanted a dictionary; after sending her detailed information on the two kinds of unabridged Websters available, Katharine ordered one at *The New Yorker*'s 30 percent discount, and had it hand-delivered by one of the office boys. Checks were put through quickly, once to lift Jean's spirits about a "big new rent" she was paying. Jean was planning a trip abroad; Katharine had the office arrange steamer accommodations, and wrote her a letter of introduction to the English writer Mollie Panter-Downes, and a detailed letter filled with tips on hotels, etc. Katharine took Jean to lunch, invited her to parties. She loved Jean Stafford, loved her writing so much that she would edit a Stafford story on vacation. "One of the first things I'm going to do after the New Year's," Katharine wrote in December of 1948, "is spend two days by myself on your pieces." Such compliments were hard for a writer to resist.

Not every writer worked well with Katharine White. Niccolò Tucci, who had begun writing for *The New Yorker* after the war, was assigned to her in 1947. Having previously written in his native Italian and in German, he found English very difficult, and in 1947 was feeling torn between writing in Italian and writing in English. Though "a good person" and very understanding of Tucci's feelings, Katharine White "was extremely insistent" that Tucci rewrite, and that he write in proper English. Tucci told her that it took twice the amount of inspiration for him to write in English that it took for him to write in Italian, and Katharine thought she could help him by making her own changes in his manuscripts, and then presenting them to him with "Now you write it your way." Her method disturbed Tucci, and he found himself unable to work with her. Tucci was then assigned to William Maxwell, whose editorial method was better suited to him. (Maxwell would discuss Tucci's story with him, but not the writing itself. He would simply request that Tucci amplify something, or ask him how he looked at things.)

Clearly, Katharine White liked Niccolò Tucci, and admired his writing. She worried about his health, and she regarded his story "The Blue Horse" as not only "a perfect comedy," but "the modern Italian counterpart of *The*

Vicar of Wakefield"—an assessment that none of her colleagues shared with her, she wrote Mary McCarthy.

Niccolò Tucci later regretted his inability to work with Katharine White, which he attributed to *his* being difficult, though she had sometimes been impatient with him. She wanted him to write more stories about his children, and once lost her temper with him when he presented her instead with a story titled "Henry VI." "Will you stop pestering me?" she said. *"Why* have you done this?" She was "very irritated" by Tucci's habits. When it got back to her that Tucci was on a diet and going off to the public library each day with only a carrot or a head of lettuce for lunch, "Mrs. White said, 'That's not right.' " (To Mary McCarthy, she added: "What Tucci needs is a good hot meal in the middle of the day, and Andy thinks so too.") But Katharine was not annoyed with Tucci when he brought her an amusing piece on an Italian Hurdy-Gurdy player, though she would not accept it. She called him and said "No."

"No? Mr. Ross doesn't want it?"

"No. I don't want it."

"Why?"

"Because we have an Italian shoeshine man who comes here every week, and I think it would hurt his feelings."

Katharine ended the decade feeling remade by her new back, which allowed her to sail and garden and swim again. There were now four grandchildren to swim with: Nancy's three children, Kitty (Katharine's namesake), aged six; Jonathan, aged four; Sarah, eighteen months; and Roger's daughter, fifteen-month-old Caroline (after Aunt Crully), called Callie. The summer of 1949 arrived with a happy invasion of Stablefords, who were staying in a nearby cottage, and a brief visit from Joel, home between semester's end at Cornell and a summer job as a camp counselor. There were heifers boarding in the pasture, along with a neighbor's flock of sheep.

But in a letter to Bryn Mawr, in June of 1949, Katharine offered a somewhat weary sketch of the Whites.

> Andy resigned his job as editorial writer for *The New Yorker* last January and now does "Notes and Comment" only occasionally, but he still writes, of course, and does various *New Yorker* jobs. His health has not been very good the past few years but I hope and think it is improving. The state of the world is what makes most people sick these days, I am convinced. My particular way of "saving the world" is rather indirect, I must admit, since it mostly involves

trying to make *The New Yorker* a good magazine, but I like what the magazine stands for and for a few years more hope to keep going on this particular task. One of my recent incidental chores has been helping to compile another collection of *New Yorker* short stories. It will appear in the fall and is a *New Yorker* Twenty-Fifth Anniversary volume. Twenty-five years of working on a weekly magazine certainly makes one realize the passage of time!

7

"Do You Remember When All We Worried About Was Love?"

NINETEEN FIFTY WAS TO BE a year of celebration, the year *The New Yorker* turned twenty-five, the year Katharine and Andy, partly in celebration of her mended back, were to sail to England, from whence they would visit Scotland, Paris, the Riviera; Italy had regrettably been abandoned because of the crowds coming to observe the Holy Year. Janet Flanner, living in Paris on the Rue de Castiglione, was appealed to for hotel recommendations. Katharine and Andy wanted something comfortable, with firm mattresses and "decent" meals—"but as you know, we hate enormous and over-deluxe places and don't want top luxury prices." They did not want to have to dress up all the time. Katharine worried about her vanished ability to speak French—"I still, after all these years, work such long hours for this magazine of ours that I have no time to polish up my vocabulary." And Andy was monolingual.

But the steamer tickets were returned, the hotel accommodations and rental car canceled, the new dress bought for *The New Yorker*'s anniversary party left hanging in the closet. Katharine came down with influenza, followed by a relapse and a month of missed work. The man who ran the farm was dying, their cook, hospitalized. Perhaps they would go abroad next year.

On December 6, 1951, Ross died. His death, coming with shocking suddenness during an operation to remove a malignant tumor, followed a long battle with lung cancer and a year in which he had been much absent from the office. (When Ross had become ill, a staff meeting was held, during which Katharine suggested that the editors divide up Ross's work to make things easier for him. St. Clair McKelway concluded that Katharine was trying to take over, and resented her for it.)

The effect of Ross's death on Katharine White is incalculable. He had been the dominant chord in her life for twenty-six years—he, and *The New Yorker,* and of course Andy. *The New Yorker* had become her fate, and *The*

New Yorker was Ross. They had worked hard together, struggled, argued, laughed together, been in constant communication, all those years. He was so funny, so kind. "He was ever on the *qui vive* to help the writer, prose or poet, in hard luck. Once I remember he even bought poems he never planned to run just to help a poet who was going blind and then after a decent interval turned them back to her to sell and get published elsewhere if she could." Katharine respected him, trusted him, and ultimately loved him. "He was one of the few really great men I have known well & one of the best educated." She was greatly indebted to him. He had hired her, given her the chance to use and stretch her talents, the opportunity to make her own special contribution to the world. He had developed her interest in editing, taught her almost everything she knew about editing (at least according to what she said later). He was a loyal friend, a contemporary born just fifty days after she was, in 1892. He was only fifty-nine when he died —"Remember," he had said to her, "you're only as good as your replacement." One could not measure such a loss; Katharine did not try. We have only Andy's description of the shock to them both—that they felt "disembowelled."

As Harold Ross had wished, he was succeeded as editor-in-chief by forty-four-year-old William Shawn, a succession that pleased Katharine and Andy, who gave a huge party for him in Turtle Bay. Shawn, a gentle, soft-spoken man, was as responsive as Ross had been to his editors' enthusiasm for new writers, and like Katharine, he valued poetry highly. He was immensely considerate of Katharine, who would later observe that "my years of work with [Shawn] were some of the happiest ones of all."

"Do you remember when all we worried about was love?" Thurber, now blind and suffering from other ailments as well, dictated a letter to Katharine in August of 1952, comparing symptoms. She had come down with infectious hepatitis. "As mad as a hornet," she unhappily resigned herself to a ruined summer vacation, to long days of rest, days nevertheless spent reading manuscripts. "I seem to have a genius for picking up long-term ailments!" she wrote Jean Stafford. Two months later, in mid-October, she had still not recovered, and she was "often disheartened about the future." She had not yet returned to the office. How glad she would be to be healthy! Like the girl in a recent Jean Stafford story, "she might . . . decide . . . that after all she was glad . . . to be . . . healthy."

"The Day of Cleansing," retitled and published as "The Healthiest Girl in Town," is Jean Stafford's story of a young girl named Jessie, who lives with her widowed mother in a Western town populated mostly by tuberculars and their families. Jessie's mother, a nurse, has come there to make a living, and she eventually goes to work for a sickly family whose two slight and precocious daughters become Jessie's schoolmates and her psychological tormentors. Longing for acceptance by the unwholesome little sisters, the robust Jessie begins to fantasize that she and her mother are, like the others, diseased, and she finally invents the story that her late father died of leprosy.

> Of course you yourself can decide better than I where to have the little girl break down and confess her lie [wrote Katharine]. As a matter of fact I decided to get another editor to read this without giving him my thoughts, just to be sure of whether my advice to you on it had made sense. He, too, liked the story enormously up to the last incident, on which he made the comment that . . . [Having related the other editor's opinion, Katharine continued:] You see that this last is almost what I said and I really believe that for the "I" of the story to break down and confess her lie about leprosy . . . with all the suffering that confession would bring her, would make it a stronger story. From that suffering, perhaps at the Boston girls' house, she might walk home and decide on the way that after all she was glad, instead of humiliated, to be a healthy child. This last sounds ham, as I describe it, but I know it won't be as you write it for it is sound. Also the mere fact of owning up to a lie gives a child a sense of euphoria.

Jean Stafford revised the story accordingly. The result was a triumph, and convincing.

Jean Stafford was unusually receptive to criticism; Katharine White, uncommonly inspiring. It was partly her letters, their precise attention to detail, the rush of warm responsiveness and enthusiasm and praise that embraced the writer like a favorite child. (The maternal metaphor is inescapable; May Sarton described Katharine White as *The New Yorker*'s "Mother Superior," and herself as one of Katharine's children; Marianne Moore perceived the editor's "New Yorker protégées clinging to [her] like opossums.") Writers—Nancy Hale, Whitney Balliett and S. J. Perelman, to name a few—felt nurtured and sustained by Katharine's letters and "occasional chats . . . in the early days when it seemed [they'd] never be able to get that toe in the door." Joseph Mitchell kept one of her letters in the top drawer of his desk "as a kind of touchstone" to reread when he became discouraged. "I think I shall ask to have your letter buried with me," wrote Robert Hale. A few words briefly but emphatically bestowed at a party could have the same effect. A young writer named Edith Iglauer had written a few articles for *Harper's;* Katharine asked her when she was going to write for *The New Yorker.* Miss Iglauer said that she was taking a writing course at Columbia. Throwing back her head in laughter, Katharine said, "Whatever are you doing that for? Of course you can write, you don't need to take any courses!

Just write about what you know, and send it to me." Edith Iglauer dropped the course and continued to write.

Katharine White was perceptive—to Elizabeth Bishop, "unfailingly perceptive"—about a writer's work and intentions; she discerned a writer's unique qualities, and appreciated his interests. "She was particularly enthusiastic about my weird choice of writing subjects, which was the Canadian Arctic," said Edith Iglauer, who added that Katharine White was "one of the few people who seemed to understand me, and my choice." The choice was then treated with great seriousness and respect: Faith McNulty's work "might have been the crown jewels instead of just a couple of beginning stories."

Remarkable to Joseph Mitchell was that Katharine White treated each writer as if he were as important as any other—as Nabokov, Wilson, or any of the really big names. This was true even of the writers Katharine did not work with, including promising young college students. In January of 1953 she took the time to write a thoughtful letter to the daughter of *New Yorker* writer Joel Sayre.

Dear Nora:

Your mother sent me a copy of the issue of the *Advocate* that contained your story. Andy and I read it aloud one night and liked it so much that it made me hope you would have some short fiction to send the New Yorker. It is certainly the best piece of writing in that issue of the *Advocate* and it made me hope that you would continue to write. I rather doubt that we'd have bought this particular story, but if we had had the chance to and have turned it down, I think it might have been largely due to the soliloquy form in which you cast the story. Everything about your piece convinced me except this one thing—that the museum guard would have ever recited all these thoughts and it is also hard for a woman to write as man and sound wholly convincing, or for a man to write as a woman, for that matter. The first person soliloquy is of course a time-honored device, but it is a device, and therefore it tends to sound a trifle artificial. We have published some stories that have used it but as a form it peculiarly is difficult for us, as is all first-person fiction. This is because the New Yorker publishes so many first person factual pieces— reminiscences, "casuals," and so forth. Because of this a New Yorker reader tends to be confused if a short story is told in the first person, and it is necessary to establish right at the start of the story that the "I" is not the author. We do publish first person fiction and always shall, since some stories are more effective if told this way, and this may be true of your "Museum," but just because I hope you will contribute, I thought I'd give you a steer that with first person fiction, and perhaps particularly the soliloquy form, you would have a couple of strikes against you at the start.

I want to remind you that many of our writers sold us their first manuscripts while still in college. We bought E. J. Kahn's first piece, for instance, when he was at Harvard. Speaking of Harvard, I thought that you Radcliffe girls had it all over the Harvard men in that issue of the Advocate. I liked Winifred Hare's poem, for example, especially its first stanza. If you know her, I hope you will ask her to send me some poetry. Perhaps she has done so already.

It's exciting to have another Sayre writing and I send you my congratulations for "Museum." It raised my spirits.

For many, evidently most, of her writers, Katharine White's qualities as an editor—chief among them her enthusiastic interest in them as people—inspired them, made them eager to work. "Without her help I'm sure I would never have believed in myself as a writer; would never have kept on trying"—the testimonials are overwhelming. And yet at least one writer thought that Katharine White did not care about her as a person. "It was *good writing* she liked—loved with a passion," said Mary Cable.

> And the magazine. The kindness and encouragement were for someone who might turn out to write well for *The New Yorker*. Certainly this is the best way for an editor to be. On the other hand, she was no psychologist. I think I would have written volumes for her if she had seemed to perceive me as a person. (Not that I'm defending that childish attitude.)

Mary Cable, who as young Mary Pratt had worked at *The New Yorker,* recalled an incident reminiscent of the time Katharine lost her temper with Niccolò Tucci. Having one day opened the door to Katharine's office and walked in unannounced, Mary Pratt was greeted with a glowering expression and a " 'WHAT DO YOU MEAN, walking in here without asking!' I stammered that the secretary had told me to, but she really seemed furious and I hastily retreated." The next day brought an apology and an invitation to visit again, which Miss Pratt accepted. If the incident is explained partly by the writer's being unknown or nearly unknown to Katharine, by the lateness and darkness of the hour (it was perhaps 6 P.M., and Katharine was still working, with only the desk light on)—still, this rare story is revealing. Even Katharine White slipped.

At her typical best—polite, gracious, considerate, warm-hearted—Katharine White was still to many people a formidable woman. Though encouraged by Katharine's confidence in her, Edith Iglauer did not send her *New Yorker* efforts to Katharine—"I really was too frightened to deal with her directly." "My being scared of her was more my problem than anything she *did,"* said Mary Cable. "However, when I met her in the halls (I remember she had a stately and heavy tread) she was not one with a ready smile or cheery greeting." Like Niccolò Tucci, Mary Cable was inclined to blame herself for her problems with Katharine White: Mary Pratt was young and silly, not serious enough about her writing, and "it's possible that [Katharine White] just plain didn't like me."

These experiences are exceptional, in sharp contrast to what many others have remembered. Susan Edwards, who worked as Katharine's secretary for a year, never saw her lose her temper, though the tremendous pressures and difficulties of the job inevitably bore down on her, and many of the writers she worked with were difficult and did not take criticism well, which required great tact on Katharine's part. "To me, Katherine's most outstanding characteristic was her sensitive perceptiveness," wrote Buckner Hollingsworth, a Bryn Mawr friend who recalled once writing her

> a letter that can only be described as cock-eyed, a silly dissertation on a word I thought was missing from our vocabulary and only an extraordinary, sensitive person would have realized that my letter covered some trouble I couldn't put down on paper. Katherine was, of course, that extraordinary person, and her reply to me was to tell me about an experience of hers that had caused her pain and outrage. As pain and outrage had been exactly my own emotions on reading a certain letter that a relative had written me, I was able to relax. Also, I was then able to tell Katherine what had been the cause of my own great distress.

Having admired John Updike's work in the Harvard *Lampoon* and hoped that one day he would contribute to *The New Yorker,* Katharine had become his editor at the magazine in 1954. Updike bombarded her with light verse ("one of our most precious ingredients," Katharine wrote, "and light verse writers are rare nowadays") and occasionally fiction, for which Katharine and *The New Yorker* were equally eager. After several acceptances and slightly more rejections, Updike was offered a first-reading agreement—a "rather unusual" step, Katharine told him, given Updike's short standing as a contributor. It was also prudent: during his first seven years as a *New Yorker* contributor (the years when Katharine served as Updike's editor), the magazine published more than a hundred of his poems and stories. In twenty-two-year-old John Updike Katharine realized that the magazine had hold of something special. She was at her attentive best, answering his questions patiently and in detail, quickly acknowledging the receipt of his manuscripts, whether or not they had been accepted or rejected. The rejection of an early submission the editors had found promising was carefully explained.

> The lines at 1), we feel are not quite as good as they might be and we wonder whether they could be improved. They might even be expanded to a whole stanza since the wife seems to be a bit unceremoniously sandwiched in between the light filament and death—so much so that one editor felt she sounded like an object, not a person. However if you can do it without adding, that would be even better.
>
> At 2), the adjective "down-directed" seems a bit awkward.
>
> At 3), we feel that this should be changed to "tossed in magazines." Most people do not burn uncut books as trash and the words bring in a new element, or red herring of a sort, suggesting book-burning or that this man is un-balanced or something not quite right, which we feel sure you do not intend. And we felt that "flipped," though a more unusual word, was perhaps not quite as good as the more usual "tossed" here.
>
> These are all just suggestions, of course, but I send them along for what they are worth and to show you that the poem interested us.*

Katharine was not always at such pains to explain a rejection. Poems that she and other editors did not think could be reworked for *The New Yorker* were returned with less fuss: "Alas, I have another poem to return. None of us like 'Song for Thomas Aquinas,' I am sorry to say. Thank you, though, and I hate to be so discouraging."

Updike responded to it all with characteristic good humor and compli-ance; he would "try to do better." He could scarcely have been more cooperative or grateful. He was happy to revise, even cut a piece to size. A poem whose opening line Shawn wanted changed ("Wakes wet; is promptly toileted") was cheerfully withdrawn and submitted to the *Ladies' Home Journal.* "The patient and abundant attention you have paid to my offerings this summer is one of the nicest things that has happened to me in my brief and lucky life," he wrote Katharine. He and Katharine nevertheless engaged in some polite struggles over the punctuation of his poetry, and *The New Yorker*'s "minor editing." Updike's use of the colon was a particular problem.

> There is no precedent for your use of the three colons, I'm afraid, and we feel that they would just be misleading [wrote Katharine]. Colons, as Fowler says, are used to "deliver the goods." I suppose you do own and read Fowler's

---

*Titled "Burning Waste."

"English Usage." If you don't, I recommend it as one of the funniest and most useful books in the language.

"Yes, I do own a copy," answered Updike,

> but along with my parents, pet cat, rubber basketball, and other steadying influences, I left it in America. Colons tend to be a weakness with me ever since I took a course in the works of George Bernard Shaw. They look so pert and snappy, somehow. I always think of a semi-colon as dragging one foot. I fear in poetry I use punctuation improperly, to indicate the degree of "stop" I want. Thank you for correcting me.

This did not end the colon question. From England, where he was studying at Oxford's Ruskin School, Updike wrote:

> About the dash . . . I went down to the Oxford Public Library, seeking Fowler's opinion, but neither *English Usage* or *The King's English* seemed to contain a sentence of the shape of "Sunflower," which is, "You with the red hair:/—what time is it?" However that sentence is punctuated, so should "Sunflower." Since I can invoke no authority, let me *beg* you to make it a colon. A colon is compact, firm, and balanced: a dash is sprawling, wishy-washy, and gawky. The colon suggests the Bible: the dash, letters and memoirs of fashionable ladies.

Katharine replied to Updike's three-page letter with a "treatise on punctuation" amounting to two and a half single-spaced typed pages.

> You seem to have a special feeling about the appearance of colons but on the score of their meaning, you seem to me to interpret them in a way that no one else does. The colon *looks* very nice, I admit, is "compact, firm, and balanced." I agree with you that a dash is less elegant-looking, but I can't believe that a dash is "wishy-washy." Often it is very emphatic. On a separate piece of paper, since you don't seem to own Fowler's "Dictionary of Modern English Usage," I enclose a copy of his little paragraph on the colon, to refresh your memory. . . . We string along with Mr. Fowler in thinking that the colon in general usage nowadays has the special function of delivering the goods. Yet here you are delivering no goods. The line where you want the colon *could* carry a comma if you prefer it to a dash, but we think the dash makes for clearer reading. Do, please, try to feel more kindly toward the dash and admit it here! After all, punctuation is only a means to the end of easy reading, clarity, and quick comprehension. If you use it too oddly, it is a red herring to your readers.
>
> The other poem is more of a problem since it is timely. Because of this, I am afraid we are going to have to go over your head and punctuate it in

a sensible way rather than in the quite odd and eccentric way you would like to have it punctuated. A punctuation mark comes, from habit, to have almost the value of a word. Therefore if used too untraditionally it impinges just the way a misused word does.

Now about our suggested commas in this poem: one thing you don't seem to realize is that a comma in prose has a different weight than a comma does at the end of a line of verse. It was my husband, a light verse writer, who first pointed out to me that stops at the end of lines of verse should be very light because the very fact that a line of verse *ends* makes a natural stop, both for the eye and for the ear. This is why I believe that your complaint that commas at the ends of all the lines would make the reader read the poem in too great a rush and too great a flurry is not sound, for the commas have much more weight than they do in the same lines, set as prose.

And so on, in the same vein.

All this detail is absurd and I am afraid you will think I am crazy to have gone into it. Actually, what it all comes down to is that we really must ask you to give us more freedom to use our own judgment when you are at such a long distance. When a contributor who is overseas makes changes on a timely proof, changes that we can't find acceptable, we usually just have to stet the changes to our way. We *try* to accept their changes, but we can't accept yours in this case and there is not time to return the proof. I hope this won't break your heart. Please let me know how to act in the future. Will you trust us to use our best judgment in small things when there is not time to consult you? And are we forgiven for overruling you?

I want to add that I am delighted to find anyone who cares as much as this about punctuation and who is as careful as you are about your verse. Do write me that I am forgiven and send back the "Sunflower" proof again. And I thank you for a very interesting and amusing letter.*

The new decade, which had begun with her influenza and a canceled trip to England, continued to be punctuated by illness for Katharine. Ross's illness and death had been followed by her hepatitis the next year. In the

---

*Writing to John Updike after rereading her own letters to him in 1970, Katharine was "appall[ed]" and "overwhelmed by how much I did 'cuff' you during those first few years. My pedantic and petty queries and wrangles, mostly over punctuation, make me blush with shame. My only excuse is that Ross had died only two years before I bought your first manuscript and we were still under his aura and the absolute rule of 'Fowler's English Usage'—a book I still go back to and am amused by, to this day. I now believe that a poet is entitled to use his own eccentric punctuation unless it is downright confusing to the reader or unless it is pretentious. I am also alarmed by the vast number of rejections you got and I'm willing to bet that nearly all of your rejected poems of that era would be far better than most of the light or serious verse that we're getting now."

winter of 1954 came a four-week attack of mumps and flu while Andy was suffering from shingles, a broken toe, and other troubles. Then Katharine's sister Rosamond, to whom she had remained close since childhood, suddenly died in Florida, leaving ninety-two-year-old Aunt Crully homeless. "I have never known our lives to be as complex as at this moment," wrote Katharine, who was getting Aunt Crully and a nurse settled in at the North Brooklin house. Though happy to care for her elderly aunt, Katharine felt confined by the responsibility of having to relieve the nurse and trying to make Aunt Crully happy. She returned to New York from that summer's vacation without feeling rested, and a couple of months later found herself in the hospital for eleven days with an infection. "Far from reading as a complaining letter, the one you wrote from Maine again made me conscious of the selfishness and smallness of my own attitude toward responsibilities of an irksome nature imposed on me from outside," wrote Nadine Gordimer. She marveled at Katharine's unresentful willingness to take in her aged aunt rather than put her in an old ladies' home.

> *You* never once thought of blaming or resenting your aunt for her excessive claims on you; blamed and resented only your own inability to meet them. I can't help marvelling at this. It's so rare to meet with a nature which honestly does regard other people's right to a share of life on a par with her own. I'm not flattering you; I wouldn't dare. It's simply that, with every letter we exchange, I realise that it isn't only as an editor that I've learnt from you.

That Katharine was not entirely selfless about Aunt Crully is suggested by the number of times she wrote of the problems of caring for her—besides Nadine Gordimer, she mentioned it to Vladimir Nabokov and John Updike, among others. Katharine loved her aunt—loved her family—deeply, but she was used to putting her own needs first, and Andy's. Even visiting grandchildren, though a delight, were noisy; they also brought colds, Aunt Crully caught one, and Katharine "had a siege of nursing her."

Katharine had never coped easily with domestic problems; she had always been frazzled by housework and its occasional intrusions, as when, several years earlier, her cook had died, she had been unable to find a replacement, "and for a few days . . . had all the housework and cooking for four" (Joe and his college roommate were visiting). A family dinner, which she would orchestrate but not cook, could so deplete her that she was unable "to face the typewriter"; and Sundays in Maine, when she was without household help and did the chores herself, were "always a strain," though Andy was more apt to push a carpet sweeper across the rug than she, and her cooking amounted to spaghetti or scrambled eggs.

By 1955 Katharine was the proud grandmother of seven. Roger and

Evelyn Angell's second child, Alice, had been born in 1951. In 1953, during his junior year at MIT, to which he had transferred after two years at Cornell, Joel had married Allene Messer; they now had two children, Joel Steven and Martha. Having taken a degree in naval architecture in 1954 and having worked at the Newport News Shipbuilding and Drydock Company, Joel had been drafted and was now in the army, stationed in Germany. Katharine and Andy hoped to visit there later in the year.

They were now ready to try again to go to England. Though they had booked a cabin on the *Mauretania* for the last week of May, neither one of them was sure the trip would occur. Andy had been ill; they were alarmed about Roger's younger child, five-year-old Alice Angell, who was hospitalized with spinal meningitis; and a nurse had to be found to stay with Aunt Crully. And Katharine was worried about her own health holding up. Katharine nevertheless wrote to Mollie Panter-Downes, whose *New Yorker* fiction she edited, for recommendations about places to stay. She also wrote to John Updike, whom she hoped to meet in person before he returned to the United States.

"Katharine is so nervously ill (says herself) she is having a nervous breakdown and so totally unrealistic about factual problems that I must see Nancy," wrote Elsie to her friend Hetty Goldman that spring. Elsie was having her own problems. Katharine had helped to supplement Elsie's inadequate income (for how long and in what amounts is unknown) until January of 1954, when she suddenly ceased giving her money. Elsie told Hetty Goldman that she had "carried a heavy load of anxiety about money" ever since. By the spring of 1955 she felt that her situation and her relationship with Katharine were reaching a crisis.

> K. has gone to Maine for a week . . . & the only time to talk with her, if she will do so at all, will be the end of April before she leaves for the whole summer. I have seen her only twice this winter & she has been totally subjective—not aware apparently that my fellowship comes to an end next November; and that the family relationship is deteriorating so fast it will break if not discussed with insight and humanity.

Katharine was troubled about Elsie, and less than a week before Elsie's letter to Hetty Goldman, she had confided in her doctor, Dana Atchley. "Just talking to him yesterday for a long while has helped me enormously," she wrote Jean Stafford. "He thinks states of mind about sisters, etc, are just as important as infectious hepatitis or a kidney stone."

Elsie had long been hurt by Katharine's lack of admiration for her work; clearly, her youngest sister's approval was necessary to her, for in 1953 she wrote Hetty Goldman:

It was especially helpful and cheerful to have your opinion [on Elsie's new biography of Willa Cather]. . . . But my gift to Katharine and Andy . . . elicited only a rather disparaging and excessively lukewarm comment—on the telephone, the night before I left. I was *dead* tired . . . and was very much crushed—tho' I didn't say so at the time.

Katharine did not, in fact, think much of Elsie's writing. The month after Elsie's letter to Hetty Goldman, Katharine wrote a letter to Edmund Wilson in which she thanked him for his compliments about a piece Elsie had written about Justice Holmes. She added: *"Your* piece on the Holmes-Laski Letters was brilliant."

Elsie regarded Katharine as not only afflicted with nervous trouble but lacking in feeling—in a "feeling function," in the Jungian sense. "I have to accept that she has *no* feeling!" Elsie said to a friend. We can only speculate about what Katharine imparted to Dr. Atchley: the money problem between the two sisters remains, like the core of that complex relationship itself, unanswered and ambiguous.

Alice Angell began to recover from the spinal meningitis, and Katharine and Andy proceeded with their travel plans. Then Aunt Crully had a cerebral hemorrhage and Katharine waited for the inevitable in Maine. Writing a letter to John Updike on May 12 to accompany a proof of one of his poems, Katharine said that she was again uncertain of being able to meet him in Oxford that summer. In addition to attending her aunt, she herself had been a little ill. Writing again on May 19, Katharine reported the death of Aunt Crully. She and Andy would sail on the 26th.

Caroline Belle Sergeant, who was born at 82 Bridge Street on April 30, 1862, died in the Blue Hill Memorial Hospital, Blue Hill, Maine, on Friday, May 13, at the age of 93. She had been ill only a few days.

Thus began the obituary Katharine wrote for the Northampton, Massachusetts, *Daily Hampshire Gazette,* published just three days after Aunt Crully's death. After outlining the notable events in her aunt's life, the events, like graduations and changes of address, that are the stuff of obituaries, Katharine opened her heart a bit.

Caroline Sergeant's life followed a familiar pattern of New England devotion and sacrifice—a spinster who took on the role of mother by force of circumstances and who brought to children and friends alike the rectitude of a Victorian upbringing and the warmth of a generous and spirited character.

Although she never wrote for publications, her letters and communications were small masterpieces of English prose—the sort of exact and elegant expression that is rare in our times and that is the work of a disciplined mind and a feeling for whatever is beautiful and true.

England was London, and London was the Connaught, *Punch,* and Joe Liebling. They came to London by way of taxi from Southampton, where they had docked with their trunk and ten pieces of luggage during a rail strike and following an unpleasant sail on the *Mauretania.* (One of the vessel's customs was to push the ship's paper under the passenger's cabin door in the very early morning, with instructions to fill out a word puzzle and rush it to the purser's office. "I always did the puzzle," Katharine wrote Jean Stafford, "—that was as low as I sunk—but I was never up in time to win a prize for solving it first.")

Imagining it to be "a sort of British Algonquin," they had come to Mayfair's "much too swish and much too expensive" Connaught Hotel on the recommendation of Andy's editor at Harper's, Cass Canfield, who promised a good martini. But the martinis disappointed and Andy, feeling "at all times unsuitably dressed and unable to speak properly," was afraid to go into the bar anyway. He came down with hay fever and a bad cold, begged off from an invitation to be the first American writer since Mark Twain to attend a *Punch* staff luncheon, and, having failed to understand a word of what Rebecca West's husband was saying on the telephone when he invited the Whites to visit Henley, stopped answering the phone. "K. & E. B. have been & are in England—upset by the strikes," Elsie wrote to Hetty Goldman, "—K. wrote as usual that Andy was 'very ill' but this last note was more cheerful."

A few days after the missed *Punch* luncheon, Katharine and Andy were persuaded to attend a cocktail party at the *Punch* office, given in honor of them and *The New Yorker* writer A. J. Liebling, whom they knew only slightly. The remainder of their week's stay in London was spent much in the company of Liebling, who introduced them to the city's interesting back alleys and to his favorite restaurants, attended them to evening entertainments, and to lunch at Mollie Panter-Downes's lovely Elizabethan house in Surrey, where the threesome parted.

From London Katharine and Andy traveled by chauffeur-driven car to Devon to recuperate, and were rewarded by an uneventful stay at the Easton Court Hotel. Steeped in literary lore—Evelyn Waugh had written *Brideshead Revisited* here; "a poet was murdered here, but not recently"—the small fifteenth-century Tudor house, with its thatched roof, flowering chestnut tree, and lovely garden, revived them. Mornings, announced by "a chorus of ring doves and cuckoos," began, at the Whites' request, with breakfast served in their rooms, and drifted into lazy afternoons. Katharine and Andy walked along the banks of the River Teign and through woods filled with bluebells to the old stannary town of Chagford, a mile away, where they drank gin and tonic and played darts at the pub. At the Ring O'Bells pub they encountered an elderly gentleman named Eric Day, who got into the habit of bringing his drink over to the table next to theirs. His wife was a writer of children's literature and in London on business, and one afternoon the solitary Mr. Day began to complain loudly about married women who wanted careers. Having long enough withstood his vociferousness and his assumption that she was one of "the dutiful homebody group" to whom Mr. Day referred, Katharine informed him that she herself was a career woman with three children, and that she had "never felt I had neglected them or my husband." Mr. Day apologized and two years later sent Katharine a rare book from his personal library.

Before leaving the Easton Court Hotel and England, Katharine and Andy made two more excursions in a hired car—to visit the English writer Elizabeth Taylor, whose *New Yorker* fiction Katharine edited, and to have dinner with John Updike and his wife and infant daughter.

Something had been happening inside Katharine, some internal adjustment or conversion, telling her that it was time to let go of New York and her all-consuming editorial work, to leave finally. Andy was not really happy in their New York life; he was never as well in New York as he was in Maine (she herself smoked less when working in Maine). For Katharine to remain at her *New Yorker* desk would have meant continuing to see him suffer, and thus suffering herself. She began to think of working for the magazine in a general or advisory capacity, helping to effect magazine policy, generating new ideas, continuing to look for new talent. This way she and Andy would be free to live in Maine year round again, and to travel when Andy wished. But her decision oppressed her—"I especially hate to give up my work with all the poets," she wrote to Louise Bogan. Though the editor Howard Moss now carried most of this work, Katharine had "read and written opinions on all the verse and poetry we have considered at all, have worked on the editing details and the final proofs, and have encouraged and corresponded with many poets." In the many letters Katharine wrote to her writers explaining her change in job, she sounded as if she were trying to convince herself that this was what she wanted.

"It has been a positive pleasure to work with you," wrote Mary McCarthy, "even in those long gruelling sessions over fine points of proof. Your understanding and feminine patience and serenity have made a most tremendous difference. And I had come to think of our lunches as one of the regular amenities of life. You will leave the fiction department with this contributor's love firmly attached to you." Mary McCarthy would never again have an editor at *The New Yorker* in the sense that Katharine White had been: there would be no more working afternoons in an editor's office, no more of the fine detail work that she and Katharine had hovered over —such as the uses of "grey" and "gray." "Katharine believed, as I did, that 'grey' with an 'a' or an 'e' depended on what shade one meant," recalled Mary McCarthy. "We both thought 'grey' was lighter; *The New Yorker* preferred a uniform 'gray.' We amused ourselves over such points," over *The New Yorker*'s fussiness about stories being seasonal ("a fall story couldn't have tulips. We both knew this was funny"). She and Katharine were "of a common mind on many things." For Mary McCarthy, who also felt "a certain sisterhood" with Katharine (McCarthy had gone to Vassar, Katharine, to Bryn Mawr), Katharine White "was the ideal editor."

"I know that it is selfish to regret this move of yours, since certainly exercising your extraordinary talents in this new capacity will be for the author's general good as well, but how I shall miss you," wrote the literary agent Bernice Baumgarten. "No editor I've worked with has been so quick to recognize new talent and so sympathetic toward its development." It was perhaps the loss of sympathy, of a sympathetic interest in their work, that Katharine's writers feared most. Sensing this, Katharine tried to reassure Nabokov: "You need not worry in the least about my disappearance as your editor here, because Shawn, Lobrano, and Maxwell—every editor there is, for that matter—are your great admirers, and things will go on for you as always." But Nabokov was distressed by Katharine's decision. "Your kindness, your gentleness and understanding have always meant so much to me."

As 1955 drew to a close and Katharine prepared to leave her editorial job, Gus Lobrano was seriously ill. She agreed to remain in her job until he returned. Only a few people knew how ill Lobrano was when he was hospitalized in January. Unbeknown to Katharine, who was in frequent communication with him about the office, Lobrano was dying of cancer. One of the last phone calls he made was to Katharine, "and it was full of affection," she later wrote. "His death came as a terrible sorrow to me." Andy wrote *The New Yorker* obituary. At William Shawn's request, on April 1, 1956, Katharine resumed the job she had given up to Gus years earlier, head of Fiction. Shawn asked her to remain in the job until new editors could be found and trained, for two years or longer. At the age of sixty-three, Katharine began to work harder than ever before.

Her office day began promptly at ten A.M., and ended, as promptly, at six. In her adherence to these hours she was as exact as a Swiss clock. It would not have occurred to her to depart from them, to leave early, unless she had a medical appointment. Looking unhurried and elegant in a silk blouse, tailored skirt, and pearl earrings, she would begin the day with the mail, reading and perhaps answering it all before she began editing manuscripts, all of which was gone about in a patient, orderly fashion, without obvious hurry, without confusion. She opposed disorder; in her work, her speech, her dress, in everything she undertook she was "a precisionist of the first order"—and yet she could tolerate imperfection in others. A new secretary just out of college who transcribed a dictated letter so quickly that she could not read her own shorthand, and rewrote the letter herself and left it on Katharine's desk, found it there later with numerous revisions, left to be typed. Katharine never mentioned it.

There were the inevitable days when she worked through lunch, having her secretary order her a turkey sandwich and milk, but most days she went out, usually to the Algonquin, conveniently located in the next block. A writer scheduled to come to Katharine's office that afternoon to go over a story would first meet her at the Algonquin, where lunch would be preceded by a single cocktail, a martini perhaps. Katharine's friendship with Mary McCarthy centered on this friendly ritual, when they would gossip, discuss common friends like Elizabeth Bishop, Elizabeth Hardwick, Edmund Wilson, and Niccolò Tucci, talk of gardening, recent *New Yorker* writing, a little about Mary's personal life, but not the older woman's. After lunch they typically worked the rest of the afternoon in a single sitting in Katharine's large office, "Katharine often rising to consult the big Webster on the lectern. . . . She was very fond of the Webster."

The work that Katharine brought home in an overstuffed paper portfolio preoccupied her throughout the evening, the page proofs and books scattered across the bed sometimes annoying her admiring husband, who retired early, and, unless troubled by insomnia or various symptoms, for the night, while his wife worked late and slept in spurts, often waking up to turn on the light and begin reading and smoking again, stopping to buff her nails, the cuticles of which, along with her toes, were red from picking. She sometimes fell asleep with a cigarette in her hand, her night clothes and manuscripts bearing small singe marks. Waking up, she was briefly disturbed by the scorched manuscript, but not, perhaps, by the damaged clothes; her day clothes were always immaculate, like the quality of her work itself, and bereft of the layer of ashes that lay unheeded upon her desk and papers, like the dirty reading glasses which she was also too absorbed to notice, and which a daughter-in-law was wont to clean for her when she was not looking.

When she was not looking, her husband composed a love song to her in which she was caught, like some rare and exotic songbird, in all her endearing absorption.*

This is a ridiculous assignment. The sensations of a Bryn Mawr husband are by their very nature private. Even if there were some good excuse for parading them in public, a prudent male would hesitate to make the attempt, so greatly do they differ from common sensations. But as far as that goes, a prudent male wouldn't have married a Bryn Mawr girl in the first place—rumors would have reached him of the wild fertility revels that take place on May Day, of the queer ritual of the lantern, of the disorderly rolling of hoops, and of all the other racy symbols and capers of the annual Elizabethan hoe-down. A sober male, sifting these disturbing tales of spring-time debauchery, quite properly would have taken stock of the situation. A girl who has spent her senior year dancing around a Maypole and beating a hoop might easily take a lifetime to cool off. A prudent male would have boarded the first train for Poughkeepsie and sought out some simple, modest maiden with daisies in her hair.

I do not, in fact, recommend that any young man enter into a marriage with a Bryn Mawr girl unless he is sure he can absorb the extra amount of emotional experience that is involved. To awake to a serene morning in a green world; to be overtaken by summer thunder while crossing a lake; to rise bodily from earth, borne aloft by the seat of one's pants as a plane passenger is lifted from the runway—unless a man can imbibe these varied and sometimes exhausting sensations, can profit from them, can survive them, I recommend that he take the easy course and marry into Wellesley or Barnard or Smith. But if he is ready for anything, if he wants to walk straight into the jaws of Beauty, if he aspires to rise above the fruited plain and swing by his heels from the trapezes of the sky, then his course is clear and the outskirts of Philadelphia are his hunting ground.

Bryn Mawr graduates, in their appearance and their manner and their composition, are unlike all other females whose minds have been refined by contact with the classics. They have long hair that flows down over their bodies to below their waist. They rise early, to sit in the light from the east window, brushing their tresses with long, delicious strokes, and then twisting them into an intricate series of coils and loops and binding them with pins made from the shells of tortoises, or, more lately, from the plastics of duPont. The husband's day thus begins with the promise of serenity, of order. But there is nothing static about Bryn Mawr. As the day advances, the pins grow (as

*White's essay ("Call Me Ishmael, Or How I Feel About Being Married to a Bryn Mawr Graduate") was undertaken at the request of Bryn Mawr College's Alumnae Bulletin, and appeared in that publication's summer, 1956, issue.

though nourished by the soil of intellect), thrusting up through the warm, lovely hair like spears of crocuses through the coils of springtime. When fully ripe, the pins leap outward and upward, then fall to earth. Thus does a Bryn Mawr girl carry in her person the germinal strength of a fertile world. Once a week she makes a trip to a hairdressing establishment that used to go by the name of the Frances Fox Institute for the Scientific Care of the Hair, where she is restored and cleansed by three ageless nymphs named Miss Abbott, Miss Nelson, and Miss Robinson, usually (as near as I can make out) while sitting in a booth next to the one occupied by Lillian Gish.

Bone hairpins are not the only things that fall, or pop, from a Bryn Mawr graduate. There is a steady cascade of sensible, warm, and sometimes witty remarks, plus a miscellany of inanimate objects, small and large, bright and dull, trivial and valuable, slipping quietly from purse and lap, from hair and ears, slipping and sliding noiselessly to a lower level, where they take refuge under sofas and beds, behind draperies and pillows—pins, clips, bills, jewels, handkerchiefs, earrings, Guaranty Trust Company checks representing the toil of weeks, glasses representing the last hope of vision. A Bryn Mawr girl is like a very beautiful waterfall whose flow is the result of some natural elevation of the mind and heart. She is *above* paperclips, above Kleenex, above jewels, above money. She spends a large part of each day *making* money, and then comes home and rises above it, allowing it to fall gently through the cracks and chinks of an imperfect world. Yogi Berra would be the perfect husband for a Bryn Mawr girl, but I am no slouch myself; I have come a long way in the catcher's art and am still improving my game.

I have known many graduates of Bryn Mawr. They are all of the same mold. They have all accepted the same bright challenge: something is lost that has not been found, something's at stake that has not been won, something is started that has not been finished, something is dimly felt that has not been fully realized. They carry the distinguishing mark—the mark that separates them from other educated and superior women: the incredible vigor, the subtlety of mind, the warmth of spirit, the aspiration, the fidelity to past and to present—girls like Helen Crosby, Diana Forbes Lloyd, Laura Delano Houghteling, Evelyn Shaw McCutcheon, Claire Robinson, Nancy Angell Stableford, Emily Kimbrough, Elizabeth Shepley Sergeant, Sheila Atkinson, Evelyn Washburn Emery, Edwina Warren Wise, Frances Fincke Hand, Cornelia Otis Skinner. What is there about these women that makes them so dangerous, so tempting? Why, it is Bryn Mawr. As they grow in years, they grow in light. As their minds and hearts expand, their deeds become more formidable, their connections more significant, their husbands more startled and delighted. I gazed on Pembroke West only once in my life, but I knew instinctively that I was looking at a pile that was to touch me far more deeply than the Taj Mahal or the George Washington Bridge.

To live with a woman whose loyalty to a particular brand of cigarettes is as fierce as to a particular person or a particular scene is a sobering experience. My Bryn Mawr graduate would as soon smoke a cigarette that is not a Parliament as sign a check with an invented name. Not long ago, when a toothpaste manufacturer made the wild mistake of changing the chemical formula of his dentifrice, he soon learned the stuff Bryn Mawr is made of. My wife raised such hell that our pharmacist, in sheer self defense, ransacked the country and dredged up what appears to be a lifetime supply of the obsolete, but proper, paste.

You ask me how I feel to have undertaken this union. I feel fine. But I have not recovered from my initial surprise, nor have I found any explanation for my undeserved good fortune. I once held a live hummingbird in my hand. I once married a Bryn Mawr girl. To a large extent they are twin experiences. Sometimes I feel as though I were a diver who had ventured a little beyond the limits of safe travel under the sea and had entered the strange zone where one is said to enjoy the rapture of the deep. It was William Browne who most simply and accurately described my feelings and I shall let him have the last word:

> *Briefly, everything doth lend her*
> *So much grace, and so approve her,*
> *That for everything I love her.*

Katharine reacted to Andy's love song with blushing pleasure and needless agitation at her classmates' expected reactions, which she imagined to be "disgusted" and even "outraged by so personal a piece of writing about another alumna." The Bryn Mawrtyrs were, in truth, delighted.

After Gus Lobrano's death, Katharine threw herself into the business of getting the Fiction Department on its feet again, with an eye toward the day when she would no longer be there. She continued to look for talented new editors in the Gibbs-Maxwell-Lobrano mold (and had found one in Rachel Mackenzie, whom May Sarton had recommended), and in long memos to William Shawn concerned herself with problems of office space and new ideas for *The New Yorker*—specifically, the publication of letters, one of Katharine's favorite kinds of reading. Ross had never published letters, but Katharine thought that as long as they "weren't too purely literary" *The New Yorker* should publish them. She thought in particular of Clarence Day's wonderful illustrated letters (which even Ross had been willing to consider), the letters of F. Scott Fitzgerald, Max Perkins, Colette, George Bernard Shaw, Max Beerbohm, Frank Sullivan, James Thurber (those of the latter two likely to be funnier than the casuals they were now producing), the letters and diaries of Virginia Woolf—the possibilities were endless. She suggested that *The New Yorker* send a letter to publishers and agents asking for a first look at any interesting letters coming up, and that the editors themselves make a vigorous effort to find them. Katharine's memos easily ran to several typed pages.

She was soon exhausted from overwork, writing to Vladimir Nabokov, who had just sent her an inscribed Olympia Press edition of *Lolita,* "I lead a crazy existence nowadays, with work that is all out of proportion to a normal life. I keep thinking that I'll get caught up but I suppose I never shall till I stop entirely." And she could not stop when there was so much to be done, so much even on the periphery of *The New Yorker* with which to be concerned: publishers' preferences for novels rather than short stories, the effect of television on the written word. "I sometimes despair for the written word, as against the spoken word, in this country," she wrote Nadine Gordimer. In the past several years there had been a gradual decline in the quantity and quality of manuscripts *The New Yorker* received, except in poetry. Katharine thought that television and radio were luring writers away from the magazines, and she asked both Nadine Gordimer and Vladimir Nabokov to steer any writers they knew, including talented students, to *The New Yorker.*

Augmenting Katharine's worries, Andy had not been well, and for two months, late in 1956 and early in 1957, the Whites had stayed close to home.

> The trouble [Katharine wrote Nadine Gordimer] is a constant discomfort in Andy's throat and right ear and sinuses, which so far the doctors have done little for except to prove that he has no growth there. It makes him feel nervous, low, and lacking in energy and it prevents his writing. They did turn up that his mastoid process protrudes on that side and found, too, that he'd strained his vocal cords reading aloud to a dear old lady friend of ours.

Katharine was reaching a final break with New York. Before she decided to leave, she enjoyed the satisfaction of seeing her son Roger leave his job at *Holiday,* where he had been an editor for ten years, and come to work as an editor for *The New Yorker.* Thirty-seven-year-old Roger Angell was a writer, too; he had long been selling stories to *The New Yorker,* beginning shortly after his graduation from Harvard, and had published books, including a collection of stories. Terribly proud but determined to be fair when Roger first submitted a story to *The New Yorker,* Katharine had insisted that another editor read it.

Roger Angell was present when the Fiction Department held one of its infrequent meetings, during which the probability of a dream in a John Updike story was discussed. The dream, which was probably from Updike's short story "Incest," contained sexual suggestions, and Katharine, in a spontaneous outburst, said, "I don't believe in dreams!" Writing to John Updike in April of 1957, she did not betray her reservations:

> We are all of us tremendously grateful to you for the new ending for "Incest," and think it is very much better than the first one. The dream is more dreamlike, for one thing. In the first version, it seemed to some of us more a planned ending than a dream, even though now we know it was an actual dream. This story, is, I think, an extraordinary piece of writing and in it you are at your very best in the thing you do so superlatively well—the domestic scene and the subtleties and affectionate and agonizing complexities of husband-wife-children relationships. And on top of this you've tackled a theme that almost no one could have handled so well. I suppose it may offend the immature person or the elderly spinster, but we can't publish the magazine for them and I have no doubts on that score. I am proud that we have so remarkable a short story to publish.

Jean Stafford was writing better than ever—in Katharine's opinion, only Mary McCarthy and May Sarton were then writing stories as well as Jean —and she was happy. After two failed marriages each, Jean and A. J. Liebling had begun spending time together after Katharine encouraged a meeting in London, and they were now thinking of marriage. But Joe had first to secure a divorce from his second wife, and Jean was still contending with Robert Lowell, with whom she had decided to sever communication. "I would have spared myself a lot if I had done the same thing years ago whereas for years I communicated often with Ernest," Katharine wrote in August of 1956.

> And at this very moment he and his present wife are in this village [in Maine] for two nights with my daughter, Nancy, and I'm to hear from Nancy tomorrow whether her father would like or would not like to come to cocktails with Andy and me tomorrow. This semblance of politeness is really far worse than an out and out break. Nowadays, though, our paths seldom run afoul. Much of the time I forget I ever was married before yet how I can with Ernest's daughter and son so much a part of my life is astonishing. He is up here now to see our mutual grandchildren.

In November of 1957, the first of a series of articles on Harold Ross appeared in the *Atlantic*. Titled *The Years with Ross*, they were James Thurber's version of Ross and of Thurber's years at *The New Yorker*. Initially undertaken with the assistance of many of *The New Yorker*'s staff, including Katharine and E. B. White, the Thurber *Years* signaled the beginning of the end of the Thurber-White friendship.

The Years with Ross, * which Katharine later described as "distasteful," "unfactual and malicious," upset her for several reasons. Essentially, she objected to it as a careless and irresponsible work about "a great editor, recently dead." It was careless in that it was replete with factual inaccuracies which could easily have been avoided had Thurber bothered to check his information with *The New Yorker*. Ross, of course, had been "a demon on fact, *exact* fact, and this alas was unimportant to Jim in his book about Ross." "The book," Katharine added, "[was] a distortion, both of Ross and of the magazine, and of Jim's relationship to Ross and the magazine." Ross was not as naive about sex as Jim described; neither was he the "illiterate boor" of Thurber's portrait. She was offended by Jim's emphasis on Ross's lack of literary education, a view of Ross that failed to comprehend his brilliant mind and editorial gifts, and completely discounted his humility about his own lack of reading and knowledge, which he had "spent his life correcting." Thurber's memoir was altogether patronizing, and, like Rebecca West, Katharine was "almost willing to label it a subconscious book against Ross." It almost seemed a subconscious book against Andy, too: she thought Jim had "downgrade[d] the importance of Andy's work on the magazine and also the importance of the Newsbreaks," and she considered his description of "Notes and Comment" "one of the most outrageous parts in the whole book." It is in her reaction to Thurber's remarks about Andy that Katharine, always a sensitive and protective wife, loses her perspective.

If *The Years with Ross* today seems a harmless and amusing book, one need only remember that its subject was not fictional to understand how someone like Katharine White, who loved Harold Ross, could be offended by its caricature portrait of him, its emphasis on his eccentricities and deficiencies rather than on his talent and his humanity.

For some time before the publication of the *Atlantic* pieces, Thurber's relationship with *The New Yorker* had been deteriorating. He took rejections hard, was touchy about editing (he felt that *New Yorker* editing was mutilating his work), and he had become increasingly and outspokenly hostile toward the magazine's editors and toward Katharine in particular, on whom he pinpointed the blame for his *New Yorker* troubles. They exchanged agitated letters about the magazine's editorial practices; she was openly critical of his *Years with Ross*. Andy also disliked the *Atlantic* pieces (and later the book), but Thurber blamed Katharine for Andy's attitude too.

---

*Published as a book in 1959.

During this time, Katharine took her eldest grandchild, Kitty Stableford, to the Algonquin for lunch. Kitty spotted Thurber at another table and wanted to go over and say hello. Katharine would not let her.

"I have . . . written a letter to my sister about what will happen when I die, a subject she is interested in," Katharine wrote Jean Stafford in the summer of 1957. "Katharine's bad nervous health is very much more serious, at least in its effect on me, and has been for months," wrote Elsie to Hetty Goldman, six months later. At about this time, eighteen months after she had assumed the head of Fiction post, Katharine left the job and New York for Maine, where she would read manuscripts and give her opinions and suggestions on them to Shawn, do her own writing, and considerably more than she had planned. E. B. White later thought that Katharine's break with editing—precisely, the change in her contact with writers—stimulated the curious new project she now took on: the writing of garden essays, which began as a review of seed catalogues.

Katharine, wrote White, had discovered

> that the catalogue makers—the men and women of her dreams—were, in fact, writers. Expression was the need of their souls. To an editor of Katharine's stature, a writer is a special being, as fascinating as a bright beetle. Well, here in the garden catalogues, she stumbled on a whole new flock of creative people, handy substitutes for the O'Haras, the Nabokovs, the Staffords of her professional life. . . . She began reading Will Tillotson, Cecil Houdyshel, Amos Pettingill, Roy Hennessey ("Oregon's angry man"), H. M. Russell (the daylily man of Texas), and many others. She was out of the *New Yorker* office but back among writers again, and in a field that had endless allure for her —the green world of growing things.

The New Yorker published the first of these charming and eloquent essays on March 1, 1958, under the "Onward and Upward" heading it had used in other contexts, at Katharine's suggestion: "Onward and Upward in the Garden."

"You did not tell me . . . you were resigning as Fiction Editor," wrote John Updike some time later.

> I am very sad, for myself and for the magazine, for I think as an editor you are irreplaceable, and probably personally responsible for a giant part of the magazine's excellence in the last thirty years. I don't know much about editors, but you have a freshness of reaction to printed words whose effect on me has always been tonic. I've enjoyed everything we've done together.

Having received a supportive letter from Katharine, Rebecca West wrote "with many thanks, and, if I may say so, an affection altogether out of proportion to the number of times we have met."

Katharine's health would gradually deteriorate; in four years more, she would retire as an editor altogether. But North Brooklin had its compensations. Joe and Allene and their three children lived nearby and "life on the farm has such a fable-like quality that it often makes me think of you," she wrote Marianne Moore, "and La Fontaine."

PART THREE

8

Only Half a Life

SHE HAD NOT REALLY LEFT *The New Yorker*. There were still her gardening articles, one planned for spring; she would probably be consulted on manuscripts from time to time; and of course in her heart she could never retire. "After 35½ years of it," Katharine wrote John Updike, "I'll never stop being a New Yorker editor and will have strong opinions on everything." And yet that life which she had long ago called "infinitely more satisfying than any I have yet known" was over. Her face reflected it. On January 2, 1961, the day on which for so many years she had returned to work, she looked "a little as though she were entering Leavenworth," wrote Andy. "Although I've always been ready to bleed and die for the magazine, her own attachment to it has been much more solid, steadier than mine, and I think the breakup will be unsettling for a while."

Katharine was possibly unsettled by the affectionate letters of tribute she was receiving from her former writers and colleagues—by the words "pension" and "many splendid services" in Fleischmann's letters—words that sounded altogether like a eulogy. Words that sounded like good-bye. Though it was gratifying to be missed—indeed, she had "wanted to quit while I'm still wanted and will be missed"—she was not ready for a swan song. With perhaps more reason than she realized, she had not yet cleared out her office. A letter from the writer Elizabeth Cullinan arrived: "I don't like to think of that office not being yours anymore. It makes me feel a bit uneasy—as if the whole building must be in danger; as if, when I come back from Ireland, nothing at all will be there."

Katharine had her own fears about leaving that office.

As Katharine would remember it, she had been "in blooming health" on January 1, 1961, the day her retirement became official. Things began to go wrong on January 2, with a near accident at the stove. She was frying bacon when she managed to twist her knee and fall, the pan in her hand, safely into the arms of Andy. The next day, January 3, she "keeled over at [her] desk, very dizzy, and one arm went totally dead for a short time. Of course Andy and I thought I had had a slight stroke but it wasn't that at all," she wrote to Louise Bechtel, one of her writer friends. By January 19 two more "strokes" had occurred. Told first that she had a slow-growing brain tumor, then that the problem might lie in her cervical spine, she was hospitalized for neurological tests.

Had she known this was coming, had she sensed it somehow? Even during her vacation the previous summer her mind had felt "empty as a sieve." She had of course been sick with infections for two months before then, but that did not seem to explain the way she felt.

The possibility that her "strokes" were psychosomatic occurred to her, and it troubled her. On January 19 she wrote a revealing letter to Mary McCarthy.

> Dear Mary:
>
> I shall at least start this letter, but whether I can complete it seems uncertain, for I have been very sick since Christmas and just to string two sentences together is an effort. I had an attack, which scared Andy and me to death. It seemed exactly like a small stroke, for I lost the use temporarily of one arm and get [sic] very dizzy. But there is nothing wrong with my heart, circulation, or blood pressure. Since then I have had two others, and the doctor here feels sure it is a neurological mechanical difficulty, perhaps in my cervical spine, where I had trouble once before, and alas, deep x-ray therapy. It would not be given to me today. I must have felt this coming on earlier, for in November, I resigned as a New Yorker editor, as of Jan. 1st. The daily work was getting to be too much. I had so looked forward to having more time for writing and for a book, based on the garden pieces, which various publishers seem to want. Instead, I am headed for Harkness and neurological tests, and go there on Feb. 4 if I don't get worse before then. I am dizzy all the time and this month, when I should be writing my spring Onward and Upward in the Garden piece, I sit here in a sea of catalogues that I've read but can't write about; it is maddening.
>
> This is why I have not been able to tell you how honored I felt to have your letter and how happy I was for you and for James West, and yet how miserable that you should be beset by all these problems and frustrations. Divorce is Hell, as I well know. I have a great feeling for Mr. West already —coming from our nearby Orono, and a graduate of Bowdoin (where my Maine grandfather, James Shepley, got his A.B., and where Andy got an honorary degree)—and with such a distinguished career and all in all so fine a person. I am very happy for you, Mary, and I do earnestly hope that by the time you get this letter things will have straightened out. Don't wait out too decent an interval. What does it matter?

It is small wonder that you have been unable to write the novel but I trust it is now in your possession. Possibly you have already sent Bill Maxwell some sections of it. I am not entirely off the staff for Bill Shawn wanted me to continue and hoped I would change my mind, but I did not, luckily. However, we have made an arrangement by which he and the other editors can consult me on any manuscript they wish to when I am well. At the moment I'm not well enough to be much use. I shall keep a small office at 43rd St. and my secretary and at the moment the office is my best address as I'm leaving here soon.

I shall end this dreary note but I did at least want you to know that I was thinking of you and with much affection. . . . We hope to go to Florida in February and were all set to go on the 14th, to the house we love on Fiddler's Bayou, but now we don't know. It may all turn out to be nothing. I hope so, and of course I know everyone at first will think it is psychosomatic. But neither the doctor nor I do. You can imagine that I hope it is in my spine and not in my cranium. I would not write this last to anyone in this country. I don't know why one always takes out everything on a person who is at a distance. Forgive me, and please do not braodcast [sic] my craven remarks.

Much love, Katharine

I shall struggle to write at least a token garden piece, to hold the franchise and keep the catalogues coming. At the moment, though, I have two small grandchildren here while their parents are away.

Among Katharine White's letters, this one is unique in its frank admission of her fear that her brain, not the rest of her body, is diseased. If we are to attempt to understand Katharine's state of mind during these years, the time following her retirement as a *New Yorker* editor, we must consider this letter: her concern about what other people will think of her latest ailment; her willingness to subject herself to more of the physical agony she has endured in the past rather than cope with psychological ills; her insistence that she really is physically sick.

Though Katharine White was part diarist in her letters, often intimate and increasingly vulnerable, she exposes her fears here. One senses what an effort it is for her to let go of her editorial work, to stop being McCarthy's editor. After reflecting that McCarthy has perhaps sent some of her new novel to William Maxwell, Katharine immediately asserts that she is not entirely off the staff, that she still has an office at *The New Yorker,* and that she is available to the editors for consultation—"when I am well. At the moment I'm not well."

That Katharine offered these "craven remarks" to Mary McCarthy and not to "anyone in the country" probably, as Mary McCarthy thought, had more to do with her dread of being talked about and giving rise to speculation about psychosomatic illness than with anything else. Living in Paris, McCarthy was at a safe remove, unlikely to discuss the letter with mutual friends. (To her mind, her former editor was understandably "sending this bad news out of the country like a message put in a bottle and dropped into the sea.") There was also the shared outlook on many things which made Katharine feel comfortable with McCarthy, the sympathetic bond between the two women which would have been deepened for Katharine by McCarthy's divorce: Katharine was fiercely sympathetic to anyone passing through the "Hell" of divorce, particularly women. Divorce touched a nerve in Katharine, especially as she aged. That one of her friends was in the midst of a divorce at this time when she herself was so vulnerable may have triggered her fearful outburst. Her advice that McCarthy not "wait out too decent an interval" before remarrying ("What does it matter?") betrays her weariness. The question is also, of course, defensive: she had not waited out too decent an interval before marrying Andy (a fact she tended to gloss over, though she never forgot it).

Despite her confidence in McCarthy, Katharine could not help reminding her that her remarks were not to be repeated. As the letter makes clear, she was aware of the way people regarded her health problems—"of course" they would think her present trouble psychosomatic; "everyone" would think so. Katharine was at times painfully sensitive to criticism, anxious about the image she projected to others (when, in 1957, Frank Sullivan teasingly wrote that she had once "snarled" at him when returning one of his pieces, she had taken it amiss). She cared intensely about what other people thought of her, especially if their ideas were incorrect. She hated to be misrepresented. And *this,* the notion that she suffered from psychosomatic illness, was especially and deeply troubling: at the heart of it lay the possibility that it was true.

Katharine's acute discomfort with this idea is variously explained. Essentially, she seems to have associated emotional disturbances with Elsie— indomitable, complex Elsie; a woman "paralyzed by indecision much of her life"—and this oppressed and frightened her.* Elsie was emotion gone awry, a living, pathetic testimony to what one could become if one failed to keep one's feelings in check. "There were always snide remarks about Elsie in the family," said Nancy Stableford, "that she went so heavy for psychotherapy she could never stand on her own feet emotionally, could never make a decision on her own." Making decisions, standing on one's own—emotion-

*E. B. White said that Katharine "was more afraid of Elsie than of anyone else in the world."

ally and financially—was crucial to Katharine, to the foundation upon which her life had been built. This had to do not only with her fear of vulnerability (what she really feared in Elsie, who was too vulnerable) and her resulting need to protect herself psychologically, but with the great importance she placed on strength of mind.

"I cherish *ideas* more than anything," she would write to the garden writer Elizabeth Lawrence in 1962.* She seemed to feel that her ability to form ideas—her mind, which she prized most in herself—was threatened if she was suffering from psychological problems: that psychosomatic illness denoted a weak mind. She was understandably frightened by diseases affecting the brain. In a letter to Elizabeth Lawrence written from Sarasota one year, she explained that her doctors were giving her Dilantin "on the *guess* that I have a scar on the surface of my brain. It's the drug they give after strokes or for epilepsy, neither of which I have or have had. They say this is *proved.*" And she added, "But because of its connotations, please do not use the word 'dilantin.'"

Elsie was not the only psychologically troubled person whom Katharine feared. Katharine had seen many of her *New Yorker* friends and colleagues suffer from psychological problems, Thurber and Wolcott Gibbs among them. She had seen how their problems had affected their lives and work, and she had heard people gossip. Mary McCarthy recalled a visit with Katharine in Maine during which Katharine confided that she was absolutely terrified of Robert Lowell, who was coming to visit the Whites. "I'm so frightened of him, and Andy is too," she said. McCarthy thought this may have had to do with Lowell's manic episodes, though Lowell would hardly have "jumped at the Whites over their teacups." (It is noteworthy that Robert Lowell had also been a violent husband: Katharine was aware that he had been rough with Jean Stafford. Edmund Wilson, whom Katharine also feared, had sometimes been physically violent with Mary McCarthy.)

Furthermore, Katharine was suspicious of psychiatrists. She had had a bad experience in her youth working for a psychoanalyst whom she considered more disturbed than her patients. Still, Katharine tried to be open-minded about society's need for psychiatrists. She would say to a granddaughter seeking psychotherapy that "psychological or psychiatric help is good—if you find the right person, one that you like. It's easier to get loads off one's mind often to a total stranger than to a parent . . . and many people have

---

*The remark echoes a description Elsie once gave of herself for Bryn Mawr College's Alumnae Association. She wrote that she was "more of an artist than a journalist yet always with social & sociological interests. . . . Bryn Mawr formed me as a writer and I shall never escape her particular stamp—e.g. I care too much for solid learning and research to be a very successful magazine writer from the money standpoint. I write slowly & care for style & have no interest in mere surfaces of any sort."

received a lot of help from it." As Roger Angell observed, Katharine believed in many things which she herself was not at ease with—like the benefits derived from unburdening oneself to a "stranger" or psychiatrist. She had rarely unburdened herself to anyone. And on the occasions when she had, such as in the letter to Mary McCarthy, she was likely to feel guilty and excuse herself, often on the grounds that she was ill. Like many people, Katharine White felt that psychiatrists were fine—for others. She herself had "never been to a psychiatrist and [had] never felt the need for one."

And the person closest to Katharine—her husband—suffered from "nervous head troubles." She had for some time realized that Andy would "never be too well nervously," and that his health was greatly affected by his surroundings: she knew that "he [was] better and happier when [in Maine]." She had long known this and deferred to it, moving to Maine so that he would be able to work and live in better health.

It is in this year (1961) that Katharine appears to have begun to differentiate between the causes of her ill health and the causes of Andy's. Eight months after the letter to Mary McCarthy, Katharine wrote to Louise Bechtel, beginning with a history of her recent illnesses. "You can imagine how frustrating all this has been, and how hard on Andy. He has been absolutely wonderful and his own nervous head troubles, though still with him, have not been so bad as sometimes. It's a mess to have two bad heads in the family, one neurotic, the other mechanical." In time, she would become more insistent about the difference in their health problems. "No doctor I have ever had would say that I have ever had an imaginary ill. Poor Andy is saddled with a decrepit wife who has now become terribly expensive because of nursing care but whose mind hasn't entirely given up. I myself don't consider Andy a hypochondriac and think he is a neurotic and is onto himself about his fears. Curiously enough most of his fears have turned out to be true." (They were, in fact, *not* true.)

It is surprising to find Katharine White—generally the most protective of wives—talking this way. For, although she is compassionate toward her husband, defending Andy in her latter remark, she is also uncharacteristically selfish—in effect, sacrificing her husband's image and protecting her own. This small betrayal occurs when Katharine is thinking about a published article that has described both Whites as preoccupied with imaginary ills.* Katharine's fear of being considered a hypochondriac is so great, her self-

---

*By Brendan Gill, in a preface to an interview with E. B. White in *The Paris Review*. His remarks would later be repeated in his 1975 book, *Here at the New Yorker*.

image so threatened by the possibility, that she cannot help thinking first of herself.

Katharine's fears, meanwhile, were not being allayed by her doctors. As her symptoms persisted, so did their uncertainty about the cause. She waited and underwent a wearying round of tests.

After a month of dizziness and alarm, neither of which was relieved by her doctors' frightening speculations about brain tumors and neurological disorders, in February she entered Harkness for neurological tests and a spinal tap. By April a diagnosis had still not been made, and she was sent to the hospital for another week. Further neurological tests then revealed that there was no tumor. But shortly after leaving the hospital she began to suffer such severe headaches that she was forced to take to her bed. On May 16 she wrote to Elizabeth Lawrence:

> Now I spend most of my time in bed, trying to get up three times a day for an hour. I am at my desk now, feeling less bad because of some new caffeine pills they are trying for my headaches, but in a few minutes I shall have to retreat to bed and continue this in pencil while lying down.
>
> . . . We have a good local doctor and he keeps in touch with the two in New York who are watching over me, but all three of them are puzzled and they still don't know whether my headaches and nausea come from the small focal point of irritation on the coating of my brain or from an injury to my spinal cord when I had the spinal tap in February . . . more and more it seems as if it were the other, or so the local doctor thinks. *I* think it's my spine, as this now hurts a great deal. I have been told to wait it out for another four or six weeks if I can, and I certainly want to. The last thing in the world I want to do is to go back into a New York hospital.

Seven months had elapsed by the time Katharine began to feel better. Throughout the spring and early summer she seemed to be getting worse, and her doctors were then theorizing that she had a benign tumor. By July 1 she felt much better, and on the 4th she felt well enough to drive into Blue Hill "to watch the town's funny annual shindig and homecoming day for one hour." But two days later, "writhing in pain,"* she was taken to the hospital for an emergency appendectomy. The appendix was gangrenous and was removed just before it perforated. "After fifteen really horrible days," she was able to leave the hospital and return home.

In this trying year, it seemed particularly cruel that so many of the things

---

*"Which had nothing to do with my head," she added.

that gave Katharine pleasure, and which would have helped distract her, or at least given her solace, were denied her. "The real trouble," she wrote Elizabeth Lawrence, "is I can do no gardening yet (even flowers, if low, must be picked for me) and I have to breakfast in bed and sleep half the afternoon, so Henry's [Henry Allen, the Whites' handyman] and my hours seldom coincide. His are 7 to 3:30. I've been living only half a life." Even the view from her window had diminished in beauty when Andy sold "our beautiful Herefords." "How sad to have no cows in the landscape and no manure for the garden and compost heap," she wrote to Elizabeth Lawrence. "Oh, dear, we are crumbling badly! But just writing you gives me hope and I am determined that I shall get back to normal again. We really feel encouraged."

Katharine recovered well from the appendectomy and there were even periods when she suffered less from the headaches and dizziness. Then, in early August, she "had another bad neurological attack involving [her] arm," and her doctors arranged for her to have what would be her third series of neurological tests. Finally, in September, she was given an angiogram, an x-ray of the arteries, which revealed a blocked carotid artery.

Considering the wealth of information that can be got from an angiogram —the detection of abnormalities in the organs and blood vessels; displaced blood vessels caused by injury, tumors, or disease; blood clots; internal bleeding—it is curious that Katharine White's doctors had not earlier thought to give her one. At the age of sixty-eight, at a time when she had made a critical transition in her life, she had been subjected to eight months of uncertainty, fear, and immobilizing symptoms. And then, having prepared herself for a brain tumor, she was informed that she had something altogether different, and told to go to Rochester for an operation.

The correct diagnosis had not dispelled her fears about her mind's being affected. The blockage in the artery prevented blood from reaching the brain, and there was a possibility that she had suffered brain damage. Her doctors' speculations that she had not were small comfort to Katharine. A letter she wrote to Elizabeth Lawrence shortly before her surgery was to take place reveals her uneasiness. She was to be operated on, she wrote, by a British surgeon "who has done more such operations on people who have not suffered brain damage. I am not supposed to have, but the fear is I will unless this is done." Another letter to the same friend, written a couple of weeks after the operation, again mentioned brain damage—she had "supposedly" not suffered any.

The days preceding the operation were harrowing. Shortly after an arteriogram, while staying in a hotel in New York, Katharine suffered a seizure of several hours' duration. Andy wrote to Katharine's doctor in Blue Hill that "the slightest excitement seems to bring on an attack." From New York, the Whites, accompanied by Nancy Stableford, went to Rochester, where Katharine was operated on in early October.

The operation was a success, though it was not without the high drama that increasingly became characteristic of Katharine's illnesses. After the surgery she "went into shock and almost died in the recovery room. . . . I was there for hours with a very low blood pressure but a transfusion brought me back," she wrote Elizabeth Lawrence. Then, in exquisite detail, she described "the sordid details" of the surgery itself, how Dr. Rob had "slit me from ear to chin, opened up the carotid and removed the fatty block which was as big as a raisin, and closed it up again without ever clamping off the artery, all in a matter of minutes." Aside from feeling "quite weird" and looking, with her swollen throat, "like a pelican," she was suffering from post-operative headaches, which the doctor thought would leave her soon.

The psychological effects of the last ten months would not leave her. The incessant worrying and waiting; the physical suffering and enforced rest; the shuttling from doctor to doctor; the hospitalizations and tests—all had taken their toll. Furthermore, the experience had confirmed and nourished her preoccupation with her health, thrusting her more deeply into it.

Hypochondriacs are widely regarded as people who suffer from imaginary illnesses. But as long ago as 1928 a British psychiatrist, R. D. Gillespie, proposed that the preoccupation was not only with imagined ills but with actual "physical or mental disorder[s]" as well.

What distinguishes the hypochondriac from anyone who is normally anxious about his health is that he is, in the words of Robert Meister, "*preoccupied* excessively; he is not merely interested in his condition, but interested with conviction, which makes him immune to all influences that are contrary to it."*

One can therefore be both physically sick and hypochondriacal. But a distinction is to be made between pure, or primary hypochondria, which exists independent of other illnesses, and secondary hypochondria, a direct result of mental or physical illness. Katharine White was probably right when she said that none of her doctors would say she had ever suffered from imaginary ills. Even the people who considered her a hypochondriac acknowledged that she had suffered from a number of serious illnesses. Her hypochondria was certainly the result not only of real ill health but of a number of complex influences.

One influence was questionable judgment on her doctors' part. It is

*From *Hypochondria: Toward a Better Understanding* (1980). The book is based on the medical records of more than 400 hypochondriacs and interviews with 300 of them; interviews with 175 physicians, 63 psychologists, and other professionals; and additional sources.

impossible to calculate precisely how much damage Katharine White's doctors did her, physically and psychologically, but at the very least, their misdiagnosis of her blocked carotid artery, and their imprudent speculations about brain tumors during this critical first year of her retirement—this year when any experience must have been magnified—seem to have aggravated her health problems, and fueled her hypochondria.

Robert Meister discusses the damaging effect physicians sometimes have on their patients, particularly those in whom there exists "an already established hypochondriacal conviction." Such patients, by being referred to too many physicians and specialists, can become hypochondriacs.

> [Oscar] Bumke noted that psychiatrists almost daily see patients who owe their hypochondriacal complaints to incautious remarks by a physician. In an apprehensive patient, thoughtless remarks such as "Your arteries are getting clogged," or "Your heart is a bit enlarged," often have devastating results. Such patients may be seriously damaged over a considerable period of years by an otherwise able physician.

When Katharine White's illness was misdiagnosed, her doctors may also have damaged her by prescribing the wrong medication (other than caffeine pills, she does not mention what she was taking)—and not only in 1961. Throughout her adult life, Katharine was in the habit of mixing medications, taking a new medicine in combination with an old. Nancy Stableford observed that her mother's doctors apparently never seemed to question her about what she was taking, or caution her against this dangerous practice. And Katharine had long taken "lots" of milk of magnesia and several antacid tablets after every meal. Her diet was rich, her lifestyle increasingly sedentary. Without knowing precisely what medications Katharine was taking and in what combinations, it is, of course, impossible to determine the physical and emotional effects of all this. But they may have been considerable.

Katharine's marriage also fueled her preoccupation with her health. Nancy Stableford would say of her mother, "When Andy came into her life, he was already a pretty good hypochondriac, and she quickly caught it." Several family members confirmed the impression of another relative, who said, "You'd never find both of them sick at the same time. If one was down, the other was up." There were, of course, times when both Whites were down, but there is some truth in the impression that their ailments cooperated in seesaw fashion. Deeply caring for each other, they were each able at times to transcend their illnesses, both physically and psychologically, in order to attend to the other. But as Roger Angell has pointed out, the Whites also engaged in an unconscious contest as to which of them was the more ill. The marriage was thus "a sado-masochistic tangle."

In a way, Katharine *did* catch hypochondria from her husband. As a result of living with Andy and his absorption in his health, her own physical ailments had become magnified. Preoccupied with his health, she had become increasingly preoccupied with her own. Sharing his ill health unconsciously served several purposes. To begin with, it helped her marriage. Her husband's devotion to her was unquestionable, but he was also devoted to his symptoms, and this mentally took him away from her. By sharing his anxieties, she could remain emotionally close to him, participate more fully in his life. (Arguably, she could remain physically close to him as well: one remembers White's aborted "year off" in 1937. Had Katharine been an unsympathetic wife, the outcome might have been very different.) Andy needed her in a way that Ernest had not, and she needed to be needed. Andy also respected her defenses, the tears that she would not discuss when she awoke in the morning crying over something she'd been thinking about, or dreaming. Andy helped her remain psychologically strong. Recognizing that he would never be too well "nervously," she had to remain strong for him. She mothered him, and he in turn took care of her, made her feel secure in a way that Ernest never had.

The marriage backfired for Katharine in that it was too insulated, ultimately severing her from the work she needed and the friends she loved. The Whites' absorption in their health was socially alienating, and increasingly, in the years to come, prospective visitors would be discouraged from visiting them in Maine. As Roger Angell observed, Katharine and Andy White had created an exclusive world of two inhabitants who spoke their own special language—the language of illness. It was a world that left other people on the outside.

However her marriage and illnesses may have stimulated Katharine's hypochondria, a predilection in her own psyche allowed it to happen. It is tempting to speculate about the jobs Katharine held before she came to *The New Yorker,* easy to interpret her work with occupational diseases, her survey of the crippled and handicapped of Cleveland, and her job as a factory inspector, as evolving from an excessive interest in health. But this in fact was not the work to which Katharine was most drawn; it was the work— the interesting work—available to her at the time. And two of the jobs had evolved from the first. If a purpose was unconsciously served by these jobs, it may have been Katharine's mothering impulse: ministering to the sick, even in the remote capacity of an interviewer or inspector, was a way of satisfying that need—though not to the extent that being an editor, and the wife of E. B. White, was. And certainly Katharine's exposure to these health problems would have made her more conscious of her own.

One catches glimpses of the elderly, health-absorbed Katharine White in those provocative early writings, "Living on the Ragged Edge" and "Home and Office." The latter touches only lightly on the subject of health; it is particularly noteworthy in its glimpse of the young Katharine Angell, who felt under pressure to do everything well: "And for most women, very much so for me, there is the problem of health, of how to achieve so busy a life without becoming overtired or ill, or so submerged that existence loses its finest qualities." In the former piece, illness is offered, however legitimately, as a partial excuse for the Angells' financial burdens. Particularly striking is the anonymous author's defensive comment about not spending money needlessly on herself—even when ill. "In the two years we have had two definite pieces of ill luck—illnesses. The first winter in town I had what just missed being a real breakdown. For the next year I devoted myself to the dull business of getting well. I did get well without the expense of trips to the south or any very heavy doctors' bills, but I could not earn during that time." (Nothing more is known about her illness.) She then mentions the costly serious illness that Nancy had (a mastoid operation), after mentioning her own illness first. This early writing just faintly foreshadows the self-centered passages in her letters that would dominate her correspondence in later years, when her own health (followed closely by Andy's) had to be described before she could turn her attention to someone else, or to other subjects.

One senses a compulsion in Katharine White to make clear that she has indeed been ill, that she has an excuse for not answering a letter promptly, or, as in the case presented in "Ragged Edge," for not earning money. What is significant, of course, is that she felt she needed an excuse. Illness and money, the connecting, in Katharine's mind, of one with the other, marked the letters of Katharine's old age. Herein lay the conflict: illness provided a socially acceptable reason for not earning money, and yet earning money was vitally important to Katharine's self-esteem.

Essentially, hypochondria is a matter of self-esteem. Psychiatrists see it as a way of protecting self-esteem by avoiding personal or professional evaluation. Lacking self-confidence, hypochondriacs are much more reliant than others on the outside world for their sense of self-worth. Sickness becomes a way of attracting attention to oneself as someone who needs help.

Katharine White's preoccupation with her own health was a white flag, a way of drawing attention to herself as someone who was vulnerable. She wanted people to see the velvet hand in the iron glove. The long paragraphs in Katharine's letters devoted to her health, the constant reminders to her correspondents that she was not well—this was a way of keeping in touch with people, "the only friends I have left," the kind of contact Katharine sorely needed. It was also the route by which her mind sought relief from what troubled her. But, like the prescription drugs she took, which gave her only temporary relief, the response she got from others offered her only a brief distraction from herself.

Katharine White's illnesses possibly served an even deeper need: the need to suffer in order to atone for her biggest mistakes. Roger Angell considered his mother guilt-ridden about her Angell children, about having, in a way, abandoned them when she gave Ernest custody and married Andy. Illness allowed Katharine to make a statement to her children: that yes, she was guilty, but she was also sick, and you cannot be too hard on a person who is sick. "Her worrying," said Roger Angell, "was a way of proving to herself that she really loved these people; worrying justified that. Of course she *did* genuinely love them."

For Katharine, the suffering was not relieved by confiding in someone, because she never really confided. She appears never to have bared her heart or told all to anyone. The letters she wrote to Elizabeth Lawrence are noteworthy not only because of their relative frankness but because Katharine had never met Miss Lawrence—a fact that probably made it easier for Katharine to write to her unchecked. Mary McCarthy was in Paris; Elizabeth, in North Carolina, was also at a distance. She was not in contact with Katharine's other friends. It was safe to write to her. Like the letter to Mary McCarthy, the letters to Elizabeth Lawrence were as messages in bottles.

Katharine needed people, and being cut off from them, especially following her retirement as a *New Yorker* editor, deprived her of a necessary sense of community or kinship; paradoxically, by holding back from others the inmost part of herself, she deprived herself of comfort. It was hard for Katharine to lean on another person: she was the editor, the nurturer.

Katharine was, essentially, an editor, and she remained an editor after her retirement, illness providing her with another focus for her talents. In a way, Katharine's preoccupation with her ill health was her literary self refocused. As an editor (and sometimes writer), she was fascinated with the description of things. Her descriptions of her surgeries (Dr. Rob "slit me from ear to chin"), the exhaustively detailed accounts of her health and her altered appearance, were not only a way of remaining in control of what was happening to her but another way of expressing herself creatively.

Katharine White was not a hypochondriac in the classic sense. There is no evidence that she fancied herself ill when well; her diseases were not tailored to fit her symptoms. But she was hypochondriacal in that a part of her thrived on being ill, and on getting attention. Illness had a place in her life. She made room for it, accommodated, if not invited, it.

What finally matters, as Katharine wisely realized of her husband, is the suffering; whether organic or psychological in origin, suffering is suffering.

"The whole illness may be nervous tension, as Andy is the first to admit," Katharine would write to Elizabeth Lawrence (1963). "For years he's had a pyloric valve that closes up the exit to his stomach when under nervous stress and strain, and he and everyone knows it may all be nerves. But this has made him no less ill, and one of course has to be *sure.*" She too had to be sure, sure about her own health.

Though she had suffered serious illnesses and been hypochondriacal before retiring, it was only after Katharine left *The New Yorker* that her health collapsed. Almost overnight she was transformed from a vigorous sixty-eight-year-old into an old woman. Her illness, of course, was real, but one wonders whether she might have been able to stall it a while, or prevent its overtaking her, if she had retired a year later. Scientists are still learning about the relationship between the human mind and body. Until recently, only a limited number of illnesses were considered psychosomatic; now virtually everything "from the common cold to cancer and heart disease" is thought to be influenced by the mind.

Katharine White's work as an editor and the habit of working had helped keep her on an even keel emotionally. For Katharine, work was not only a passion but therapy. She was made happy, and fulfilled, through work. Retirement quickly made her feel useless and restless. Leaving her job, she was suddenly forced to confront her failings. Her absorbing work had helped her avoid doing that before.

Katharine White's was a deeply private nature, her life, essentially creative. Much of her time was spent alone in a room—reading, writing, and editing. Her personality is perhaps finally understood in this context: as one who needed this kind of solitary activity, and consequently more replenishment than the ordinary person needs from the world outside. That time spent alone prohibits us from knowing certain things about Katharine White's inner life. Some things she did not communicate.

Katharine was recuperating from her surgery in Rochester when James Thurber died on November 2. He had been ill for a long time, suffering from arteriosclerosis and a large hematoma on the brain, undiagnosed and untreated until a month earlier, when he suffered a massive brain hemorrhage and collapsed. After being operated on in Doctors Hospital in New York, he had lingered for some weeks in a state of half-consciousness and partial paralysis. Then pneumonia set in, a blood clot on one of his lungs was discovered, and he fell into a coma before finally dying.

We can imagine Katharine's conflicting feelings upon hearing of her old friend's death. Jim was associated not only with her first years at *The New Yorker,* but with the time she fell in love with Andy. "Jim could be so wonderful and also such a wonderful friend, as he was to me in the 1920's when I had been struggling for seven years over a bad marriage, that I feel horrible to write down these things about his book," she would write, after attacking *The Years with Ross*. "I also admire him for his spirit as a man going blind, and as a blind man. He was the least *blind* blind man I ever knew, and the most independent. He should be given great tribute for that. I think he will live forever in American letters both as a writer and an artist." But they had seen little of each other in recent years, and their last encounters had been decidedly cool.

E. B. White may have reflected both his and Katharine's feelings about Thurber in the obituary he wrote for *The New Yorker* with William Shawn (Shawn wrote the first half, White the second). The few paragraphs White wrote are pure White: generous, touching, and sure; graced with the perfect and perfectly enchanting metaphors: "he wrote the way a child skips rope, the way a mouse waltzes." Regarding Thurber's book *The Last Flower*, White's favorite, he said, "of all the flowers, real and figurative, that will find their way to Thurber's last resting place, the one that will remain fresh and wiltproof is the little flower he himself drew, on the last page of that lovely book." But one also notices a trace of anger in the piece, a consciousness of what the once gentle and wildly funny man had become. Quoting a remark from a recent Thurber letter in which he compared his own writing to the work a surgeon does, White dwelt briefly on Thurber's anger at someone's remarking that humor was a shield rather than a sword— "it made him mad. He wasn't going to have anyone beating his sword into a shield." It is in his opening sentence that White probably came closest to capturing his wife's feelings: "I am one of the lucky ones; I knew him before blindness hit him, before fame hit him." Fame, and Thurber's appetite for it, had hit him hard, nearly ruining him and destroying his character. White was alert to the dangers of fame, and had himself managed to dodge them—this was the crucial difference between him and Thurber. *Hit* is a telling verb in another sense, as well. Katharine might have added, "Before Thurber hit me." Her affectionate memories of Thurber notwithstanding, Katharine was and would remain conscious of the smarting verbal blows she had received from her late friend.

But now was not the time to dwell on such things—not on Thurber, nor on this strange half-life she had been living. Her surgery was pronounced a success. Now was the time to concentrate against pain and on getting well, on getting back to her garden writing and the many things she had not had time for before retiring.

9

The Garden

I T WAS, PERHAPS, the finality of Katharine's retirement as much as the terror of her undiagnosed illness that had stirred her awareness of her own mortality: leaving her full-time editorial job had marked the beginning of her feelings of uselessness, and her uncomfortable new dependency on Andy. One senses that to her the "strokes" signaled the beginning of the end of her life—the end of the only kind of life that mattered to her. We find her making wistful remarks to friends about how she had looked forward to having more time to write her garden pieces, how she had hoped to put together a book of them, as if she will never again be able to work. Now she begins to compose the record that her lawyer and friend Milton Greenstein called her "Victorian Will," a catalogue of her and Andy's possessions, which not only bequeathed "every stick of furniture and inkwell in the house," but told the history of each piece.

It is a revealing document, funny, anecdotal, characteristic of its meticulous, generous author. Katharine White's love of tradition and family come alive here, at this time when she must have felt herself clinging to the familiar for her very life. One imagines her sitting at the antique cherry desk in her study, or under the canopy of her four-poster mahogany bed late at night, mentally traveling the rooms of her house, traveling back in time. The china duck bowl, "said to be unusual and of value but I have forgotten what kind of china it is," would go to her granddaughter, Alice Angell. It "always stood on the mantlepiece [sic] in Uncle George's room in Northampton." The horsehair trunk "belonged to the Barrows side. I don't know who the A.D. is whose initials are on it and it is full of antique smelly garments. We used to dress up in these when I was a little girl, at which time the trunk was in the attic of the Brookline house." The "old print of the Public Garden in Boston" recalled less happy memories. It "was given to me by James Thurber after he had been particularly insulting when intoxicated one night. He thought it showed where I used to go to recess from Miss Winsor's School and it almost did, except it shows the corner of Charles and Beacon instead of Arlington and Beacon. Evelyn."* "The clock that doesn't run was in this house [when the Whites moved in]. It is an antique but no good and ugly and I don't know why I've left it there. [No bequest.]"

She must be fair distributing all this, of course, and she must be practical. The things inherited from Andy's side of the family and those that belonged to both her and Andy should naturally go to Joe. And it made sense that, in addition, Joe should have the things that complemented or came with the house, like the "blue and white mug in the corner cupboard"—these were Maine things and Joe was a Maine man, having permanently settled in Brooklin with his family in 1962. Most of the *New Yorker* artifacts should of course go to Roger: the bound copies of the magazine dating from the 1920s, most of the framed *New Yorker* covers, and the artist Helen Hokinson's ceramic Thurber Man and Woman, which Hokinson had given Katharine. The highboy in her office should go to Nancy, "as she has no John Sergeant red cherry furniture; Joe and Roger each have one John Sergeant apiece." A portrait of John Shepley to Joe's youngest son, John Shepley White, "for obvious reasons"; likewise a silhouette of Nancy Perley, "for whom [Nancy] was named, at least she was so named in my mind, if not in her father's," should go to Nancy. "Two mahogany arm chairs in heavy Empire style" would be left "to Roger, as they go with the table" he was to have too. Her own "child's Windsor arm chair painted black" should belong to her granddaughter, "Martha [White], who has used it most." But had she been unfair to someone? she would wonder, waking up in the middle of the night. And she would set about making changes.

The silver cigarette box given her by Nancy and Roger should go to Louis Stableford. Did he still smoke? Well, "for Louis if he still smokes. If not, for anyone who does." Would Roger know how to correctly stand the mahogany card table that was to be his? "It looks best if set with the single leg folded in and the leaf up against the wall." The "gold mirror between the windows" was to be Kitty Stableford's. It was a "Shepley piece given me by Aunt Poo. . . . This is gilded in real gold leaf and can be brightened when necessary by the same process. Never use a gold paint." She would remember to warn Joe about gold paint too: he was to have the smaller mirror decorated with gold leaf. "The Encyclopedia Britannica was a wedding present to us from Mr. and Mrs. White. It should go to Joe eventually if he wants it. It is as good as ever except on science and history and modern biography."

*Roger's first wife, Evelyn Angell, had also attended Miss Winsor's.

As always, Andy's comfort was not far from Katharine's thoughts. If she should die before he did, her bequests were to remain in the house until he no longer had any use for them.

It was the writing of garden essays that Katharine was chiefly concerned with following her retirement. That she had been able to produce a piece for the March 11, 1961, issue of the magazine, when she was suffering from her undiagnosed "strokes," was a tribute to her psychological strength and her determination. (Part of it was written from her hospital bed at Harkness.) The 8,100-word essay, titled "Green Thoughts in a Green Shade," ("Onward and Upward in the Garden") ranges, characteristically, over a variety of topics—from water lilies and roses to flower painting and English gardens, with digressions on Jane Austen, Elizabeth Lawrence, Katharine's Northampton aunts, and her latest garden-book reading sprinkled happily throughout. If not at her spirited best, she is nevertheless chatty and opinionated, amused and amusing in places (on gladiolus: "I can *not* be glad about glads"). And the essay contains one of the most eloquent passages in all of her writing.

> The lake was Chocorua, and picking water lilies was not an unusual event for my next-older sister and me. We spent the best summers of our girlhood on, or in, this lake, and we picked the lilies in the early morning, paddling to the head of the lake, where the water was calm at the foot of the mountain and the sun had just begun to open the white stars of the lilies. The stern paddle had to know precisely how to approach a lily, stem first, getting near enough so the girl in the bow could plunge her arm straight down into the cool water and break off the rubbery stem, at least a foot under the surface, without leaning too far overboard. It took judgment to select the three or four freshest flowers and the shapeliest lily pad to go with them, and it took skill not to upset the canoe. Once the dripping blossoms were gathered and placed in the shade of the bow seat, we paddled home while their heavenly fragrance mounted all around us. I know now that their lovely Latin name was *Nymphaea odorata,* but at the time I knew only that they were the common pond lily of northeast America.

The writing of garden essays—any kind of writing except letter writing —was for Katharine "an agonizing ordeal." As her husband observed, she edited as she wrote, and was incapable of relaxing enough to allow a first draft of even a paragraph to emerge before she began revising. The struggle was not relieved by careful reading and thorough preparation before she sat down to write, and it intensified along with her infirmities.

The Garden

Katharine hoped that the new year would find her "less of a burden" to Andy than she had been the previous year. "The thing that matters," she wrote John Updike in January of 1962, "is that Andy gets back to writing." Still, she herself was "not yet able to write anything worth reading." In February she wrote the poet Elizabeth Bishop that she was still feeling unwell from her surgery the previous October—"the after effects of having an artery slit open in the throat are fairly brutal." And in February, still trying to write a garden piece, she was beset by a severe cough. There was also septic-tank trouble in the Maine house. And Katharine worried about the orbiting astronaut, John Glenn. "Apparently I worried more about him than his mother did," she wrote to a friend. "How simple life would be if one could have that sort of faith in God!"

(Though not a religious woman, Katharine confessed to praying "in my queer way," prayer of a sort that "wouldn't be called official in any church." By her husband's definition, she was spiritual without being a churchgoer. Katharine was frankly uncomfortable with religious zealots and the newly converted, whom she seems to have equated with the former. She loathed the term "Catholic writer," and once refused to indulge a zealous writer who had returned to the Catholic Church and wanted to be so labeled. In 1950, after hearing a rumor that Mary McCarthy had become a Catholic, and then hearing from Mary herself that it wasn't true, Katharine had written her in relief: "I felt certain from the start that you had not joined the Catholic Church and told everyone so. . . . These are frightening times and the growth of rumors nowadays is one of the most frightening aspects of it." Later, when Nancy Stableford announced her intention of being baptized and confirmed in the Episcopal Church, Katharine replied that that was all right as long as Nancy didn't try to convert *her*.)

Despite the discouraged tone of Katharine's letters, another garden piece appeared in the June 9th issue. Titled "For the Recreation & Delight of the Inhabitants," it was, like the essay of the previous year, an informative, rambling reverie, this time on lawns and lawn mowers; garden books and Jane Austen (never far from Katharine's thoughts); blueberries, bamboo, bonsai trees, marigolds, and goldenrod—the last prompting another of her most charming passages. She was again taken back in memory to Lake Chocorua and to one memorable, Tennyson summer.

> On that bright New Hampshire mountain day so long ago, a parade of decorated canoes and rowboats was the first event in an afternoon of water sports, and, like every other family on the lake, we wanted to be in the parade. My sisters and I began the day by gathering bucketfuls of goldenrod, which my aunt spent the morning stitching onto a sheet in an intricate pattern—no

stems or leaves showing, only the plumy golden blooms. Geoffrey Taylor points out that although Tennyson's Queen had little interest in flowers, her Poet Laureate was the most garden-conscious of all the Victorian poets. Perhaps this was why he was so much read by my nineteenth-century garden-loving elders and why it was entirely natural for the family to decide to make our canoe represent the death barge that carried "Elaine the fair, Elaine the loveable, / Elaine, the lily maid of Astolat" down the river to Camelot, bearing in her white hand her last message to Lancelot, who, to his shame, at the moment loved only "the wild Queen" Guinevere. So while Aunt Caroline sewed, the rest of us were busy all morning draping our green Morris canoe in black and devising costumes for Elaine and the dumb oarsman. I, only because I was the smallest and weighed the least and had the fairest hair, was to be Elaine, dressed in white cheesecloth, and my father, cloaked in black, the spellbound oarsman. (I remember swathing a peaked Mexican straw hat with my big black silk middy-blouse tie, to make a suitably lugubrious covering for his bald head.) We had taken a heavy wooden bathhouse door off its hinges and laid it on top of the gunwales of the canoe, leaving open only the stern seat. So, after my sisters had covered my summer-tanned face and arms with a heavy coating of white talcum powder, to achieve the pallor of a defunct lily maid, I was gingerly laid out on the door and my long hair, which I usually wore in pigtails, was spread out under my shoulders. My arms were crossed on my breast, the letter to Sir Lancelot was placed in my right hand, and the goldenrod cloth of gold was drawn up over me and my bath-house-door pallet. Then it became my father's terrible task to seat himself in the stern and paddle this top-heavy, teetery craft and his youngest daughter a mile or more, from the head of the big lake, where we lived, through the narrows to the small lake, where the regatta was assembling. The sun beat down upon us, and my powdered face and nose grew redder and redder. My father couldn't stand the weight and heat of his hat, so he laid it at my feet. A light breeze sprang up, and the overladen canoe became even harder to handle. His usually cheerful round face was soon as "haggard" as the oarsman's of the poem, and he constantly cautioned me not to move a muscle. I didn't; I was scared stiff. As we drew in sight of the judges' float, my father resumed his peaked hat, and I, closing my eyes, put on what I hoped was a demurely lovelorn expression. Then we circled endlessly in the parade. At one point, the oarsman removed the letter from my tanned fingers (all the powder by now had melted away), paddled up to the float, and handed it to one of the judges, who read it aloud to his colleagues, just as King Arthur read out Elaine's message to his assembled knights:

The Garden

"Most noble lord, Sir Lancelot of the Lake,
I, sometime call'd the maid of Astolat,
Come, for you left me taking no farewell,
Hither, to take my last farewell of you.
I loved you, and my love had no return,
And therefore my true love has been my death."

Without this message, I fear we would not have been recognized and would not have won first prize. For years, I kept it—a framed photograph of Mount Chocorua with the lake at its foot—knowing all along that it was my aunt's lovingly sewn goldenrod cloth of gold that had won it for us.

On June 5 (1962), four days before the essay appeared in *The New Yorker,* Katharine wrote a slightly agitated letter to Elizabeth Lawrence about what she thought was wrong with the piece, as though forewarning her friend that the essay she would soon read was not good. The letter reads like an apology, Katharine alternately criticizing her own writing and offering excuses for not doing better—illness, as usual, being emphasized. Because of the illnesses of the previous year, she writes, she has "a whole year's work to catch up on." She *is* feeling better: "instead of being an invalid with breakfast in bed and a whole afternoon of sleep, I'm now back to being up and around all the time, though I still can't write well or easily or really bear down on desk work." Her deadline had been moved up a month, preventing her from getting much gardening information into the piece. And the Whites were "in a state of turmoil domestically." Their cook of eleven years had died, and the boy who mowed their lawn had gone into the Navy.

Katharine had originally hoped to review the spring gardening catalogues in her essay, but it was too late for that, "so what it mostly turned out to be was the usual New Yorker memory piece stuff, which I had not intended." It is, of course, the "memory piece stuff" that comprises many of the most affective, graceful, and lyrical passages in Katharine White's gardening essays. Katharine's reaction to the personal passages in her work suggests not only that she was blind to the strongest virtues in her own writing, but that she was uncomfortable about communicating some of her tenderest feelings, even in this gentle vein. She continued defensively to Elizabeth Lawrence that it had been "a dreadful effort to get anything down on paper and I persisted, perhaps, only to prove to myself that I could. I am ever so much better than I was, but still have my bad days and my strength does not last very long—either at my desk or in the garden."

The letter purports to be concerned with Katharine's anxieties about a book she had briefly reviewed in the essay. The book was written by an old friend with whom Katharine had lately corresponded. The friend, who had become blind, sent her a review copy of her new book, and though Katharine had not thought much of it, she felt obliged to mention it in this latest gardening piece.

Katharine's review comprises only a short part of the long essay. With qualifications, the review is favorable. Though Katharine clearly finds the book wanting in several respects, she seems to be struggling to like it and be able to recommend it.

In reviewing her friend's book, Katharine had meant to be kind, but the price of kindness was dear. It pained her to have to review a friend's book less than enthusiastically. And she resented the claim of friendship, the claim of a blind friend upon her sympathy, which had caused her to sacrifice her own integrity as a reviewer. "Friendship, blindness, can't enter into honesty in reviews," she wrote Elizabeth Lawrence. She thought perhaps she oughtn't to have mentioned the book at all. The book had also, she felt, reflected badly on her own credibility. What really made her "mad" was her "poor" friend's having acknowledged her in the book (as a result of some errors Katharine had pointed out to her after receiving some of the proofs). Though Katharine had told her she should check some of her facts, "she didn't, quite, and now I'm pinned with the responsibility for that inaccurate and weak chapter." And that particular chapter was about the great English gardener Gertrude Jekyll, whom Katharine's friend hated and Katharine didn't, causing her further embarrassment. Two years after the incident, Katharine wrote to Elizabeth: "I still burn at [my friend's] inaccurate little diatribe, though I have to forgive her because she is blind."

Katharine White's language is startling. Her attitude toward her blind friend, and her compunction about having publicly tempered her opinion of the friend's book, are surprisingly uncharitable. But, in her letters to Elizabeth Lawrence, one is struck by Katharine's frequent use of the word "horror"—though she often used the word indiscriminately. Reviewing the book "with less than great enthusiasm" was a "horror," the horror compounded by the friend's blindness; "I did have the horrors," Katharine wrote —all in the same letter to Elizabeth Lawrence. Given Katharine's integrity, and her compassionate regard for the feelings of others, her horror is natural. Blindness, too, would have been a horror to her. It would not only have meant losing the ability to read, as well as the other visual pleasures, but— most profoundly troubling to a woman of Katharine's temperament—nearly total dependency on Andy and others. Her preoccupation with her friend's book appears to have been a way of shifting her fear of old age and her worries about her own declining powers, including her literary powers, to her friend. It is only after devoting nearly a full typed page to a discussion of her friend's book that Katharine is able to speak directly to Elizabeth Lawrence about what she views as the weaknesses in her own writing.

Despite Katharine's worries about the latest garden piece, it was well received by her friends. The complimentary letters that followed the essay's publication were a salve to Katharine's wounded confidence. Even William Shawn's acceptance of the piece had been "the greatest comfort" to her.

On the day the essay appeared in *The New Yorker,* Marianne Moore dispatched a characteristic panegyric from her home at Cumberland Terrace: "The *lawn* lures me from captivity—from letters extorted!* *How* compress such worlds of romance into *one* essay!" She wished Mrs. White would collect the pieces, publishing them as *Onward and Upward,* Volume 1. Raoul Fleischmann wrote that he was "delighted" by the essay. "If I didn't think so highly of you and have great respect for you, [an] old phrase comes to my mind: 'Well, there's life in the old girl yet.' "

Marianne Moore's letter revived an old hope: that the garden pieces would make a worthwhile book. Katharine in turn confided that Alfred Knopf had long been encouraging her to do just that, but she was afraid she was no longer up to the task. It would mean putting together a whole new book, only borrowing in places from the garden pieces, and "rais[ing] the book out of the 'garden book' category into the general reading category." Katharine was beset by the usual doubts. "I'm afraid it is now beyond my capabilities, for every paragraph is a struggle and has to be done over and over." But Marianne's letter had taught her to think, perhaps for the first time, that the essays could be published in book form much as they stood, only brought up to date, and with the addition, Katharine thought, of "a first chapter setting the Maine scene." Katharine was anxious to know whether Marianne thought there would really be an interest in this kind of book. She thought she might be up to doing that much, still, "It is maddening to be so full of ideas and with so little remaining ability to bear down and work well and constantly. I've been less well since doing this article."

Katharine's hopes of producing another garden piece for late August or early September were extinguished when Andy became ill. Tests at the Blue Hill Hospital were apparently inconclusive, and the Whites removed to New York, where Andy underwent further tests. (In letters to Elizabeth Lawrence, Katharine wrote that Andy was suffering from a "chronic thing that is very troublesome," and that "part of his trouble is a deteriorating spine." The remark was a typical wild exaggeration of the Whites' common medical

---

*"For the Recreation & Delight of the Inhabitants" contains a long idyll about the tending of the lawn at 4 Hawthorn Road, and the games the Sergeant girls played there.

talk about themselves and each other.) Katharine assumed the task of answering Andy's mail, and took over most of the work on the proofs of his next book, *The Points of My Compass.* She was herself feeling poorly again, and following tests at the local hospital, her doctors told her that she was suffering from a mild form of diabetes. To Elizabeth Lawrence she wrote, "I begin to feel like Job, when I add this to a back put together with screws, a chronic urological problem requiring regular treatment, an artery block and the horrid results of having it removed." By early October she was ready to undergo more tests to see if the pains she was experiencing in her "unreliable head" were "due to the [spooky character] who now presides in the kitchen or to a new clogging of the defective circulation system." Her doctors were now saying that the diabetes "was probably a false alarm, or at least if I have it, it is very mild. Thanks to no sugar & a little starch I've lost an elegant eleven pounds, which is also good."

The year in which Katharine hoped to regain her health and her footing in life had been merely an adjunct to the disastrous first year of her retirement. "We are crumbling badly!" she had written in 1961. And the rural Maine surroundings sounded an answering chord: first the beloved Herefords had gone. Then, in 1962, a killing drought and Hurricane Daisy laid waste to the garden and water supply. Finally, after the Whites consulted a tree surgeon, "the two ancient Balm of Gilead trees which were the chief beauty of the home yard" were claimed by the ax. "One," sighed Katharine, "was the coon tree."

But the Whites had each other. For Katharine's seventieth birthday, her husband presented her with a copy of *The Points of My Compass,* with the following poem written on the flyleaf.

A COMPASS FOR KATHARINE

I turn to the East, I turn to the West,
I turn to the one that I love best,
You are my Cove, my leafy Bay,
My North, my South, my night, my day.
All signs suggest I'm growing older:
The heat-pad draped on the Poet's shoulder,
The slowed step, the girdled waist—
(Remember the years of fire and haste?)
The searching wind now finds the bone,
And there is still so much to be done!
What gets me up? What gets me dressed?
I wake to the one that I love best.

Katharine and E. B. White, around 1930.

*Katharine White walking
infant Joel and Daisy.*

The White farmhouse in North Brooklin, Maine, at about the time they bought it (early 1930s).

Katharine White and her children: Joel, Nancy, and Roger.

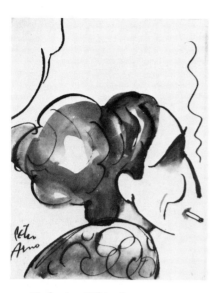

Katharine White by Peter Arno.   *Harold W. Ross.*

Katharine and E. B. White, early 1940s.

Katharine and E. B. White,
probably early 1940s.

Katharine and E. B. White.

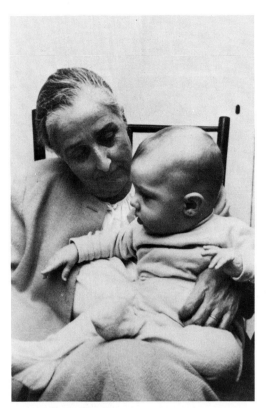

Katharine White with grandson Steven, early 1950s.

Katharine White and Aunt Crully.

Katharine White.

*Katharine White
at her desk at*
The New Yorker.

Katharine and E. B. White.

E. B. White with Joel.

Katharine and E. B. White.

The Garden

Katharine continued to follow *The New Yorker* closely, often reading stories and articles first in proof. During the summer of 1962 she was urging friends to read Rachel Carson's "remarkable" series on the chemical industry, "Silent Spring," which she "consider[ed] . . . the most important thing the New Yorker ha[d] published in years." To Rachel Carson, Katharine wrote, "[I]n all my years as a New Yorker editor I've never been prouder of anything we published than of 'Silent Spring.' "

Katharine's former writers continued to remember her with letters and copies of their latest books. Perhaps most gratifying was the surprise dedication to her and Andy of John Updike's new book of poetry, *Telephone Poles*. In September of 1963 Katharine wrote to Updike that it was "one of the few *pleasant* things that has happened to me in the past two and a half years and more." She had not only found the book "a great pleasure to read," but thought it *"good,* every bit of it." For months she had meant to write him about his new novel, *The Centaur,* which she considered his "best book and [which] contains some of your very best writing. The novel moved me almost constantly."

To Mary McCarthy, who had directed her publisher to send Katharine a copy of *The Group,* Katharine wrote with less enthusiasm. Though she had "galloped through it with fascinated attention," found it filled with "humor, wit, satire, and irony, and keen memory behind the documentary material," she disliked the book's explicit sex scenes (something she would come to deplore in John Updike's writing as well), which she thought "went over that thin line of taste 'between candor and shame.' "* And she found it "too much a social document and too little a novel about six or eight young women." As for the women themselves, "only one or two of them seemed to me really to come alive in the way most of your characters in other books and stories have." Though her criticism of the novel was heavily balanced with praise, Katharine typically suffered second thoughts about her candor, and was "greatly relieve[d]" when a sensitive note from Mary McCarthy arrived, assuring her that she was not angry, and that she loved her "for taking all these pains to tell me the truth."

Nineteen sixty-three dragged on in the now familiar way. In January, on the advice of Katharine's doctors, the Whites removed to Florida for the winter, both suffering from ill health. During the previous October Katharine learned that she had developed another artery block, this time in the left femoral artery (her thigh). She had thus far been well enough to avoid another arteriogram, and her doctors thought that the warmer climate would

*Still, she was happy for Mary that the book had become a best-seller. A later letter contains the following postscript: "It was certainly a pleasure to see 'The Group' displace 'The Shoes of the Fisherman' as Number 1."

improve her circulation, and possibly prevent a second operation. But she was not feeling much better. Katharine's "head swims and prevents her from doing another garden piece, which she dearly wants to do," Andy wrote his brother, Bun (Stanley Hart White), in February. And she had bursitis in her writing arm. Since she was also without secretarial help "or even an amanuensis," her letter writing to friends had to be severely curtailed. Nearly all her little writing energy was taken up with business and family letters, and Andy's mail. She seems to have assumed Andy's mail partly out of the guilty feeling that she was responsible for his illness, and because he appeared to be the more ill of the two of them. Andy was suffering from an ulcer, caused, Katharine was sure, by the strain of her illnesses of the past two years. Though she could not have helped being ill, she was willing to assume some of her husband's work, even at the sacrifice of her own work. She hoped that, by freeing Andy of letter-writing duties, she could clear a path for him back to his writing, which he had not been able to do for two years. She insisted that her own inability to write "doesn't matter, except to me."

"I sometimes think I would give everything I own for one garden piece, one book, and one restored lady," Andy wrote Roger Angell. Andy was convinced that Katharine's lack of progress during the winter was his fault. In January, before his ulcer was diagnosed, he had "developed a truly spectacular array of ailments and miseries extending all the way from gout to an ulcerated tooth. I lost my voice and I lost my nerve," he wrote Bun. ". . . I put [Katharine] over the jumps . . . with my total collapse, and she's now busy trying to recover from ME. No small assignment."

The Sarasota winter was chilly. The Whites' area was recovering from the worst freeze in its history. About them lay the ruins of once beautiful trees and plant life: the coconut and royal palms, the Australian pines, the great, stringy banyans—"their corpses are heartbreaking to look at," wrote Andy. The hibiscus and bougainvillaeas did not bloom; much of the remaining foliage was brown; and Katharine's footlocker full of garden literature lay untouched. "She hasn't quite given up," Andy wrote Roger, "but her spirit is badly cracked, and it is the saddest thing I have ever had to live with, to see her this way, after having done so much for so many, and now unable to do a small thing for herself." Warmer weather came at last, mocking them with a red tide. The beaches were awash with dead fish. It was in this melancholy landscape that Katharine and Andy took their first precarious steps toward recovery, he swimming in the bayou "within stroking distance of dolphins," she taking brief walks and cautious steps to and from the car that they drove to baseball games, her sole source of pleasure that season.

By the time the Whites arrived home in May, Katharine could report to

Elizabeth Lawrence that she had "fooled the vascular surgeon who thought I would need an operation on my blocked femoral artery this spring." Her faithful walking throughout the long exile in Florida had paid off and she now had "less pain walking and can walk further than last fall. However, the same thing is now starting in my right leg." The second week in July found the Whites in New York, where Katharine was undergoing tests to determine whether another operation for her arterial trouble was needed. Her doctors thought that surgery could be postponed at least until fall; then, in September, more tests indicated that surgery was not needed.

Life brightened a bit shortly before Andy's sixty-fourth birthday, in July, when he was awarded the Presidential Medal of Freedom. Andy was taking a bath when the news arrived by Western Union over the telephone. "The President was a bit long-winded," Andy recalled, "and after K had dutifully scribbled the first thirty or forty words on a scratch pad, she said to the girl, 'Is this a practical joke?' (There's a wife for you!) 'No,' said the girl a little stiffly, 'Western Union is not allowed to transmit practical jokes.' "

To Katharine's mind, the assassination of President John F. Kennedy on November 22 was one of two events that contributed to her continuing ill-health. Like many Americans, Katharine was captivated by Kennedy's youth and vigor, and found him a refreshing new political force.

The other depressing event was a family matter. After twenty years of marriage, Roger and Evelyn Angell had separated, and were now divorced. Added to the grief that Katharine naturally and empathically felt for her son were feelings of uselessness, of being unable to help him. Roger's annual summer visit to Maine with his daughters had been "extra hard this year as they are all displaced and unhappy," Katharine wrote John Updike. "The real trouble was me of course, for I am now in such poor health that I'm a hazard to all my family and to myself."

Most disheartening, and most debilitating to Katharine's spirits, she was still unable to write a garden piece. To John Updike she wrote that she could not write "anything worth reading—not even a letter, as you can see." She remained convinced that the artery surgery had not only affected her brain, "which doesn't work as well as it did," but also impaired her ability to do any sustained piece of writing, and to "write *well.* "

During the winter of 1963–64, Katharine was overtaken by the worst physical affliction yet. It began as "a mild skin outbreak" just after Christmas, shortly before the Whites departed from Maine for Florida, where they had rented a house for four months. Once installed in the Florida house with Andy and their domestics, Mr. and Mrs. Cook, Katharine became seriously ill. The skin outbreak had escalated into something wild and hideous. The

Whites flew immediately to New York, where Katharine spent the next two weeks at the Harkness Pavilion. Though her case was misdiagnosed, the skin trouble responded well to the drug she was given, prednisone, and she was released. She and Andy returned to Sarasota at the end of January. Four weeks later the eruption was again out of control and she returned to Harkness.

Katharine's case, which at first baffled the dermatologists, was eventually diagnosed as subcorneal pustular dermatosis ("a horrible name," Katharine thought), also known as Sneddon and Wilkinson disease: a rare disorder that had been defined only seven years earlier, in 1956, by Drs. Ian B. Sneddon and Darrell S. Wilkinson of Great Britain. Twenty-three years after its discovery only 150 cases would be reported worldwide. SPD is "chronic and recurrent," lasting for decades in some cases. It is most commonly found in women between the ages of forty and seventy. Its cause is unknown. Katharine White would have been wryly amused had she known that the disease not only resembles a disorder found in dogs, which, like SPD, also responds to the drug dapsone, but that (report Sneddon and Wilkinson) "examination of the skin of the groin of an Egyptian mummy of the 22nd dynasty (945–715 B.C.) revealed a picture reminiscent of subcorneal pustular dermatosis."

The disease, whose appearance Katharine likened to second-degree burns covering her body, is characterized by soft bubbles half-filled with pus. These pea-sized pustules form without warning, in a matter of hours. They appear either singly or in clusters, and tend to coalesce, sometimes shaping themselves into "bizarre" round or serpentine patterns, mainly in the areas of the groin, armpits, and abdomen, sometimes on the upper arms or upper legs. The pustules are easily ruptured upon contact; the eruptions mar the skin with round, scaly lesions.

Katharine spent most of the winter of 1964 in the hospital, remaining at Harkness for nearly nine weeks the second time, when the disease was correctly diagnosed. She could let nothing touch her skin—no garments, no bedclothes—and, in this uncomfortable and humiliating state, lay in a private room where the sheets were "supported and held away" from her body, visited only by doctors, nurses, and Andy, who stayed at the Algonquin. In most patients, SPD is controlled by sulfones or sulfapyridine. The sulfa Katharine White was given immediately produced a severe allergic reaction: she developed a high fever, "blistered all over," and shed her entire skin— "like a snake," observed Andy. The doctors again resorted to prednisone, a cortisone derivative, to suppress the disease, and the massive doses Katharine was given produced side effects that for her were worse than the disease itself:

her skin swelled, most of her molars fell out, and, most heartbreaking, she lost large chunks of her lovely hair and acquired hair "where it does not belong—a freak no less," she wrote Elizabeth Lawrence.

Still, ever-attentive to her writers (they would always be *her* writers), Katharine managed to keep informed about their lives, and even to send out an occasional dictated message. "From [her] bed of agony in Harkness" on March 11, she sent John Updike a congratulatory letter on his winning the National Book Award for *The Centaur.* Writing briefly about her latest affliction, she noted that Updike "looked handsome and without any [skin trouble] in [his] photograph in the Times." She was proud of her young protégé, and pleased to see his work thus recognized. She may also have been struck by the irony: *The Centaur*'s young author was himself afflicted with psoriasis.

Katharine's doctors gradually reduced the dosage of prednisone, but the disease returned as soon as she wore clothes. Back in Maine in the spring, she was forced to increase the dosage again, and dress only in loose cotton.

E. B. White later spoke of what "a humiliating (for a woman) and lonely time" Katharine's second, nine-week stay at Harkness was, when she had been unable to wear any clothes or be visited by friends and family. A male friend of the Whites who asks not to be identified recalled a related incident that underlines an essential feature of Katharine White's nature: that for her, vanity—and illness—were always subordinate to her more urgent need to be a fully functioning human being. Once, Katharine's disease confined her to a New York hotel room, and she called the friend, saying she had some business to discuss with him. He asked if he should come over to her hotel and she hesitated, saying she was afraid of how he'd feel about seeing her: she could wear only the thinnest nightgown, which made her body extremely visible. The friend said that he understood and didn't mind. The meeting filled him with admiration: upon his arrival at the hotel, Katharine plunged right into business, waving aside her appearance. The man marveled at her ability to transcend her embarrassing infirmity; this, he recalled, was only one, if the most remarkable, instance of her refusing to let illness get in the way of work.

Writing to her friends and family about her infirmities and her changed appearance was a means of coping with what had happened to her. One is continually struck by her graphic and frequently ugly descriptions of herself in old age, the fascinated disgust with which she came to view herself. Attacking her own appearance was a way of remaining in control of her life: if *she* said she looked horrible, no one else could. It was also a way of asserting that she was still lucid enough to see how she looked, that she still had her wits about her. Katharine's need to be in control was never stronger than when she was in the grip of the rare dermatosis (one recalls Roger Angell's memory of his mother rising from her chair on being admitted to the hospital as a *housewife:* the semi-retired fiction editor was not going to take *that* sitting down). She literally shed her skin—a grotesque, symbolic peeling away of her defenses. (She was once, at the age of seventy-six, even required to stand naked before twelve dermatologists who were being lectured to by her doctor. She was unable to climb into the bathtub, and Andy had to bathe her—an act that troubled him because of his wife's immense dignity: it did not seem right that Katharine be bathed by anyone other than herself.) But in her letters she continued to function creatively. A letter she wrote to John Updike in early May suggests that her feminine awareness of herself and the world around her also remained alive.

> I slop about all ungirdled and wearing loose cotton but at least I have the pleasure of picking my daffodils and tulips and supervising the spring transplanting. (It's more fun to do it oneself.) We have a Baltimore Oriole in the pear tree. And since writing this his mate has arrived, so I strew my hair combings about each day, hoping to induce them to nest in our elm tree as they did a few years back.

Katharine's image of herself as a freak was typical of someone with her illness. One skin doctor has described this "leper complex," a state of mind present in similarly afflicted people, who view skin diseases as dirty and themselves as untouchables. Other specialists have pointed out that to the victims and society alike skin diseases "are repugnant because they seem to suggest an outbreak of decay comparable to the decomposition of tissues after death." Katharine White had not needed this disease to make her aware of her declining strength and powers. She had agonized as, piece by piece, she had fallen into a ruin of her former self. But the dermatosis was the final insult. She was not even left with her beautiful hair (so she saw herself: she actually had plenty of hair left).

Roger Angell speculated that the rare skin disease was an emotionally triggered fallout from Katharine's retirement. Diseases of the skin have long been viewed as psychosomatic, the skin itself looked upon as "an organ of expression." But experts caution against regarding all skin disorders as psychosomatic, and one dermatologist, Dr. Frederick A. J. Kingery, points out that nothing indicates that SPD (in contrast to hives, for instance) is affected by stress or the emotions. Although Katharine White would have felt vindicated by this statement, she thought that her "horrid affliction" was brought on "by the shock of Kennedy's assassination. . . . I still can't bear a world without him."

Casting a backward glance over 1964 in November of that year, Katharine White found that she remembered very little of it—such were the effects of illness and medication. She was now taking tranquilizers "to lower the nervous tension caused by the cortisone [prednisone] plus the anxieties."

Her anxieties, as usual, were not confined to her health. She continued to gather material for another garden piece and "the mythical book," as she was now calling the planned collection of essays; but she felt the same frustration about her ability to write. She thought that unless she could discontinue the tranquilizers, she could never write again; she would "never be able to write anything *good* again, & so I won't write. And 'good' for me isn't *really* good, at best." After losing some weight and regaining a little strength earlier in the summer, Katharine again found herself beset by family problems. This time, Elsie was seriously ill. Now eighty-three years old, Elsie had "hardening of the arteries of the brain with queer mental aberrations, a bad heart, and many digestive problems," Katharine wrote Elizabeth Lawrence. In addition, she had recently suffered "*six* falls (& never broke a bone!)" With typical feelings of duty mixed with wary affection, concern, and resentment, Katharine applied herself to the considerable task of sorting through her eldest sister's possessions, and disposing of the things that Elsie had not taken with her when she moved from her house in Piermont, New York, to a nursing home. It troubled Katharine to think of her sister in a nursing home rather than "in mine or somewhere else in a family." But, she added to Elizabeth Lawrence, Elsie "is at least still surrounded by the best pieces of old family furniture."

As 1964 drew to a close, the Whites again prepared to leave Maine for Florida—this time, in advance of Christmas. Apparently, Katharine's doctors had speculated that the cold Maine December of the previous year, together with "the excesses and labors of a family Christmas with the younger grandchildren" had contributed to her dermatosis. This year she was "not to send a single Christmas card or wrap a single gift."

The previous winter had been unusually expensive. In addition to the cost of flying back and forth from New York to Florida, and the many weeks Andy stayed in a hotel while Katharine was being treated at Harkness, the Whites had had to pay Mr. and Mrs. Cook's wages for four months in Florida, and the rent for the winter house as well. This year they planned to economize by dividing the winter between Sarasota and a boarding house called Tidalholm, in Beaufort, South Carolina, an old plantation house which was now an inn, to which they would repair first, and to visit their friends, Dr. and Mrs. Joe Wearn, who had a plantation in Beaufort. Katharine hoped that a detour to Charlotte would be possible, where she would at last meet her dear correspondent Elizabeth Lawrence. But the meeting was not to take place until several years later.

The Whites were in Beaufort, soon to depart for Sarasota, when on January 27, 1965, they learned of Elsie's death. Elsie had been in New York for some dental appointments, staying at the Cosmopolitan Club, at 122 East 66th Street, when she collapsed on January 26. She was found dead the next morning, an advance for her next book in her pocket.

When Katharine heard of her sister's death she took up her pen to write a long letter to two of Elsie's long-time friends, Ellen and Hildegarde Nagel. Her acknowledged object in writing so quickly was to protect the Nagels from the shock of learning of Elsie's death from the newspaper. (Katharine had first tried telephoning the sisters.) But she was also, of course, dealing with the shock to herself in her own way. "For the first few days after Elsie died," Andy later wrote Roger Angell, ". . . K practically never mentioned Elsie. It was as though nothing had happened, except that she seemed withdrawn and wore a look of quiet interior concentration." Then the Whites arrived in Sarasota, and Katharine immediately set to work on the memorial service Elsie had requested in place of a funeral: "a secretary named Mrs. Rupprecht came in, mornings, for dictation and copying, and the volume of mail, in and out, grew to almost unbelievable proportions. We've been here for more than a month, and in that time I don't think K has been out of the house for a total of four hours. Her skin erupted, the cortisone had to be stepped up, and for a while she was in a state of near collapse."

Despite Elsie's failing health, Katharine had been unprepared for her sister's death. After a sad visit with Elsie at Harkness in September, when she was confused and suspicious (apparently of Katharine, as well as others), the sisters had had a happy reunion in December, when the Whites were en route to Beaufort. Elsie had then "seemed so utterly different a person . . . that I had rejoiced," Katharine wrote the Nagels. And up until her death Elsie's letters to Katharine were lucid and brimming with literary plans.

"Death ends a life, but it does not end a relationship, which struggles on in the survivor's mind toward some resolution which it may never find." So muses the narrator-son of Robert Anderson's play *I Never Sang for My Father*. Remembering the period following Elsie's death, when Katharine was so absorbed by the planning of Elsie's memorial service, E. B. White observed that "Elsie, even after she was dead and gone, had an extraordinary hold over her little sister." Elsie's psychological grip on Katharine is observed, partly, in Katharine's scrupulous attention to the details of the memorial service Elsie had several years earlier outlined to Katharine in a letter. Elsie's wish to be cremated, and have the ashes buried near her mother's grave in the Shepley-Sergeant plot in Winchester, Massachusetts, required a series of painstaking letters to the Winchester Department of Records, a task complicated by Elsie's apparently having misplaced the deed to the plot. Elsie's desire that her closest Jungian friends be consulted about and invited to the memorial occasioned many letters to the Nagels for help with names (as Katharine explained to the sisters, she had been excluded from the Jungian part of her sister's life and was at a loss about whom to contact). The site for the memorial presented special problems. There was, for instance, to be no church service. And Elsie had desired that the memorial be held at her own home on Piermont Avenue. Since it was now impossible to honor the latter request, Katharine had to come up with a place that she thought would have been agreeable to Elsie. The Cosmopolitan Club was finally decided on. Elsie had also requested that Paul Nordoff play the piano; that could be arranged—and so on.

Elsie's death left Katharine the sole surviving member of Charles Sergeant's family. This lonely and perhaps frightening position undoubtedly added a sense of urgency to the arrangements for Elsie's memorial. But Katharine was driven by a more compelling force: Elsie had spoken. Elsie had called her to the task. Things were no different than when Katharine was newly married to Andy and Elsie would telephone, bringing the household to a halt. And yet Katharine's letters suggest that a sort of calm had settled over her warring emotions about Elsie, that a ceasefire had been called.

> About Elsie's and my relationship I could write a book [Katharine wrote to Hildegarde Nagel] . . . it was always a fond one, & especially in the early years & the last ten years when she & I were the last of our generation. Our temperaments were different but our tastes were united. I owe her a great deal & have never regretted being able to help her financially since the 1920s. It was a pleasure, but unlike my Aunt Caroline, she was a hard person to give to—I suppose inevitable when a younger sister has to help support an older one, who wanted to be independent & hated to be helped.

Had Katharine forgotten that in the 1950s she ceased giving Elsie money? Or had she resumed support at a later date? Unfortunately no records of these transactions exist. We can only speculate that Katharine's description of her relationship with her eldest sister as "always a fond one" is evidence that Katharine was capable of repressing not only certain feelings but the memory of some of her own actions as well. That she deliberately misrepresented herself to her sister's friends is unlikely; she was too honest for that. She was, of course, defensive about Elsie, and she continued to defend her. Exasperated by the tedious process of obtaining permission to bury Elsie's ashes in the Winchester cemetery, Katharine wrote the Department of Records that "the ashes to be interred are those of Miss Elizabeth Shepley Sergeant, born in Winchester and a distinguished writer. Winchester should be honored to have her buried there."

The comment to the cemetery department reflected Katharine's weariness, too. By mid-February, her dermatosis and the high dosage of prednisone she was taking had forced her to turn over the final arrangements for the memorial to Roger Angell and Elsie's friend and executor, Anne Gugler (Nancy Stableford had not become Elsie's executor after all.) Still, Katharine's condition did not prevent her from writing detailed letters to those concerned in the memorial, including Nancy Hale, whom she hoped to engage as a speaker (Nancy Hale had known Elsie at the MacDowell Colony).

The memorial was set for April 12. Robert Frost's daughter, Leslie Frost Ballantine, would speak about Elsie's friendship with Frost and her book about him; Bryn Mawr College President Katharine McBride would introduce her and the other speakers.

Years later Roger Angell recalled that his mother had been deeply offended by a comment made by Glenway Wescott, one of the speakers at Elsie's memorial, who referred to Elsie's having prepared for death. Katharine was much younger than her eldest sister, and one didn't, to her mind, prepare for death. She seems to have equated the idea with giving up on life; she was certainly not about to do that. And yet it is a curious reaction in light of her own preparations for death (begun as early as 1961 with her Victorian Will) and what she wrote to the Nagels the day she learned of Elsie's death: "[Elsie] has never wanted to talk about her possible death & has often been too depressed for me to want to bring the subject up." But Katharine's reaction is perhaps explained by her tendency to believe in certain things even though she herself was not comfortable with them.

Katharine suffered another loss during the summer, when Susan Lyman Wearn, her closest friend in Maine, died. But, before that happened, she had had to contend with a professional blow.

In April of 1965, Katharine and E. B. White were angered and insulted by a two-part article on *The New Yorker* written by Tom Wolfe, published in the New York *Herald Tribune*. Citing differences in the editorships of Ross and Shawn, denouncing *"The New Yorker* style" of writing and editing, and the formula plot of *New Yorker* short stories, Wolfe was sharply critical of the magazine. But it is the tone of the piece that is a startling departure from earlier anti–*New Yorker* articles—a tone that J. D. Salinger, in an objecting letter to the *Tribune,* called "sub-collegiate and gleeful and unrelievedly poisonous." Part I ("Tiny Mummies! The True Story of the Ruler of 43d Street's Land of the Walking Dead!") is almost wholly devoted to an unremittingly vicious and tedious parody of William Shawn. Shawn the man, rather than Shawn the editor, is held up as an object of special ridicule as Wolfe harps on Shawn's speech, Shawn's dress, Shawn's good manners, Shawn's fears, and Shawn's shyness. The attack is incessant, the author's motive ambiguous. Shawn is apparently despised for what Wolfe sees as his attempts to preserve Ross's magazine rather than improve it; Shawn is portrayed as "the smiling embalmer," "the museum curator," the portrait embellished with a wooden, corpselike sketch of William Shawn, hands folded in front of him, and a drawing of a hollow-eyed Eustace Tilley in a casket, a butterfly resting on the rim of the opened lid.*

In his letter to the *Tribune,* E. B. White ignored Wolfe's criticisms of the magazine, its writers and contributors (White himself had been dismissed as one of *The New Yorker*'s "tiny giants"), and addressed himself to the "journalistic delinquency" of the piece, the personal assault on Shawn—an assault White found "all the more contemptible" because of "the virtuosity of the writer." To White, it seemed that "the spectacle was of a man being dragged for no apparent reason at the end of a rope by a rider on horseback—a rider, incidentally, sitting very high in the saddle these days and very sure of his mount." Katharine White appears not to have written the *Tribune,* but she did write to Shawn. "You and Andy were the first people I heard from," replied William Shawn on June 7. "I thought at the time that it was characteristic of you to offer your support and affection immediately, and I know now that one reason I was able to weather the crisis as well as I did was that both of you were standing alongside me. The wonderful letter you wrote me, dear Katharine, is one I will cherish."

Apart from the attack on Shawn, Katharine would have taken exception to Wolfe's criticisms of *"The New Yorker* style" of editing, and his merry effusion on the stories' formula plots. This particular *New Yorker* criticism was, and would continue to be, painfully familiar to her. As Katharine later wrote Corey Ford, she had "winced over the sentence" in his book *The Time Of Laughter,* which described *The New Yorker*'s fiction as "the self-analytic pastel-stories-without-plots" which had become "a New Yorker 'standby,' which is the fashionable cliche to my mind, but is a matter of opinion, not fact."

Katharine must have winced more at Wolfe's assertion that Roger Angell

---

*The picture of Shawn was drawn by Tom Wolfe. A class picture of William Shawn is also included.

was expected to be Shawn's successor at the magazine as editor, and that by virtue of Angell's mother, her marriage to E. B. White, and the Whites' close relationship with Ross, Katharine's son was peculiarly well fitted for the job. These statements were made worse by Wolfe's sly reference to Katharine White as "Katherine Angell," and his account of her romance with Andy: "They grew close right there in the offices of *The New Yorker*." But we have no record of Katharine's response to these comments in particular. Her letter to Shawn seems to have expressed only the worry that her many years of editing had been in vain. Shawn sought to reassure her.

> ... nothing Wolfe wrote can detract even minutely from what you have done for American letters, or for the world, in your great and unique work as an editor. Numberless writers have written better because of what you were able to give them, and many editors, including me, have been able to be of more service to writers and artists because of what you have taught them. In your integrity and passion and dedication and generosity, in your energy and your never-ending youth, you have inspired us all. The Tribune articles have altered none of that. The significance of your work grows as time passes. This country has a few things it can be proud of today, and one of them is The New Yorker, and nobody has done more than you to make that true.

In the last months of 1965 Katharine was reading *The New Yorker*'s serialization of Truman Capote's book *In Cold Blood* with fascinated attention. She wrote S. N. Behrman that she considered the work "outstanding," and "a feather in Shawn's cap."

Behrman himself had recently published a collection of his own pieces. Titled *The Suspended Drawing Room,* the book contained a charming preface about Harold Ross (to whom the book was dedicated), in which Behrman expressed his hope of someday writing a memoir of Ross. Katharine responded with a long, affectionate letter of encouragement. She thought that his preface and Rebecca West's review of *The Years with Ross* had begun to correct "[Thurber's] horrible distortions" of Ross, and that Behrman was just the writer to finish setting the record straight. Furthermore, she was plagued with the fear that soon all those who knew Ross best and had daily observed him at the magazine during its early years would be dead. A memoir must be written now. If Behrman wished, and if her health and various obligations permitted, she would gladly set down her own memories of Ross to help with Behrman's memoir; and she began setting them down in the letters. But was Sam well enough to do this project? "Shawn told me ... that your health, like Andy's and mine, was not too good and that, like us, a lot of your time was spent on just keeping going."

Missing the warning implicit in Katharine's comparison of Behrman's health with her own, Behrman wrote back enthusiastically, saying that he was willing to tackle a memoir of Ross, but only if Katharine would help him, serving as his collaborator as well as his editor. They should share the royalties if Katharine wished. Katharine's reply, which is not available, appears to have reflected her alarm in the face of Behrman's strenuous plans. Behrman's next letter was contrite. He had not known about "what [she] had been through, that [she] had been hospitalized and so threatened," and that she was overwhelmed with Elsie's papers and Andy's. Katharine had apparently backed out of her offer and suggested that Behrman find another collaborator; but without her help, Behrman felt that he couldn't possibly do the book and said he would forget about it.

The remainder of Behrman's letter consists of an intriguing comment on his and the Whites' differing views of the war in Vietnam (Katharine seems to have said something about this in her letter). Behrman's letter is worth looking at because it exemplifies the reverential feelings both Whites, who had by then become legendary, had come to excite in certain of their *New Yorker* friends. It evokes the attitude with which some of those friends went to visit the Whites during their later years in Maine, visits undertaken in a spirit that Roger Angell likened to pilgrimages to Lourdes. Behrman writes:

> I was really startled by the fact that you and Andy don't agree with me about Viet Nam. I had thought that you would. Now I feel that I have been wrong because you know what I think of Andy's instinct and knowledge. I am really quite mystified. A few months ago I went up to visit Brooks Atkinson in Durham, New York. He is one of the decentest men I know. He gave me a booklet gotten out by that outfit in Santa Barbara that thinks things over. There was a piece about it in the New Yorker. Hutchins, is, I believe, the head. Has Andy seen this booklet? It says that we never belonged in Viet Nam and shouldn't be there. I remember JFK saying in a press conference which I heard myself that it was not our war; it was their war and that the most we could do would be to supply a few advisors. Of course I showed Elza your letter and she begs, as I beg, for one or two sentences of clarification from Andy. I am prepared to say, and so for Elza, and so for my secretary, Mrs. Wherry (a daughter of the late Senator Maloney of Connecticut), who feels about Andy the way I do, that we will acknowledge our mistake and confess that we have been entirely wrong.

Katharine's reply is not available, but she is likely to have felt dismayed by Behrman's letter, since it required another long reply. She may have been a little embarrassed, too: neither she nor Andy had ever assumed the role of a political sage. They would not have felt comfortable dispensing such advice to anyone, let alone an intelligent person like S. N. Behrman.

Nineteen sixty-five had begun as a year of loss for Katharine; it ended with a small gain in the form of another garden piece. Titled "An Idea Which We Have Called Nature" (borrowed from John Donne), the piece was essentially a series of book reviews. Katharine typically thought her latest effort not well written, and, furthermore, that "like many New Yorker writers, [she was] beginning to write more than anyone wants to know about any subject." If this piece seems to justify her disparagement, it is rather because of its limited range than because of the quality of the article, which is as clear, scrupulously researched, and carefully considered as are her other writings. But one misses the fussy, spirited opinions, the personal reminiscences and lyrical evocations of a New England girlhood that elevate the other essays above the ordinary and set them apart. That she was still capable of this caliber of writing was made evident earlier in the year, when she penned a charming letter to the editor for *The New Yorker*'s "Department of Amplification" (June 23, 1965). In response to a recent editorial on seaweed, Katharine recalled a dessert made in her childhood home by the family's "talented and tyrannical cook, Mary Hillen, that I couldn't stomach," Irish-moss blancmange.

Writing the latest garden piece as a book review was the easy way out, but nevertheless a triumph. It was a beginning, and it was hopeful: if she could do this much, perhaps she could do more. The mythical garden book might, after all, become a reality.

10

Matriarch

SPRING CAME LATE to Maine in 1966; and for Katharine White a gentler season had arrived. During the next couple of years her health improved slightly. Though still plagued with the dermatosis, she managed to stay out of the hospital. From 1966 to 1968, she was given enough of a reprieve from ill health to be able to produce six more pieces for *The New Yorker:* one letter for the "Department of Amplification," and five new garden pieces.

Written a year after her last letter to the editor, the new letter (published June 18, 1966) was even better than the previous one. In response to an M.F.K. Fisher piece about "children's food and drink, past and present," Katharine recalled the medicinal hot whiskey lemonade of her own youth served by her father, and the baby foods she herself had prepared for Nancy, which, in turn, reminded her of the eating habits of her youngest grandchild. It was one of her best letters, prompting William Shawn to exclaim in a written message that "these reminiscent letters of yours can become an institution."

The latest garden essays frequently departed from the book-review format, taking up the thoughtful writing that had distinguished Katharine's earlier efforts. Some of her most charming passages are found in these last essays. From Part I of a two-part essay titled "The Flower Arrangers" (published November 4, 1967), one of the best gardening pieces she ever wrote, comes the following recollection.

> A friend has reminded me of the very tall vases, shaped like umbrella stands, that were especially designed to hold the long-stemmed fragrant American Beauty roses when they were the rage. We owned no such vase because we seldom indulged in American Beauties. My father considered them a bit "gross," with their great size and strong blue-pink coloring, but this may have been an aesthetic verdict influenced by the pocket-book; the Beauties were very costly for their day. I remember the tall vases, though, in the houses of friends where the American Beauty happened to be the most prized rose. It was indeed so much in vogue that one of the bolder debutantes of my five-years-older sister's generation had a costume made by her dressmaker for

her year of "coming-out" balls that was designed to be worn with two choice American Beauties. The floor-length gown, as I recall it, was made of rich white satin with a very low neck, and with it she wore, of all things, bright-green silk stockings. In the V of her low neckline she tucked two huge American Beauty roses. If one of her partners commented on their fragrance or their rich color, this saucy girl was reputed to lift her floor-length skirt daintily to show her pretty green ankles and maybe even a bit of her slim green calves, and say demurely, "Yes, lovely. And here are the stems."

One of the highlights of this period occurred in 1967, when a meeting with Elizabeth Lawrence finally took place. Katharine later wrote her friend, "Meeting you in person at last—you who have been my guide and mentor and my envy and admiration because of your knowledge and your wonderful books and writing—was a nervous moment for me so if I acted jumpy, I hope you can forgive me. The wonderful thing for me was that I loved you at once as a person and wanted to stay on and talk for hours. Forgive me if I have written all this before." It was to be the friends' only meeting.

Katharine continued to suffer severe doubts about her ability to write, and to disparage the essays she did write as insignificant, badly written diatribes. She still maintained that she could no longer write letters, or letters that were worth reading. "I sneaked a look at K's letter to you and was delighted with that sentence about how she is no longer able to write letters," Andy wrote his brother, Bun. "She knocks them off ten or twelve a day, of approximately the length of the one you received. Her production staggers me."

But Katharine felt age "pressing down on [her]," time pressing down on her, the problems of daily life frustrating and increasingly oppressive. "Household and secretarial help, i.e., the lack of it, is my greatest enemy," she wrote May Sarton. "Each year brings more rather than less responsibility, it seems," she wrote another friend early in 1966. There had been another of the domestic disasters that seemed to dog her. While in Sarasota that winter, the Whites' cook's husband had had a mental breakdown, and after sending the couple home to Maine, Katharine had fallen, badly wrenching her back and spraining her foot. She and Andy reached Maine "in a battered condition of nerves and body." And time pressed down on her in other ways. Advancing age inevitably brought the deaths of friends and long-time *New Yorker* associates. Dorothy Parker died in 1967; for Katharine that meant "one less left of the very early team. Alas."

The annual winters in Florida had long seemed like a banishment (and "I really *despise* everything that Florida stands for but it *is* beautiful," Katharine had long ago written Jean Stafford), but neither Katharine nor Andy could tolerate the long, hard winters in Maine, and they considered buying a second home in Florida. But they thought they could not afford it, and even if they could, they had reached a time of life when they wanted to simplify, not further complicate their lives. In a letter Katharine wrote to her Bryn Mawr class in 1967 she summed up her life of the past few years and her feelings about the present.

> A sense of urgency presses all of us, I suppose, because there are more things we hope to accomplish than we may have time for. I recently said to a friend that I'd be mad as all get-out if I died or became incapacitated. She thought it was funny but I meant it. In other words I am still in love with life and with my life with my husband. His health has been an anxiety, but like all real writers, he never stops writing. . . . My proposed book of the New Yorker garden pieces, plus some new material, is still a dim hope, but growing dimmer. Too little time, too many goat feathers, and too much interest in the sad state of the world we live in, both natural and political. Really to read *The New York Times,* and I never fail to, uses up many hours a week.

The sense of urgency Katharine felt pushing her on during these years was sadly justified during the winter and spring of 1969, which marked the beginning of her life as an invalid. The fall she had taken after sending off her domestics resulted in a fractured vertebra. This was followed by a severe case of shingles on top of her dermatosis. In late February of 1969 Katharine returned to Harkness, where she remained for thirteen weeks, developing a staph infection while there.

Katharine was now found to be suffering from the debilitating bone condition osteoporosis, a disease that may have been aggravated by years of high dosages of prednisone (a warning on the drug's label says that those who have osteoporosis should use it cautiously), and the antacids and medications she took (those containing aluminum can interfere with the body's ability to metabolize calcium).

After "a long, cold, grim winter," the Whites finally returned to Maine, Katharine by ambulance plane. Andy slept in a separate room now; Katharine's room was fitted up with a hospital bed, and nurses were hired to attend her, transforming the house into what Andy only half-jokingly referred to as White's Nursing Home. In July of 1969 E. B. White described his wife in a letter to Frank Sullivan: "She walks with a walker, gets boosted upstairs and down by my skillful laying on of hands, and is at this moment presiding at the morning ritual of flower arranging. Her borders still bloom, her spirit is still unshattered. The rest of her is in a thousand pieces."

Spring was followed by "a horrible summer": a kidney infection, "a touch of pneumonia" for which Katharine was briefly hospitalized. Most of the time she remained in bed, or moved cautiously about with her walker, an attendant always behind her. The simplest tasks were now beyond her. She could not bend down to look for an address in her files, pluck a deadhead from a stem, or pick her own flowers. When someone was available to do the picking for her, she would lean on her walker, or sit in a chair by her flower beds and point. Now was a long way from *The New Yorker*'s Tuesday art meetings, when, armed with knitting needles, she and Gibbs had pointed at drawings.

She loathed this life now centered around "tending [her] disintegrating carcass," but she did not intend to resign herself to it. Through dictation or with her own shaky hand she still managed to write letters, many of them on *New Yorker* stationery. Her identification with the magazine was abiding, and (at least until 1968) she continued to receive occasional proofs from *The New Yorker*. "Like an old elephant, I don't forget and I can't stop being an editor," she wrote to Jean Stafford. "I feel exiled without you," wrote Marianne Moore.

During the summer of 1969 Katharine was again unsettled by the United States forays into outer space. Following a mission that brought Apollo 10 astronauts within 9.4 miles of the moon, in July Apollo 11 landed on the moon and Neil Armstrong stepped onto its surface. This was followed by an Apollo 12 mission, which returned to earth with lunar samples. Katharine felt these dramatic events as keenly as she had experienced the assassination of John F. Kennedy six years earlier. "I'm afraid your letter crossed a brisk telegram from my wife to you demanding that you call off the moon shot," Andy wrote to President Nixon, who had sent him a congratulatory telegram upon his seventieth birthday. In a letter to Frank Sullivan following the death of Sullivan's friend Corey Ford, Katharine wrote: "Thinking back over the last week of terrible tension for all of us because of the men in the moon, I can't help wondering whether the very act of watching the lunar landing may not have raised his blood pressure. I know that just to look briefly at the landing, the walk itself, the lift off of the Eagle and the boys climbing onto the Hornet nearly killed me. I have been sick in bed ever since, and with unexplained sudden high fevers."

Eighteen hours a day Katharine was accompanied by a nurse, aide, or neighbor; such steady attendance was necessary in order to relieve Andy, so that he could get a good night's sleep and at least eight hours a day to himself for writing, chores, and leisure. Andy, who was finishing his third children's book, *The Trumpet of the Swan,* felt under terrific financial pressure to keep the Thanksgiving deadline he had promised Harper's. To the writer Robert Coates he wrote, "The book will have to net me about half a million dollars, otherwise I won't be able to pay off all the registered and unregistered nurses that tend K every day and every night. They are a nice bunch of girls, but the payroll is fantastic. And Maine has just decided on top of everything else to collect a state income tax." In addition to all Katharine's other woes, her "heart is acting up and she has been put on digitalis—foxglove to her. All in all, a sad time."

"My chief source of woe is Katharine's long illness," Andy wrote to the artist Garth Williams on the last day of the year. The Whites had remained in Maine that winter, Katharine being too ill and frail to travel. Still, her hospital bed was laden with garden books—another source of woe to her husband, since she was not supposed to lift anything heavy. Katharine had her own worries about Andy. That fall he had suffered several migraines and blurred vision. Writing to Elizabeth Lawrence, Katharine assured her friend that Andy had *"not"* had a stroke. "There has been *no* brain damage and his arteries are good for his age, not hardened." Katharine's dermatosis was again troubling her and the high dosage of prednisone she was taking had affected her ability to read. "I'm trying to make hay while I have the extra energy of the raised dose, but I know it will all be in vain."

Early in 1970, Katharine completed her last garden piece for *The New Yorker,* and with it resigned her post as garden writer and critic. "Knots and Arbours—and Books" appeared in the March 28th issue. Katharine typically thought it bad—her "poorest ever" (in fact, it was not). It had been a great struggle to complete the piece, and she thought it would have been better not to have done it. "I should have had the guts never to submit [it]," she wrote Elizabeth Lawrence, "but I couldn't bear to waste nearly a year of working toward it." Katharine intended to continue working to produce enough material for the mythical garden book, but she had come to a resolution about the *New Yorker* pieces: that she was now too ill to write well or to write against a deadline. A sad letter to Elizabeth Lawrence written in late March of 1970 suggests that she had reached a more profound resolution as well. "As I now have some heart trouble my main job should be to help Andy and tidy up this house, which is still in chaos so far as my files go." Nancy and Louis Stableford had just left the United States to teach in the Philippines for a year. Nancy Stableford later recalled her mother bidding her good-bye: "If I die, don't come back for the funeral." Nancy promised that she would not. She was left with the impression that her mother had thought this through, realizing not only that it would be too expensive for the Stablefords to return home but that they would not be able to help her by doing so.

It had helped her to have her children and their spouses and children around during the summer: Roger and Carol and Roger's daughters; Nancy and Louis and their three children. Each summer, both families rented or had owned houses nearby; Nancy and Louis eventually sold their house. And Joe and Allene and their children, Steven, Martha, and John, had of course lived in Maine year round since Joe was discharged from the army and had returned home from Germany in 1956. It was wonderful to have the family there, to watch the children growing up. And dear Allene sometimes served as Katharine's secretary, taking dictation as Roger's first wife, Evelyn, had done one winter during the war, when she stayed with Katharine and Andy while Roger was in the army.

It said something about her children's affection for her that they chose to spend their summer vacations near her, that one had settled nearby, though this physical proximity presented inevitable problems. To the summer children, Mother could seem demanding. Evelyn Angell remembered Katharine as having been less demanding in Maine than she was in New York, when Evelyn and Roger lived outside the city and Katharine would call at the last minute and say that so-and-so was coming for cocktails and she wanted Evelyn and Roger to come. Roger was working in the city, so it wasn't difficult for him to go over at the last minute, but Evelyn was home with the two kids and would have to get a sitter. In Maine, Katharine's fear of being cut off from her children in an emergency once led her to interfere. Katharine was upset that Evelyn and Roger had not had a phone put in their Brooklin cottage, and she would have to drive over if she wanted to talk to them. Mother had gone a step further with Nancy and Louis and had a phone installed in their summer house against their wishes. She said she couldn't stand the thought of not being able to call if she needed them.

As a mother-in-law, Katharine White's faults were slight, despite her tendency to be obtrusive and occasionally exasperating ("If you told her you used a certain kind of mustard, she'd use five or six sentences to tell you why you should use the kind she uses"; she had advised both of Roger's wives how to make a home for a writer: they should overlook a lot of his moods; they should say a lot of funny things). To Carol Angell, who had happily come into Katharine's life when she was elderly and no longer formidable, and who had at the outset established that she would not run paid errands for her, Katharine was "a perfect mother-in-law": fond and confiding (taking Carol out to lunch and telling her all about her divorce), amusing, interested and interesting, never interfering, and generous, showering Carol with gifts when she became Roger's wife. Katharine had been generous with Allene and Evelyn as well. Each daughter-in-law felt that she benefited from having Katharine as a mother-in-law. While taking dictation from her, Allene had learned a lot and found it an enriching experience, though it ultimately became too much with three children to take care of and office duties when Joe took over the Brooklin boatyard. In the early years of Allene and Joe's marriage, Katharine would stop by with flowers from her garden;

when Evelyn stayed with the Whites during the war, Katharine placed fresh flowers in her room. Evelyn Nelson, who remarried after her divorce from Roger Angell, regarded Katharine as very gracious, though difficult to get close to, and "a remarkable person." Louis Stableford, who called Katharine "Mater," thought she had "a brilliant mind," and liked her very much.

Shortly before Easter, 1970, the heart trouble Katharine had been having degenerated into congestive heart failure. In a letter to a friend E. B. White described the aftermath of an attack.

> I got our doctor and he whizzed over here and after examining her put in a call for our local ambulance, which is a volunteer affair. Very soon the Corps arrived, with the old DeSoto and an oxygen tank. They gave K a few whiffs of oxygen, then loaded her into the ambulance. Meantime her nurse and I were wildly trying to assemble all the one thousand things she would need in the hospital.
>
> Once we got there, our doctor gave her three shots and then put her in an oxygen tent. True to form, K wanted to take everything into the tent with her: morning paper, latest *New Yorker,* cigarettes (!! bang bang). Anyway, she responded beautifully to the treatment, slept all night in the tent, and was dramatically improved by Easter morning. There was very little left of me, as I had been sick myself with a springtime resurgence of the old ulcer. But I was so pleased to see the way she bounced back, I didn't mind, and I felt very lucky that we had been able to get such prompt attention on the Saturday before Easter. The three corpsmen who showed up were (1) the editor of our weekly paper—at the controls, (2) the parson of the Congo church in Blue Hill—oxygen, and (3) the industrial arts teacher at the Academy—heavy lifting. It makes a lot of difference, at such moments, to have your friends drive in and go to work. And our doc was marvelous.
>
> K is on complete bed-rest (she's as busy as a monkey from morn till night), looks well, and will probably be returned to me on Saturday.

The friends who had always been welcomed and encouraged to visit the Whites in Maine were now warned away; too much bedroom space was inhabited by Katharine and her army of nurses to accommodate overnight guests. Ever conscious of her own ravaged appearance, Katharine could not help preparing potential visitors for the shocking change in herself. Even those who were unlikely ever to visit her in Maine were told that they would hardly recognize her (she did not, in truth, look bad). She was now commonly referring to herself as "a bent and horrible looking old crone" who was "a burden to myself and to poor Andy." Because of the dermatosis, she could not wear nylons and took to wearing white ankle socks. In a letter to John Updike in late July, Katharine described the skin disease, which had doctors coming "from all sorts of places to look at [her]"; she wryly noted that in future her "only claim to fame would come under the heading 'Annals of Medicine.'"

In July Andy had a car accident. After taking an antihistamine with a glass of whiskey and water, he had fallen asleep at the wheel and smashed into a telephone pole. Though he escaped with only minor injuries, the accident left him depressed and shaken for weeks. He could not sleep most nights, and the little sleep he did get was inhabited by nightmares about the accident. In addition to a broken nose and rib, he was experiencing pain in one of his ears and, wrote Katharine to John Updike, "a feeling that he could not control his own mind any more." He feared that his driver's license would be taken away from him. Both Whites continued to feel the after-effects of the accident for months. In September Katharine wrote Frank Sullivan, "I trust that you are in much better health than this old pair of crocks who are nearing the end of the worst year of bad luck in our married life."

Katharine now climbed the stairs to her bedroom only twice a day. Moving slowly to the stairs with her walker, she would grab hold of the banister and push the walker aside, pulling herself up the rest of the way, an attendant or Andy behind her to catch her if she fell. Her life thus circumscribed, she set up two bases of operation from which she worked in the house: a card table beside her hospital bed, and a long, collapsible desk in the living room. Turning to her left in spring and summer, through the ruffled organdy curtains on the living-room windows she could observe her flowers blooming against the white picket fence; in fall, the maple along the road at the foot of the driveway was brilliant red. She disliked the fall, which reminded her that winter was coming and she would soon "be shut in entirely."

Katharine typically arose at six-thirty in the morning, pushing her walker back and forth across the hall to get her bowels moving, her hair in a long braid down her back. Andy would carry up her breakfast tray, having first made a trip to the small greenhouse he gave her in 1975 for their forty-sixth wedding anniversary. "Oh! How pretty!" Katharine would exclaim at the flower on the tray, though privately disapproving Andy's choice of a southern flower, a camellia (why had he surprised her with an order of plants not indigenous to New England?). While Andy went about his chores Katharine would eat her breakfast in bed, sometimes reading the Ellsworth *American*. At nine o'clock the nurse arrived, and bathed and dressed her. Katharine went downstairs at ten, read the mail, and dictated letters to the nurse or a part-time secretary.

Katharine's work now consisted almost entirely of letter writing—on behalf of Andy, and her own prodigious correspondence with her former writers and colleagues, friends, relatives, and nurserymen. Her dictated letters and many of her handwritten scrawls were later typed on *New Yorker* or Mrs. E. B. White stationery by one of her helpers. She was also busy assembling her hundreds of *New Yorker*–related books and letters, which would go to Bryn Mawr as a bequest in her will, a task that included writing notes about many of the writers and *New Yorker* staff members with whom she had worked and corresponded. In the course of sorting and reading through these letters, she found herself writing additional notes and anecdotes in letters to the Bryn Mawr college library's director, James Tanis.

Katharine White was eighty-four years old in 1976. Her hair was thinner now, but still ample, her hairline having receded from years of cortisone. The pure white hair, still worn in a knot at the nape of her neck, was becoming, softening the deep shadows ringing her intelligent gray eyes, the deeply lined face upon which were written years of illness and too little sleep. Sitting by day at the heavily laden makeshift desk in her book-lined living room, pillows supporting her back against the chintz sofa, and by night at the card table in her bedroom, she took up her pen and remembered the active years, "the dear dead days" when nothing was too much for her. The cigarette burned, the light burned late as she sat at her desk remembering, reliving her young years as a *New Yorker* editor, as wife to Ernest Angell.

Ernest was dead now, since 1973, having survived his wife Betty by two years. "We were married for fourteen years, 1915 to 1929, and the first seven years were happy ones and before that we had been engaged to be married for four years," Katharine had written Callie Angell shortly after Ernest's death.

> He proposed to me on my eighteenth birthday just before I went off to college as a Freshman and when he was starting his senior year at Harvard and had three years of Law School to accomplish before we could be married. He went into his father's old law office in Cleveland when he graduated from law school and by the next spring we married, the spring of 1915. I go into all this only to tell you of the eleven happy years we had together. These are the ones I remember now; while I try to forget the seven unhappy years that ended our marriage for reasons I won't go into except to say that I really did try to save the marriage and that my divorce had nothing to do with Andy.

Now, three years later, she was more candid. She began by writing about Andy's college sweetheart, Alice Burchfield.

Apparently they had hardly ever even kissed. The morals of that decade are very different from that of today and every one [as] green and innocent . . . the 20s made a big break and pretty soon marriages were a mess—wife swapping and so on. World War I soldiers who went to France, as your grandfather Angell did, came back with the French idea that a wife and a mistress was the way to live. I tried it seven years with your grandfather but in the end it was making me sick—to have him live with a much older woman all his working week and come to me and the children in Sneden's for the weekends. I hung on, for the sake of Roger and Nancy, as long as I could. Finally I said it was not my idea of marriage and he bravely gave up his mistress. We went on a good many more years in [93rd] St. but it was no use—he was too highly sexed or something and began having affairs with other men's wives, with women who were *my* friends, etc. So I began to work and held down several jobs before the New Yorker was founded then we got to quarreling (and this was bad for Nancy and Roger) and when one day he slapped my face and knocked me down to the floor I walked out for good and all. This was *before* Andy and I fell in love.*

Ernest Angell had never quite recovered from Katharine's leaving him; and though she was given to saying that she was an Angell before she was a White, Katharine was never comfortable with her status as a divorced woman, or with the circumstances of her divorce. Now, in her old age, she felt compelled to repeat this part of her history, assuring her granddaughter and others that her divorce had had nothing to do with adultery on her part —nor had Roger's divorce from Evelyn had anything to do with his second wife, Carol, nor did Kitty Stableford's divorce from her first husband, Michael, a year earlier (1975) have anything to do with Kitty's second husband. Divorce and adultery were something of an obsession with Katharine White. ("The latest news in my family," Katharine wrote a friend, "is that Kitty Stableford, who was divorced two years ago, is remarrying next Saturday—just a small wedding in Easton. . . . The man she is marrying is named Roger Bennett . . . and she did not meet him until after she had left Michael.")

Though fully sympathetic with the feelings of divorced women, Katharine had distanced herself from her former daughter-in-law after Evelyn Angell's divorce from Roger, though she continued to send Evelyn Christmas cards and to inquire about her in letters to Callie. (By contrast, after the Roger

*Katharine closed the letter by asking Callie to "forgive this great outpouring" and to burn the letter. "I have never been so frank with your father [ând Nancy] as I have with you because I wanted them to love and respect their father." And then, in a postscript: "The new morals are probably much better in the long run even though I sometimes feel they may destroy 'the family.' But I am not against unmarried couples living together. It's often a wise arrangement and it may result in fewer marriages that end in divorce."

Angells' divorce, Ernest often took Evelyn to the symphony.) Katharine's relative unfriendliness toward Evelyn Angell (later, Evelyn Nelson) probably resulted from loyalty to Roger and to Roger's second wife, Carol, though neither one of them desired that Katharine drop Evelyn. Whatever the explanation, Katharine suffered for and felt embarrassed by her own behavior. She was furious with Roger when, years after his divorce, he discouraged Evelyn from paying a call on the Whites in Maine (because they would work themselves into a tizzy planning meals and getting things ready).

Shortly before lunch, Katharine would rise from her desk to go out to the garden and point to the flowers she wanted the nurse or Henry Allen to cut. She would arrange the flowers herself, on newspapers spread out on the old round settle table in the enclosed north porch, where Andy had mixed the martini he was quietly sipping in the corner while he watched his wife deftly arrange the flowers into four or five vases.

If she had no doctor's appointment that day, after lunch Katharine would return to the living-room sofa and desk. Many of the letters she now wrote were to biographers of the *New Yorker* writers she had known and edited. She herself loved biographies and collections of letters; among the books she had devoured during the last few years were *Zelda,* by Nancy Milford, R.W.B. Lewis's monumental *Edith Wharton* ("utterly fascinating"), *The Book of Abigail and John,* and Virginia Woolf's *Letters.* She no longer read all of *The New Yorker*— "I don't have time and my eyesight is dimming, and there are some departments I can't stand and seldom read, but almost always there is something in an issue I would not have missed for anything."

On John O'Hara: "I think he wrote better when he was drinking than he did later. His subject matter and style seemed fresher then."

And of Louise Bogan:

> The amazing thing, when one thinks of it, is that she became so learned a scholar and so distinguished a critic, since she was so largely self-taught. . . . The drinking matter is absurd. Thank God she *could* drink! . . . I join in some of her detestations, especially of Horace Gregory, with whom I served as a judge of a Houghton Mifflin Poetry contest. I don't know whether the man is alive or dead, and I rather hope he is dead because her unkindest words were for him, but I feel just the same way. I never could stand the man or his writing.

To a biographer of Herman Mankiewicz she wrote, "to be honest, I was scared of him. He talked very loud, he typed very fast and loud, and acted as if he owned the place. In the very few hours he was in the office during the week I merely stayed out of his way."

And she wrote of the responsibility of being an editor. "If he is an office boy I would include him in my list of those who need TLC just as much as one's own children and grandchildren do."

Katharine White was an obliging source for biographers, even when she had not known their subjects well. But she was cautious, too, insistent upon accuracy— "Ross brought me up that way," she explained to one biographer; and there had been so many "terrible inaccuracies in all the books thus far written on *The New Yorker* or members of its staff." She required not only that biographers give her approval of direct quotations from her and that they allow her to see the passages in which her comments appeared, but also that she be allowed to approve her own facts or opinions, even when she was not quoted directly.

Katharine was especially cautious now, since the publication of Brendan Gill's *Here at The New Yorker* in 1975. A mixture of autobiography, *New Yorker* history, and anecdote—much of the latter, Katharine contended, inaccurate, unsubstantiated gossip—Gill's book had had a devastating effect on her. She was most acutely pained by his characterization of her; by his mention of a supposed rumor that she had once "prepared to lead a palace revolution" against Harold Ross; and by his account of the suicide of Wolcott Gibbs's second wife. She was especially hurt because she had considered Brendan Gill a friend. Why did he feel that way about her? she wondered. She had bought his first piece, and just a few years earlier (in 1972) commended him for an obituary of John O'Hara he wrote for the *Century Club Yearbook*. Thanking Gill for sending her a copy of the obituary, she wrote down some of her own memories of O'Hara, and suggested that Gill write a biography of him. Reading about herself in *Here at the New Yorker*, a book written by a man she knew, liked, and trusted, was therefore a greater blow than it would have been otherwise. And it was made still worse by a revelation of Roger Angell's: that he had read the book in galleys and begged Gill to remove the offending and wholly inaccurate parts about Katharine White, saying that she would cry for months if they were published, that it might kill her. But it was too late to make any changes, said Gill. The book was ready to go to press.

Measured against the depictions of others in the book, the portrait of Katharine White seems harmless, if not wholly flattering. Examined by itself and from the subject's point of view, the picture looks different. The technique applied here is the barbed compliment: Katharine White is a rose, but roses have thorns. She is a silver fountain, but silver fountains have mud. "Katharine White is a woman so good-looking that nobody has taken it amiss when her husband has described her in print as beautiful," writes Gill, "but her beauty has a touch of blue-eyed augustness in it, and her manner is formal."* The brushstrokes are applied point, counterpoint: Katharine White is painted as a woman of class, breeding, background—Boston roots, a Bryn Mawr education.† A woman of taste with an eye for quality, she was "militantly proud . . . of her fitness to take part in matters of importance in the world"—in contrast to the young White, Ross, and Thurber, who had not yet defined themselves. Her self-confidence takes the form of stubbornly "pushing for the acceptance of her opinions" around the office (she is likened to a "weighty glacier" moving down "a narrow Alpine pass")—but by being this way she did the magazine good, writes Gill, did Ross good, in fact "gave him" an "intellectual conscience," was an Edmund Wilson to his Fitzgerald.

The effect of all this is curiously Thurberish. Note the word choices: "militantly proud," "weighty glacier," the sense of her heavy forcefulness, which is contrasted with the lighter, weaker sex: White, Ross, and Thurber. In case one has missed the point Katharine is then portrayed as holding the influential *New Yorker* writer E. B. White "as a sort of hostage"—again, to push for the acceptance of her own opinions at the magazine. Elsewhere in the book, she is seen casting a shadow over Gus Lobrano when she gives up her title as head of Fiction (writes Gill, "she had given up her position but not her interest"); and she similarly oppresses St. Clair McKelway.‡ According to Brendan Gill, the Whites retired to Maine in the thirties with Katharine's "reluctant consent." Paraphrasing Janet Flanner, Gill said, "Mrs. White believed herself to be giving up the best job held by any woman in America when she followed her husband to Maine, and no doubt she was right. The retirement proved temporary, but Mrs. White was unable to regain her lofty place in the editorial hierarchy of the magazine."

In the many letters Katharine White wrote to her friends, family, and *New Yorker* colleagues about the Gill book, it is striking that she scarcely mentioned Gill's gleeful description of her and Andy as hypochondriacs.§ Instead, she focused on the alleged "rumor" that she was prepared to lead a palace

---

*"[H]e hasn't even looked at me, apparently, because he says my eyes are blue and they are not," Katharine wrote Milton Greenstein.

†To Geoffrey Hellman: "Gill is maddeningly inaccurate although I suppose it is insignificant that he calls me an old Bostonian. Actually my family came from central Massachusetts and Maine although I was born and brought up in a suburb of Boston."

‡In Gill's words, McKelway agreed to become Ross's managing editor "on three conditions: one, that [the job] be set up in a new fashion, establishing for the first time a division between fact and fiction and thereby insuring that Mrs. White would no longer be concerned with editing factual material."

§*Here at The New Yorker* repeated, word for word, some of the same remarks Brendan Gill had made in the preface he penned for a *Paris Review* interview with E. B. White in 1972—remarks that elicited a good-natured but clearly offended response from Katharine White, denying that she had ever suffered from imaginary ills and seeking to explain her husband's health problems. Her letter to Brendan Gill, which was mostly about her memories of John O'Hara, was personal, touching, admiring, and supportive of him, making his repetition of the offending remark the more astonishing.

revolution against Ross, and on Gill's version of the suicide of Elizabeth Gibbs. (Brendan Gill does not dwell on the former, mentioning it only briefly, in the context of Harold Ross's problems with Raoul Fleischmann. He also states that the rumor about Katharine White is "highly implausible, though it may contain a germ of truth.") The following comment typifies the response Katharine felt driven to give the people to whom she wrote about the book.

I especially resented the totally untrue "rumor" about me, saying that I led a "revolt" against Ross and tried to get him fired by Fleischmann because I and some others thought he was neglecting his editorial work [she wrote Frank Sullivan]. I, for one, never heard of *any* revolt against Ross (except by Fleischmann) and the exact opposite was true. As you surely know, I was fanatically devoted to Ross and three times over I *prevented* or rather, I *persuaded* Fleischmann not to fire Ross when Raoul was in a fit of anger or annoyance against HWR. The difficulty between them always came when Raoul forgot his initial promise to Ross not to interfere with Ross's editorial decisions. It happened once when Benchley wrote a piece spoofing a Lucky Strike ad, if I remember right, and Raoul suddenly said it couldn't run because they were such important advertisers. Ross showed the piece to everyone of us editors and we all agreed it was fine and should run. Well, it ran, and that irked Raoul, and incidentally Lucky Strike didn't withdraw their advertising. Once when Andy spoofed Elizabeth Arden (another row) she did withdraw her advertising but in six months it was back again. She couldn't get along without New Yorker advertising. Anyway, the first time Fleischmann came to me it was a tentative approach. He asked me what would I think of Arthur Krock as Editor. I replied that I could hardly think of anybody less suitable, and that besides Ross *was* the magazine and that if he were fired most of the rest of us would leave. Then one day when I was still Mrs. Angell (so it was in the early days) I was sick at home with an ear abscess and Raoul called me up and said he had to see me at once and could he come up—and come up he did. He said he simply could not work any more with Ross and would I be the Editor. This, by the way, is only for you, because it sounds boastful —but it was merely a bribe. I said of course I wouldn't, and that I wouldn't have time because of my young children, and didn't consider myself competent anyway. Again, I said that Ross *was* the magazine and that if he went I would also leave and so, also, I thought, would many others. Then some years went by and Fleischmann made still another approach, and this time he took Andy and me out to dinner and the whole rigamarole was repeated over again. He offered the editorship to Andy and me jointly and we just laughed in his face. It was a ridiculous idea. But I do consider myself libeled in other sections. I hope, if you get the book read to you, that you will not agree that I was a conniving, power-hungry, glacier, moving slowly and unbendingly to get my way. I couldn't think of anyone with whom I ever had that sort of experience. It was always give and take and Ross was the final decision maker on every manuscript just as Shawn was after him.

Despite Katharine's comment that the information about Fleischmann offering her the editorship of *The New Yorker* was "only for you," she informed other correspondents of this. She was so overwhelmed by what Gill had written about her, so fearful of what others would believe when they read *Here at The New Yorker,* that she simply could not help herself. She would recount this story many times in her letters, often in the same detail and with the same language, avowing her fanatical devotion to Harold Ross.

Katharine expended nearly the same amount of energy retelling the suicide of Wolcott Gibbs's wife. She was indignant that Gill had recounted this private and painful chapter in her late friend's life, relying on hearsay, and she was outraged by the flippant and offhand manner in which he told it. Brendan Gill does not mention Katharine White in connection with this story, and yet it was her story too, part of her history. She had been with Gibbs that day, and her memories of the day were perhaps more poignant, her reaction to Brendan Gill's rendition of it more resentful, because of the intimate associations the event evoked: she had been pregnant with Joel then, Andy's and her only child. Thus to come across the story in print, inaccurately and disrespectfully told, not only angered her as Wolcott Gibbs's friend, it violated her privacy by cheapening a piece of her own experience, by trespassing on her life. Like her defense against the palace-revolution charge, her rendition of this story was nearly the same in letter after letter.

> The whole thing about Gibbs, and the insinuations and guesses about his wife's suicide upset me greatly because I was there, unfortunately, and know what happened [she wrote Geoffrey Hellman]. That very morning Gibbs called me on the phone and said, "Could you come right over—Elizabeth has just killed herself!" Previously, promptly at 10, he had called to say she was sick and he couldn't leave her. The call to come over happened to be between 12:30 and 1:00 when I was eating a sandwich lunch at my desk. I went, of course, and since he hadn't told me on the phone how she had killed herself, I went with some fear, especially because I was then pregnant with Andy's and my first child. I spent the whole day with Gibbs and finally got him to let a doctor come and put him in a hospital under sedation. I absolutely know that O'Hara was out of town and that there had been no riotous party at the Gibbs apartment the night before; and Gibbs was completely sober when I saw him. Also, I'm sure that he never said the awful remark Brendan reports as a rumor. When I got to the apartment, Gibbs was moaning over and over "I never

should have left the room." He had been up all night with Elizabeth and had had no breakfast, and he had given her a sleeping pill and thought she was asleep. After watching her quite a while, he stepped out into the living room or kitchen to get a bite to eat or to have a cigarette. She was only pretending to be asleep; when he left, she got up and locked herself in the bathroom and jumped out a small bathroom window. Anyway, I finally persuaded the police and the detectives who were swarming around to let Gibbs go or else he would be the next suicide. He was already threatening to kill himself and he kept emphasizing what bad publicity this was for *The New Yorker* and said he could never return to the magazine. I won't go back over the long hours before Gibbs at last let us call a doctor.

And so Katharine wrote her friends and relatives, imploring them not to believe what Brendan Gill had written about her. And she began annotating the book for inaccuracies—a task which she was not up to mentally or physically, but which preoccupied her nearly until the end of her life, until Andy finally insisted that she put it aside.

It is to Katharine White's credit that even at her most passionate she did not resort to attacking Gill personally, and that she even acknowledged that he had been very valuable to the magazine. (Still, she was human, and a couple of comments slipped through. "If he had kept it to his own autobiography it might have been quite charming. But he is no longer a charming man; he's a writer who showed more promise than he could fulfill." And to another friend: "I bought his first piece, and I must say I was ashamed of it when I read it in the Gill New Yorker book, but at least I did see promise, and of course he has turned out to be a very valuable person for the magazine.") Katharine was delighted by a piece Nora Ephron wrote for *Esquire* in June of 1975 in which Brendan Gill was given his comeuppance ("Brendan Gill and The New Yorker"). But she refused an offer from George Core of the *Sewanee Review* to review the Gill book; she realized that she was too personally involved to do it objectively.

During the first months following the book's publication, Katharine contemplated suing Brendan Gill for libel, an action from which she was dissuaded by her lawyer, Milton Greenstein, Andy, and Roger Angell. They told her that others had been more seriously maligned than she, and that Gill had protected himself from libel suits anyway, by telling anecdotes with the cushioning phrase "There was a rumor that . . ." or "One story goes that . . ." Still, Katharine could not shrug the book off. "I know my friends will know that all these things said about me are untrue," she wrote unconvincingly to William Shawn, "and I have had quite a number of letters to that effect, but it does worry me that thousands and thousands of people I don't know will be pitying Andy for having such a horrifying, glacial, and power hungry wife." Gloom settled over her; her distress was made worse by a feeling of powerlessness. "[I] even have nightmares at night," she wrote William Shawn in April, 1975. Convinced that "there [was] nothing that [could] be done to correct the matter," she came to feel that she "would press no libel suit even if I had one." But she would write a friend that the book had "[come] near to killing me."

"The horrible old Brendan Gill book, which gives such a ghastly picture of your old Grandmother," Katharine wrote to Callie. It was a hurt from which she would never fully recover. Protesting too much, in letter after letter she insisted that she was no longer troubled by the book, no longer depressed. Meanwhile, she went on with her copious annotations.

Another book had also preoccupied Katharine White during these years. Since 1972, she had been helping Andy with a volume of his letters; in late 1976 they were published by Harper & Row as the *Letters of E. B. White*. The November 21st issue of the *New York Times Book Review* carried a front-page review of the book by Wilfrid Sheed. Katharine's heated reaction to the review recalled her response to *Here at The New Yorker*.

She was deeply offended by Sheed's eloquent and laudatory review, calling it, in a letter to Callie, a "dreadful putdown . . . so full of inaccuracies and malice." Others, Katharine wrote, "seem[ed] to find [the *Letters*] amusing and readable despite" Sheed's review. Katharine aired her grievances to Wilfrid Sheed as well, in a letter that unfortunately is unavailable. But in Sheed's responding letter to Katharine and in her letter to Callie, the source of Katharine's grievances becomes clear.

She was naturally disturbed by Sheed's suggestion that Andy was a "minor" writer, and she complained to him for using the word.* Katharine also took exception to Sheed's observation that White refused to lecture and join certain literary organizations, disregarding Sheed's acknowledgment that Andy had his "good reasons." And she was hurt by his description of a Dear John letter White had written Alice Burchfield as "icy": Katharine was understandably disturbed by such a portrait of her loving husband.

Katharine's defensiveness about Andy is of course characteristic. But she is far from being reasonable (Sheed's review, as has been pointed out, was

---

*Katharine apparently confused Wilfrid Sheed's words with some in the article on *The New Yorker* by Tom Wolfe, for nowhere does Sheed use the word "minor." Sheed pointed out that White was not at his writerly best when he took up political writing during the forties, and he questioned White's motives for doing so. "Why? Perhaps because this country is merciless to good small talents. A writer who doesn't take chances and swing for the fences (whether or not he has a prayer of reaching them) is less than a man. White must surely have been aware of this."

highly favorable; he obviously enjoyed and recommended the book). She not only compares Sheed's review to Anne Carroll Moore's campaign against the *Charlotte* and *Stuart* books, she theorizes to Callie that Sheed, like others who have written unfavorably about *The New Yorker* and its writers, had himself been rejected by the magazine or denied a job there. It is an old lady's letter, the grumbling of a person who has withstood too many disappointments, too many battles with illness, too many useless years (so Katharine had felt since her retirement). The shaky, wandering, handwritten letter to Callie shows it. Though not yet worn out, Katharine was worn down, and the *Letters* had contributed to this weary state of mind and body.

Like *The Trumpet of the Swan,* the *Letters of E. B. White* had been undertaken to earn money. Collections of Andy's essays and verse were also planned, Andy not being up to writing anything new. From the beginning, the project was beset by problems. Gus Lobrano's daughter, Dorothy Guth, was appointed collector and editor of the letters. Mrs. Guth had done an admirable job of retrieving White's letters, but her work had been hampered by her own family's illnesses. There had been a turnover at Harper's of editors assigned to the book, and both Katharine and Andy had put many hours into the project as well—the effect of all this, of the delays and the several years spent on the project, had tried them both.

In her early eighties Katharine still found it hard to slow down. She had never accepted old age and its attendant infirmities; she was not resigned to the loss of her young and vigorous self, the Lady Before Breakfast, who "by eight o'clock" in the morning had "rewritten noon." And when in this unsettled state of mind she was confronted with a young woman who must have seemed to her to possess that lost energy and confidence, she responded —not directly, but in her personal letters—with uncharacteristic captiousness.

The young woman was Corona Machemer, the last editor Harper's assigned to the book. Miss Machemer had been assistant to Cass Canfield before swiftly ascending to the position of editor at Harper & Row. Thirty-three years old at the time she met the Whites—the same age as Katharine when she began her editorial career at *The New Yorker*—she was hard-working, with a single-minded and passionate intensity about her work that reminds one of Katharine White years earlier. There was a physical resemblance as well—faintly, in the face, and in her nice legs and dainty, small feet, like Katharine's before she became old and ill. Corona Machemer laughed hard at Andy's jokes, the way Katharine did. Katharine's reaction to her was, from the start, severely critical.

Katharine thought Miss Machemer bright and a good organizer, but she considered her "lacking in humor," and too young and inexperienced for the job. To begin with, she had been "trained only to teach Biology," Katharine complained to Frank Sullivan.

> She had read only two of Andy's books (one of them a children's book) and it appears to us that she has read practically nothing anyway. (Never read *The New Yorker,* for instance; never heard of Frank Sullivan or Wolcott Gibbs or Harold Ross et al, or anything that happened in the '20s, '30s, and '40s.) Well, naturally, although she is bright, she asked innumerable foolish questions but some good ones.

Miss Machemer's questions led to a heavy apparatus of footnotes, which Katharine thought unnecessary and inappropriate for a book of this kind, and many of which White later removed. All of this, said Katharine, had created a lot of extra work. Katharine objected.

> During her week here she drove Andy so hard, expecting him at his age to work morning, afternoon, and late into the evening, that after four days of this Andy had an attack of tachycardia and had to retire to bed for a day taking nicotinic acid—the specific for a fast and irregular heart. After twenty-[four] hours, he rose and went at it again.

Katharine's complaints sound legitimate, and her concern for her elderly husband is understandable. It is her harping that gives one pause: from late 1975 until the end of the following year, the same grievances about Corona Machemer appear in Katharine's letters. One is particularly struck by Katharine's constant references to Miss Machemer's youth. She is "the young woman from Harper's"; "a thirty-three year old girl"; "this crazy new young editor"; "this silly young editor"; "an over zealous young editor"; "the new baby editor." She is also, of course, the Lady Before Breakfast; not, perhaps, exactly as Katharine White had been, but Katharine may have seen just enough of her young self in Corona Machemer, and enough that was different and objectionable, to feel jealous of her. After Katharine's death, Andy White and Corona Machemer became affectionate friends, White finding in her much that reminded him of his late wife when she had been "in full editorial flight." Katharine likely observed something in Andy's response to Miss Machemer that troubled her, or at least saw the potential for such a response.

Though Katharine had no reason to feel insecure about her husband's love and fidelity, she had often been made uncomfortable, and perhaps jealous, by Andy's flirtatiousness with other women—for him, a natural, inherently innocent, but at times obvious display of affection or admiration. Katharine may have been reminded of Ernest; and she was possibly unsettled by such free behavior anyway, of which she, with her New England reserve, was incapable. And Katharine herself was old now; her face was wrinkled. She could never again be as she had been—nor could her marriage, which seems to have long since ceased to be sexual. Even conversation was now difficult, she talking in a faint old lady's voice, he being hard of hearing. Andy was not only seven years her junior; he was still youthful, despite his ailments, still charming. He was a romantic man whom one might find out picking wild rose hips for his wife. His wife doted on him. Callie Angell remembered the phone ringing once when Andy was in the Blue Hill Hospital for tests, and Katharine flinging her walker aside and rushing to answer it: "That must be Andy!"

Another, or an additional, explanation for Katharine's response to Corona Machemer is that Katharine was offended that Harper's had not asked *her* to edit the letters. Though she would certainly have refused the job because of precarious health and lack of time, she may have wanted to be asked. It was hard to watch from her sofa as Andy collaborated with someone else, hard to observe another woman helping him as she herself had done for so many years and was no longer able to do. They consulted her—should this letter be used? should this be cut?—but it was not the same.

To be sure, Corona Machemer's first visit with the Whites had not been auspicious. On her last night in their home, without informing her hosts, she left her contact lenses and lens case to steam on the stove. Andy entered the kitchen to find the lenses, case, and a sieve on fire, the result being a dusting of black ash that wafted through the house, settling on walls, drapes, bookcases, etc. "Little does she know how many days' work had to go into cleaning it up again," Katharine wrote to Callie, exaggerating the mess. It was a story she would repeat, not without satisfaction. In younger, vigorous years, she might have laughed at the incident.

September 6, 1976

Dear Jill:

I am really overwhelmed by your gift to me of that perfectly beautiful huge album, filled with pictures of those I love the best. (I should add that there are a daughter and her three children, and Joe's wife and their three children who are equally loved, and I only wish they could have been here when you were.) You have many excellent pictures of Andy.

Katharine was writing to the photographer Jill Krementz, who had presented the Whites with an expensive leather-bound album of photographs of Katharine and Andy, Roger, Carol, Callie, and Alice Angell, after a recent photographic session in Maine.

> As for the pictures that include me, I'm such a ghastly object nowadays that I can hardly bear to look at myself but I shall give Roger the better one of myself and him as one in his collection. One trouble is that I always forget to rearrange my garments before you get shooting. In this instance my belt had slipped down around my hips and my silk dress was rumpled up at the top and what appears to be an enormous belly protrudes disgustingly. Because of all the cortisone I have had to imbibe for my dermatosis, I do have what is known medically as a cortisone belly, but it is actually a rather small protruding belly and not that great huge one shown, because the belt had slipped down to my groins. I don't know whether the pictures could be cut off to cover this up but I suppose not.

She rambled on about the photographs she was ordering, and other matters:

> I think we may use some of the photographs of Andy for gifts to his remaining brother and sisters. We just haven't got as far as thinking much about Christmas yet, and it makes Andy angry to have it mentioned in September.

"The big thing I lack, after health, is money these days and this particular Christmas season seems to be particularly costly because all my nurses and household help (except Edith) have so many children or grandchildren," Katharine wrote to Callie in December of 1976. "I give books to the children of all of them. It's my one big splurge." The want of money had become a familiar refrain. Ever conscious of the great expense she was to Andy, she was compelled to explain to friends and family that, lacking money, she must sell a slice of land (she didn't); that she needed the tax deduction her donation of treasured letters and books to Bryn Mawr would bring her; that she could not keep up the garden—"I'm broke all the time and while Andy isn't, we just can't keep adding manpower." She had for several years felt deeply guilty about the terrible animated film version of *Charlotte's Web*, Andy having sold the book in order to help pay Katharine's enormous medical bills. (When the movie was televised, Katharine was more upset about it than Andy—"That's not the way our barn looks!") At Christmastime, recalled Nancy Stableford, "she was one to consistently say, 'I'm sending too much money. I can't afford it.' And she'd say she was therefore sending less than she had last year. But she always sent exactly the same amount—a check for

$100." "I never thought I would have to borrow from savings to give my Christmas presents but that is true this year," Katharine had written to S. N. Behrman several years earlier. "I figure it's better to give away my savings while I'm alive because inheritance taxes will take most of them. I have a terrible lot of little hostages to fortune and I am a real matriarch."

More than twenty years earlier Katharine White had described herself as "happily matriarchal" when surrounded by children and grandchildren in summer. Her children were a source of pride to her, both because she loved them and because each one of them had become successful and happy in his or her chosen career. Roger Angell had not only become a first-rate writer most widely celebrated for his baseball writings and books, he was also a senior editor at *The New Yorker,* and a very good one, and had inherited some of Katharine's own former writers—including John Updike, Vladimir Nabokov, and, in Roger's early years at the magazine, Thurber.

Having devoted the early years of her marriage to the rearing of her three children, Nancy Stableford had since worked as a teacher and head of the science department at the Moravian Seminary for Girls in Bethlehem, Pennsylvania; as a lay missionary teacher of biology at Trinity College in Quezon City, the Philippines; as a teacher at various Pennsylvania colleges; and as an active volunteer and member of many boards—including Planned Parenthood in recent years.

Joel White had followed an altogether different course, settling in Maine and satisfying his lifelong love of boats by becoming a master craftsman and designer of wooden boats and owner of the boatyard in Brooklin's Center Harbor. Having taken Maine to heart and wanting to settle there, having attended to Andy's frequent assertion that it's important to enjoy what you do, Joe had not only created a satisfying life for himself but had done it with his parents' aplomb, distinguishing himself in his chosen profession and earning the admiration of boat lovers and naval architects alike. He had inherited his father's love of carpentry and small boat sailing and both parents' high standards and capacity for hard work. His reputation as a boat builder was equaled by his fame as a naval architect, and he was an expert sailor as well—a fact that never prevented his enormously proud mother from worrying about him so much whenever he was away in a boat that she often wanted to send the Maine coast guard after him.

Katharine now had nine grandchildren, and six great-grandchildren, the great-grandchildren all from Nancy's children: Kitty Stableford Bennett had two children, Joshua and Rachel Hecter, from her first marriage; Jon Stableford was the father of Jennifer and Jason; and Sarah Stableford Albee had two sons, Benjamin and Jacob.

Katharine had perhaps never appreciated her family more than she did now, when time seemed short and her life was so restricted. No longer able to travel to Florida, she found the long Maine winters especially confining. Now, during the winter of 1976–77, the *Letters of E. B. White* having at last been published, she sought the company of a granddaughter; in February (1977) Callie Angell paid her a visit. Callie would have happy memories of this last visit with her grandmother, of an evening when Andy got out all his old records and played them for her—Benny Goodman and old love songs—and he and Grandma serenaded her. Grandma was certainly more in tune with the bygone era of Benny Goodman, the age of radio, than she was with today's entertainment. (Her television viewing was confined to the World Series, which she watched while polishing gourds.) There had been another evening during that visit when Callie and Andy were watching television, and Goldie Hawn's name was mentioned. From her bedroom across the hall Katharine called out, "Who's Goldie Hawn?" Andy called back that he couldn't explain Goldie Hawn.

Katharine White was in some ways an old-fashioned grandmother, old-fashioned in her sense of tradition, in her notions of propriety. Christmas would be greeted with the traditional plum pudding, which nobody liked. As youngsters, the country-reared White grandchildren had been required to dress for dinner with their paternal grandparents. (The dinners were always good and predictable: there was, for instance, the roast beef dinner, with deep-dish apple pie.) Martha White might wear a dress her grandmother had given her; that was the only occasion she would have to wear such a dress. The grandchildren, especially the boys, rather hated going there for dinner—they would have to dress up, and it was boring. They would have to sit at the table for a long time before going off to play, read, or watch television. Grandchildren were forbidden to chew gum in the White house, and were told by their parents to spit it out before they got there. The farmhouse, with its barn, its woodburning stove for cooking, its fireplaces, and its wonderful cooking smells, was itself old-fashioned, and the leisure-time activities of spring and summer likewise belonged to an earlier era. There were picnics at the shore: soggy mayonnaise-and-tomato sandwiches, watercress sandwiches with the crusts cut off, stuffed eggs, lemonade (made with fresh lemons), iced tea or coffee, all got up in a large wicker hamper. There was the proper, orderly game of croquet (Martha White recalled that Uncle Roger kept things light). As a young girl, Martha would help her grandmother in the garden:

> That was proper too. I would go out in my little pink dress, carrying a flat basket with a handle. She'd have shears this long. . . . Usually, her arrangements were perfect. She'd have just the right amount of flowers to fill the vases with,

but occasionally she'd need more flowers. She'd tell me to get five more *scabiosa,* or whatever—sometimes referring by name to a flower I didn't know. I was always afraid I'd do the wrong thing, bring the wrong kind, but I never did.

It was not that Katharine's granddaughter was afraid of getting in trouble with her, but, as Kitty Stableford put it, "her approval meant a lot."

Katharine White was a grandmother to be looked up to. She had had an office at *The New Yorker* and she had an office in her house—"There was no crashing into her or Andy's offices uninvited," recalled Kitty Stableford. Usually, if a grandchild was called into Katharine's office, it was for "a serious talk—very serious business." Kitty was conscious of her grandmother's being someone important, just as important as Andy, though she was not a famous writer the way he was. Kitty never felt that her grandmother was at all inferior to Andy, or in any way less important. As a child Kitty would tell her friends that she too was going to go to Bryn Mawr. She was proud of both her mother and her grandmother, and she wanted to follow in their footsteps.

Katharine was keenly interested in her grandchildren, questioning them about their interests and schoolwork (Martha White said that her grandmother always knew her grades), correcting them in conversation. If Kitty said "my sister," Grandma would say, "Your sister has a name." Martha White thought it was probably harder for Katharine to be close to the boys: Martha could cut flowers with her, and it was always she who sat next to Grandma on the couch. ("I think the boys thought that if *I* sat next to her, she wouldn't ask them as many questions.")

To the young grandchild, Katharine's interest in her could be daunting. She would ask the Stableford children which one of their parents they liked best. As a child Kitty had visited her grandmother at her Turtle Bay apartment. Grandma would ask, "Have you had a bowel movement today?" and in this was rather formidable, expressing great concern. Kitty would enter Grandma and Andy's bedroom, where both would be reading newspapers in bed. Grandma would sternly instruct her that if she had a bowel movement she was to let her see it before flushing the toilet. Kitty summoned her courage to lie, saying she'd flushed it before she remembered to show her.

On the other hand, this kindly, formidable, and proper grandmother sent a congratulatory telegram to Martha White when she made honors in college; allowed Kitty Stableford to smoke and drink in the White home; gave Martha a copy of *The French Lieutenant's Woman* when she was in high school, though she worried about its being a bit racy for her. In her younger years, she had gone sailing and swimming with her grandchildren, and was in the water almost as much as they were: she was no stay-on-the-beach grandma. Kitty remembered Katharine as very demonstrative, able to say, "I love you." Kitty believed her. Grandma was, of course, a worrier. She worried about her grandchildren and their happiness as much as she worried about everyone she cared about. Kitty recalled Katharine giving her a hard time about driving and sailing, though Kitty was old enough to drive and had been sailing since she was a child.

Katharine's interest in her grandchildren was generous. When her granddaughters became young women, Katharine wrote them long, warm letters, entering into their lives and interests, sharing with them her own history and interests. (Katharine's letters to Callie Angell are far more personal than are most of the letters she wrote to her friends.) She gave them unexpected cash gifts. She had heard that Callie needed contact lenses and she sent her a check for $100. She also took it upon herself to do some reading about contact lenses, and to inform Callie that the soft lenses could hurt the eyes. She thought carefully about gifts for them, ordering books with their interests in mind, or books she thought they should read, like the novels of Jane Austen and Elizabeth Gaskell (one granddaughter had several editions of the same Gaskell novel, which Katharine kept forgetting she had sent her); ordering sweaters from catalogues with their hair and eye color in mind. In her effort to send them what was appropriate, she could be unintentionally funny: when Nancy's son Jon Stableford was living in the ancestral town of Winchester, Massachusetts, Katharine gave him a cemetery plot for his birthday.

Katharine White tried to be modern, and, most of all, literate, in her approach to the changing times and the dilemmas confronting her grandchildren and their generation. She was, for instance, familiar with Maine's stiff new marijuana law and she informed at least two of her grandchildren about it in case they happened to smoke marijuana and planned to carry it with them to Maine in their car. In a letter to Callie and Alice Angell, Katharine devoted several long typed paragraphs to a discussion of the law and how it was enforced, repeating herself, and assuring her granddaughters that she herself did not think marijuana "wicked," or the Maine law fair. Still, she hoped they did not smoke it. While trying not to lecture her granddaughters (twenty-three and twenty-six at the time of their visit), she could not help recounting the story of a local couple who were seriously injured when a girl who was high on marijuana drove her car into theirs. And Katharine wrote of what a doctor had told her: that the marijuana plant has many varieties—both harmless and harmful—and the danger in legalizing the stuff is that one cannot be sure of where it has come from.

Katharine's generosity with her grandchildren had its limits. At the request of one of her children, she once agreed to help pay for psychotherapy for a grandchild, which she did for a while, then abruptly announced that she wanted to stop—as abruptly, apparently, as she had ceased giving money to Elsie. But she didn't stop. When the grandchild's parents threatened to remove one of their other children from college in order to pay for the therapy, Katharine continued to pay her share. Katharine was "prone to do that kind of thing," said Nancy Stableford. She would be thinking about something, and would suddenly come to a decision and act on it. What appears to have been selfish or cold behavior is probably attributable to Katharine's nagging insecurity about money, her persistent fear that she would run out of money or leave Andy without enough money if she should die before him. It was the fear of a retired woman who was by nature a working woman, the fear of the old.

Katharine spent the first months of 1977 in her quietly busy way. Andy was feeling oppressed by the flood of mail his *Letters* had prompted, and had turned most of them over to her to answer. Katharine managed to keep up her personal correspondence while generously responding to these countless friends and strangers alike.

Unless she had a visitor or a doctor's appointment, there was little variation in Katharine's daily routine. After lunch, she typically remained downstairs until two o'clock, when she went to her bedroom for a nap. She was down again at four, brewing herself a very thick coffee to be poured into a tall glass filled with ice. Except for a token sip of a celebratory cocktail or the wine someone had brought for dinner, she never touched alcohol, had not since the late 1960s, when she found herself taking too much medication.

Physically, Katharine continued to deteriorate. Discovered to be suffering from senile macular degeneration, a condition that could lead to blindness, she was now forced to use both a magnifying glass and glasses with special magnification to read. She insisted that she could not see what she wrote, as it was impossible to hold both a magnifying glass and a pen in her hands; nevertheless, her dictated, typed letters continued to bear her own handwritten, nearly illegible interlined words and emendations. "If I had been warned, I could have learned touch typing and other things to aid the blind," she wrote Elizabeth Lawrence. A kind friend was coming to read to her once a week; the friend had picked up where Katharine left off in *The Letters of Virginia Woolf.*

Katharine still struggled with feelings of uselessness and the fear that she would become financially dependent on Andy. Writing, she would contend, was still a need. "I *need* to write and earn because I have become such an expensive creature for Andy to maintain, with my eight-hour day nurses and my ten-hour night nurses, that if I could manage to write and earn something I'd be happy." But she realized that her professional writing days were over. She did not think it in her power to produce even one more garden piece. Having climbed into her hospital bed at nine or ten o'clock with the assistance of her nurse and the little wooden step Joel had built for her, she would still be writing letters or talking to the nurse at midnight.

A visitor to the Whites' home would be warmly and graciously received by the elderly woman who sat nearly immobile on the living-room sofa, her constrained body in marked contrast to her alert and beautiful dark eyes, and the slender and still agile man with white hair and mustache who watched her so closely, jumping up occasionally to adjust the pillow behind her back or push an ashtray beneath the long curl at the end of her cigarette. "No, Kay, you're wrong," he would say, and then begin telling his version of the story. She would insist that she was right, he wrong, and as he continued with his tale, a grin would begin at the corners of her mouth, and then she would laugh, a smoker's laugh, chesty, faintly wheezing, and pleasant.

The spring thaw began. The roadways began to clear, and Katharine looked forward to getting out to walk. Gripping her walker, she would proceed carefully along the highway in front of her house, "facing the traffic as one is counseled to do." One day, she and her nurse had been confronted by a

> ruffian-looking fellow in a huge truck [who] swung right over in front of us on the wrong side of the road, where there was a curve ahead. He leaned out and said to me "Are you prepared to meet your Maker?" I replied, "If you stay on this side of the road I expect to meet him any moment." I refused the literature he held out because I knew that he was probably one of the Holy Roller sect of which we have quite a number in this region. My nurse was more sensible and accepted the literature and thanked him and said "I have my own church but I will read about yours."

In late spring or early summer of 1977, Katharine suffered another attack of congestive heart failure, which left her feeling weak but anxious to recover for the upcoming annual visit of Roger Angell and his family, which included a much-loved six-year-old son, John Henry. She continued to smoke the cigarettes she claimed she had never inhaled (she partially inhaled them), realizing that if she had she would have died long since.

Katharine was soon picking up her correspondence, writing a letter of condolence to Véra Nabokov on July 11, following the death of Vladimir.

I still think back with longing and pleasure to my contacts with him while editing, for *The New Yorker,* the chapters of "Conclusive Evidence" and "Pnin." And I still cherish the two paperback volumes of the Olympia Press Edition of "Lolita," which he gave me. Eventually, all my books by *New Yorker*-contributors are to go to my college, the Rare Book Room of Bryn Mawr

—and she was briefly distracted, lapsing into an account of her collection. She had a tendency now to sit with her head cradled in her hands, a melancholy posture that troubled Roger, who told her to stop.

I hope Dmitri is there to help you. Andy sends you his sorrowful greetings and his sympathy.

We live the year round in Maine now because I can no longer travel and I am subject to spells of congestive heart failure, i.e. when I can't breathe, I'm given oxygen at home—our local volunteer ambulance rushes me over to the intensive care unit of the Blue Hill Hospital. I get about on a walker quite well but need day and night nurses, so I am an expensive bother. What is worse is that now my eyesight is failing. I have peripheral vision, but I can't read or see what I write without the aid of a magnifying glass. Andy, too, is slowing up, but we both work hard, in one way or another, in the mornings and evenings. Andy's greatest problem is high blood pressure.

Dear Vera, do keep up your legendary courage

—and she drifted back, fondly, to memories of Vladimir.

Two days later, on July 13, Katharine wrote to Jean Stafford: "I think about you often and do wish to know how you are—I don't even know where you are and no one has sent me news of you." Jean had had a stroke.

Here we are in something of a mess too. I have lost my eyesight so far as reading and writing goes. I have plenty of peripheral vision and walk around without hitting the furniture, and I can even see the view of the cove, though less distinctly. Distance vision is easier than near, but if a fox crossed the pasture I wouldn't be likely to see it.

After a little more talk about her eyesight, Katharine returned to her concerns about Jean's health, the enormous medical bills she was faced with (a fund to which Katharine contributed had been established by Stafford's friends to help with the bills), and whether Jean had someone to care for her and feed her. Did she have some land she could sell to help pay her pressing expenses? If Jean couldn't answer this letter herself, did she have a friend or neighbor who could telephone Katharine collect and let her know how Jean was?

Two of Andy's sisters . . . are living in a nursing home. One is in Saint Johnsland. . . .

Andy, himself, has not been at all well this summer because of high blood pressure. . . . He had his 78th birthday this week. . . .

Did I tell you that Roger has bought the cottage he is living in but will not sign the deed until September because his landlady had an August tenant. This is nice for me because it means they will be coming back each summer.

Excuse a dull and feeble letter. The next thing I have to do is to read a lot of letters from ancestors & my aunt.

Perhaps Bowdoin College, the repository of Shepley family papers, would want some of her Maine grandfather's letters. "He was the grandfather who was murdered. Lots of love—Katharine."

Six days after her letter to Jean Stafford, on a hot day in late July, Katharine's heart failed her once more. It happened early in the morning. A nurse was with her. Someone called the fire department, who rushed to the White house with oxygen. It had happened several times before, but there was something different about this time; sensing it, Katharine said to Andy, "I'm sick." She did not usually say that. Katharine was rushed by ambulance to the hospital. She was running a high fever and was beyond the reach of medication. The doctor told Andy that the signs were not very good. Katharine was moved out of the room where infectious people were kept, and into intensive care. There was no communication between Katharine and Andy that afternoon. As the day wore on and she gradually lost consciousness, her husband of almost forty-eight years sat nearby, watching the flashing light of the monitor. Roger and Carol Angell and Joe and Allene White were with him. Katharine died at five o'clock on the afternoon of Wednesday, July 20, after a day's struggle. As Andy would recall later, she had seemed beautiful to him the first time he saw her, and she seemed beautiful when he gave her the small kiss that was good-bye.

At Katharine's request, there was no funeral service, just a simple committal service on July 23 at the gravesite in Brooklin's small cemetery, about three miles down the road from the White home. Unable to bring himself to attend the service, Andy remained at home. In attendance were Katharine's three children and their spouses, and several of her nine grandchildren.

Andy wrote the service, which was read by Roger Angell. As Katharine had requested, it included a reading of the poem her husband had long ago written about her, which she had always loved, "Lady Before Breakfast." "It is a judgement about me—it's me as I was when I was vigorous, and I like it."

To the writers Katharine White never lost touch with, she had remained that woman, her vigorous spirit unchanged, her passion for good writing undiminished. On the desk in her study at home lay a letter from one of them: "To have your affectionate and warm letter made me feel nurtured, as you did indeed always nurture me."

Acknowledgments

Had E. B. White not decided to take a chance on me nearly ten years ago and cooperate in my pursuit of Katharine, I would not have attempted the project. Andy White's assistance over the years amounted to dozens of letters and notes, to me and others on my behalf, full access to Katharine White's papers at the Bryn Mawr College Library and to the letters I wished to see in his own collection at Cornell, and a number of weekends spent talking and socializing in Maine, where I was a frequent guest at his table and a welcome visitor (so he made me feel) to his home. He was unfailingly generous with his time and his memories of Katharine. He was a friend whom I quickly came to love. By encouraging me and helping me with this book he forever changed the course of my life. I could never adequately thank him. I will always miss him and be indebted to him.

Without Roger Angell, Nancy Angell Stableford, and Joel and Allene White, who were always available to answer questions and patiently and at great length discuss my subject with me, I would have been so seriously handicapped as to make it foolish to proceed with the biography. I am deeply grateful to them for their willingness to talk openly, for their intelligence and their psychological perceptions (which guided me in my own thinking and made my work a lot easier), and for their hospitality. I thank them for allowing me to make a selection from their family photographs for use in the book. All of them—together with Carol Angell, Louis Stableford, and Martha White Temple—read the completed manuscript as well, caught me in errors, and made valuable suggestions. Roger Angell taught me some important things about good writing and reporting, told me much about *The New Yorker* and corrected my misinformation about the magazine, and did me the favor of thinking up the title of this book. And his help at *The New Yorker*—his cheerful willingness to talk to people on my behalf and get a hold of pertinent research material—made a great difference. He was a wonderful friend and ally, enormously patient with this fledgling biographer. My conversations with Nancy Stableford were among the liveliest, most memorable, and most helpful, and I owe much to her sharp memory and her generosity. Allene White, as I have stated in the notes at the back of the book, clarified and corrected some of the genealogical information and told me a lot about the Whites' life together in Maine. Joel White, Carol Angell, and Louis Stableford were extremely helpful and accommodating, and very enlightening about KSW. Certainly no biographer was ever luckier in his subject's living relatives than I have been in the White, Angell, and Stableford families.

With their kind and tireless interest, my family and friends boosted my spirits and made me feel less alone in the solitary work—no small thing in the long journey to book's end. I thank them all. Several of these people have been exceptionally helpful. My grandmother, Honor Lister, to whom this book is dedicated, financed the early research trips needed to produce enough pages to obtain a contract. She did this as a gift, attached only to her love and good wishes. And she was ever interested, always constant in her faith in me. My friend Betty (Mrs. R. B.) Early was another patroness, and because of her my life and work were made easier. My mother-in-law, Julie Yanikoski, came to my house to babysit for my daughter, Alexandra, one morning a week to give me some precious extra hours to work—this she did faithfully for more than a year. My other grandmother, Claire Davis, traveled all the way from Oregon to Massachusetts to help care for my daughter for two weeks as I was finishing the book. All of these wonderful people were supportive and helpful far beyond the call of friendship or family duty.

My good friends Leo Dolenski and D. Elise Brian were of invaluable help. Leo, who is curator of manuscripts at Bryn Mawr College's Canaday Library, was always available to help me in every possible way with Katharine White's large collection. He not only guided me through it during my research trips to Bryn Mawr, but in long, delightful letters and sometimes over the telephone, he patiently and thoroughly answered my frequent questions, and, along with his wife, the writer D. Elise Brian, became a good personal friend. From the beginning, both cheered me on, and I came to depend upon their support. There were times when, lacking confidence, I might not have persisted without their encouragement and assistance. I cannot thank them enough.

My dear friends Anne Jones and John R. Davis (who is also my brother) steadily conveyed their great enthusiasm for my work and their belief in my ability to do it well, which was more important to me than they know.

I thank my agent, John Ware, for his energetic and excellent work on my behalf; my editor, Larry Ashmead, for his good humor and sensible guidance and for leaving me alone to work; Larry's assistant, Margaret Wimberger, for her hard work and her many efforts to accommodate me in some particular wish for the published book; Maggie Cheney, who

Acknowledgments

copyedited the book with great skill; and Debra Orenstein, legal counsel.

Without the suggestion of my graduate school adviser, Dr. Wylie Sypher, that I forget about writing a thesis on Katharine White and write a biography instead, this book would probably not have been written. Dr. Sypher's counsel and interest during the past eight years, his prompt answers to my letters and the questions I asked, helped sustain me more than he realizes.

Many others contributed to the book by granting me interviews, answering letters, providing information of various kinds, putting me in touch with other people, and offering personal assistance. I appreciate their help more than I have space enough to say. They include: Kenneth Allen, Alice Angell, Callie Angell, Henrietta Bancroft, Greta Lee and Parker Banzhaf, Louise Seaman Bechtel, Ruth Beckwith, the Beinecke Rare Book and Manuscript Library (Yale University), Kitty Stableford Bennett, Bernard Bergman, Burton Bernstein, Gardner Botsford, the Bowdoin College Library, the Bryn Mawr College Library's Rare Books Room, Mary Cable, Richard Chapin, Marian and Stuart Chase, Louise Collins, Joseph H. Cooper, Cornell University Library's Rare Books Room, Malcolm Cowley, Elizabeth Cullinan, Edith Iglauer Daly, Jean Davis, Patricia H. Davis, Peter De Vries, Liz Dickinson, Donald Eddy, Susan Edwards, Scott Elledge, Katharine Fernstrom, Leah Cadbury Furtmuller, Donald Gallup, Penelope Gilliatt, Arthur Goldschmidt, Julia Gray, Mr. and Mrs. Thornton Gray, Milton Greenstein, Julie F. Grey, Dorothy Lobrano Guth, Dianne M. Gutscher, Beulah Hagen, Nancy Hale, Katherine Romans Hall, Mark Harris, Shirley Hazzard, Dr. Joseph Henderson, the Historical Society of Saratoga Springs, Buckner Hollingsworth, Dr. Frederick A. J. Kingery, Jill Krementz, Elizabeth Lawrence, Barbara Ellen Leighton, Dr. S. Monte Levin, Susan Lovenburg, Corona Machemer, the Kristine Mann Library, the Seeley G. Mudd Mann Library (Princeton University), the library of the Massachusetts Bay Transportation Authority, William Maxwell, Mary McCarthy, William McGuire, Faith McNulty, Joseph Mitchell, Véra Nabokov, Evelyn Nelson, *The New Yorker,* Mrs. George J. Openhym, Francisca Warren Paine, Mollie Panter-Downes, Pennell C. Peck, Polly Pierce, Nora J. Quinlan, Lillian Ross, George M. Sanborn, May Sarton, William Shawn, Hayden Shepley, Dr. Patricia G. Simmons, Carol Smith, the Sophia Smith Collection (Smith College), Jonathan Stableford, Francis Steegmuller, Richard Sterne, the Stockbridge Library Association, James Tanis, Martha White Temple, Niccolò Tucci, the Rare Books Room of the University of Colorado at Boulder, John Updike, Harriet Walden, Robert Ward, Eugene P. Watson Memorial Library (Northwestern State University of Louisiana), Carol Wells, Lucy Fischer West, Elena Wilson, Joan H. Winterkorn, and Mrs. Rachel P. Young.

Acknowledgments

Last, and with special pleasure, I thank my husband, Charles Yanikoski. Without this marriage of true minds, without Chuck's astonishing confidence in me and his insistence that I keep writing, I certainly could not have finished the book when I did, and might not have finished it at all. Our frequent conversations about KSW, Chuck's infinite patience and his tireless efforts on my behalf—which included research, and copyediting and proofreading many times over—affected the biography more than anything else. If I have achieved something of importance or beauty in this book, it is because of Chuck.

Notes

The following abbreviations are used throughout these notes:

CA	Caroline (Callie) Angell
KSA	Katharine S. Angell
RA	Roger Angell
BMC	Bryn Mawr College
LHD	Linda H. Davis
RE	"Living on the Ragged Edge"
H&O	"Home and Office"
EL	Elizabeth Lawrence
MMcC	Mary McCarthy
APM	Aunt Poo's memoir
VN	Vladimir Nabokov
HWR	Harold W. Ross
O&U	"Onward and Upward in the Garden"
CSS	Charles Spencer Sergeant
ESS	Elizabeth (Elsie) Shepley Sergeant
KS	Katharine Sergeant
NAS	Nancy Angell Stableford
JS	Jean Stafford
FS	Frank Sullivan
JT	James Tanis
JTh	James Thurber
JU	John Updike
EBW	E. B. White
LEBW	*Letters of E. B. White*
KSW	Katharine S. White
NYer	*The New Yorker*
HATNY	*Here at The New Yorker*

Prologue

1 **pretty, like a cameo:** LHD interview with William Maxwell, 3/8/79.

1 **low and strong:** Faith McNulty to LHD, 11/18/77.

1 **on general magazine policy, new ideas:** KSW to Henry Volkening, 11/28/55.

1 **really obsessed:** KSW to Ida Treat Bergeret, 11/25/55.

2 **the loveliest apartment:** KSW to Ruth Limmer, 11/6/73.

2 **both as an actress:** KSW to James Tanis, 6/23/75.

2 **dream-duplex:** Louise Bogan quoted in Susan Edmiston and Linda D. Cirino, *Literary New York, A History and Guide,* Houghton Mifflin, Boston, 1976, p. 228.

2 **big sweet gum tree:** KSW to Ruth Limmer, 11/6/73.

2 **narrow and secret-looking** and following: Nadine Gordimer to KSW, 12/28/55.

2 **They are about the only friends:** KSW to May Sarton, 11/28/55.

2–3 **The new work will give me:** KSW to Nadine Gordimer, 11/30/55.

3 **have the pleasure of reading:** KSW to Mrs. H. H. Nash, 11/28/55.

3 **[becomes] too much for everyone:** Henry Volkening to KSW, 5/12/55.

3 **broody hen:** EBW, *Paris Review* interview (see bibliography)

3 **eating only a carrot:** MMcC to LHD, 9/29/78.

3 Footnote: **It tickled Sam pink:** KSW note on SNB, BMC.

4 **On Friday p.m.:** KSW Note on VN, 1977, BMC.

5 **I have read "Lolita":** KSW to VN, 3/25/57.

5 **in her refined quality:** LHD interview with Joseph Mitchell, 2/16/78.

7 **walking about in distress:** KSW note on letter to JS dated 12/22/55.

7 **its corners neatly:** "The Mountain Day," *The Collected Stories,* Jean Stafford, p. 245.

7 **the most dreadful:** KSW to JT, undated.

8 **too close to the actual:** KSW to JS, 5/4/56.

8 **too close to reality:** *Ibid.*

8 **not nearly as good as:** KSW to JT, undated.

8 **giddy:** "The Mountain Day," p. 233.

8 **Jean took this dreadful:** *Ibid.*

8 **My mother [Phyllis McGinley] has told me:** Julie Hayden to KSW, 1976.

8 **long-winded *old* lady:** KSW to JU, undated.

1. Hawthorn Road

Genealogical research for this chapter is based on the Sergeant papers at the Beinecke Library, Yale University, and the Shepley papers at Bowdoin College. I am also indebted to Allene White, who has done her own genealogical research and corrected many errors for me. For the story of Aunt Poo's marriage I have relied on Aunt Poo's own account in her memoir, and on E. B. White's essay, "Aunt Poo," June, 1942 (published in *One Man's Meat,* Harper & Row, New York, 1982).

13 **To me:** Nancy Hale to LHD, 12/18/77.
13 **First the pilgrims:** LEBW, pp. 174–5.
13 **in a company of Puritans:** From Sergeant summary, Beinecke Library, Yale University, pp. 1–2.
13 **personal attraction:** *Ibid.*
14 **apply your mind:** *Ibid.*
14 **such a severe dose:** ESS, autobiographical fragment.
15 **cultivated their own gardens** and following: O&U, 3/11/61.
15 **The fourth John Sheple:** Caleb Butler, *History of the Town of Groton,* MS/GRO/30.
16 **extreme poverty** and following: APM.
16 **masses of pale hair** and following: APM.
17 **maddeningly vague:** To NAS from KSW, 1/5/73.
17 **had a clear understanding** and following: APM.
17 **Bessie, with her beauty:** Shepley papers, Bowdoin College Library.
17 **a quiet young man** and following: APM.
18 **the three huge English hawthorn** and following: O&U, 6/9/62.
19 **Nobody can say:** APM.
19 **When my Aunt Caroline died:** To EL from KSW, 1/15/66.
19 **a marvelous person:** LHD interview with EBW, 6/19/79.
20 **too upright:** *Ibid.*
20 **had rages:** *Ibid.*
20 **a flawed personality:** LHD interview with NAS, 5/15/79.
20 **did not easily slip:** LHD interview with EBW, 6/19/79.
20 **silent:** *Ibid.*
20 **I have always tended:** KSW to Mr. Sokolov, undated.
20–21 **talented, tyrannical** and following: KSW, "Department of Amplification," NYer, 7/10/65, p. 71.
21 **impressive** and following: LHD interview with EBW, 6/19/79.
21 **the hell out of** and following: LHD interview with NAS, 5/15/79.
22 **I was the youngest:** KSW, "Books," NYer, 12/7/46.
22 **very low** and following: ESS, autobiographical fragment (unpublished).
22 **Boutet de Monvel's:** KSW, "Books," NYer, 12/7/46.
23 **first taste of realism** and following: *Ibid.*
23 **dearly loved:** KSW to JS, 1/13/75.
23 **the best picture:** KSW to Edmund Wilson, 6/21/44.
23 Footnote: **All my life:** *Ibid.*
24 **the long nest** and following: KSW to EL, 3/21/77.
24 **Katharine never did** and following: Mrs. Leon Little to LHD, 1978.

24 **with the boys from:** Mary Louise Hill Coolidge, *The Winsor Bulletin,* Spring, 1977, p. 3.

24 **Winsor girls:** Katharine P. English, *The Winsor Bulletin,* Spring, 1977, p. 9.

24 **when I came home:** KSW to EL, 1/20/69.

25 **Miss Winsor's stimulating:** KSW, *Winsor Alumnae Publication.*

25 **and unharvested:** O&U, 12/16/67.

26–27 **I was the third:** KSW to James F. Powers, July, 1958.

27 **queen of the May:** LHD interview with EBW, 6/19/79.

27 **Everything Elsie did:** *Ibid.,* 11/4/77.

27 **didn't think Elsie:** EBW to LHD, 10/22/81.

27 **in very bad shape:** APM.

27 **highly entertaining:** *Ibid.*

27 **rather a hero:** KSW to Morris Bishop, 10/5/72.

27 **condition:** APM.

28 **who was in pursuit** and following: KSW to Bessie B. Poor, 9/10/73.

28 **a great psychologist:** ESS, autobiographical fragment (unpublished).

28 **long nervous illness:** APM.

28 **an extraordinary thing** and following: *Ibid*

28–29 **It became apparent:** EBW, "Aunt Poo," June, 1942, *One Man's Meat,* Harper & Row, New York, 1982, pp. 240–41.

29 **this formidable new:** Theodore Roosevelt quoted in Howard K. Beale, *Theodore Roosevelt and the Rise of America to World Power,* Collier Books, New York, 1968, p. 284.

30 **broke the story:** EBW, "Aunt Poo," p. 241.

30 **[I]n the end:** APM.

30 **celestial** and following: EBW, "Aunt Poo."

31 **had taken the then:** O&U, 11/4/67.

31 **I can hardly remember:** H&O.

2. The Inner Shrine

For this chapter, I am particularly indebted to Roberta Frankfort's excellent and informative book, *Collegiate Women* (New York University Press, New York, 1977).

32 **Germantown stone:** Buford Pickens and Margaretta Darnall, *Washington University in St. Louis: Its Design and Architecture,* School of Architecture, Gallery of Art, Washington University, St. Louis, Missouri, 1978, p. 9.

32 **give a sense of quiet:** *Ibid.*

33 **become as well known:** M. Carey Thomas quoted in *Collegiate Women,* p. 32.

34 **was delighted to learn:** KSW to Mrs. Gummere, 11/7/62.

34 **intellectual renunciation:** Frankfort, pp. 33–34.

35 **It is undesirable:** M. Carey Thomas quoted in Frankfort, pp. 33–34.

35 **both economically and:** Frankfort, p. 37.

35 **I'm engaged:** LHD interview with Leah Cadbury Furtmuller, 4/4/79.

35 **Fine, frank, judicious:** ESS, *Shadow Shapes, The Journal of a Wounded Woman*, Houghton Mifflin, Boston, 1920, p. 40.

36 **the privacy of the two:** LHD interview with RA, 5/16/79.

36 **I guess there's no** and following: KS to CSS, 2/16/13.

37 **proudly:** KSW to CA, 10/9/72.

37 **one of the leading:** LHD interview with Leah Cadbury Furtmuller, 4/4/79.

37 **called "The Inner Shrine":** KSW to MMcC, 12/3/63.

37 **Merit in Greek** and following: KS to CSS, 2/6/13.

38 **to a group:** KSW, BMC Alumnae Information, undated.

38 **passionately for or:** KSW to Claire Robinson Jacobus, 6/23/75.

38 **Endless people are:** KS to CSS, 4/6/13.

38 **to wheedle a:** KSW to Sheila Atkinson Fisher, 2/10/59.

38 **She took exception:** NAS, "Bryn Mawr," 4/4/79 (unpublished paper).

39 **summoned me about:** KSW Collection, BMC.

39 **We are growing old:** KS, *Tipyn O'Bob*, 1913.

39 **We cannot now:** *Ibid.*

39 **acquired the greatest:** KS, "The Bullet Head," *Tipyn O'Bob*, 1913.

39 **always effective** and following: KS, "The Theorist," *Tipyn O'Bob*, 1914.

40–41 KSW's shame about Lake Chocorua incident: KSW note on letter to JS, dated 12/22/55.

41 **was so big that:** KSW, BMC Alumnae Information, undated.

41 **When Katharine said:** LHD interview with Leah Cadbury Furtmuller, 4/4/79.

41 **When we poor** and following: KS, "May Day," The Book of the Class of 1914 (BMC), pp. 61–63.

3. Divertissement

For information about the Cleveland Play House, I have relied heavily on Julia McCune Flory's book, *The Cleveland Play House, How It Began* (Press of Western Reserve University, Cleveland, Ohio, 1965). My account of Elsie's misadventure in France is based partly on Amy Lowell's book review, "A Mirage of Experience," *New York Times Book Review and Magazine*, 11/40/20.

43 **which is really:** NAS to LHD, 4/5/79.

43 **in general practice:** EA, Harvard College Class of 1911, Twenty-fifth Anniversary Report, Cambridge: The Cosmos Press, 1936, pp. 18–20.

44 **outstanding legal ability:** Joseph W. Bishop, 5/7/69.

44 **infinite patience:** Stephen C. Vladeck, 5/20/69.

44 **willingness to take risks:** Eugene V. Rostow, 5/19/69.

44 **the man of the family:** LHD interview with RA, 5/16/79.

44 **tall and thin:** *Ibid.*

44 **Mrs. Angell, long:** KSW to Bessie B. Poor, 9/10/73.

44 **to earn a maid:** RE.

45 **its relation to art** and following: Julia McCoun Flory, *The Cleveland Play House: How It Began.*

45 **their first roughening:** KSW to CA, 2/4/71.

45 **completely breathtaking:** Flory.

46 **the first insurance:** KSW to CA, 2/4/71.

46 **taught [her] a great:** *Ibid.*

46 **Usually in a tenement** and following: *Ibid.*

47 **in a fever of:** RE.

47 **a young girl:** KSW to CA, 2/4/71.

47 **evenings were for letters:** RE.

47 **a true Red Sox fan** and following: Roger Angell, *Late Innings,* Simon and Schuster, 1982, pp. 374–75.

47 **A color harvest:** KSA, "To a Child, In a Garden," 1918.

47 **for the golden:** KSA, "Thanks for a Friend," 1918.

48 **indefensible:** Proceedings of the Massachusetts Special Commission to Consider the Financial Condition of the Boston Elevated Company, Boston, 1917, p. 129.

48 **genius for organizing** and following: Boston *Sunday Globe,* 2/27/38, p. 10.

49 **I don't know what:** LHD interview with NAS, 6/25/79.

49 **Nancy Stableford has surmised:** LHD interview with NAS, 8/5/85.

49 **I have and always have had:** H&O.

50 **easily tired:** *Ibid.*

50 **except if you'd skinned:** LHD interview with NAS, 5/15/79.

50 **the affection in:** ESS, *Shadow Shapes: The Journal of a Wounded Woman,* p. 40.

50 **Your grandfather:** KSW to CA, 2/4/71.

51 **After twenty long:** *Ibid.*

51 **a pleasant place:** EA, Harvard College Class of 1911 Decennial Report, June, 1921.

51 **of an unending** and following: *Ibid.*

51 **the parochialism** and following: RE.

51 **We were very short:** *Ibid.*

52 **Ernest: he will have:** ESS, *Shadow Shapes,* pp. 80–81.

52 **World War II soldiers:** KSW to CA, Christmas, 1976.

52 **an amusing place** and following: KSW to BMC, 1921.

52 **almost on the East River:** RE.

53 **bad mathematics:** KSW to CA, 2/4/71.

53 **if not so tragic:** KSA, "The Great Ditch in Haiti," *The New Republic,* 3/22/22.

Notes

53–54 **The Dominicans have:** KSA, "On Trial in Santo Domingo," *The New Republic,* 7/5/22.

54 **a psychoanalyst whose:** KSW to CA, 2/4/71.

54 **Amy's idea of:** *Ibid.*

54 **domesticity, gayety:** KSW to BMC, 1924.

55 **Before applying at:** KSW to CA, 2/4/71.

4. Rewriting

For this chapter, I am particularly indebted to Scott Elledge's *E. B. White: A Biography,* on which I have relied heavily, and on E. B. White's obituary of Wolcott Gibbs (*The New Yorker,* 8/30/58).

60 **Being a sensitive:** Raoul Fleischmann to KSW, 1/6/61.

60 **doing everything—as we all:** KSW to CA, 2/4/71.

60 **Ross felt that artists:** KSW note, April, 1973, re: *New York Times* obituary of Rea Irvin.

60–61 **never felt any attraction:** KSW, quoted in Scott Elledge, *E. B. White: A Biography,* W. W. Norton, 1984, p. 118.

61 **the barrier reef:** EBW, Harold Ross obituary, NYer, 12/15/51.

61 **endless curiosity:** KSW to Mr. Kinney, 3/23/73.

61 **Send me a Dickens:** *Ibid.*

61 **best of all:** KSW quoted in Jane Grant, *Ross, The New Yorker and Me,* Reynal & Co. in association with William Morrow, New York, 1969, p. 259.

61 **All right:** Grant, p. 258.

61 **I have two entirely:** HWR to KSW, early '40s, Monday.

61 **ambiguous:** LHD interview with William Shawn, 2/16/78.

62 **This is to introduce:** Elledge, p. 118.

62 **the highest personal:** *Ibid.*

62 **from the highest** and following: RE.

66 **She always licked:** RA to LHD, 5/20/86.

66 **lousy at handling money:** LHD interview with NAS, 7/5/83.

66 **naive about money:** *Ibid.*

66 **above money:** EBW, "Call Me Ishmael, Or How I Feel About Being Married to a Bryn Mawr Graduate," Bryn Mawr Alumnae Bulletin, Spring, 1956.

66 **When I re-read** and following: RE.

67 **And now after eleven** and following: H&O.

69 **For most of the time:** NAS, Bryn Mawr Alumnae Bulletin, Spring, 1981.

69 **terrible nuisance:** LHD interview with NAS, 8/5/83.

69 **Roger Angell . . . never felt that he wanted his mother not to work:** LHD interview with RA, 12/20/85.

69 **honest attempts at** and following: H&O.

71 **a much older woman:** KSW to CA, Christmas, 1976.

71 **So I began to work:** KSW to CA, *Ibid.*

71 **all the time:** LHD interview with NAS, 7/5/83.

71 **very argumentative:** *Ibid.*

71 **a scary, violent:** LHD interview with RA, 1/27/83.

71 **didn't scream so that:** LHD interview with NAS, 7/5/83.

72 **didn't intersect:** LHD interview with RA, 1/27/83.

72 **was not very good:** LHD interview with NAS, 8/5/83.

72 **We all had a very:** KSW to FS, 2/1/75.

73 **Ideally . . . all editors:** KSW to Ruth Rogin, 11/19/76.

74 **Like every good writer** and following: KSW to Matthew Bruccoli, 5/17/71.

75 **stormed into:** KSW to Brendan Gill, 1/17/72.

75 **prickly qualities** and following: KSW to Matthew Bruccoli, 5/17/71.

75 **Go back and put:** LHD interview with RA, 1/27/83.

76 **Old Foolish this:** Further notes by KSW on Woollcott and The NYer and "Shouts and Murmurs" (probably 1973).

76 **silly:** KSW to S. N. Behrman, 10/12/65.

76 **half in love:** LHD interview with EBW, 10/14/83.

77 **Are you Elwyn** and following: LEBW, p. 72.

77 **have they guessed:** EBW, "Notes from a Desk Calendar," NYer, 1/14/28.

77 **And if I love:** *Ibid.*

78 **Too small a heart:** EBW, "Belated Christmas Card," NYer, 1/7/28.

78 **absolutely livid:** LHD interview with NAS, 7/5/83.

79 **had to become:** LHD interview with EBW, 10/14/83.

79 **the sound of someone:** EBW quoted in Elledge, p. 156.

79 **guard[ing] the most:** EBW, "This Is a Prayer Before I Sleep," The Conning Tower, New York *World,* 12/4/28, p. 15.

79 **nearness** and following: "Soliloquy at Times Square," The Conning Tower, New York *World,* 8/20/28, p. 11.

79 **walk[ed] with love:** EBW, "This Is a Prayer Before I Sleep."

80 **I am very much grieved:** CSS to ESS, 4/27/29.

80 **that wounded me more:** LHD interview with RA, 1/27/83.

81 **Ernest . . . was always:** LHD interview with EBW, 10/14/83.

81 **all mixed up:** KSA to EBW, Friday, 5/31/29.

81 **healthy and normal** and following: *Ibid.*

81 **By the time you:** KSA to EBW, 5/27/29.

82 **The pilot, unable to see:** EBW, "Writer's Faith," Nieman Reports, March, 1972.

82 Nevada's and New York's divorce laws: Swift Paine, "As We See It in Reno," *The North American Review* 229 (6): 720–26. June, 1930.

82 **that joint custody was:** KSW to CA, Christmas, 1976.

82 Divorce statistics, 1930: Elaine Tyler May, *Great Expectations: Marriage and*

Divorce in Post-Victorian America, Chicago and London: University of Chicago Press, 1980, pp. 167, 173.

83   **the sage was bright:** KSA to EBW, 5/29/29.

83   **at huge stakes:** KSA to EBW, *Ibid.*

83   **All morning was:** KSA to EBW, *Ibid.*

83   **A regular Ring:** KSA to EBW, 5/27/29.

83   **superb; religiously:** *Ibid.*

83   **to become thoroughly:** KSA to EBW, 5/29/29.

83   **Ross writes me:** KSA to EBW, 5/27/29.

83   **a flourishing vegetable:** *Ibid.*

84   **Mr. Angell was unfaithful:** Pennell C. Peck to LHD, 6/8/83.

84   **And yet to Andy Katharine confided:** LHD interview with EBW, 10/14/83.

84   **there was not one admirable:** LHD interview with RA, 1/27/83.

84   **I went to Reno:** KSW to CA, Christmas, 1976.

84–85   **two bad days** and following: KSA to EBW, 5/31/29.

86   **is so good of Snowball:** *Ibid.*

87   **The hot desert summer:** KSA to EBW, 6/29/29.

87   **as good as Greek:** KSA to EBW, 6/22/29.

87   **a distinction of which:** KSA to EBW, Friday [June, 1929].

87   **wholesale handling:** KSA to EBW, 6/22/29.

87   **Sustenance, birth:** *Ibid.*

87   **as engaging a person:** KSA to EBW, 6/5/29.

87   **Bobby I hate** and following: KSA to EBW, 6/22/29.

87   **most of their time:** KSA to EBW, 6/18/29.

88   **for which I'd been:** KSA to EBW, Friday [June, 1929].

88   **abandoned, antagonized:** KSA to EBW, 6/7/29.

88   **most of my life:** KSA to EBW, 7/12/29.

88   **still, in spite of:** KSA to EBW, 6/5/29.

88   **homesick for a:** KSA to EBW, Tuesday [May–June? 1929].

88   **too disgusted:** KSA to EBW, 7/17/29.

88   **for my own satisfaction:** KSA to EBW, Wednesday, 6/26/29.

88   **Jim on sex:** KSA to EBW, 6/15/29.

88   **perhaps that's the kind** and following: KSA to EBW, 6/22/29.

89   **It would be kind of:** KSA to EBW, 6/5/29.

89   **far less homeless:** KSA to EBW, 6/8/29.

90   **On account of the fact that** and following: LEBW, p. 86.

90   **You may dislike:** KSA to EBW, undated, [1929].

90   **I can't and won't:** KSA to EBW, 7/17/29.

91   **You say you're:** KSA to EBW, Friday, June 21 [1929].

93   **will be everything:** KSA to EBW, 7/28/29.

5. Real and Incontrovertible

94 **official home:** LHD interview with NAS, 6/30/83.

94 **act like an adult:** LHD interview with NAS, 8/5/83.

95 **the handsome new canoe** and following: EBW to KSA, 9/11/29.

95 **I don't remember:** Elledge, p. 170.

96 **It was a very:** LEBW, p. 83.

96 **an endless round:** *Ibid.*

97 **Part of their philosophy:** LHD interview with NAS, 5/15/79.

97 **Father could never:** LHD interview with NAS, 8/15/83.

97 **She left me for:** *Ibid.*

97 **Pretty soon . . . after we:** LHD interview with NAS, 8/12/83.

97 **the most beautiful:** EBW to KSW, November, 1929, Interoffice memo.

97 **all blows around:** LHD interview with EBW, 10/14/83.

97 **yellow lamplight:** EBW, "For Serena, Keeper of the Draw Curtains," *Poems and Sketches of E. B. White,* Harper & Row, New York, 1981, p. 69.

99 **If it lasts only:** Ann Honeycutt to EBW, August, 1977.

99 **would get kind of rigid:** LHD interview with Arthur Goldschmidt, 3/28/83.

100 **There's a man who:** *Ibid.*

100 **Tex really saved:** RA to LHD, 5/20/86.

100 **brilliant:** LHD interview with RA, 1/27/83.

100 **Some of it may have:** LHD interview with NAS, 8/5/83.

100 **terribly nice:** LHD interview with Arthur Goldschmidt, 3/28/83.

100 **She was a great** and following: *Ibid.*

102 **[held] himself back** and following: LEBW, pp. 91–92.

102 **it was always more fun:** LHD interview with RA, 1/6/78.

103 **but it is foolish:** LEBW, p. 95.

103 **bounced back after:** Elledge, p. 178.

103 **"Note at Fifth Avenue":** KSW, NYer, 10/29/32.

104 **with my left hand:** KSW to Janet Malcolm, 2/13/66.

104 **my three year:** KSW, "Books for the Children," NYer, 12/9/33.

104 **ingratiatingly simple** and following: *Ibid.*

104 **the artists have it:** KSW, "Books for Younger Children," NYer, 11/30/35.

104 **This book is worthy:** *Ibid.*

105 **It is a pity that:** *Ibid.*

105 **With a few exceptions:** KSW, "The Children's Harvest," NYer, 11/25/39.

105 **The rank-and-file:** *Ibid.*

105 **There are too many coy:** KSW, "Books for Younger Readers," NYer, 11/30/35.

105 **The child has become:** KSW, "Children's Books: Between the Dark and the Daylight," NYer, 12/7/46.

105 **It has always seemed:** KSW, NYer, 12/8/34.

Notes

105–6   **You wonder how:** KSW, "Books for Boys and Girls," NYer, 12/8/34.

106   **The hardy, and we:** KSW, "Books for the Babies," NYer, 12/1/34.

106   **listed for parents who:** KSW, "The Children's Harvest," NYer, 11/25/39.

106   **The only youthful:** KSW, "Summer Reading for the Children,"· NYer, 5/29/43.

106   **I don't feel that children:** KSW, "The Children's Harvest," NYer, 11/25/39.

107   *The Travels of Babar:* KSW, "Books for the Babies," NYer, 12/1/34.

107   *The Pied Piper: Ibid.*

107   **a sinister little set:** KSW, "Spring Books for Children," NYer, 5/13/39.

108   **was a habit [she]:** KSW to William Maxwell, 7/27/70.

109   **Now what do you:** KSW to Clarence Day, 4/19/35.

109   *Please* **don't get:** *Ibid.*

110   **My God, if I:** Clarence Day to KSW, 7/8/35.

112   **finally persuaded him** and following: KSW to Professor Perlmutter, 6/14/75.

113   **And she, along with a few:** KSW to Matthew Bruccoli, 5/17/71.

113   **Nuts! . . . which still retained:** *Ibid.*

113   **I do not believe:** KSW notes on HATNY.

113   **For instance, Ross:** KSW to Corey Ford, 9/23/67.

113   **Gibbs and I rebelled:** KSW to EBW, Tuesday [1934].

114   **Katharine was soon:** EBW, *Paris Review* interview.

114   Footnote: **I had a good tho. brief:** CSS to ESS, Sunday, August 5.

115   **It's almost worth:** KSW to EBW, Tuesday [1934].

115   **frightful grind:** LEBW, p. 126.

115   **You say nothing:** KSW to EBW, Tuesday [1934].

115   **prepared for the end:** LEBW, p. 118.

115   **I have long thought:** JTh to KSW, 4/30/38.

115   **It is probably wrong:** EBW to KSW, 10/18/35.

116   **to start fresh:** KSW to EBW, September, 1935

116   **Whenever the subject** and following: LEBW, pp. 154–56.

117   **with his expended fire** and following: EBW, "Zoo Revisited, Or, The Life and Death of Olie Hackstaff," *Poems and Sketches of E. B. White,* Harper & Row, New York, 1981, p. 112.

118   **KSW's NYer stock** and **This arrangement** and following: Raoul Fleischmann to KSW, 1/12/37.

119   **I am sorry that:** KSW Collection, BMC.

119   **friend at court:** KSW to Professor Perlmutter, 6/14/75.

119   **As a critic:** KSW confidential memo to Ross, Gibbs, McKelway, and Shuman.

121   **the basic absurdity** and following: KSW memo to Ross, 8/4/47.

122   **It would embarrass:** LEBW, p. 161.

122   **You can't take it** and following: LEBW, p. 159.

122   **He wished Kay could share:** LEBW, p. 163.

122   **he enclosed in his letter:** LEBW, p. 165.

122   **saying she was:** LEBW, p. 168.

123   **in a limp:** LEBW, p. 170.

123   **I read today** and following: KSW to EBW, 12/30/37.

123   **This is the last:** EBW to KSW, LEBW, p. 169.

123   **an unholy mess:** LEBW, p. 170.

123–24   The NYer's stock arrangement with KSW: Raoul Fleischmann to KSW, 5/2/38.

6. The Imperfect Script

125   **leaped on our:** KSW to EBW, March, 1937.

125   **not their lives:** KSW to EBW, September, 1936.

125   **If someone had said:** LHD interview with RA, 1/6/78.

125–26   **"Lady Before Breakfast":** EBW, *Poems and Sketches of E. B. White,* p. 70.

126   **there have been times:** Patricia Collinge to KSW, 5/13/38.

126   **the fountain and shrine:** JTh to KSW, 2/23/38.

127   **when she was on:** Daise Terry to KSW, 1938.

127   **Mrs. White believed:** HATNY, p. 130.

127   **I wanted to go:** KSW, notes on HATNY.

127   **I wasn't at all:** *Ibid.*

128   **rang[ed] from:** LEBW, p. 184.

128   **Am convinced that:** EBW to KSW, 4/28/38.

128   **Glad to hear Nancy's:** JTh to KSW, 1/22/38.

129   **Well now, what courses:** LHD interview with NAS, 8/12/83.

129   **good enough at:** KSW to BMC, 1931.

129   **One of my three:** KSW to Maddy Vegtel, 3/10/61.

129   **I think I told:** ESS to Hetty Goldman, 8/26/[57?].

130   **Are you sure you:** LHD interview with NAS, 8/12/83.

130   **Yes. How often:** LHD interview with NAS, 5/17/86.

130   **To negate my** and following: NAS to LHD, 8/17/85.

131   **not at all unpleasant:** KSW to FS, 1/9/74.

131   **I give up:** KSW to EBW, Friday [early 1942].

131   **a little too remote:** KSW to Gene Saxton, 1/15/42.

131   **I'd rather be near:** *Ibid.*

131   **I could hardly go:** KSW to EBW, March, 1942.

131   **own special literary:** Ralph Ingersoll to KSW, 4/30/42.

133   **trying to make:** KSW to BMC, 1949.

134   **One of the most:** HWR to KSW, 1939–40?

134   **wise and constructive:** HWR to KSW, 3/6/42.

134   **putting a writer like:** HWR to KSW, 10/19/42.

134   **Your remarks about:** HWR to KSW, Wednesday, 1942?

134   **I have a proof:** HWR to KSW, Wednesday [probably 1939].

Notes

135   **Mrs. White: As to:** HWR to KSW, [1939].

135   **the time would be:** HWR to KSW, 11/4/46.

135   **in these meetings:** Note by KSW, December, 1970.

136   Ross's dislike of rejections; he did not work directly with writers and artists: EBW, *Paris Review* interview (see bibliography).

136   Ross's reaction to Janet Flanner letter: KSW to EBW, 1937.

136   **silly or unimportant** and following: Note by KSW, December, 1970.

136   **No two people:** EBW, *Paris Review* interview.

136   Joel White's impression of KSW and HWR: LHD interview with Joel White, 10/8/78.

136   **I didn't give a hoot:** HWR to KSW, Thursday [1943].

137   **It takes an old-timer:** HWR to KSW, 4/10/42.

137   **Dear Mrs. W: The tooth:** HWR to KSW, [1941–42?].

137   **wanted to know what:** HWR to KSW, Friday [1939 or 1940].

137   **Thurber did a piece:** HWR to KSW [1941 or 1942].

137   **Comment is by far:** HWR to KSW [1941 or 1942].

137   **Andy did not do:** HWR to KSW, Friday [1939 or 1940].

137   **warped by self-consciousness:** HWR to KSW, Wednesday [1942?].

138   **better to take it:** HWR to KSW [1943?].

138   **How are you doing:** KSW to Gus Lobrano, 2/15/41.

138   **I know (because he:** Gus Lobrano to KSW, Thursday, [1941 or 1942].

138   **baffle** and following: KSW to Gene Saxton, 6/23/40.

139   **"I never did hold":** KSW to H. L. Mencken, 6/26/41.

139   Footnote: **He asks me:** Rosalind C. Lohrfinck to KSW, 5/13/55.

139   **more or less dispassionately:** Wolcott Gibbs to KSW, Friday (early closing) [1941?].

139   **get right after it:** EBW to KSW, Monday night [Summer of 1941].

139   **would not want to tangle** and following: LHD interview with EBW, October 7 and 8, 1978.

139–40   **the terrible responsibility:** KSW to EBW, 4/23/45.

140   **The tone and:** KSW to Mrs. George F. Murray, 4/27/49.

140   **Katharine "detested" Anne Carroll Moore . . . the false sentimentality:** KSW to Louise Bechtel, 9/12/61.

141   *The scenic points:* EBW, "Wedding Day In the Rockies," *Poems and Sketches of E. B. White,* p. 92.

141   **all the trials of Job** and following: KSW to EBW, 2/26/43.

141   **She gave an impression:** Faith McNulty to LHD, 11/18/77.

142   **a difficult, sticky** and following: KSW notes on HATNY.

142   **When I'm at long:** KSW to Edmund Wilson, 6/21/44.

142–43   Bernard Bergman's view of KSW: LHD interview with Bernard Bergman, 4/6/79.

143   **the most ravishing:** Nancy Hale to LHD, 12/18/77.

143   **an excellent teacher:** LHD interview with William Maxwell, 3/8/79.

143   **Don't fire until:** Nancy Hale to LHD, 12/18/77.

144 **a strong woman:** LHD interview with Niccolò Tucci, 3/23/83.

144 **It is very hard:** Louise Seaman Bechtel to LHD, 2/7/78.

144 **a velvet hand:** LHD interview with Nancy and Louis Stableford, 8/30/78.

144 **hard, suave:** "The New Yorker," *Fortune,* August, 1934, p. 88.

144 **New England and austere:** KSW to FS, 2/1/75.

144 **She had a lot of armor:** LHD interview with Gardner Botsford, 1/27/83.

144 **on all [Nabokov's] output:** KSW to Edmund Wilson, 6/2/44.

145 **electrifying:** KSW to Véra Nabokov, 7/11/77.

145 **It will be of the greatest:** KSW to Edmund Wilson, 6/23/44.

145 Joseph Mitchell's impression of KSW and Edmund Wilson: LHD interview with Joseph Mitchell, 2/16/78.

145 **was not the kind** and following: LHD interview with MMcC, 10/18/83.

145 **anti-editing campaign:** Edmund Wilson to KSW, 11/12/47.

145 **all the literary writers:** LHD interview with MMcC, 10/18/83.

146 **didn't care for:** MMcC to LHD, 9/24/83.

146 **pointless and inane:** Edmund Wilson to KSW, 11/12/47.

146 **What are we going:** KSW to Edmund Wilson, 5/11/44.

146 **At last . . . I enclose:** KSW to VN, 3/1/49.

147 KSW thought VN's use of obsolete words perhaps inevitable: *Ibid.*

147 **a very long and:** KSW to EBW, Saturday, 4/28/45.

148 **Mrs. White: Would appreciate:** HWR to KSW, 1948.

148 **I do not understand:** VN to KSW, 3/17/51.

148 **I think it's fine:** KSW to VN, 3/21/51.

148 **You want to say:** KSW to VN 3/7/50.

148 **All right, I surrender:** VN to KSW, 3/13/50.

148 **suggested editing and queries** and following: KSW to VN, 3/22/48.

149 **[Nabokov] was merely:** KSW note, 1970, on letter to KSW from William Maxwell, Monday [February, 1971].

149–50 **I think this is perhaps:** KSW to VN, 11/25/49.

150 **I am getting more:** KSW to VN, 4/13/50.

150 **It is a devastating:** KSW to VN, 7/29/50.

150 **There has been a long:** KSW to VN, 2/11/57.

150 **Dear Vladimir: Where are you?:** KSW to VN, 7/30/54.

150 **his quantity bonus** and following: KSW to Véra Nabokov, 4/7/50.

150 **It is characteristic:** Andrew Field, *Nabokov: His Life in Part,* Penguin, New York, 1978, p. 265.

150–51 **occasional emendations** and following: KSW note (1972) on Ross memo to Nabokov.

151 **the very, very:** *The Nabokov-Wilson Letters, 1940–1971,* edited by Simon Karlinsky, Harper-Colophon Books, New York, 1980, p. 210.

151 **told poor Mrs. White off:** Karlinsky, p. 145.

151 **had the gall to:** Karlinsky, pp. 144–45.

151 **such a subtle and loving:** VN to KSW, 3/17/51.

151 **cloudless association:** VN to KSW, 11/24/55.

151 **who didn't worship:** LHD interview with Evelyn Nelson, 2/21/83.

151 **I hope you like:** Janet Flanner to KSW, 1930.

151 **You are one of:** KSW to James F. Powers, 10/18/62.

151 **an energy I find:** JU to KSW, 12/12/57.

151 **Her praise . . . was the best:** Faith McNulty Martin to EBW, 7/29/77.

152 **attempted improvements** and following: MMcC to LHD, 9/29/78.

152 **upset by the fear:** LHD interview with MMcC, 10/18/83.

152 **one of [Katharine's] best friends:** KSW to Raymond Sokolov, 3/16/76.

152 **without agonizing sciatica:** KSW to Mavis Gallant, 6/30/78.

153 **I find myself unable:** KSW to JS, 1/15/48.

153 **I was delighted with:** KSW to JS, July 26 [1949].

154 **Every time we use:** KSW to JS, 9/29/48.

154 **entirely apt:** KSW to JS, 1/15/48.

154 **a remarkable reviser:** KSW to JT, 10/28/75.

155 **It seems to swing back:** HWR comment, 1/10/49.

155 **big new rent:** KSW to JS, 12/3/48.

155 **One of the first:** KSW to JS, 12/20/48.

155 **Niccolò Tucci's work** with KSW, and quotations: LHD interview with Niccolò Tucci, 3/23/83.

155 **a perfect comedy** and following: KSW to MMcC, 7/25/60.

156 **What Tucci needs:** LHD interview with MMcC, 10/18/73.

156–57 **Andy resigned his job:** KSW to BMC, 1949.

7. *"Do You Remember When All We Worried About Was Love?"*

158 **decent** and following: KSW to Janet Flanner, 2/13/50.

159 **He was ever on:** KSW note, December, 1970.

159 **He was one of the few:** KSW to CA, December 20, [1969?].

159 **Remember . . . you're only as:** KSW quoted Jane Grant, *Ross, The New Yorker and Me.*

159 **disembowelled:** LEBW, p. 346.

159 **my years of work:** KSW to JT, 11/11/74.

159 **Do you remember:** JTh to KSW, 8/1/52.

159 **As mad as** and following: KSW to JS, 8/11/52.

159 **she might . . . decide:** KSW to JS, 1/19/51.

160 **Of course you yourself:** KSW to JS, *Ibid.*

160 **Mother Superior:** May Sarton to KSW, 9/17/61.

160 **New Yorker protégées:** Marianne Moore to KSW, 8/10/60.

160 **occasional chats:** Whitney Balliett to KSW, 8/5/59.

160 **as a kind of touchstone:** Joseph Mitchell to KSW, 10/22/64.

160 **I think I shall ask:** Robert Hale to KSW, 1/20/72.

160–61 **Whatever are you doing:** Edith Iglauer Daly to LHD, 12/15/77.

161 **unfailingly perceptive:** Elizabeth Bishop to EBW, 7/27/77.

161 **She was particularly:** Edith Iglauer Daly to LHD, 12/15/77.

161   **might have been:** Faith McNulty to LHD, 11/18/77.

161–62   **Dear Nora:** KSW to Nora Sayre, 1/23/53.

162   **Without her help:** KSW Collection, BMC.

162   **It was *good writing:*** Mary Cable to LHD, 8/31/83.

162   **WHAT DO YOU MEAN:** Mary Cable to LHD, 6/16/83.

162   **I really was too:** Edith Iglauer Daly to LHD, 12/15/77.

162–63   **My being scared:** Mary Cable to LHD, 7/14/83.

163   **Susan Edwards, who worked as Katharine's secretary:** LHD interview with Susan Edwards, 11/30/77.

163   **To me, Katharine's most:** Buckner Hollingsworth to LHD, 11/16/77.

163   **one of our most precious:** KSW to JU, 7/17/54.

163   **rather unusual:** KSW to JU, 9/15/54.

164   **the lines at 1):** KSW to JU, 7/21/54.

164   **Alas, I have:** KSW to JU, 11/23/54.

164   **try to do better:** JU to KSW, 7/27/54.

164   **The patient and abundant:** JU to KSW, 9/2/54.

164–65   **There is no precedent:** KSW to JU, 9/15/54.

165   **but along with my:** JU to KSW, 9/30/54.

165   **About the dash:** JU to KSW, 11/26/54.

165–66   **You seem to have:** KSW to JU, 12/1/54.

166   Footnote: **appall[ed]** and **overwhelmed:** KSW to JU, 9/23/70.

167   **I have never known:** KSW to Morris Ernst, 4/2/54.

167   **Far from reading as:** Nadine Gordimer to KSW, 11/14/54.

167   **had a siege of:** KSW to JS, 10/18/54.

167   **and for a few days:** KSW to JS, 7/28/58.

167   **to face the typewriter:** KSW to JS, 8/8/57.

167   **always a strain:** KSW to JS, 6/16/57.

168   **Katharine is so nervously:** ESS to Hetty Goldman, 3/23/55.

168   **carried a heavy load:** *Ibid.*

168   **K. has gone to:** *Ibid.*

168   **Just talking to him:** KSW to JS, 3/18/55.

169   **It was especially:** ESS to Hetty Goldman, 8/8/53.

169   **Your piece:** KSW to Edmund Wilson, 9/2/53.

169   **I have to accept:** Dr. John Henderson to LHD, April, 1985.

169   **Caroline Belle Sergeant:** KSW, Northampton, Mass, *Daily Hampshire Gazette,* 5/16/55.

170   **I always did:** KSW to JS, June 18 [1956?].

170   **a sort of British:** LEBW, p. 409.

170   **much too swish:** KSW to JS, 8/31 [1956 or 1957].

170   **at all times:** LEBW, p. 409.

170   **K. & E.B. have been:** ESS to Hetty Goldman, Saturday [Summer, 1955].

170   **a poet was murdered:** LEBW, p. 407.

170   **a chorus of:** *Ibid.*

171   **the dutiful homebody:** KSW note on Eric Day letter.

171 **I especially hate** and following: KSW to Louise Bogan, 12/5/55.

171 **It has been a positive:** MMcC to KSW, 12/10/55.

172 **Katharine believed, as I did** and following: MMcC to LHD, 9/29/78.

172 **I know that it is selfish:** Bernice Baumgarten to KSW, 12/2/55.

172 **You need not worry:** KSW to VN, 11/21/55.

172 **Your kindness:** VN to KSW, 11/24/55.

172 **and it was full:** KSW notes on HATNY.

173 **a precisionist of:** LHD interview with Harriet Walden, 3/13/83.

173 **A new secretary just out of college:** LHD interview with Susan Edwards, 11/30/77.

173 **KSW's lunches with MMcC:** MMcC to LHD, 9/29/78.

173 **Katharine often rising:** *Ibid.*

176 **disgusted:** KSW to Lysbeth Boyd Borie, 9/13/56.

176 **outraged by so:** KSW to Mrs. Henry Peter Borie, 9/21/56.

176 **weren't too purely:** KSW to William Shawn, 11/12/56.

177 **I lead a crazy:** KSW to VN, 11/27/56.

177 **I sometimes despair:** KSW to Nadine Gordimer, 1/21/57.

177 **The trouble:** KSW to Nadine Gordimer, 1/27/57.

178 **I don't believe in:** LHD interview with RA, 1/6/78.

178 **We are all of us:** KSW to JU, 4/23/57.

178 KSW opinion that only Mary McCarthy and May Sarton were writing stories as well as Jean: KSW to JS, 7/14/56?

178 **I would have spared:** KSW to JS, 7/26/56.

179 **distasteful:** KSW note on letter: JTh to KSW, 2/18/58.

179 **unfactual and malicious:** KSW to CA, 12/20/69?

179 **a great editor** and following: KSW to Mr. Kinney, 3/23/73.

179 **New Yorker editing was mutilating his work:** JTh to KSW, 5/3/57.

180 **I have . . . written:** KSW to JS, 6/16/57.

180 **Katharine's bad nervous health:** ESS to Hetty Goldman, 12/15/57.

180 **that the catalogue makers:** EBW, introduction to *Onward and Upward in the Garden,* Katharine S. White, Farrar, Straus & Giroux, New York, 1979.

180 **You did not tell me:** JU to KSW, 12/27/59.

181 **with many thanks:** Rebecca West to KSW, 8/7/59.

181 **life on the farm:** KSW to Marianne Moore, 11/7/57.

8. Only Half a Life

185 **After 35½ years:** KSW to JU, 1/2/61.

185 **infinitely more satisfying:** H&O.

185 **a little as though:** LEBW, p. 474.

185 **Although I've always:** *Ibid.*

185 **pension:** KSW to RF, 1/10/61.

185 **wanted to quit while:** KSW to JU, 1/2/61.

185 **I don't like to think:** Elizabeth Cullinan to KSW, 2/7/61.

185   **in blooming health:** KSW to Louise Bechtel, 9/12/61.

185   **keeled over at:** *Ibid.*

186–87   **Dear Mary:** KSW to MMcC, 1/19/61.

188   **sending this bad news:** *Ibid.*

188   **paralyzed by indecision:** LHD interview with RA, 1/27/83.

188   **There were always snide:** LHD interview with NAS, 6/30/83.

188   Footnote: **was more afraid of Elsie:** LHD interview with EBW, 6/19/79.

189   **I cherish** *ideas:* KSW to EL, 7/13/62.

189   **on the** *guess:* KSW to EL, undated [1961?].

189   **I'm so frightened:** LHD interview with MMcC, 10/18/83.

189   **jumped at the Whites:** *Ibid.*

189   Footnote: **more of an artist than:** ESS to BMC, undated.

189–90   **psychological or psychiatric help:** KSW to CA, 3/22/74.

190   **never been to a psychiatrist:** *Ibid.*

190   **nervous head troubles:** KSW to Louise Bechtel, 9/12/61.

190   **never be too well nervously:** KSW to Frances Gray Patton, 8/30/57.

190   **he [was] better and:** *Ibid.*

190   **You can imagine how:** KSW to Louise Bechtel, 9/12/61.

190   **No doctor I have ever had:** KSW to Brendan Gill, 1/17/72.

191   **Now I spend most of:** KSW to EL, 5/16/61.

191   **To watch the town's funny:** KSW to EL, 8/13/61.

191   **writhing in pain** and following: *Ibid.*

191   **After fifteen really horrible:** *Ibid.*

192   **How sad to have no cows:** KSW to EL, 5/16/61.

192   **Oh, dear, we are crumbling:** KSW to EL, 8/13/61.

192   **had another bad:** KSW to EL, 8/25/61.

192   **who has done more such:** KSW to EL, 9/27/61.

192   **supposedly:** KSW to EL, 10/18/61.

192   **the slightest excitement:** LEBW, pp. 483–84.

193   **went into shock:** KSW to EL, 10/18/61.

193   **the sordid details; slit me from:** *Ibid.*

193   **physical or mental disorder[s]:** Robert Meister, *Hypochondria: Toward a Better Understanding,* Taplinger Publishing Co., New York, 1980, p. 56.

193   **preoccupied excessively:** *Ibid.*

194   **an already established:** *Ibid.,* pp. 55–56.

194   **[Oscar] Bumke noted:** *Ibid.* pp. 63–64.

194   **lots:** LHD interview with Evelyn Nelson, 2/21/83.

194   **When Andy came into:** LHD interview with NAS, 6/30/83.

194   **You'd never find both:** LHD interview with Martha White Temple, 10/15/81.

195   **As Roger Angell observed:** LHD interview with RA, 1/6/78.

196   **And for most women:** H&O.

196   **In the two years:** RE.

197   **Her worrying:** LHD interview with RA, 1/27/83.

198 **The whole illness may be:** KSW to EL, 1/25/63.

198 **from the common cold:** Jane E. Brody, "Emotions Found to Influence Nearly Every Human Ailment," *New York Times,* 5/24/83.

198–99 **Jim could be so:** KSW to Mr. Kinney, 3/23/73.

199 **he wrote the way** and following: "James Thurber," NYer, 11/11/61.

9. The Garden

200 **Victorian Will:** LHD interview with Milton Greenstein, 6/7/78.

200 **every stick of furniture:** *Ibid.*

200 **said to be unusual** and following: KSW's Victorian Will.

202 **I can *not* be glad:** O&U, NYer, 3/11/61, p. 158.

202 **The lake was Chocorua:** O&U, NYer, 3/11/61, p. 138.

203 **less of a burden** and following: KSW to JU, 1/18/62.

203 **the after effects of having:** KSW to Elizabeth Bishop, 2/8/62.

203 **Apparently I worried more:** KSW to WM (?), 2/24/62.

203 **in my queer way:** KSW to JS, Memorial Day, 1960.

203 **wouldn't be called:** KSW to JS, 3/18/77.

203 **By her husband's definition:** LHD interview with EBW, 11/4/77.

203 **I felt certain:** KSW to MMcC, 1/10/50.

203–5 **On that bright:** O&U, NYer, 6/9/62.

205 **a whole year's work** and following: KSW to EL, 6/5/62.

206 **Friendship, blindness:** KSW to EL, *Ibid.*

206 **I still burn at:** KSW to EL, 11/18/64.

206 **horror** and following: KSW to EL, 6/5/62.

207 **the greatest comfort:** KSW to Marianne Moore, 6/18/62.

207 **The *lawn* lures me:** Marianne Moore to KSW, 6/9/62.

207 **delighted:** Raoul Fleischmann to KSW, 6/14/62.

207 **rais[ing] the book out of** and following: KSW to Marianne Moore, 6/18/62.

207 **chronic thing:** KSW to EL, 7/13/62.

207 **part of his trouble:** KSW to EL, 8/6/62.

208 **I begin to feel like Job:** KSW to EL, 8/23/62.

208 **unreliable head:** *Ibid.*

208 **was probably a false alarm:** KSW to EL, 10/13/62.

208 **the two ancient:** *Ibid.*

209 **remarkable** and following: KSW to Helen Bevington, 6/25/62.

209 **[I]n all my years:** KSW to Rachel Carson, 11/21/62.

209 **one of the few *pleasant:*** KSW to JU, 9/5/63.

209 **galloped through it:** KSW to MMcC, 9/23/63.

209 **greatly relieve[d]:** KSW to MMcC, 11/6/63.

209 **for taking all these pains:** MMcC to KSW, 10/26/63.

209 Footnote: **It was certainly:** KSW to MMcC, 11/6/63.

210 **head swims:** LEBW, p. 496.

210 **or even an amanuensis:** KSW to Elizabeth Taylor, 3/15/63.

210 **doesn't matter, except:** *Ibid.*

210 **I sometimes think:** LEBW, p. 499.

210 **developed a truly spectacular:** LEBW, p. 495.

210 **their corpses are:** LEBW, p. 496.

210 **She hasn't quite given up:** LEBW, p. 499.

210 **within stroking distance:** LEBW, p. 498.

211 **fooled the vascular surgeon** and following: KSW to EL, 5/17/63.

211 **The President was:** LEBW, p. 503.

211 **extra hard this year** and following: KSW to JU, 9/15/63.

211 **which doesn't work as well** and following: KSW to EL, 5/17/63.

211 **a mild skin outbreak:** LEBW, p. 520.

212 **a horrible name:** KSW to EL, 11/18/64.

212 **chronic and recurrent:** Ian B. Sneddon and Darrell S. Wilkinson, "Subcorneal Pustular Dermatosis Differs from Subcorneal Pustulosis," *American Journal of Dermatology* (Winter 1981), 3 (4): 377.

212 **examination of the skin:** Sneddon and Wilkinson, "Subcorneal Pustular Dermatosis," *British Journal of Dermatology,* (1979), p. 64.

212 **bizarre:** *Ibid.*

212 **supported and held away:** LEBW, p. 520.

212 **blistered all over:** KSW to EL, 11/18/64.

212 **like a snake:** EBW to LHD, 7/7/83.

213 **where it does not belong:** KSW to EL, 11/18/64.

213 **From [her] bed of agony** and following: KSW to JU, 3/11/64.

213 **a humiliating:** LEBW, p. 520.

214 **I slop about:** KSW to JU, 5/13/64.

214 **leper complex; are repugnant because:** Eric Wittkower, M.D., and Brian Russell, M.D., *Emotional Factors in Skin Disease, A Psychosomatic Medicine Monograph,* Paul B. Hoeber, Harper & Brothers, 1953, p. 23.

214 **an organ of expression:** F. A. Whitlock, *Psychophysiological Aspects of Skin Disease,* W. B. Saunders, London, 1976, p. 37.

214 **horrid affliction:** KSW to EL, 11/18/64.

215 **by the shock of:** KSW Collection, BMC.

215 **to lower the nervous tension** and following: KSW to EL, 11/18/64.

215 **in mine or somewhere else** and following: *Ibid.*

216 **For the first few days** and following: LEBW, p. 529.

216 **seemed so utterly:** KSW to Ellen and Hildegarde Nagel, 1/27/65.

216 **Elsie, even after:** EBW to LHD, 8/24/83.

217 **About Elsie's and my relationship:** KSW to Ellen and Hildegarde Nagel, 2/5/65.

218 **the ashes to be interred:** KSW to the Cemetery Dept., Town of Winchester, 3/2/65.

218 **[Elsie] has never wanted:** KSW to Ellen and Hildegarde Nagel, 1/27/65.

219 **sub-collegiate:** J. D. Salinger, "To the Editor," New York *Herald Tribune,* 4/25/65, p. 20.

219 **the smiling embalmer:** Tom Wolfe, "Tiny Mummies! The True Story of the Ruler of 43d Street's Land of the Walking Dead!" New York *Herald Tribune,* April, 1965.

219 **journalistic delinquency:** EBW, "To the Editor," New York *Herald Tribune,* 4/25/65, p. 4.

219 **You and Andy were:** William Shawn to KSW, 6/7/65.

219 **winced over the sentence:** KSW to Corey Ford, 9/23/67.

220 **"Katherine Angell"** and following: Tom Wolfe, "Lost in the Whichy Thicket, The Whichy Thicket, The New Yorker—II," New York *Herald Tribune,* 4/18/65.

220 **... nothing Wolfe wrote:** William Shawn to KSW, 6/7/65.

220 **outstanding** and following: KSW to S. N. Behrman, 10/12/65.

220 **[Thurber's] horrible distortions** and following: *Ibid.*

221 **what [she] had been through:** S. N. Behrman to KSW, 10/26/65.

221 **I was really startled:** *Ibid.*

222 **like many New Yorker writers:** KSW to Nancy Hale, 7/24/65.

222 **talented and tyrannical cook:** KSW, "To the Editors," NYer, Dept. of Amplification, 7/10/65.

10. Matriarch

223 **children's food:** KSW, "To the Editors," NYer, Dept. of Amplification, 6/18/66.

223 **these reminiscent letters:** William Shawn to KSW, 6/3/66.

223–24 **A friend has reminded me:** O&U, NYer, 11/4/67.

224 **Meeting you in person:** KSW to EL, 11/16/67.

224 **I sneaked a look:** LEBW, p. 559.

224 **pressing down:** KSW to EL, 1/17/67.

224 **Each year brings more:** KSW to Ida T. Bergeret, 1/1/66.

224 **in a battered condition:** KSW to Janet Malcolm, 6/18/66.

224 **one less left:** KSW to Ogden Nash, 6/10/67.

224 **I really despise:** KSW to JS, 1/31/51.

225 **A sense of urgency:** KSW to BMC, 1967.

225 **a long, cold:** LEBW, p. 579.

225 **She walks with:** *Ibid.*

225 **a horrible summer** and following: KSW to EL, 10/17/69.

226 **tending [her] disintegrating:** *Ibid.*

226 **Like an old elephant:** KSW to JS, 8/20/68.

226 **I feel exiled:** Marianne Moore to KSW, 7/12/68.

226 **I'm afraid your letter:** LEBW, pp. 579–80.

226 **Thinking back over:** KSW to FS, 7/30/69.

226–27 **The book will have to net me:** LEBW, p. 584.

227 **My chief source of woe:** LEBW, p. 592.

227 *not* and following: KSW to EL, 10/27/69.

227 **poorest ever:** KSW to EL, 3/25/70.

227 **I should have had:** *Ibid.*

227 **As I now have some heart trouble:** *Ibid.*

227 **If I die:** LHD interview with NAS, 8/15/83.

228 **If you told her:** LHD interview with Evelyn Nelson, 3/21/83.

228 **a perfect mother-in-law:** LHD interview with Carol Angell, 4/18/86.

229 **a remarkable person:** LHD interview with Evelyn Nelson, 3/21/83.

229 **a brilliant mind:** LHD interview with Nancy and Louis Stableford, 5/15/79.

229 **I got our doctor:** LEBW, pp. 598–99.

229–30 **a bent and horrible** and following: KSW to JU, 7/21/70.

230 **a feeling that he could not:** *Ibid.*

230 **I trust that you:** KSW to FS, 9/16/70.

230 **be shut in entirely:** KSW to FS, 9/23/74.

230 **Oh! How pretty!:** EBW Introduction to Katharine S. White, *Onward and Upward in the Garden,* Farrar, Straus & Giroux, New York, 1979.

231 **the dear dead days:** KSW to Mr. Healey, 3/29/71.

231 **We were married for:** KSW to CA, 1/20/75.

232 **Apparently they had hardly:** KSW to CA, Christmas, 1976.

232 **The latest news:** KSW to Katharine Fernstrom, 3/10/75.

233 **utterly fascinating:** KSW to Howard M. Teichmann, 10/1/75.

233 **I don't have time:** KSW to Charles Cooke, 2/2/76.

233 **The amazing thing** and following: KSW to Ruth Limmer, 11/6/73.

233 **to be honest:** KSW to Richard Merryman, 6/10/75.

234 **If he is:** KSW to Ruth Rogin, 11/19/76.

234 **Ross brought me up** and following: KSW to Howard M. Teichmann, 6/19/75.

234 **prepared to lead a palace revolution:** HATNY, p. 210.

234 **Katharine White is a woman:** HATNY, p. 310.

235 **militantly proud** and following: HATNY, pp. 310–11.

235 **as a sort of hostage:** HATNY, p. 312.

235 **she had given up:** HATNY, p. 313.

235 Footnote: **[H]e hasn't even looked:** KSW to Milton Greenstein, 7/2/75.

235 **Mrs. White believed herself:** HATNY, pp. 129–30.

235 Footnote: **Gill is maddeningly inaccurate:** KSW to Geoffrey Hellman, 10/3/75.

235 Footnote: **on three conditions:** HATNY, p. 159.

236 **highly implausible, though:** HATNY, p. 210.

236–37 **I especially resented:** KSW to FS, 2/1/75.

237–38 **The whole thing about Gibbs:** KSW to Geoffrey Hellman, 10/3/75.

238 **a very valuable person:** KSW to JU, 12/10/75.

238 **If he had kept it to:** KSW to Claire Robinson Jacobus, 6/23/75.

238–39 **I know my friends** and following: KSW to William Shawn, 4/2/75.

239 **[come] near to killing me:** KSW to Claire Robinson Jacobus, 6/23/75.

239 **The horrible old Brendan Gill book:** KSW to CA, 3/10/75.

239 **a dreadful putdown** and following: KSW to CA, Christmas, 1976.

239 **good reasons; icy:** *Ibid.*

239 Footnote: **Why? Perhaps because:** Wilfrid Sheed, "The Letters of E. B. White," *New York Times Book Review,* 11/21/76.

241 **lacking in humor** and following: KSW to FS, 9/19/75.

241 **the young woman:** KSW to CA, 9/12/75.

241 **a thirty-three:** KSW to FS, 9/19/75.

241 **this crazy new:** KSW to CA, 1/2/76.

241 **this silly:** KSW to EL, 4/18/76.

241 **an over zealous:** KSW to Katharine Fernstrom, 5/19/76.

241 **the new baby editor:** KSW to JS, 6/10/76.

242 **Little does she know:** KSW to FS, 9/19/75.

243 **The big thing I lack:** KSW to CA, Christmas, 1976.

243 **I'm broke all the time:** KSW to EL, 3/11/74.

243 **she was one to consistently say:** LHD interview with NAS, 8/15/83.

244 **I never thought I would:** KSW to S. N. Behrman, 11/3/72.

245–46 **That was proper too:** LHD interview with Martha White Temple, 10/15/81.

246 **her approval:** LHD interview with Kitty Stableford Bennett, 8/24/78.

246 **There was no crashing:** *Ibid.*

246 **I think the boys:** LHD interview with Martha White Temple, 10/15/81.

247 **wicked:** KSW to CA and Alice Angell, 4/24/74.

248 **prone to do:** LHD interview with NAS, 8/12/83.

248 **If I had been warned:** KSW to EL, 5/31/77.

248–49 **I *need* to write:** KSW to EL, 3/21/77.

249 **facing the traffic** and following: *Ibid.*

250 **I still think back:** KSW to Véra Nabokov, 7/11/77.

250 **I think about you:** KSW to JS, 7/13/77.

251 **she had seemed beautiful to him:** EBW to Stuart Chase, undated [1977].

251 **It is a judgement about me:** EBW, committal service for KSW (unpublished).

252 **To have your affectionate:** NYer obituary of KSW, 8/1/77.

Selected Bibliography

"A Master-Mistress of Education," *The World's Work* 26 (5), September 1913.

Angell, Katharine S., "Home and Office," *The Survey,* December 1, 1926.

————, [published anonymously] "Living on the Ragged Edge, Family Income Vs. Family Expenses," *Harper's Monthly,* Vol. 152, December 1925.

Beale, Howard K., *Theodore Roosevelt and the Rise of America to World Power.* Collier Books, New York, 1968.

Beard, Charles A. and Mary, *The Rise of American Civilization.* Macmillan, New York, 1930.

Bernstein, Burton, *Thurber: A Biography.* Dodd Mead, New York, 1975.

Boas, Louise Schutz, *American Education: Its Men, Ideas, and Institutions.* Arno Press & New York Times, New York, 1971.

Boston Elevated Railway Co., *Fifty Years of Unified Transportation in Metropolitan Boston,* 1938.

Chimenti, Sergio, and Ackerman, A. Bernard, "Is Subcorneal Pustular Dermatosis of Sneddon and Wilkinson an Entity *Sui Generis?" American Journal of Dermatopathology* 3 (4), 1981.

Coolidge, Mary Louise Hill, *The Winsor Bulletin,* Spring, 1977.

Day, Clarence, *Life with Father.* Alfred A. Knopf, New York, 1935.

Donaldson, Scott, "The New Yorker, Old and New," *Sewanee Review* 83 (4), Fall 1975.

Edmiston, Susan, and Cirino, Linda, *Literary New York: A History and Guide,* Houghton Mifflin, Boston, 1976.

Elledge, Scott, *E. B. White: A Biography.* W. W. Norton, New York, 1984.

Field, Andrew, *Nabokov: His Life in Part.* Penguin Books, New York, 1978.

Finch, Edith, *Carey Thomas of Bryn Mawr.* Harper & Brothers, New York, 1947.

Flory, Julia McCune, *The Cleveland Play House, How It Began.* Press of Western Reserve University, Cleveland, Ohio, 1965.

Frankfort, Roberta, *Collegiate Women.* New York University Press, New York, 1977.

Gill, Brendan, *Here at the New Yorker.* Random House, New York, 1976.

Grant, Jane, *Ross, The New Yorker, and Me.* Reynal & Co. in association with William Morrow, New York, 1968.

Guth, Dorothy Lobrano (Ed.), *Letters of E. B. White.* Harper & Row, New York, 1976.

Hyman, Stanley Edgar, "The Urban New Yorker," *The New Republic,* June 20, 1972.

[Ingersoll, Ralph], "The New Yorker," *Fortune,* August 1934.

Kendall, Elaine, *Peculiar Institutions.* G. P. Putnam's Sons, New York, 1976.

Kramer, Dale, *Ross and "The New Yorker."* Doubleday, New York, 1951.

May, Elaine Tyler, *Great Expectations: Marriage and Divorce in Post-Victorian America.* University of Chicago Press, 1980, New York and London, 1980.

Meigs, Cornelia, *What Makes a College? A History of Bryn Mawr.* Macmillan, New York, 1956.

Meister, Robert, *Hypochondria: Toward a Better Understanding.* Taplinger, New York, 1980.

Newcomer, Mabel, *A Century of Higher Education for American Women.* Harper & Brothers, New York, 1959.

Niemtzow, Annette, " 'I Ain't Ladylike . . .' The Early Journals of M. Carey Thomas," Bryn Mawr Alumnae Bulletin, Spring 1979.

Paine, Swift, "As We See It in Reno," *The North American Review* 229 (6), June 1930.

Pickens, Buford, and Darnall, Margaretta, *Washington University in St. Louis: Its Design and Architecture.* School of Architecture, Gallery of Art, Washington University, St. Louis, Missouri, 1979.

Plimpton, George A., and Crowther, Frank H., "The Art of the Essay, I: E. B. White," *Paris Review,* 48, Fall 1969.

"Proceedings of the Massachusetts Special Commission to Consider the Financial Condition of the Boston Elevated Company," Boston, 1917.

"Random Notes on H. W. Ross," Talk at the Grolier Club, by Geoffrey Hellman, May 14, 1975.

Rittenhouse, Caroline S., and Dolenski, Leo M., *Bryn Mawr College,* Bryn Mawr College Library, 1985.

Rook, Arthur, Wilkinson, D. S., Ebling, F. J. G., (Eds.) *Textbook of Dermatology.* Blackwell Scientific Publications, Oxford, 1972.

Sergeant, Elizabeth, *Shadow Shapes: The Journal of a Wounded Woman.* Houghton Mifflin, Boston, 1920.

[Shawn, William], "Katharine S. White," *The New Yorker,* August 1, 1977.

Sneddon, Ian B., and Wilkinson, Darrell S., "Subcorneal Pustular Dermatosis," *British Journal of Dermatology,* 1979.

———, "Subcorneal Pustular Dermatosis Differs From Subcorneal Pustulosis," *American Journal of Dermatology,* Winter 1981.

Stafford, Jean, *The Collected Stories.* Farrar, Straus & Giroux, New York, 1969.

Teichmann, Howard, *Smart Aleck: The Wit, World and Life of Alexander Woollcott.* William Morrow, New York, 1976.

Thurber, Helen, and Weeks, Edward (Eds.), *Selected Letters of James Thurber.* Little, Brown, Boston, 1981.

Thurber, James, *Men, Women & Dogs.* W. H. Allen, London, 1977.

———, *The Years with Ross.* Little, Brown, Boston, 1959.

Thurber, James, and White, E. B., *Is Sex Necessary? Or Why You Feel the Way You Do.* Harper & Brothers, New York, 1929.

White, E. B., "Call Me Ishmael, Or How I Feel About Being Married to a Bryn Mawr Graduate," Bryn Mawr Alumnae Bulletin, Spring 1956.

———, *Essays of E. B. White.* Harper & Row, New York, 1977.

Selected Bibliography

————, *One Man's Meat.* Harper & Row, New York, 1982.

————, *Poems and Sketches of E. B. White,* Harper & Row, New York, 1981.

White, E. B., and White, K. S. (Eds.), *A Subtreasury of American Humor.* Coward-McCann, New York, 1941.

White, Katharine S., *Onward and Upward in the Garden.* Farrar, Straus & Giroux, New York, 1979.

Whitlock, F. A., *Psychophysiological Aspects of Skin Disease.* W. B. Saunders, London, 1976.

Wilson, Edmund, *Letters on Literature and Politics 1912–1972.* Selected and edited by Elena Wilson, Farrar, Straus & Giroux, New York, 1977.

Wilson, Jonathan, "Craftsmanship Lives: Master Boat Builder," *Mercedes,* Vol. 9, Mercedes Benz, North America Inc., 1983.

Wittkower, Eric, and Russell, Brian, *Emotional Factors in Skin Disease, A Psychosomatic Medicine Monograph.* Paul B. Hoeber, Harper & Brothers, New York, 1953.

1910 Bryn Mawr College Calendar.

Index

Andy   FOR   E. B. White
EBW   E. B. White
"For the Recreation . . ."   "For the Recreation and Delight
of the Inhabitants"

Katharine   Katharine White
KSW   Katharine White
Letters   *Letters* of E. B. White
Subtreasury   *A Subtreasury of American Humor*

Index

Index

Index

Index

Index